C000103239

OXFORD STUDIES IN METAETHICS

Oxford Studies in Metaethics

VOLUME 4

Edited by
RUSS SHAFER-LANDAU

OXFORD UNIVERSITY PRESS · OXFORD

OXFORD
UNIVERSITY PRESS

Great Clarendon Street, Oxford, OX2 6DP,
United Kingdom

Oxford University Press is a department of the University of Oxford.
It furthers the University's objective of excellence in research, scholarship,
and education by publishing worldwide. Oxford is a registered trade mark of
Oxford University Press in the UK and in certain other countries

© the several contributors 2009

The moral rights of the author have been asserted

First Edition published in 2009

All rights reserved. No part of this publication may be reproduced, stored in
a retrieval system, or transmitted, in any form or by any means, without the
prior permission in writing of Oxford University Press, or as expressly permitted
by law, by licence or under terms agreed with the appropriate reprographics
rights organization. Enquiries concerning reproduction outside the scope of the
above should be sent to the Rights Department, Oxford University Press, at the
address above

You must not circulate this work in any other form
and you must impose this same condition on any acquirer

Published in the United States of America by Oxford University Press
198 Madison Avenue, New York, NY 10016, United States of America

British Library Cataloguing in Publication Data
Data available

Library of Congress Cataloging in Publication Data
Data available

ISBN 978–0–19–956630–3

Links to third party websites are provided by Oxford in good faith and
for information only. Oxford disclaims any responsibility for the materials
contained in any third party website referenced in this work.

Contents

Notes on Contributors

Dorit Bar-On is Professor of Philosophy, University of North Carolina–Chapel Hill

Paul Bloomfield is Associate Professor of Philosophy, University of Connecticut

Matthew Chrisman is Lecturer in Philosophy, University of Edinburgh

David Copp is Professor of Philosophy, University of California–Davis

Luca Ferrero is Assistant Professor of Philosophy, University of Wisconsin–Milwaukee

Gilbert Harman is Professor of Philosophy, Princeton University

Stephen Kearns is Visiting Assistant Professor, Sage School of Philosophy, Cornell University

Brad Majors is a Graduate Student in Philosophy, University of Wisconsin–Madison

Jacob Ross is Assistant Professor of Philosophy, University of Southern California

Andrew Sepielli is a Graduate Student in Philosophy, Rutgers University

Daniel Star is Assistant Professor of Philosophy, Boston University

Nicholas Sturgeon is Professor, Sage School of Philosophy, Cornell University

Pekka Väyrynen is Senior Lecturer in Philosophy, Leeds University

Introduction

Russ Shafer-Landau

Oxford Studies in Metaethics is designed to provide an annual selection of some of the best new work being done in this exciting field. I think that the articles collected here have done an excellent job in fulfilling the aims of this series. They also display, perhaps more than any previous volume in the series, the breadth of issues that nowadays falls within the boundaries of metaethics.

We begin with Andrew Sepielli's "What To Do When You Don't Know What To Do." Sepielli considers a little-discussed problem in metaethics—how to behave when we are unclear about which normative considerations are most relevant to the situations we encounter. We often receive differing advice from competing normative theories, while unsure of which (if any) theory is correct. When each of them has some credibility, how are we to go about making a decision? In this article, Sepielli offers us his advice on how to choose under circumstances of what he calls "normative uncertainty."

Next we turn to two articles that concern the relationship between the natural world and its normative, or more specifically ethical, features. Such concerns often focus on relations of supervenience. In "The Natural and the Normative," Brad Majors distinguishes among a variety of supervenience relations, and argues that much of the literature on this topic is misguided, as its discussions fail to mark the needed distinctions. Once we distinguish between global and local supervenience, and weak and strong versions, we can see, says Majors, that many statements of moral supervenience, most of which are intended as conceptual truths, are actually false. Majors also critically discusses Simon Blackburn's influential anti-realist arguments based on supervenience, and argues that they are unsound, owing to a failure to attend to the important distinctions that Majors notes.

Nicholas Sturgeon registers his own "Doubts about the Supervenience of the Evaluative." Like Majors, Sturgeon begins by noting that the supervenience of the evaluative is regarded by nearly everyone in the field as an uncontroversial truth. But Sturgeon invites us to think about what the evaluative is meant to supervene *on*. Common candidates include the nonevaluative, the natural, the descriptive, and the factual. Each of these, argues Sturgeon, will be rejected by at least one prominent camp of metaethical theorists. Sturgeon concludes that there is no neutral and widely acceptable specification of the supervenience base for the evaluative.

Pekka Väyrynen follows with a continuation of his research program into the nature of moral standards. In "A Theory of Hedged Moral Principles," Väyrynen seeks to offer a view of moral principles that enable them to play both explanatory and epistemological roles, while also showing how they can admit of exceptions (when they do). He is not himself offering a list of such principles, or a normative ethic from which these principles may be derived. Rather, he seeks to show that if we conceive of moral principles as having a certain hedged structure, then they will be able both to explain why actions are (among other things) right and wrong, and also explain how we can come to know them. Both explanatory and epistemological roles are crucial. A theory that implies that each moral rule will admit of indefinitely many exceptions *may* be satisfying in theory, but, since we can never know its contents, it will hardly do in practice.

Moral semantics has garnered a good deal of attention from metaethicists, who tend to rely on increasingly complex, technical arguments to develop their ideas. By contrast, the next two articles are non-technical and quite accessible. Dorit Bar-On and Matthew Chrisman pair up to offer us "Ethical Neo-Expressivism," a new take on the expressivist view that ethical claims directly express motivational states. This view has usually led either to simple subjectivism, a view endorsed only by introductory students, or to noncognitivism, the view that the semantic content of ethical claims is given by a nonpropositional motivational attitude that receives expression in moral utterance. Bar-On and Chrisman argue for a third alternative, which requires us to attend to an ambiguity in the notion of a moral claim. Understood as sentences, moral claims express propositions. Understood as utterances, moral claims express motivational states. Distinguishing these two roles enables us, they argue, to solve several outstanding problems in moral semantics.

David Copp next discusses an intriguing semantic view, realist-expressivism, that he first introduced almost a decade ago. In "Realist-Expressivism and Conventional Implicature," he further develops this hybrid view, possessed of two essential constituents. First, it holds that moral assertions express motivating attitudes (e.g., approval and disapproval). But unlike traditional subjectivism or noncognitivism, such assertions, like non-ethical assertions, are capable of truth and falsity—indeed, Copp sees moral assertions as possessed of truth conditions that we can construe as realists would prefer. The key to making this work is seeing sincere moral assertions as conventionally implicating the existence of the speaker's motivating attitude. This idea has come under fire from various quarters. Here, Copp takes up two prominent criticisms, one by Kent Bach, and the other by Stephen Finlay, and tries to undermine their force.

Gilbert Harman next offers us the sort of counsel that many of us have longed to hear—Leave Guilt Behind! In his "Guilt-Free Morality," Harman focuses on guilt as a form of internalized self-punishment. He argues that morally good people need never feel such an emotion, and that the best sort of moral education will avoid any effort to inculcate such an emotion into our children. To the extent that we are susceptible to guilt, we ought to try to rid ourselves of this sort of vulnerability.

The next article is a joint effort of Daniel Star and Stephen Kearns. Their paper, "Reasons as Evidence," attempts to offer a unified theory of practical and theoretical reasons. The unification is effected by means of conceptualizing of reasons as a kind of evidence. So-called theoretical reasons, i.e., reasons for belief, can be analyzed as evidence for the truth of the proposition in question. Practical reasons can be analyzed as evidence that an agent ought to act in a certain way. Star and Kearns focus on the practical side of things, and lay out the attractions of their view as an analysis of practical reasons, before considering, and rebutting, a host of objections.

Jacob Ross then offers us his "How to be a Cognitivist about Practical Reason." This sort of cognitivism is a view about intentions. The view tells us that intentions involve beliefs, and that our intentions are subject to certain rational requirements that also apply to the beliefs that figure in our intentions. Ross devotes the bulk of his very wide-ranging paper to discussions of two of these rational requirements. The first is one of consistency, which demands that our beliefs and intentions not conflict with each other. The second is a means–end coherence requirement, which (roughly) demands that we intend what we know to be the needed means to our intended ends. The key here, according to Ross, is to offer an account of the beliefs that figure in intentions. Part of his article is designed to show how and why this task is as difficult as it is.

Paul Bloomfield's "Archimedeanism and Why Metaethics Matters" offers a large-scale view of the nature and value of the metaethical enterprise. Metaethics has come in for criticism recently from a variety of quarters, some arguing that there really is no such thing as metaethics (alas for this series!), or that metaethics can offer no distinctive approach or insight into morality. As Bloomfield sees things, metaethics does indeed have distinctive contributions to make regarding our understanding of morality. It will not directly answer our normative ethical questions, but it will have direct implications for issues regarding moral authority, moral knowledge, moral education, and moral disagreement. It is hard to argue with the importance of such matters, and so, if Bloomfield is right, the value of metaethical inquiry can be successfully vindicated.

Our last contribution is Luca Ferrero's "Constitutivism and the Inescapability of Agency." Constitutivism is the view that the requirements of rationality and morality are, or depend upon, constitutive features of agency. Since (it is often claimed) we cannot fail to be agents, so long as we are alive and remain who we are, then we are at least implicitly committed to certain norms of morality and rationality. This can explain why such norms apply to us regardless of our contingent desires and aims. Constitutivism thus promises an answer to the perennial questions about the rational authority of morality. Here, Ferrero offers a limited defense of constitutivism against a number of important recent objections.

The papers collected in this volume were each given an airing at the 4th Annual Metaethics Workshop in Madison, Wisconsin, in the fall of 2007. The Program Committee for that event thus deserves a great deal of credit not only for taking the needed time to evaluate a large bundle of submissions, but also for their sharp eye for talent. My sincere thanks to committee members David Brink, Stephen Darwall, James Dreier, Don Loeb, Michael Ridge, and Connie Rosati. Once the papers were delivered, then revised, Peter Momtchiloff—OUP editor *extraordinaire*, and another very keen eye for talent—wisely asked Sean McKeever and Sarah Stroud to anonymously review these contributions. Their expert advice made a batch of strong papers stronger still. I thank them both for allowing me now to credit their invaluable efforts. The 2007 Workshop was underwritten by the generous sponsorship of the Berent Enç Fund of the University of Wisconsin Department of Philosophy. My thanks to department chair Steven Nadler for ensuring that the workshop continues to receive the funds needed to maintain its place in the metaethical firmament.

1

What to Do When You Don't Know What to Do

Andrew Sepielli

You and I are limited beings, and must therefore make our decisions under uncertainty. There are two types of uncertainty with which we must contend. One is *non-normative uncertainty*—uncertainty about matters of non-normative fact. Non-normative facts may include everything from the age of the universe to the gross domestic product of India to the health effects of drinking four gallons of Mountain Dew in one night. The other is *normative uncertainty*—uncertainty about the reasons those facts give us. For example, someone might be uncertain about the permissibility of abortion, even if she were certain about the science of fetal development, the kind of life a child born to her would lead, and so on. Similarly, someone may be uncertain whether the reasons to support a tax increase outweigh the reasons to oppose it, even if she is sure about what the economic and social effects of the measure would be. At a more theoretical level, someone may be uncertain whether utilitarianism or Kantianism or contractualism or some other comprehensive account of morality is correct.

A good deal has been written on the issue of what we should do when we're non-normatively uncertain. Most of decision theory concerns rationality under non-normative uncertainty, and it's typically seen as incumbent upon ethicists to develop theories capable of guiding agents who are uncertain about the non-normative facts. By contrast, shockingly little has been written on the issue of what we should do when we're normatively

Thanks to Lara Buchak, Tim Campbell, Pavel Davydov, Elizabeth Harman, Des Hogan, Jonathan Ichikawa, Toby Ord, Derek Parfit, Philip Pettit, Wlodek Rabinowicz, Jacob Ross, Holly Smith, Larry Temkin, Brian Weatherson, and Evan Williams, and to audiences at the Wisconsin Metaethics Workshop and the Lund-Rutgers Philosophy Conference, for helpful feedback on this chapter. Special thanks to Ruth Chang for all of the phone conversations, e-mails, and five-hour lunches in which she helped me to refine these and other ideas.

uncertain.[1] This is both unfortunate and surprising, seeing as normative uncertainty seems to pervade the life of the reflective person.

In this chapter, I'll take some small steps towards rectifying this neglect. Here's how things will proceed: Parts I and II will be devoted to setting up the problem. In Part I, I'll say a bit more about what normative uncertainty is, and explain how and why I plan to restrict my focus to a particular kind of normative uncertainty. In Part II, I'll get clearer about the sense of 'should' I have in mind when I ask what we should do when we're normatively uncertain. Then, in Part III, I'll briefly take up the question of what we should (in this more carefully formulated sense) do under normative uncertainty. I'll consider and reject what may seem like the obvious answer, and suggest an alternative. But my alternative may seem problematic, for it requires a sort of commensuration of different normative views that may appear impossible. I'll explain the nature of this commensuration and why it's thought to be especially difficult. This will then bring me to the main goal of the chapter—showing that such a commensuration is indeed possible, through a method that I'll explicate in Part IV. In Part V, I consider some objections to, and some complications that inhere in, the method I've proposed.

PART I: THE PHENOMENON OF NORMATIVE UNCERTAINTY

An agent is normatively uncertain just in case (a) her degrees of belief (or 'credences', or 'subjective probabilities') are divided between at least two mutually exclusive normative propositions, and (b) this division in her degrees of belief is not entirely due to non-normative uncertainty.[2] Consider a commander-in-chief deciding whether to go to war. If he has some credence in the proposition *the balance of reasons favors going to war*

---

[1] The only recent publications to address the issue are Hudson (1989), Oddie (1995), Lockhart (2000), Weatherson (2002), Sepielli (2006), Ross (2006), and Guerrero (2007). A very similar debate—about so-called 'reflex principles'—occupied a central place in Early Modern Catholic moral theology. The most notable contributors to this debate were Bartolomé de Medina (1577), Blaise Pascal (1656–7), and St Alphonsus Liguori (1755). The various positions are helpfully summarized in Prümmer (1957), *The Catholic Encyclopedia* (1913), and *The New Catholic Encyclopedia* (2002). I discuss the Catholic dispute, and its connections to the topic of this paper, at greater length in ch. 1 of Sepielli (unpublished-*a*). Thanks to Des Hogan for clueing me in to this body of work.

[2] These two conditions can be summarized and stated formally as follows: For at least two normative propositions, $Norm_1$ and $Norm_2$, and at least one complete non-normative description of the world, $Comp$, $p(Norm_1|Comp) > 0$, $p(Norm_2|Comp) > 0$, $p(Comp) > 0$, and $p(Norm_1) + p(Norm_2) = p(Norm_1 \text{ OR } Norm_2)$, where p(q) is the subjective probability of q.

rather than not going to war and some credence in the proposition *the balance of reasons favors not going to war rather than going to war*, and this is not fully explained by his uncertainty regarding the non-normative facts, then the commander-in-chief is normatively uncertain.

There are many different kinds of normative propositions—everything from *murder is wrong* to *the reasons of justice outweigh the reasons of piety*. I doubt there could be anything like a simple, explanatorily powerful account of what to do when your credence is distributed across propositions of all these different kinds. Since I'm after just such an account, I'm going to restrict my focus to one kind of normative proposition that seems to play an especially prominent role in many people's normative thinking—the *Practical Comparative*. Practical comparatives are propositions of the form *the balance of reasons favors doing action A rather than doing action B*.

By 'reasons', I mean *objective* reasons, as opposed to what are sometimes called *subjective*, or *belief-relative*, reasons.[3] Now, it's notoriously difficult to give an entirely satisfactory definition of 'objective' as it's used in this context, but the following should suffice for our purposes: an objective reason is a reason whose status as such is primarily determined independently of the beliefs of the subject for which it is a reason (although it may not be determined independently of other mental states of that subject; on many theories of practical reasons, it may depend on the subject's conative and/or affective states). I'll say something more about subjective/belief-relative reasons in connection with my clarification of 'should' in Part II.

Since the locution 'the balance of reasons favors ... rather than ...' is a bit cumbersome, I'll express that same proposition using the following bits of shorthand: 'Action A is better than action B', and 'Action A has greater value than action B'. We can express the same proposition with 'Action B is worse than action A' and 'Action B has lesser value than action A'. To express the proposition that A and B are supported by reasons of equal strength, I'll say 'A and B are normatively equivalent' or 'A and B have the same value'. Again, this is simply shorthand, so if you're fond of using 'the balance of reasons favors ... rather than ...', '... better than ...', and '... has greater value than ...' such that they are not equivalent, recognize that we're just using the same words to express different concepts.

Other treatments of normative uncertainty have focused on uncertainty among normative *theories*, rather than uncertainty among practical comparatives.[4] Normative theories include such ethical theories as utilitarianism,

---

[3] 'Subjective' is the term standardly used in marking off this distinction; I borrow the more transparent 'belief-relative' from Parfit (unpublished).

[4] See especially Lockhart (2000).

deontology, virtue ethics, and all the rest, as well as theories about prudence, legality, and so on. My main reason for focusing on practical comparatives rather than on theories is that, while almost everyone has beliefs about the former—which, again, are simply propositions about which actions are better or worse than which other actions—very few people think in terms of comprehensive theories like utilitarianism. Even those who do have beliefs about theories may have many beliefs about practical comparatives that are entirely independent of the deliverances of their theories. It'd be better, then, to shift the focus away from beliefs that constitute such a small part of most people's normative thinking.

With that said, there are ways of extending the account I offer in this paper to the case of uncertainty about normative theories. That's because a normative theory, on one conception at least, is just a very large practical comparative. It's a comparative of the form *Action A is better than action B, which is better than action C, which is better than action D …* Someone who has credence in this sort of normative theory thereby has credence in one or more practical comparatives. The converse, mind you, isn't true. I could think that some high-utility action is better than some low-utility action without having any thoughts about utilitarianism, or any other theory for that matter.

PART II: THE SENSE OF 'SHOULD'

In light of Part I, we may revise our animating question as follows: What should you do when you're uncertain among practical comparatives? One quick and easy answer is: Act in accordance with whichever practical comparatives are *actually true*. If, for example, going to war is in fact better than not going to war, then the uncertain commander-in-chief should go to war.

As you may infer from the length of this chapter, I don't find such a quick and easy answer entirely satisfying, even if, on one reading of the question, it's clearly right. The problem is that we cannot base our actions on the correct normative standards; our relationship to such standards is limited to mere conformity to them. This follows from a quite general point—that we cannot guide ourselves by the way the world is, but only by our representations of the world. So while there is room for an objective sense of 'should', there is also value to developing a sense of 'should' on which what one should do given one's beliefs is sensitive to those very beliefs.

The 'should' I have in mind, then, is a certain kind of belief-relative 'should'. So let's talk about kinds of belief-relativity for a moment. Start by dividing things up into the normative and the non-normative. There is a notion of 'should' that is relative to the agent's beliefs about the non-normative, but independent of the agent's beliefs about the normative. Call this the *Non-Normative Belief-Relative 'Should'*. This is what people are usually talking about when they talk about the 'subjective "should" '. But there are other subjective 'shoulds'. There is also a notion of 'should' that's relative to the agent's beliefs about the normative, but independent of the agent's beliefs about the non-normative. Call this the *Normative Belief-Relative 'Should'*. Finally, there is the most belief-relative 'should' of all—relative to the agent's beliefs about both the normative and the non-normative. Call this the *Rational 'Should'*. This is the kind of 'should' I'll be concerned with, although for expediency's sake I'll bracket issues of non-normative uncertainty, and simply ask what one rationally should do—or better, what it's rational to do—under normative uncertainty only.

Now we'll need to make a further distinction, between two ways of assessing rationality—*globally* and *locally*. What it's globally rational for an agent to do depends on all of that agent's mental states. What it's locally rational for an agent to do depends on only a subset of that agent's mental states. But while it makes sense to say what it's globally rational *simpliciter* for an agent to do, it doesn't make sense to say what's locally rational *simpliciter* for an agent to do. We first have to specify which subset of the agent's mental states we're talking about. So evaluations of local rationality will always be evaluations of what it's locally rational to do *relative to* this or that subset of an agent's mental states.[5]

Recall that in Part I, I said that I wanted to focus on uncertainty among practical comparatives. Given our latest distinction, we can say more clearly what this focus amounts to: Degrees of belief in practical comparatives (along with some other normative beliefs I'll mention later) will constitute the subset of beliefs relative to which we'll be making assessments of local rationality. So we can rephrase our animating question once again: What's it locally rational to do relative to your degrees of belief in practical comparatives? Given this way of phrasing the question, our answer will not conflict with any accounts of practical rationality that purport to be theories of global practical rationality, or that purport to be theories of local practical rationality relative to different subsets of beliefs. Such accounts are answers to different questions.

Before we move on to the next section, I'll need to introduce one more distinction. There are two different ways of answering our question as just

---

[5] For a defense of the importance of local rationality, see Kolodny (2005). Kolodny wishes to reject in particular the view that local norms of rationality are merely *prima facie* global norms of rationality (p. 516 n. 8). I share Kolodny's wish, and provide my own argument against the '*prima facie*' view in ch. 1 of Sepielli (unpublished-*a*).

stated. One way treats the credences in practical comparatives as *given*, and offers an answer of the form: 'If you have credence distribution C over practical comparatives, then it's locally rational, relative to C, to do action A.' Another way treats the credences in practical comparatives as *open to revision*, and offers an answer of the form: 'It's locally rational, relative to C, to either a) do A, or b) to revise C.'

The first of these accounts is an example of a *Narrow-Scope* rational norm, while the second is an example of a *Wide-Scope* rational norm. Suppose 'A' in these schemas is *the action that ranks highest according to the practical comparative in which you have the highest credence.* Then it's possible for someone with credence distribution C to satisfy the first norm only by doing the action that ranks highest according to the practical comparative in which she has the highest credence. By contrast, it's possible for such a person to satisfy the second norm without doing this action; he could revise his credences instead.

I want to urge that the correct answer to our animating question will be a narrow-scope rational norm. It may be that it's appropriate in many cases to revise one's credences in practical comparatives, but this does not dissolve the question of which action it's rational to do, at the present time, given one's present credences. The rational norms about how to change one's perspective are different, and in my view, independent from the rational norms about how to behave given one's perspective as it stands.[6] It's the latter to which I'll now turn.

PART III: EXPECTED VALUE AND THE PROBLEM
OF VALUE DIFFERENCE COMPARISONS

Perhaps the most natural answer to our question is: It's rational to act in accordance with the practical comparative in which you have the highest credence. That is, if your degree of belief is highest that Action A is better than Action B, then you should do A rather than B. We might offer a similar answer in the case of uncertainty about normative theories: If your degree of belief is highest in Negative Utilitarianism, you should do whatever Negative Utilitarianism says is best in any given situation. That this answer

---

[6] My thinking about this last distinction was spurred by an exchange between Kolodny and John Broome. See Kolodny (2005) and (2007) and Broome (2007). My reasons for favoring a narrow-scope rational norm in the present case are similar to some arguments Kolodny offers (2007: 379, 381). Debates about the scope of rational norms are quite complicated, and deserve more thorough engagement than, regrettably, is possible here.

seems so natural is, I suspect, one reason why so little attention has been paid to the question of what to do under normative uncertainty.

We should be leery of this approach, though, because some similar courses of action under non-normative uncertainty seem so clearly mistaken. Suppose that I am deciding whether to drink a cup of coffee. I have a degree of belief of .2 that the coffee is mixed with a deadly poison, and a degree of belief of .8 that it's perfectly safe. If I act on the hypothesis in which I have the highest credence, I'll drink the coffee. But this seems like a bad call. A good chance of coffee isn't worth such a significant risk of death—at least, not if I assign commonsensical values to coffee and death, respectively.

Similarly, suppose I am deciding between actions A and B. There's some chance that A is better than B, and an ever so slightly greater chance that B is better than A. I also believe that, if A is better than B, then A is saintly and B is abominable; but if B is better than A, then A is slightly nasty and B is merely okay. Despite the fact that my credence is higher that B is better than A, it still seems as though it's rational to do A instead, since A's 'normative upside' is so much higher than B's, and its 'normative downside' not nearly as low.[7]

Here, then, is a more promising answer: I should perform the action with the highest Expected Objective Value (EOV). We get the expected value of an action by multiplying the subjective probability that some practical comparative is true by the objective value of that action if it is true, doing the same for all of the other practical comparatives, and adding up the results.[8] This strategy is sensitive not only to degrees of belief, but also to degrees of *value*—the relative sizes of the upsides and downsides of actions.

And yet, if there's anything well-established in the literature on normative uncertainty, it's that approaches like EOV maximization suffer from a potentially debilitating problem that I call the Problem of Value Difference Comparisons (PVDC).[9] Imagine that my credence is divided between two practical comparatives—*A is better than B*, and *B is better than A*. To determine whether A or B has the higher EOV, I must know how the degree to which A is better than B if the first is true compares to the degree to which B is better than A if the second is true. For example, if my credence is .1 that A is better than B and .9 that B is better than A, the difference between A

---

[7] Acting in accordance with the hypothesis in which you have the highest credence has other drawbacks as well. I illustrate some of these in ch. 4 of Sepielli (unpublished-*a*).

[8] More formally, $EOV = \sum_i p(PC_i) \cdot v(A \text{ given } PC_i)$, where $p(PC_i)$ is the subjective probability that practical comparative PC_i is true, and $v(A \text{ given } PC_i)$ is the objective value of the action A given that PC_i is true.

[9] See Hudson (1989), Lockhart (2000), and Ross (2006). This problem is also noted in unpublished work by Andy Egan and Alan Hájek, and by Nick Bostrom and Toby Ord. Something like it seems to have been recognized in the Catholic tradition's treatment of normative uncertainty, specifically in connection with the theory of 'Compensationism'. See *The Catholic Encyclopedia* (1913) and Prümmer (1957).

and B on the former hypothesis must be greater than 9 times the difference between B and A on the latter hypothesis if A is to have the higher EOV.

I can't determine that from the comparatives themselves. Each of them tells me which actions are better than which other actions, but neither tells me how the differences in value between actions, if it is true, compare to the differences in value between actions if some other comparative is true. If it helps, we can cheat a bit and think of the problem in terms of comprehensive normative theories. Some consequentialist theory may say that it's better to kill 1 person to save 5 people than it is to spare that person and allow the 5 people to die. A deontological theory may say the opposite. But it is not as though the consequentialist theory has, somehow encoded within it, information about how its own difference in value between these two actions compares to the difference in value between them according to deontology. The problem, then, is this: Although it seems as though we ought to be sensitive to value difference comparisons across normative hypotheses, we lack a way of making such comparisons.[10]

It's tempting to try to evade the PVDC by adopting a principle other than EOV maximization. I think there are two reasons to resist this temptation. First, there are good grounds for accepting EOV maximization as the correct principle of rationality under normative uncertainty.[11] Second, it's not only EOV maximization that requires value difference comparisons. Any theory that's adequately sensitive to comparisons of degrees of value across practical comparatives will require, well, comparisons of degrees of value across practical comparatives. So chances are we'll still have to face up to this problem even if the particular theory of rationality I favor is incorrect. At any rate, I will assume for the remainder of the chapter that the PVDC is a serious problem, and suggest a way to solve it.

PART IV: A SOLUTION TO THE PROBLEM OF VALUE DIFFERENCE COMPARISONS

Now I'll outline a solution to the PVDC.[12] Specifically, I'll explain which beliefs an agent must have, in addition to her beliefs in practical

---

[10] This problem is in some ways analogous to the welfare economists' problem of interpersonal comparisons of utility. See Robbins (1938), Harsanyi (1955), Hammond (1976), Elster and Roemer (1991), and Broome (1991) and (2004) for just a sample of the work on this topic.

[11] I argue for EOV maximization in chs. 4 and 5 of Sepielli (unpublished-*a*).

[12] There are three other published solutions to this problem—one that Lockhart develops at length in his (2000), and two that Ross mentions briefly at the end of his (2006). See Appendix below.

comparatives, for her value differences to be comparable. While I think it's quite plausible that real people tend to have beliefs like the ones I'm about to discuss, I leave the defense of this psychological claim to other work.[13] Instead, think of the next two sections as constituting a conditional thesis—that if people do have these additional beliefs, then their value differences are comparable across practical comparatives. I'll start by explicating an approach suitable for highly idealized agents with very simplistic normative beliefs. After that's done, I'll add some extensions to the approach that will permit its application to more realistic agents with more complex sets of normative beliefs.

Let me introduce my solution by considering a real-life situation that may be fraught with normative uncertainty—that of a pregnant woman deciding whether to have an abortion. Suppose she believes to some degree that not having an abortion is better than having an abortion, and believes to some degree that having an abortion is better than not having an abortion. (See Fig. 1.1.) This way of putting the situation may strike some people as awkward, as they assume that nobody thinks there's a chance that having an abortion is *better* than not having an abortion; it's just that having an abortion may be *permissible* (and not having one may also be permissible). Perhaps. My goal here, though, is simply to illustrate my solution to the PVDC. If it fails to capture the way most people think about abortion, that's okay for now. But it also doesn't strike me as crazy to suppose that having an abortion is, in many cases, all things considered better than not having one. At any rate, I'm quite sure many people have at least some credence that this is so.

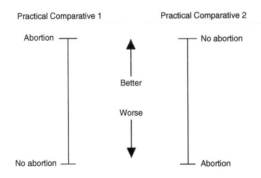

Fig. 1.1

[13] See ch. 3 of Sepielli (unpublished-*a*).

To determine which of the options has the higher EOV, we'll need to know how the difference between abortion and non-abortion, on the condition that the former is better, compares to the difference between the two, on the condition that the latter is better. To find this out, we'll have to move beyond our agent's practical comparatives, and have a look at some of her other normative beliefs. Suppose that the woman also believes that: (1) if not having an abortion is better than having an abortion, then abortion and murdering an adult human being are of equal value (i.e. that abortion is tantamount to murder); and (2) if having an abortion is better than not having an abortion, then abortion and practicing an innocuous form of birth control like the 'rhythm method' are of equal value. I'll call the contents of these beliefs—propositions of the form *If A is better than B, then A and C are of equal value*—*Practical Conditionals*. (See Fig. 1.2.)

We might imagine that the woman's practical comparatives are, in some sense, based on her practical conditionals. That is, she thinks there's some chance that having an abortion is better than not having an abortion *because* there's some chance that abortion is normatively equivalent to birth control, and she thinks there's some chance that not having an abortion is the better option *because* there's some chance that abortion is tantamount to murder. Indeed, I suspect that many people's thoughts about abortion are related in roughly this way. For the purposes of our argument, though, this basing relationship needn't obtain. The woman just needs to have credence in the practical comparatives and practical conditionals I've mentioned.

Now, abortion is a controversial issue. It divides societies, and insofar as many of us are uncertain about it, it divides minds. Murder, on the other hand, is not controversial. Its value is obviously very, very low. Likewise,

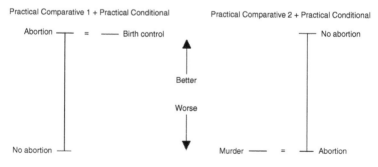

Fig. 1.2

the rhythm method is not controversial. It's clearly acceptable. So although the woman may be uncertain about abortion, she may be more confident about the relative status of murder and the rhythm method. This will all prove crucial to the next part of my solution.

I will suppose the woman has the following view regarding the respective values of (A) murdering an adult, (B) using birth control along the lines of the rhythm method, and (C) bearing a child (which, we'll just assume, is what will occur if she does not have an abortion)—that the difference in value between murder and bearing a child is (let's just say) *20 times greater* than the difference in value between bearing a child and using this sort of birth control. In other words, avoiding pregnancy via something like the rhythm method is probably the best option; getting pregnant and bringing the pregnancy to term is a little bit worse than that; but the difference between murder and bringing the pregnancy to term is enormous—as we're imagining things, 20 times greater than the difference between the latter and using some clearly benign form of birth control.[14] (See Fig. 1.3.)

This belief of hers concerns a *cardinal ranking* of the values of various actions—that is, a ranking that represents not only the *order* of the actions, but also the ratios of the value differences between them. What is interesting and important about this ranking is that it's independent of the woman's views about abortion. Whatever views she holds concerning the relative values of abortion and non-abortion, she can also believe in this ranking. (Similarly, in the interpersonal case, an ardent pro-lifer who is certain that killing a fetus is normatively equivalent to killing an adult, and an ardent pro-choicer who is certain that it is not, could both assent to this ranking.) I will call this sort of cardinal ranking a *Background Ranking*.

What this background ranking gives us is a way of comparing the difference in value between abortion and non-abortion, on the condition that abortion is better, with the difference in value between abortion and non-abortion, on the condition that non-abortion is better. The difference between murder and bearing a child, according to the background ranking, is 20 times the difference between bearing a child and using the rhythm method. So the difference between abortion and bearing a child, if abortion has the same value as murder, is 20 times the difference between bearing a child and abortion, if abortion has the same value as using the rhythm method.

---

[14] The values of these briefly described actions depend, of course, on other features of the context of choice. And so, while we're imagining that the woman believes that bearing a child is worse than using birth control in this situation, she needn't, and arguably shouldn't, believe that this would be true in other situations. Thanks to Elizabeth Harman for encouraging me to note this.

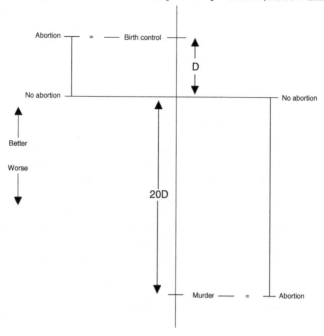

Fig. 1.3

We can then determine whether abortion or non-abortion has the higher EOV. We start with the difference between having an abortion and not having one, on the condition abortion is better. We'll assign this difference some positive value D. Now we multiply D by the woman's credence in that proposition, giving us the value (Credence1 · D). We've established that the difference between not having an abortion and having one, if non-abortion is better, is 20 times greater than this. Its value, then, is 20D. We multiply 20D by the woman's credence that non-abortion is better, giving us the value (Credence2 · 20D). Then we subtract (Credence2 · 20D) from (Credence1 · D). If the result is positive, then abortion has the higher EOV; if it is negative, then non-abortion has the higher EOV.

The imputation of a background ranking with cardinal structure is sure to raise hackles, for it may seem implausible that real people have ratios of value differences like our fictional woman's 20:1 ratio supposed here. Certainly, most of us cannot discover by mere introspection that we have such precise, informative rankings of actions. Luckily, decision theory supplies us with a template for how we might both define and discern such a background ranking. At least since Frank Ramsey's 'Truth and Probability', we have known how to define differences in value between outcomes *via* ordinal rankings of probabilistic options.[15]

Here's an example: Suppose I'm indifferent between two options: (1) a .2 chance of winning a new car, and a .8 chance of winning an apple pie, and (2) a certainty of winning a new bicycle. Then I can be represented as having a cardinal ranking of the car, the bicycle, and the pie such that the difference in value between the first pair is 4 times the difference between the second pair.

Something similar can be done for differences in value between actions: Suppose I regard the following two probabilistically described actions as having the same non-normative belief-relative value: (1) an action with a .2 chance of being an instance of killing someone, and a .8 chance of being an instance of breaking someone's finger, and (2) an action with a 1.0 chance of being an instance of paralyzing someone. Then I can be represented as having a cardinal ranking of killing someone, paralyzing someone, and breaking someone's finger such that the difference in objective value between the first pair is 4 times the difference between the second pair. All one needs in order to have a cardinal background ranking of actions is an ordinal background ranking of probabilistically described actions.

This is, of course, only the barest sketch of an account. There are plenty of objections out there to Ramsey's method and other methods that have followed in its wake. And there are additional objections that apply specifically to the use of a Ramseyian method to develop a cardinal ranking of *actions*. While I lack the space to address these here, I think they can be surmounted, as indeed I attempt to do in another paper specifically devoted to background rankings.[16] Later on in this chapter, though, I will have something to say about agents who seem to lack precise background rankings.

Let me show you another application of my strategy. It involves a good old-fashioned trolley problem. Suppose that a train will strike and kill 25 people unless its path is obstructed. At a railroad crossing, a car full of 5 people sits in the shadow of a tractor-trailer, and at the wheel of the tractor-trailer we find you, dear reader. You may either use your vehicle to push the car in front of the train, thereby killing the 5 people but saving the 25, or you can abstain from doing that, in which case the 5 people will live but the 25 will die.[17] You have some credence in the proposition that

---

[15] See Ramsey (1926).   [16] This is ch. 3 of Sepielli (unpublished-*a*).

[17] The idea for this variant on the trolley problem comes from Steven Spielberg's first movie, *Duel*.

Andrew Sepielli

killing 5 is better than letting 25 die, and some credence in the proposition that letting 25 die is better than killing 5. (See Fig. 1.4.) This is, of course, a classic battle between consequentialism and non-consequentialism. So what's an uncertain trucker to do?

Let me impute to you two beliefs in practical conditionals. One accords with traditional consequentialism; the other accords with at least one brand of non-consequentialism. According to a traditional consequentialist view, there's no normative difference between killing and letting die. So let's suppose you believe that, if killing 5 is better than letting 25 die, then letting 25 die is equal to killing 25. According to many forms of non-consequentialism, letting die is not as bad as killing, but is still sort of bad. With that in mind, let's suppose you believe that, if letting 25 die is better than killing 5, then letting 25 die is equal to killing, let's just say, one person. (See Fig. 1.5.)

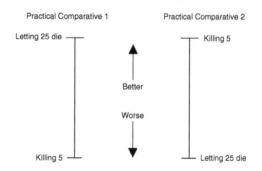

Fig. 1.4

Fig. 1.5

And now for the background rankings. You believe that the difference between killing 25 people and killing 5 people is 5 times the difference between killing 5 and killing one. This is a background ranking that you can accept regardless of your views regarding killing and letting die, for it involves only killings of different numbers of people. We can see this even more clearly by imagining a committed consequentialist and a committed non-consequentialist of a certain sort, both of whom could accept this ranking. (See Fig. 1.6.)

Finally, we can solve the PVDC as it confronts us in this situation. The difference between killing 25 and killing 5, according to the background ranking, is 5 times the difference between killing 5 and killing 1. So the difference between letting 25 die and killing 5, if letting 25 die has the same value as killing 25, is 5 times the difference between killing 5 and letting 25 die, if letting 25 die has the same value as killing 1.

EOV can be calculated in the same manner as before.

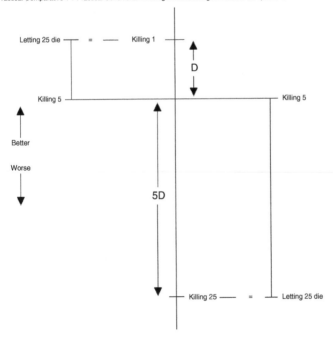

Fig. 1.6

Now, the abortion and trolley cases were useful expository devices, but each of them may have understated my method's scope of application in two ways. First, each was set up so that the actions in the practical comparatives were similar in salient non-normative respects to the actions in the background rankings with which they were 'linked'. Abortion bears obvious non-normative resemblance both to murder and to using birth control. That's why you often hear that abortion *is* murder, or that it's possible for someone to use abortion *as* birth control. Similarly, letting people die when you could have saved them is similar in obvious ways to killing them.

But this kind of similarity needn't obtain. So long as the agent has the appropriate practical conditionals, actions in his practical comparatives may be linked to very dissimilar actions in his background rankings. Consider the abortion case again. We could, in theory, replace *murdering an adult human being* with *stealing a widow's life savings*, and *using an innocuous form of birth control* with *eating an ice cream cone*, and the argument would go through just as before. (Of course, we'd now be talking about a different person.)

Secondly, I've focused on two cases where one of the actions mentioned in the practical comparative is also an action to be found on the background ranking. In the abortion case, bearing a child was in each of the practical comparatives and on the background ranking. The idea was supposed to be that the woman was unsure about where abortion stood on the background ranking—same value as murder, or same value as birth control?—but was sure about where bearing a child stood. In the trolley case, killing 5 people was in each of the comparatives and on the background ranking. The idea was supposed to be that you, the trucker, were sure about where killing 5 people stood on the background ranking, but unsure about where letting 25 die ranked—same value as killing 1, or same value as killing 25?

This was tacitly assumed in each of these cases because it seemed to fit with conventional thinking on these issues. But the assumption can be done away with. We can still compare degrees of value across practical comparatives, even when none of the actions in the comparatives are on the background ranking. However, it will require that the agent believe in slightly different practical conditionals. Let me put the point schematically: Suppose I'm uncertain whether A is better than B, or whether B is better than A. My background ranking includes *neither* A nor B, but it does include C, D, E, and F. Perhaps it includes some other actions, but these won't be relevant here. I can compare the differences across the comparatives if I believe in practical conditionals of the following form: *If A is better than B, then A is equivalent to C and B is equivalent to D*, and *If B is better than A, then A is equivalent to E and B is equivalent to F*—that is, practical conditionals that link *all* actions mentioned in the practical comparative to actions in the background ranking.

PART V: OBJECTIONS AND EXTENSIONS

Having laid out the basic framework for solving the PVDC, I now want to further explain and extend it in response to some objections.

The Multiple Act/Multiple Comparative Problem

I've been discussing situations in which there are precisely two choices—such as having an abortion or not, pushing a car full of people onto the train tracks or not. Thus described, these choices exhaust the possibility space, but one may worry that they fail to divide it finely enough. There are, after all, many ways of not pushing a car full of 5 people onto the train tracks, from the benign—keeping your truck still—to the monstrous—reversing your truck so as to crush the 6 people in the car behind you. Given all of these different ways, it will be difficult to locate *not pushing the car* on any sort of value scale, as that possibility is composed of some sub-possibilities that rank very high, and some sub-possibilities that rank very low. Sometimes, then, it will be helpful to consider the possibility space as divided up into more than two actions. The challenge is whether the proposal I've outlined can be modified to accommodate this.

I think that it can. Let's suppose we want to carve up the possibility space in a choice situation into 4 actions—A, B, C, and D. In that case, there will be 24 practical comparatives in which the agent might have some credence—from *A is better than B, which is better than C, which is better than D* to *D is better than C, which is better than B, which is better than A*. According to half of these, A will be better than B; according to the other half, B will be better than A; *mutatis mutandis* for A and C, A and C, B and C, and C and D.

We can assign all of the credence in practical comparatives according to which A is better than B to the proposition that A is better than B, and all of the credence in the comparatives according to which B ranks higher than A to the proposition that B is better than A. Call these propositions the '*New Comparatives*'. Then, we can look for practical conditionals associated with each of these new comparatives, and utilize background rankings just as we've been doing. This will tell us which of A and B has higher EOV. We can then do the same with B and C (and, if necessary, A and C), and so on down the line, until we have an ordering of the actions in terms of their expected values.

The Multiple Conditional Problem

There may also be more than one practical conditional per practical comparative. Suppose I have some credence in the practical comparative that A is better than B. I might not fully believe in the associated conditional that, if A is better than B, A is equivalent to C. Instead, I might have some credence in that conditional, some in that, if A is better than B, A is equivalent to D, some that, if A is better than B, A is equivalent to E, and so on. It's easy to think about this problem in connection with the abortion case and the trolley case. Perhaps abortion is equal to murdering an adult human, perhaps it's equal to killing a dolphin, perhaps it's equal to killing a rabbit, and so on. Perhaps letting 25 die is equivalent to killing 1, but perhaps it's equivalent to killing 2, or killing 3, or poking one in the chest, and so on. Can my approach to the PVDC handle more than one conditional per comparative?

It can, if our background ranking includes C, D, E, and whatever other actions are, according to a practical conditional, equal to some action in one of the practical comparatives. For then, we can use the background ranking to determine how the difference between A and B, if A is equivalent to C, compares to the difference if A is equivalent to D, how these compare to the difference if A is equivalent to E, and so on.

The difference in value between A and B will now depend on *both* which practical comparative is true *and* which practical conditional(s) are true. Our way of calculating EOV will need to be changed accordingly. Rather than taking as inputs the values of the action in question if various practical comparatives are true and the probabilities of the respective comparatives, our new way of calculating EOV chops up the space of possibilities more finely. It takes as inputs the values of the action in question if various practical comparative-practical conditional *pairs* obtain, and the probabilities of those respective pairs.[18]

The First Multiple Background Ranking Problem

Suppose that, in addition to being uncertain about practical comparatives, an agent is uncertain among different cardinal background rankings. She may have some credence in the background ranking according to which the difference between A and B is 5 times the difference between B and C, some credence in the background ranking according to which the first difference is

---

[18] Or, stated formally: $EOV = \sum_i \sum_j p(PC_i \ \& \ PCond_j) \cdot v(A \ given \ PC_i \ \& \ PCond_j)$.

10 times the second, some in the ranking according to which the first is one-third as great as the second. Does this sort of uncertainty threaten a person's ability to compare degrees of value across different normative hypotheses?

Not as much as you may initially think. Let me point out three reasons why.

First, a person need only be certain in a *partial* background ranking in order for her value differences in a given situation to be comparable via the stated method. Consider the trolley case once again. Here, we need only three actions on the background ranking—*killing 1 person, killing 5 people*, and *killing 25 people*. If you are not certain of how, say, *killing 300 people* ranks cardinally vis-à-vis these other actions, that's fine; we can still compare value differences in the aforementioned manner.

Second, the items ranked in the background ranking are actions *under descriptions*. It's important to keep this in mind, for the following reason: Uncertainty about the ranking of a set of actions under one set of descriptions in no way precludes certainty about the ranking of the same set of actions under a different set of descriptions. Consider a toy example involving a merely ordinal ranking. I may have some credence that worshiping Allah is better than dancing the Macarena, which is better than worshiping Jehovah, and some credence that worshiping Jehovah is better than dancing the Macarena, which is better than worshiping Allah. But this does not mean that all is uncertainty. For I may at the same time be certain that worshiping the true God is better than dancing the Macarena, which is better than worshiping the false God. It's just that I'm not sure whether Allah or Jehovah (or any other god) is the true God. The lesson of this example is that, if we can't get a certain ranking of actions under one set of descriptions, we should try another set of descriptions. That every action falls under infinite descriptions gives us a fair bit of room to work here.

Thirdly, we may partially dissolve the problem of multiple background rankings by 'combining' those rankings. Consider that different background rankings can imply many of the same value relations among actions. For example, if one background ranking says that the difference between two actions is 10 times the difference between two other actions, and another background ranking says that the difference between the first two is 20 times the difference between the second two, then each ranking implies that the difference between the first two is *at least 10 times, and no greater than 20 times* the difference between the second two.

In cases like this, where some background rankings have the same implications, we can assign all of the agent's credence in those rankings to their shared implications. If all of an agent's background rankings have some implication, then we may assign credence of 1, or absolute certainty, to this implication. We can use these *Combined Rankings*, along with practical conditionals, to compare differences in value between practical comparatives. In other words, we can use combined rankings just as we used regular background rankings.

Combined rankings will specify 'at least ... at most' value differences, rather than precise value differences, between possible actions. In some cases, this will render these combined rankings unhelpful. Suppose my credence is .07 that A is better than B, and .93 that B is better than A. I've used a combined ranking to determine that the difference in value between A and B, if A is better, is at least 10 times and no greater than 20 times the difference between B and A, if B is better. In that case, I can't determine which action has the higher EOV. But sometimes it will be helpful to know that one value difference is at least 10 times and no greater than 20 times another. If my credences in the two practical comparatives are .01 and .99, respectively, or .5 and .5 respectively, then I will be able to tell which of A and B has a higher EOV.

The Second Multiple Background Ranking Problem

There's another multiple background ranking problem—this time, involving background rankings with the same cardinal structure over the relevant intervals. Let me explain. I've been tacitly assuming that someone who believes that the difference between, say, abortion and bearing a child is 20 times the difference between bearing a child and using the rhythm method thereby believes in a single value ranking according to which this is true. But this doesn't follow. To say that an agent has credence of P that the difference between A and B is 20 times the difference between B and C is to say that P is somehow divided among cardinal rankings according to which these differences obtain. But the rankings needn't be one and the same.[19] They need only be what I shall call '*Partially Cocardinal*' rankings. (See Fig. 1.7.) Partially cocardinal rankings have the same ratios of value differences between at least some actions (although they may have different ratios of value differences between other actions; by contrast, *Completely Cocardinal* rankings have exactly the same cardinal structure as one another—the same ratios of value differences between all ranked actions).[20]

That a bit of cardinal information does not determine a single value ranking presents a problem for the EOV calculation performed above.

---

[19] Thanks to Toby Ord for presenting me with this objection.

[20] As Lara Buchak and Wlodek Rabinowicz each mentioned in conversation, it's not obviously meaningful to talk about distinct rankings that are nonetheless completely cocardinal with one another.

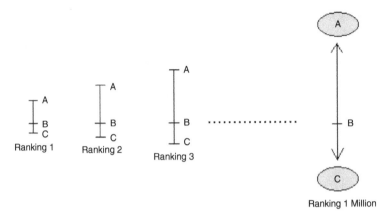

Fig. 1.7

Consider two rankings that are cocardinal with respect to the actions *murdering an adult human being, bearing a child*, and *using the rhythm method*. Call these 'Ranking 1' and 'Ranking 2'. Suppose that Ranking 2's value differences in this region are 1,000 times larger than Ranking 1's. Suppose further that these rankings are dependent on practical comparatives and conditionals in the following way: if abortion has the same value as murder, then the Ranking 1 obtains; but if abortion has the same value as the rhythm method, then Ranking 2 obtains. On these suppositions, the difference between abortion and non-abortion, if the former is better, will be *larger* than the difference between the two actions, if the latter is better. For although the difference between murder and bearing a child is larger than the difference between bearing a child and the rhythm method according to each of these rankings, the difference between bearing a child and the rhythm method according to the 'expanded' Ranking 2 absolutely dwarfs the difference between murder and bearing a child according to the 'contracted' Ranking 1. And it's the way these two differences compare that matters for our purposes.

Now, it may seem as though there's something contrived about this scenario. Why would the value differences between actions like murder, bearing a child, and using the rhythm method be larger if abortion is as bad as murder, and smaller if abortion is as innocuous as the rhythm method? Speaking for myself, nothing about my views on abortion seems to suggest anything of the sort. In cases like this, where the practical conditional seems to be unrelated to the choice among partially cocardinal rankings, the approach I'll take is to divide the agent's credence among these rankings the same way regardless of which practical conditional obtains. So if the distribution of credences on the condition that abortion is as bad as murder is, say, .01 to each of 100 partially cocardinal rankings, so should it be on the condition that abortion is as benign as birth control. If credence is distributed .01 to Ranking 1, .42 to Ranking 2, .000004 to Ranking 3, and .569996 to Ranking 34 on the condition that abortion is as bad as murder—put to one side the strangeness of such a distribution—so should it be if abortion is as benign as birth control.

When this 'equal distribution' constraint is in place, the distribution of credences over background rankings will be independent of practical comparatives and practical conditionals. Each of the background rankings, then, will be a sort of 'stand-in' for the others. This constraint will allow us to put aside the problem of multiple partially cocardinal background rankings for all practical purposes, and treat all of the rankings as though they were one and the same.

However, it may be sensible in some cases to reject this constraint, and allow the distribution of credences over partially cocardinal background rankings to be different for different practical comparatives and conditionals. But, of course, this will mean that there won't be a single difference in value between two actions if some practical comparative-practical conditional pair obtains; there will only be a difference in value between two actions on the condition that (a) some practical comparative is true, (b) some practical conditional is true, *and* (c) some background ranking of a partially cocardinal family is true.

We will have to modify our way of calculating EOV to accommodate this. The inputs will now be probabilities of practical comparative-practical conditional-background ranking *triples*, and values of actions given those triples.[21]

APPENDIX: OTHER SOLUTIONS TO THE PROBLEM OF VALUE DIFFERENCE COMPARISONS

Lockhart's solution employs something called the 'Principle of Equity among Moral Theories':

The maximum degrees of moral rightness of all possible actions in a situation according to competing moral theories should be considered equal. The minimum degrees of moral rightness of possible actions in a situation according to competing theories should be considered equal unless all possible actions are equally right according to one of the theories

---

[21] $\sum_i \sum_j \sum_k p(PC_i \ \& \ PCond_j \ \& \ BR_k) \cdot v(A \ \text{given} \ PC_i \ \& \ PCond_j \ \& \ BR_k)$.

(in which case all of the actions should be considered to be maximally right according to that theory). (2000: 84)

I criticize this principle in Sepielli (2006) and (unpublished-*b*). It is reminiscent of the 'zero-one rule' in the literature on interpersonal comparisons of utility. See Hausman (1995) for a criticism of the zero-one rule.

Ross's first solution involves assigning values to agents based on their credences in normative theories. Here's just a snippet:

> To say that the difference in value between ordering the veal cutlet and ordering the veggie wrap is one hundred times as great according to [a vegetarian moral] theory as it is according to the traditional moral theory is to say, among other things, that if one's credence were divided between these two theories, then it would be more rational to order the veggie wrap than the veal cutlet if and only if one's degree of credence in [the vegetarian] theory exceeded .01. (2006: 763)

The main problem with this strategy is that it simply assumes the rationality of maximizing EOV under normative uncertainty. But this is a position that should be argued for independently of one's solution to the PVDC, not merely assumed as a means to solving the problem. Otherwise, we prejudge the answer to our primary question — "What is it rational to do under normative uncertainty?" — in the course of solving a secondary problem. So this first solution of Ross's is unsatisfying.

Ross's second solution resembles in some ways the method I've developed. See Ross (2006: 764–5), but his is more preliminary, and differs from mine in ways that, I think, favor the latter. Those curious about the differences are encouraged to read Ross's very interesting paper, and my discussion of it in Sepielli (unpublished-*a*).

REFERENCES

Broome, John (1991) *Weighing Goods: Equality, Uncertainty, and Time* (Oxford: Basil Blackwell).

—— (2004) *Weighing Lives* (Oxford: Oxford University Press).

—— (2007) 'Wide or Narrow Scope' *Mind* 116: 359–70.

The Catholic Encyclopedia (1913), available at http://www.newadvent.org/cathen/.

Elster, Jon, and Roemer, John (eds.) (1991) *Interpersonal Comparisons of Well-Being* (Cambridge: Cambridge University Press).

Gewirth, Alan (1978) *Reason and Morality* (Chicago: University of Chicago Press).

Guerrero, Alexander A. (2007) 'Don't Know, Don't Kill: Moral Ignorance, Culpability, and Caution' *Philosophical Studies* 136: 59–97.

Hammond, Peter (1976) 'Why Ethical Measures of Inequality Need Interpersonal Comparisons' *Theory and Decision* 7: 263–74.

Harsanyi, John (1955) 'Cardinal Welfare, Individualistic Ethics, and the Interpersonal Comparison of Utility' *Journal of Political Economy* 63: 309–21.

Hausman, Daniel M. (1995) 'The Impossibility of Interpersonal Utility Comparisons' *Mind* 104: 473–90.

Hudson, James (1989) 'Subjectivization in Ethics' *American Philosophical Quarterly* 26: 221–9.

Kant, Immanuel (1785) *Groundwork of the Metaphysics of Morals*, trans. H. J. Paton (New York: Harper & Row, 1964).

Kolodny, Niko (2005) 'Why Be Rational?' *Mind* 114: 509–63.

—— (2007) 'State or Process Requirements?' *Mind* 116: 371–85.

Liguori, St Alphonsus (1755) *Theologia Moralis, 2nd edn*, trans. R. P. Blakeney. (London: Reformation Society, 1852).

Lockhart, Ted (2000) *Moral Uncertainty and its Consequences* (Oxford: Oxford University Press).

de Medina, Bartolomé (1577) *Expositio in 1am 2ae S. Thomae.*

The New Catholic Encyclopedia, 2nd edn (2002) (Washington: Catholic University Press).

Oddie, Graham (1995) 'Moral Uncertainty and Human Embryo Experimentation,' in K. W. M. Fulford, G. Gillett, and J. M. Soskice (eds.), *Medicine and Moral Reasoning* (Oxford: Oxford University Press).

Parfit, Derek (unpublished) *On What Matters.*

Pascal, Blaise (1656–7) *The Provincial Letters*, trans. A. J. Krailsheimer (New York: Penguin Books, 1967).

Prümmer, Dominic M. (1957) *Handbook of Moral Theology* (New York: P. J. Kennedy and Sons).

Ramsey, F. P. (1926) 'Truth and Probability,' in R. B. Braithwaite (ed.), *The Foundations of Mathematics and Other Logical Essays* (New York: Harcourt, Brace, and Company, 1931).

Robbins, Lionel (1938) 'Inter-personal Comparisons of Utility' *Economic Journal* 48: 635–41.

Ross, Jacob (2006) 'Rejecting Ethical Deflationism' *Ethics* 116: 742–68.

Sepielli, Andrew (2006) 'Review of Ted Lockhart's *Moral Uncertainty and its Consequences*' *Ethics* 116: 601–3.

—— (unpublished-*a*) *'Along an Imperfectly-Lighted Path'*: Practical Rationality and Normative Uncertainty.

—— (unpublished-*b*) 'Moral Uncertainty and the Principle of Equity among Moral Theories.'

Spielberg, Steven (1971) *Duel* (Universal Television).

Weatherson, Brian (2002) 'Review of Ted Lockhart's *Moral Uncertainty and its Consequences*' *Mind* 111: 393–6.

2

The Natural and the Normative

Brad Majors

It is a commonplace to observe that it is a commonplace to observe that the moral supervenes upon the natural.[1] Roughly speaking, to say that the moral supervenes upon the natural is to say that it is necessary that fixing the natural fixes the moral. This much is granted by nearly everyone working in ethical theory. One cannot, however, be much more precise than this without running into controversial issues. There is little agreement concerning, for example, the kind of modality appropriate to the formulation of moral supervenience; the kind of entity or entities the properties of which are at issue in such a formulation—whether, that is, they be actions, individual moral agents, situations, states of affairs, or entire worlds; and, finally, whether moral differences unaccompanied by natural differences are impossible across possible worlds, or merely within a single such world.[2]

The central thesis of this chapter is that moral theorists have paid insufficient attention to these distinctions. And in so doing they have made significant mistakes concerning the relationship between the natural and the normative.

Thanks to Matthew Chrisman, Terence Cuneo, Michael Ridge, Russ Shafer-Landau, and to a pair of anonymous referees for comments on earlier versions of this material. A quite different incarnation of the chapter was presented at the 4th annual Metaethics Workshop at the University of Wisconsin-Madison, in the autumn of 2007. I benefited as well from the comments of those present on that occasion.

[1] See, among many others, Brink (1989: 160), Smith (1994: 22, 40), Jackson (1998: 118), Shafer-Landau (2003: 77), Dancy (1993: 77; 2004: 87), and Huemer (2005: 202).

[2] Sturgeon (2009—Ch. 3 this volume) argues persuasively that it makes a great deal of difference precisely what one takes to be the subvenient base underlying moral properties—whether they are taken to be natural, descriptive, or factual properties, for example. His central thesis is that there seems to be no single supervenience thesis that can (or should) be accepted by all metaethicists. Since I will be dealing in this chapter only with particular versions of moral supervenience, formulated by others, I think that my methodology and conclusions are not in any tension with Sturgeon's illuminating discussion.

Neglect of the significance of two distinctions, in particular, has caused trouble. The first is that between local and global supervenience. I will contend that the most common formulations of moral supervenience fail to respect this distinction, and as a result actually state falsehoods. The second distinction is that between weak and strong supervenience. The former proscribes only the possibility of moral differences without natural differences within individual possible worlds; the latter claims its impossibility, in addition, across possible worlds. I will argue that neglect of each of these distinctions vitiates Simon Blackburn's supervenience-based argument against moral realism.

The structure of the chapter is as follows: Section 1 introduces the notion of supervenience, and briefly mentions roles it was originally called upon to play in the philosophy of mind. The purpose of this section is merely to provide introduction and orientation; it may be safely skipped by those already familiar with the relevant issues and history. Section 2 begins the substantive discussion by detailing the respects in which local and global versions of supervenience differ, one from another, including reasons for favoring the latter where the relationship between physical properties and representational mental states is concerned. Section 3 applies the lessons learned here to the issue of moral supervenience. It is argued that one very popular way of formulating moral supervenience is flawed, by virtue of neglecting the distinction between local and global versions of the doctrine. Sections 4–5 discuss differences between weak and strong versions of supervenience, arguing that clarity here points the way toward a solution to Blackburn's problem. In Section 6 I consider the suggestion that what Blackburn is really after is an explanation of the conceptual truth of moral supervenience. Finally, Section 7 contains brief concluding remarks.

1

The term 'supervene' is occasionally employed, in non-philosophical parlance, as an intransitive verb. To say that something supervened, in this sense, is to say that it came to pass. W. V. Quine employed the term in this way, in his autobiography, describing his teenage years: "Necking supervened in time, as necking will" (1985: 43). This use of the term is, however, only distantly related to its philosophical meaning. In the early part of the twentieth century, some British Emergentists, such as Lloyd Morgan, used the term in a sense intermediate between its vernacular and philosophical meanings (McLaughlin and Bennett 2005). The first clear use of the contemporary concept of supervenience, though not of the term, is in G. E. Moore, who suggested that two things cannot differ in respect of quality without differing in respect of intrinsic nature (1922: 263). The first clear use of the term, in its present sense, is by R. M. Hare, who associated it closely with his doctrine of universalizability (1952: 80). Hare later claimed that the term was frequently used in its philosophical sense at Oxford in the 1940s, though he does not remember who originated this use (1984: 1).

It was not, however, until Donald Davidson employed the term and the concept in his classic essay 'Mental Events,' in 1970, that the contemporary discussion of supervenience began. Davidson had reasoned that while any view which identifies mental and physical features or *properties* is not credible, it is nevertheless possible and plausible to maintain that mental *events*—where events are taken to be unstructured particulars—are identical with physical events. As stated, though, the resulting view is too lax: It permits the possibility that mental properties float completely free of physical properties, in the sense that there are no necessary connections whatever between them. This is not something that any physicalist, reductive or not, should be prepared to abide. In response to the difficulty Davidson appealed to supervenience:

> Mental characteristics are in some sense dependent, or supervenient, on physical characteristics. Such supervenience might be taken to mean that there cannot be two events exactly alike in all physical respects but differing in some mental respects, or that an object cannot alter in some mental respects without altering in some physical respects.   (1970: 214)

The combination of token-identity and supervenience appeared to enable Davidson's 'anomalous monism' to accommodate physicalist intuitions and inclinations, without running afoul of the alleged fact that the mental is normative in a sense incompatible with the identification of psychological and physical properties.

Supervenience theses remained popular and important throughout the next two decades, despite a growing dissatisfaction with Davidson's own views. They were, indeed, essential components of most or all formulations of nonreductive forms of physicalism during this period. The work of Jaegwon Kim was particularly influential here.

Most of Kim's work on supervenience at this time was devoted to distinguishing different varieties of supervenience—such as strong and weak, local, global, and parametric forms of supervenience—together with explorations of interrelations and implications amongst them; and to suggesting possible applications for the notion, both inside and outside the philosophy of mind, including applications in ethics and aesthetics, epistemology, metaphysics, and philosophy of science (Kim 1993*b*). But supervenience also played a key role in Kim's early account of mental causation, which employed the notion of 'supervenient causation.' The idea was that non-fundamental properties, such as mental properties, are causes in the sense that they supervene upon more fundamental causally efficacious properties. Thus mental property M 'superveniently causes' mental property M* just in case M supervenes upon P, M* supervenes upon P*, and P causes P*.

Kim soon abandoned this account, in part because it became clear that the sort of counterfactual dependence that supervenience was brought in to provide is not sufficient even for causal relevance (cf. Block 1990; Majors 2003). Indeed, Kim eventually arrived at the opinion that supervenience is of no help whatsoever in solving the mind/body problem. His current view is rather that supervenience *states* the problem—what is wanted from an account of the mind/body relation (*inter alia*) is an explanation of *why* supervenience obtains, rather than the series of empty assurances that it does obtain, which were to be found in many discussions of non-reductive physicalism (Kim 1998: ch. 2). As we will see, a similar opinion had been arrived at much earlier, in the metaethical literature, by Blackburn.

We turn now to discussion of the essential differences between local and global forms of supervenience, and to the significance of the distinction for work in metaethics.

2

Local supervenience theses specify dependency or covariation relationships between classes of properties of individual things, such as persons, states, and events. The most popular such thesis is strong supervenience, which in its psychophysical incarnation runs as follows:

(SS) $\Box$ $(\forall x)(\forall M)$ $(Mx \supset [(\exists P) Px \,\&\, \Box (\forall y)(Py \supset My)])$

This closed formula states that it is necessarily the case that, for all individuals and all mental properties, if an individual has a mental property, there is a physical property which it has as well, and it is necessarily the case that anything which has the physical property in question possesses the mental property.

It is an obvious consequence of this thesis that two individual thinkers who do not differ with respect to their physical properties cannot differ with respect to their mental properties. And it was noticed fairly early on in the debate that this consequence is in conflict with anti-individualism about the individuation of representational mental states. *Anti-individualism* is the view that the natures of many representational mental states and events are partly determined by nonintentional relations to a subject matter (Putnam 1975; Burge 1979, 1981).[3] That is to say, it is the view that part of what it is to be in certain mental states is to bear nonrepresentational relations—paradigmatically, causal relations—to the subject matter ostensibly represented. It follows from this thesis together with reasonable assumptions that two thinkers can be physically indiscernible while differing with respect to the mental properties they instantiate. This is in direct conflict with (SS).

A familiar sort of example will help to make the point clear. Suppose that Jones is a normal thinker in our world who possesses the concept *water*. Like all of us, she stands in causal relations to samples of H_2O in the local and wider environment. Suppose further that there is a microphysically indiscernible thinker, Jones*, who inhabits a world in which there is no water. The stuff in the lakes, rivers, and streams around this second thinker is not H_2O, but a distinct substance XYZ. This substance is not water, though members of the world use the word-form 'water' to refer to it. Call the substance XYZ 'twater'. Jones* has never been in contact with water, nor have any of her cohorts. They have been in contact only with twater. Neither has anyone in this world theorized about water.

Now consider a situation in which each thinker utters the sentence-form 'Water is wet' in a normal, assertive context.[4] Jones expresses thereby the thought *that water is wet*. But Jones* does not. She has never been in any sort of contact with water, and thus has had no opportunity to form a concept of it; concepts are ways of thinking about things, and Jones* has no way of thinking about water. But attitudes or thoughts are typed (individuated) by their contents. Part of what it is to be a belief that p is to be related to the propositional content p. A state with a different content is *ipso facto* a different state. It follows that Jones and Jones* are in distinct mental states, despite being microphysically indiscernible—for the propositional contents of their respective beliefs differ. Jones believes that water is wet; she is no more in a position to have thoughts about twater than Jones* is about water. Jones* believes that twater is wet. Since the two thinkers we have described are physically indiscernible, but

---

[3] It is necessary to specify that the relations in question be nonintentional (nonrepresentational) because of the fact that it is trivial, on any view, that representation requires the obtaining of representational relations.

[4] We speak of word- and sentence-*forms* here in order to respect the widely held view that words and associated linguistic items such as sentences are partly individuated in terms of their meanings. Thus Jones and Jones* do not use the same word to refer to water—and their respective sentences describing water are not the same—since the words they do use have different meanings (this is the point of the argument). But the words and sentences they employ have the same (syntactic) forms.

mentally distinct, the possibility of such a case appears to show that (SS) is false.

In response to this sort of difficulty, many have proposed replacing the *local* supervenience claim embodied in (SS) with a *global* one. Notice that it seems a necessary condition on the sort of variation in representational content in the above example, and others like it, that there be environmental differences across the two cases. Were it not for the fact that Jones's environment contains water, while Jones*'s does not, it would not be plausible to suppose that the two express different concepts with their respective uses of the word-form 'water'. This suggests that no two *worlds* can differ mentally without differing physically. The resulting thesis is called 'global psychophysical supervenience':

(GS) No two possible worlds are physically but not mentally indiscernible.[5]

Since the two worlds at issue in the example provided are not physically indiscernible, the case is not incompatible with (GS). The thesis constrains the relationship between mental and physical properties, though not in a way that is incompatible with the fact that features of a thinker's context partly determine the concepts she possesses, and therefore the thoughts she can think.

Now some have thought that global psychophysical supervenience is too lax (e.g. Kim 1984 and Grimes 1995). They have pointed out that it is compatible with the possibility of cases in which two worlds differ mentally in highly significant ways, despite there being only trivial physical differences between them. For example, (GS) is compatible with there being a world, w_1, in which there is no mentality at all, and a world, w_2, which is mentally just like our world—where the only physical difference between w_1 and w_2 is that the latter contains a single proton that the former lacks.

But it has seldom been noticed that local supervenience theses have precisely the same feature.[6] (SS), for example, is consistent with there being

---

[5] Strictly speaking, this thesis is rejected by many or most physicalists. This is because they think that two physically indiscernible worlds could differ mentally if one, but not the other, had some disembodied mind 'added-on' to it; cf. Horgan (1982), Lewis (1983), Chalmers (1996), and Witmer (1999). Such physicalists deny that our world contains anything like this, but do not think that such a situation is impossible. Though I will not argue the point here, I think it can and should be questioned whether mental states in general are possible in the absence of dispositions to behavior of a sort which would seem to require the possession of physical properties. So it may not be the case that theses such as (GS) need to be restricted in any of the usual ways, if the kind of add-on envisioned by these thinkers is a conceptual impossibility.

[6] Paull and Sider (1992: 842) make essentially the same point.

two creatures that differ physically only in that one possesses a single neuron the other lacks, but who are completely different mentally—the former has no thoughts or other mental states at all, while the latter has the mental life of a normal, adult human being. Global and local supervenience theses are precisely analogous in this respect, and so the kind of laxity in question cannot be a reason for preferring the latter over the former.

In addition, it has sometimes been contended that the difference I have been stressing between the two sorts of supervenience theses is illusory. For example, Kim had claimed at one point that (SS) and (GS) are equivalent. Now it seems clear enough that (SS) implies (GS). If there can not be any mental differences without natural differences within *individual thinkers*, then there could presumably be no mental differences across *worlds* absent natural differences. For it is only individual thinkers who instantiate mental properties. But Kim went further, maintaining that the converse implication holds as well, thus insisting that "(g)lobal supervenience ... is nothing but strong supervenience" (Kim 1984: 168). It was soon demonstrated that this claim is false. A model was described on which (GS) is true, but (SS) is false (Petrie 1987). And if they were equivalent there could of course be no such model. Consider a pair of worlds with only two individuals, a and b, and two property-types, F and G, instanced as follows:

w_1: Ga, Fa, Gb
w_2: Ga, ⌐Fa, ⌐Gb

Now consider the question whether the Fs in this model strongly supervene on the Gs. It is clear that they do not, since there is an F-difference—a difference in a's possession of F—between the worlds with no corresponding G difference—a is the same in each world, with respect to possession of property G. So (SS) is false on this model. But the model is entirely consistent with (GS), since there are G-differences between the two worlds. In w_1 b has G, and in w_2 she does not. This shows that (SS) and (GS) are not formally equivalent.[7]

The upshot of our reflections here is that there are important differences between local psychophysical supervenience theses, such as (SS), and global psychophysical supervenience theses, like (GS). The former, but not the latter, are inconsistent with the role of environmental context in determining the natures of many representational mental states and events. We will see in the next section that these lessons from the philosophy of mind have not been widely appreciated in the metaethical literature. One consequence of this is that the most common sorts of formulations of moral supervenience actually state falsehoods.

---

[7] Though see Paull and Sider (1992) for criticism and refinement of Petrie's argument.

3

Here is a standard formulation of the supervenience of the evaluative upon the natural, taken from an important recent discussion by Michael Smith:

Take any two persons, actions, characters, or states of affairs that are identical in all of their naturalistic features: every naturalistic feature of the one is a feature of the other, and vice versa. These two persons, actions, characters, or states of affairs must be identical in evaluative respects as well. There can be no evaluative difference without a naturalistic difference.   (2000: 208)

This is clearly a version of local supervenience, since the entities it is claimed cannot differ evaluatively without differing naturalistically are individuals—persons, actions, characters, states of affairs—rather than worlds. And it is false for the same reason that local psychophysical supervenience is false. Differences in context, in both the mental and the evaluative cases, can affect whether an individual possesses the relevant supervenient properties. Her physical or naturalistic properties, properly so-called, do not of themselves settle the matter.

Consider a pair of moral agents, Gottlob and Gottlob*. Gottlob inhabits world w_1, and Gottlob* inhabits distinct world w_2. The two agents are physically type-identical—they instantiate all and only the same physical properties, properties described by physical science. Suppose that the same physical laws govern each world. Then, because the agents are physically indiscernible, they make the same physical movements. On one particular occasion, Gottlob makes physical movement m_1, and Gottlob* makes type-identical movement m_2. It just so happens that the contexts are different enough that the action Gottlob performs is morally right (or morally good, or admirable), while Gottlob*'s action is not—the latter is morally neutral, or morally bad, or condemnable.

That this is possible may be seen by reflecting upon the loose relation between physical movements and intentional actions. Making a particular physical movement is neither necessary nor sufficient for performing any given action. It is not *necessary*, because it is always possible for slightly different physical movements to realize the same intentional action. Actions are multiply realizable physically. And it is not *sufficient*, because the physical movement might have been made in something other than an intentional manner. Actions are partly individuated by the mental states that give rise to them. Any given movement could have been made in the absence of any particular mental state. So no physical movement is such that its presence is sufficient for any given action.

What could be responsible for such a difference in the moral status of the actions performed in worlds w_1 and w_2? There may be morally relevant contextual differences that do not stem from physical or naturalistic features of the agent's physical movements. The morally relevant differences, that is to say, may stem from the character of the *actions* in question, rather than from the nature of the physical *movements*. Gottlob's action could have been one of helping someone in need. Gottlob*'s action could have been the aiding of someone known to be engaging in morally questionable behavior. And this despite the fact that each makes precisely the same physical movements—each agent's action could have (partially) consisted, for example, in the movement of his arm towards another. Given the supposition that physical indiscernibility entails naturalistic indiscernibility, this sort of case appears to show that naturalistically indiscernible agents can differ with respect to moral status, thus contravening Smith's formulation of moral supervenience.

Now it can be objected that the case I have described is incoherent. If Gottlob* knows, while Gottlob does not know, that the person in question is engaging in morally questionable behavior, then there must be physical differences between them. Of course, knowledge does not itself supervene upon the physical make-up of a thinker. This is because, in the general case, the truth of one's beliefs is independent of one's physical make-up. So it might be thought that the difficulty can be evaded by stipulating that, while Gottlob* knows, and Gottlob does not know, that the person in question is behaving immorally, this is simply because the belief that they share is true in the former case, but false in the latter one. But this will not work. If Gottlob *believes*, even falsely, that the person he is helping is behaving immorally, then it becomes much less clear that what he is doing is morally right; and the pointed contrast upon which the argument turns is lost.

A better way to respond to the objection is to point out that the knowledge in question need not be present in Gottlob* himself. It can be rather a piece of general knowledge, or other form of knowledge that he ought to have, and for lacking which he is epistemically culpable. Gottlob is not in this situation, because of relevant differences in context. Therefore, the latter is behaving morally, and the former is not, despite their physical and naturalistic indiscernibility. So Smith's version of moral supervenience is false.

Of course, there is nothing terribly unusual or idiosyncratic about Smith's version of the thesis. Such local moral supervenience claims are widely, almost universally, endorsed.[8] If the kind of case I have described works as

---

[8] Here are some additional examples—Klagge: "In any possible world in which [an] object or action exists and has the same naturalistic properties as it has in a given possible

it is claimed to work, it refutes all versions of local moral supervenience; just as the twin-earth type case discussed in Section 2 above refutes versions of local psychophysical supervenience.

Notice that if one is of a consequentialist bent then it ought to be obvious that naturalistically indiscernible agents can differ in moral status. For it is surely uncontroversial that naturalistically indiscernible agents and actions may cause, or result in, morally different consequences.

Another objection must now be faced. Smith and others who endorse local supervenience theses presumably intend to include *relational*, as well as *intrinsic*, naturalistic properties of the moral agents in question. And of course, if there is no restriction put upon what counts as a relational property of an agent, any difference in the environment, or moral context, across two worlds will show up in relational properties of their respective denizens. This might appear to be enough to allow the proponent of local moral supervenience to overcome the objection lodged above.

The primary problem with this line of reasoning is that many of the sorts of relational properties in question do not seem to count as naturalistic features of an agent. To the extent that we have any sort of secure grip on the concept *natural*, in this context, it is fixed by the proprietary vocabulary, concepts, and properties of the natural sciences. These sciences include physics, chemistry, biology, physiology, and neuroscience. For a property to be closely associated with the kinds of one or more of these sciences just is what it is for it to be natural. A consequence of this, I believe, is that two property-tokens which are treated by these sciences as being of the same type are necessarily naturalistically indiscernible. And a corollary of this further point is that not all relational properties count as natural properties, even when the *relata* are themselves natural properties, events, or objects. Only those properties, whether intrinsic or relational, which *make some difference* to the explanatory interests and aims of the natural sciences are appropriately considered natural properties, in this context. Furthermore, the differences in relational properties that I have allowed to obtain between Gottlob and Gottlob* are precisely not of this character. From the perspective of the natural sciences, they are indiscernible. The differences between them are of no concern to explanations in these sciences.

world, it will have the same moral properties as it has in the given possible world" (1984: 375–6); Audi: "No two things (including actions) can have the same natural properties and differ in their moral ones" (1990: 6); Shafer-Landau: "Something exemplifies a moral property entirely in virtue of its possessing certain natural features" (2003: 75); and Miller: "If two things have exactly the same natural properties, then they also have exactly the same moral properties" (2003: 31). Many more such formulations could be added to the list.

And, as I say, this is just what it is for the two agents or objects to be naturalistically indiscernible.[9]

A secondary point is that allowing all manner of relational properties to count as natural properties, in one's formulation of moral supervenience, collapses the important distinction between local and global forms of supervenience. For if no restriction is put upon the sorts of relational properties that count as natural, then local and global moral supervenience theses are provably equivalent. This may be seen as follows: Suppose that unrestricted local moral supervenience (as we may call it) were false; then there would be a moral difference across persons, actions, characters, or states of affairs, without a difference in their respective relational natural properties; but without the latter sort of difference there can be no difference in the worlds the entities inhabit—any difference in world would show up as a difference in the relevant class of relational properties; so global moral supervenience would be false. Suppose now that global moral supervenience were false; then there would be a moral difference across two worlds without a natural difference between the worlds; but then there cannot be any naturalistic difference across the inhabitants of one world and their counterparts in the other—any difference in the two worlds would show up as a difference in the relational natural properties of the populace of the two worlds; so unrestricted local moral supervenience would be false. Hence the two are equivalent.

The fact that allowing any kind of difference between two worlds to count as a naturalistic difference across the inhabitants of the worlds collapses the distinction between local and global supervenience is a very good reason to reject the proposal. Add to this the fact that the proposal loses touch with what it *means* for a property to be natural, and I think we are warranted in rejecting the response proposed on Smith's behalf.

A final, related point is that insisting that any naturalistic feature of a world makes for a relational natural property of every individual in the world makes nonsense of the corresponding debate in the philosophy of mind. As we have in effect seen, the move to global supervenience theses on the basis of the recognition of implications of anti-individualism presupposes that some principled distinction can be drawn between a thinker's physical properties, on the one hand, and properties of an environment or world that do not bear upon the correct physical description of the thinker, on the other. The Petrie-style counterexample to Kim's claim of the equivalence of (SS) and (GS), considered above, itself works only if we follow the usual and sensible practice of drawing such a distinction. This seems to me an additional reason for insisting upon some distinction between those

---

[9] See Majors (2005) for arguments that bear upon these claims.

relational properties that do, and those that do not, make for a naturalistic difference across moral agents or actions.

I do not of course suggest that Smith and the others who have endorsed local forms of moral supervenience are unaware of the fact that context often matters to morality. Their mistake concerns rather the nature of supervenience, and the implications for it of the context-dependent character of morality. To endorse the sort of supervenience thesis quoted at the outset of the section is in effect to conflate the two forms of supervenience, local and global. We will see in the next couple of sections that confusion over the distinction between weak and strong supervenience has caused trouble as well.

4

Strong supervenience theses such as (SS) are contrasted with forms of weak supervenience, such as the following version of weak psychophysical supervenience:

(**WS**) □ $(\forall x)(\forall M)$ $(Mx \supset [(\exists P) Px$ & $(\forall y)(Py \supset My)])$

This thesis claims that, for all possible individuals and mental properties, if an individual has mental property M, then it has a physical property P, and anything that has P has M. It will be noticed that the only difference between this thesis and (SS), formulated in Section 2 above, is the absence of a second necessity operator in the former. The universally quantified conditional in the conjunctive consequent of (WS) is not claimed to hold of necessity. One way to explain the difference this makes is to point out that while (SS) implies that there are no two *possible individuals* who are physically indiscernible but mentally dissimilar, (WS) implies only that no two *individuals who inhabit the same possible world* can be mentally distinct but physically indiscernible. In other words, according to (WS), it is a contingent truth that every individual with physical property P has mental property M—it might have been otherwise.

Another way to make the same point is as follows: There is a distinction commonly drawn in the philosophy of science between lawlike and accidental generalizations. It is a law that, *ceteris paribus*, heating a pot of water to 212 degrees Fahrenheit, at a certain altitude, will cause it to boil. Such laws support counterfactual claims. Not only is it true that every actual case in which a pot is so heated its water boils. But it is true as well that *were* any pot to be treated in this manner, the same sort of effect would ensue. Laws purport to state necessary regularities in the world.

Not all true generalizations are laws, however. To use a familiar example, it may be true of me that every coin in my pocket is a dime. Then it will be true that every time I reach into my pocket (on this occasion, i.e. in this world) and produce a coin, the coin will be a dime. But this is not a law. It need not be true that, *were* I (on some other occasion, i.e. in some other possible world) to produce a coin from my pocket, it would be a dime. Accidental generalizations do not support counterfactual claims. Though it is true that all the coins in my pocket are dimes, this is a contingent feature of me, or of the world, rather than a necessary one.

Of course there are related *intra*world conditionals that are not completely devoid of interest, and which may be supported by theses such as (WS). If I were simply to cross the room, for example, or make myself breakfast, it would still be the case—*ceteris paribus*—that any coin produced from my pocket would be a dime. The problem is simply that such true conditionals do not even begin to cover the range of possibilities (*inter*world possibilities) that are of concern to the moral theorist.

From the perspective of the entire space of possible worlds, then, weak supervenience theses such as (WS) are similar to—indeed, are—accidental generalizations. Suppose that (WS) were true. Then any world one might pick out will be such that no individuals within that world are physically indiscernible but mentally distinct. But it does *not* follow that there can be no mental change without physical change. Such claims about hypothetical changes are counterfactual, or at least subjunctive. They are claims about individuals' situations *across* possible worlds, and as such (WS) has no bearing on them. It is perfectly consistent with (WS) for a thinker within a world to have her mental properties dramatically altered without undergoing any physical change whatsoever. The crucial point is that *weak supervenience theses have no counterfactual implications*—they imply nothing about relations between individuals across possible worlds. And because of this they are arguably useless as theoretical tools.

This difference between weak and strong supervenience is subtle, and can be difficult to see. So I will try to explain it in one final, related way. (WS) purports to state a necessary truth. If the thesis is true, then any possible world that one might pick out is such that that portion of (WS) which is governed by the necessity operator is true of the world. *But this portion of the thesis holds only contingently.* To put the point metaphorically: (WS) can get you to any possible world; but when you get there you are stuck with a contingent truth. By contrast, theses such as (SS) can not only get you to any possible world, but when you get there you have a claim that holds of necessity. This is why the latter, but not the former, supports counterfactual claims.

These crucial differences between weak and strong supervenience have not always been appreciated, even in the philosophy of mind. Davidson himself, for example, refused to allow anything stronger than (WS), in his characterization of the mind/body relation.[10] This is because he was committed, on various grounds, to the impossibility of psychophysical laws. And, as we have seen, statements of strong supervenience are precisely lawlike statements. Like scientific laws, they support counterfactual claims. They purport to pick out necessary connections between physical and mental properties, across the space of possible worlds.

Davidson was in two ways mistaken in his commitments in this area. First, recall his initial formulation of psychophysical supervenience. He claimed therein that "such supervenience might be taken to mean that there cannot be two events exactly alike in all physical respects but differing in some mental respects, or that an object cannot alter in some mental respects without altering in some physical respects" (1970: 214). Two claims are made here. The first may or may not be implied by weak psychophysical supervenience, depending upon what precisely is meant by 'cannot'. But the second claim is certainly *not* implied by (WS). It is a claim about individuals' features across possible worlds. In fact, not only does (WS) fail to imply, or even to support, this claim, but the claim itself would be correct only if strong supervenience were true. Davidson, in common with others whom we will mention later on, failed to understand how very weak weak supervenience really is. His denial of strong supervenience is incompatible even with his own explicit statement of the dependence of the mental on the physical.[11]

Davidson's second mistake lay in failing to see the point stressed in the last couple of sections, that the dependence of thought on environmental

[10] See e.g. Davidson (1985: 242–3). As a nominalist about properties Davidson preferred a linguistic formulation of supervenience, according to which a predicate p supervenes upon a system of predicates S just in case p does not distinguish any entities that cannot be distinguished by S. Though there are some complexities here, the crucial point is still that Davidson has formulated only an accidental generalization, and so has produced another form of weak supervenience. Klagge (1990: 28 n. 4) claims that the contention that supervenience entails the existence of principles is controversial. This is false. Clearly, one need only employ universal instantiation to generate principles. What is true is that it is controversial whether necessary principles (laws), or useful principles (such as might be relevant in the debate over moral particularism), can be derived from supervenience claims.

[11] Davidson's mistake is evidenced also in an exchange between him and Kim; see Davidson (1993) and Kim (1993*a*). Kim had claimed more than once that Davidson's view of the mind–body relation is consistent with the possibility that all the mental properties could be sucked out of a world, as it were, leaving the distribution of physical properties unchanged. In response Davidson appealed to supervenience, claiming that it rules out this possibility. But Kim's point is of course that only strong supervenience rules it out, and Davidson explicitly rejects strong supervenience.

context—a dependence insisted upon by Davidson himself—refutes local supervenience theses generally. It is clear from the quotation lately provided, and from his own advocacy of something like (WS), that Davidson was committed to the truth of local psychophysical supervenience. But such a thesis is incompatible with the kind of perceptual externalism endorsed by Davidson. Furthermore, had he instead opted for something like (GS), Davidson would have been spared the kind of anxiety concerning laws that led to his denial of anything stronger than weak supervenience. For it is generally recognized that global supervenience theses are too general and inspecific to be of any use in constructing laws. I want now to show how the reflections developed in the present section provide the materials for solving Blackburn's problem.

5

In his classic article "Moral Realism," and later in an essay entitled "Supervenience Revisited," Simon Blackburn argued that considerations surrounding moral supervenience in effect refute all forms of moral realism. This ambitious agenda was pursued in the following manner: Moral realists are committed to the supervenience of the moral upon the natural, which thesis Blackburn formulated thus—

(S) $\Box ((\exists x) (Fx \,\&\, G^*x \,\&\, (G^*x \,U\, Fx)) \supset (y) (G^*y \supset Fy))$

This thesis states that it is necessarily the case that, if something has moral property F, and natural property G^*, and its possession of the former 'underlies' its possession of the latter, then everything which has G^* has F.

Now there are serious problems with this ostensible formulation of supervenience, which will be mentioned here, but not dwelt upon. First, it is not clear exactly what role the predicate letters 'F' and 'G' are playing. They are not bound by quantifiers, and yet would appear not to be constants either. Second, and more seriously, the notion of 'underlying' is never adequately explained. Indeed, on one natural understanding, for one property to 'underlie' another is just for the latter to supervene upon the former. The presence of 'U' thus threatens to trivialize the entire affair, making it seem that what is claimed is that moral properties supervene upon those properties on which they supervene. And in any case it makes it quite mysterious what (S) claims. Finally, as we will see in some detail later on, Blackburn mistakenly took (S)—which, *modulo* the recently voiced concerns, is a version of weak supervenience—to have the counterfactual consequences associated rather with theses such as (SS). Like Davidson,

Blackburn failed to understand the difference between weak and strong supervenience.

As noted, Blackburn took moral realists of all stripes to be committed to (S). The problem was supposed to be that they were equally committed to rejecting a stronger thesis, which Blackburn called 'necessitation':

(N) $\Box$ (x) (G*x $\supset$ Fx)

This thesis states that it is a necessary fact that anything which has G* has F; in other words, that their underlying bases guarantee the instantiation of moral properties, in every possible world. Blackburn assumed that realists were committed to rejecting this thesis because of the widespread acceptance of Hume's law, the view that there can be no entailments between the natural and the moral. If (N) were true, then a proposition to the effect that an individual possesses natural property G* would entail the proposition that the individual has moral property F, contravening Hume's law. But given that they must reject (N), realists are committed to accepting its denial:

(P) $\Diamond$ ($\exists$x) (G*x & ~Fx)

That is to say, it is possible for an individual to have natural property G* but lack moral property F. It is the combination of (S) and (P) that Blackburn thinks leads to trouble. As he put the point:

> Imagine a thing A, which has a certain set of naturalistic properties and relations. A also has a certain degree of moral worth: say, it is very good. This, according to the realist, reports the existence of a state of affairs: A's goodness. Now the existence of this state of affairs is not entailed by A being as it is in all naturalistic respects … That is, it is logically possible that A should be as it is in all naturalistic respects, yet this further state of affairs not exist. But if that is logically possible, *why* isn't it a logical possibility that A should stay as it is in all naturalistic respects, and this further state of affairs cease to exist?   (1971: 118–19)

(P) entails that their natural subvenient bases do not, in general, entail the instantiation of moral properties. But Blackburn thinks that it is a consequence of (S) that there can be no moral change without a natural change. And this is mysterious: If natural properties do not entail moral properties—do not suffice for them in all possible worlds—then why does retaining one's precise naturalistic make-up guarantee, for any given possible world, that one does not change in moral respects?

A way to make what is essentially the same point is to note that (P) entails that there are some worlds in which an agent has G*—which, in our world, underlies her possession of moral property F—but does not have property F. Yet (S) disallows the possibility that there are worlds in which *some*, but *not all*, agents who are G* are F. "The one thing we do not have is any mixed world, where some things are G* and F, and some things are G* but not F ... Why should the possible worlds partition into only two kinds, and not into three kinds?" (Blackburn 1985: 134–5). This is what has come to be called 'Blackburn's problem'.

Blackburn thought that no satisfactory explanation of the facts mentioned in the previous paragraph is available to the realist, and goes on to offer his own projectivistic account of why supervenience is true despite the falsity of necessitation. It is thus that he believes he has refuted moral realism. But the details of Blackburn's explanation are not important for present purposes, since my goal is simply to explain how confusion over the nature of supervenience vitiates Blackburn's case against moral realism.[12]

Blackburn is guilty of conflating each of the distinctions that has been emphasized here. His insistence that realists will want to accept (S), but deny (N), betrays confusion over the distinction between local and global supervenience. And it is clear from the above quotations, together with the structure of (S), that Blackburn confuses weak and strong supervenience. I will defend these points in turn.

Consider once again (S). Blackburn claims that realists will want to accept it. But this is not obviously the case. Everything turns on what precisely is included in G*. Blackburn is not very clear on the matter. He says that G* will typically include, not merely properties of the agents or actions in question, but facts or truths about 'other things'. As I have stressed, morality is highly context-dependent. More precisely, whether an agent or action possesses a given moral property usually or always depends, not merely on intrinsic properties the former possesses, but on features of the context. If it is to be plausible that F supervenes upon G*, then the latter must include much more than intrinsic physical or natural properties of the individual in question. It must include relevant features of the broader context. The problem, however, is that the more we add to G*—at the limit, taking it to contain all of the physical or natural properties of the entire world in question—the less plausible it becomes that the realist will want to deny (N). For if we go far enough in this direction, (N) will amount to no more than the thesis that fixing the naturalistic character of the entire world fixes also its moral character. And this is something no realist should be prepared to deny.

In effect, Blackburn has confused local and global moral supervenience. We saw in Section 3 that allowing all manner of relational properties into

---

[12] Earlier treatments of Blackburn's problem include Klagge (1984, 1987), McFetridge (1985), Dreier (1992), Shafer-Landau (1994, 2003), Zangwill (1995), and Sobel (2001). I will not comment upon Sobel's paper, because I do not understand it. Commonalities and differences with the other writers will be noted as the discussion proceeds.

the subvenient base in a claim of local supervenience makes it provably equivalent to global supervenience. So the key question to ask is what precisely does Blackburn propose to include in G*? If only intrinsic properties of the individual, then (N) will indeed be rejected by realists, but so will (S)—for, as has been stressed more than once already, moral properties do not supervene upon intrinsic naturalistic properties of the individual or action in question. If he means rather to include enough of the context in G* to make (S) plausible, then (N) will be plausible as well. After all, if G* truly does suffice for F, in any given situation, then a quantified conditional binding the two will be necessarily true. Therefore, it is only by a kind of equivocation concerning the subvenient bases of moral properties that Blackburn is able to make it seem plausible that the realist will want to accept (S) but reject (N)—the base is viewed narrowly, when (N) is at issue, but broadly when it comes time to consider (S). And if the realist is not so committed then the explanatory burden upon which Blackburn rests his argument against moral realism does not exist.

What of the suggestion that Hume's law prohibits the realist from accepting (N)? The answer is that no one who has upheld this alleged law has meant to deny that naturalistic propositions describing *entire worlds* fail to imply moral propositions; such a denial would be manifestly incompatible with any plausible version of moral supervenience, whether it be local or global. They have been concerned rather to deny that relatively simple, ordinary naturalistic propositions—such as propositions describing an action as one of lying, or of killing—imply moral propositions. And this denial is in no tension with (N). As we noted just above, (N), like (S), is plausible only so long as we pack a great deal into the specification of G*, and in effect abandon the claim of local moral supervenience.[13]

The suggestion, then, is that, had Blackburn borne in mind the crucial distinction between local and global supervenience, he would have seen that (S) and (N) stand or fall together, as far as the moral realist is concerned. And, as indicated, since Blackburn's problem precisely is how to reconcile

---

[13] Dreier builds a device into his formulation of moral supervenience that may be meant to deal with the problem of context-sensitivity. He assumes that the relevant classes of properties are closed under Boolean operations such as disjunction and conjunction (Dreier 1992: 14). (Though this assumption is certainly not necessary for the mere formulation of supervenience theses generally, or for that of moral supervenience in particular, as Dreier seems to imply.) McFetridge makes essentially the same presupposition with his employment of the notion of 'maximal naturalistic properties' (1985: 248), as does Zangwill (1995: 1). (Klagge (1984), by contrast, fails to recognize the need for some such device.) These assumptions are highly controversial, and are rejected by many who nevertheless accept supervenience. But as I am understanding them, their employment does at least signal some awareness of the problem that context-dependence poses for local formulations of moral supervenience.

the acceptance of the one with the rejection of the other, the problem dissolves.

Furthermore, we noted earlier that Blackburn's (S), to the extent that we can make any sense of it at all, is a version of weak moral supervenience. The claim is merely that, *within* any given possible world, that naturalistic property which underlies any moral property suffices for it. It implies nothing whatever about property dependence or covariation across worlds. But we saw that Blackburn wants to know why, for the realist, moral change without naturalistic change is impossible, given that natural properties do not necessitate moral ones. He asks, "*why* isn't it a logical possibility that A should stay as it is in all naturalistic respects, and this further state of affairs cease to exist?" (Blackburn 1993: 119).

As has already been pointed out, it is an error to think that (S) proscribes this possibility. It is perfectly consistent with the thesis the weak supervenience claim embodies that an individual should cease to have any moral properties at all, or to change radically in respect of her moral properties, while remaining precisely as she is in all naturalistic respects. This possibility concerns a comparison *between* worlds, and as such (S) is completely silent on the matter. It is, again, the fact that weak supervenience theses like (WS) are completely devoid of counterfactual implications that makes them uninteresting, and essentially useless as theoretical tools. (More or less the same mistake—failure to understand the difference between weak and strong supervenience—is made in addition by Hare (1984: 4).)[14]

The upshot is this: Blackburn asks two questions of the moral realist. First, how can she explain why (S) is true, if (N) is not true? Second, why can there be no mixed worlds, given that no particular world can

[14] Thus Blackburn wants to be talking about strong supervenience, as his informal glosses on the notion show, but formulates only a weak version of the doctrine. Dreier seems to recognize this point, claiming that Blackburn is committed to strong supervenience; but he does not explain why he thinks this (1992: 36 n. 12). McFetridge suggests, plausibly, that ordinary moral thought, and presumably therefore moral realism, is committed to something stronger than weak supervenience (1985: 249). Klagge claims that the moral realist ought to accept strong supervenience (1984: 378). This would be correct were it not for the fact that strong moral supervenience is a version of local moral supervenience, and therefore false for the reasons stated in Section 5.

I have heard it suggested that Blackburn's informal glosses on moral supervenience may be consistent with the rejection of strong supervenience, if we restrict the notion of change in question to diachronic, intra-world change. I do not believe this is a plausible understanding of the relevant passages, but even if it were the devastating problem would remain that Blackburn failed to discuss the kind of supervenience theses that moral realists have always had in mind, whether explicitly or tacitly, cf. Zangwill (1995: 9). Weak supervenience theses—*pace* Davidson, Blackburn, and Hare—are of no interest to anyone, certainly not the moral realist.

contain individuals who differ morally without differing naturalistically, and given also that naturalistic properties do not logically suffice for moral ones? The answers are, first, that it is only if one confuses local and global supervenience that one would think that (S) is true but (N) false. And second, it is only if one conflated weak and strong supervenience that one would think that there is a problem of mixed worlds. There cannot be mixed worlds because, if one builds into moral properties' subvenient bases enough to make the claim of supervenience plausible, these bases effectively necessitate instantiations of the relevant moral properties. In effect, as these formulations of the answers suggest, there is just one large confusion here, evenly distributed over the two questions. But I believe that this way of dividing it up is illuminating.

6

It sometimes appears as if Blackburn wishes to acknowledge certain of the points made above. On these occasions he insists that what he is really after is an *explanation* of why the moral supervenes upon the natural, as a matter of *conceptual necessity*. Why is it that the nature of moral concepts dictates that two worlds which do not differ in respect of their natural properties cannot differ morally? As before, Blackburn believes that the realist has no adequate explanation to offer here:

> we could say that ... when we deal with analytically possible worlds, we are dealing with beliefs we have about competence: in this case the belief that the competent person will not flout supervenience. But this belief is only explained by the further, anti-realist nature of moralizing. If moralizing were depicting further, moral aspects of reality, there would be no explanation of the conceptual constraint, and hence of our belief about the shape of a competent morality.   (1985: 64)

The idea here seems to be that the anti-realist can explain the 'analytic' nature of moral supervenience, inasmuch as she pictures moralizing as agents responding to patterns of natural property instances. If this is what moral agents are doing, then there seems to be a clear kind of incoherence involved in reacting differently, morally speaking, to identical natural patterns. But the moral realist, as Blackburn is envisioning matters, does not view moralizing in this way. For the realist, moral agents are reacting to properties distinct from natural properties. And this raises the question: Why is it incoherent, on such a view, to treat as morally different two naturalistically indiscernible situations? If it were replied that the moral cannot vary independently of the natural, Blackburn would presumably insist that this is the fact to be explained. The realist cannot simply help herself to it in this context.

Let us grant, for the sake of argument, that Blackburn's projectivist anti-realist can adequately explain the conceptual necessity of moral supervenience. She does so by appealing to an indispensable feature of our use of moral terms. The question I want to raise in this section is why the realist cannot do the same. There are two primary views on the source of conceptual truths. Crudely speaking, empiricists have traditionally viewed such truths as grounded in usage and convention. Hume's doctrine that the only true necessities concern mere relations of ideas; Kant's insistence that analytic judgments are vacuously true; and the positivistic notion that necessary truths are one and all tautologies are each instances of this point. Naturally Blackburn's moral anti-realist falls into this camp as well. She explains the conceptual truth of moral supervenience as falling out of features of moral practice. Rationalists, on the other hand, have often taken conceptual truths as simply mirroring necessary features of non-conceptual reality. For Leibniz, for example, every truth is one of conceptual containment; but every true proposition is at the same time made true by the nature of the world. It is the fact that concepts are what they are partly owing to the character of that world which keeps this view from being incoherent, or unprincipled. On such a conception, to take just one example, if it is a truth about the concept *bachelor* that it applies only to entities in the extension of the concept *unmarried male*, then it is equally a necessary feature—at the level of reference, rather than of sense—that bachelors are necessarily unmarried males.

For our purposes, there is no need to try to adjudicate between these two kinds of views concerning the source of conceptual truths. The crucial point is that the moral realist is just as well off as the anti-realist, in respect of explaining supervenience, on either view. If what it takes to explain conceptual truths is to advert to patterns of linguistic usage, then the realist can do this as well as can Blackburn's projectivist. If, rather, there is no deep, reductive explanation to be had of conceptual truths—if they are simply mirrors in thought of necessities obtaining in the mind-independent world—then neither the realist nor the anti-realist will have much to say in explanation of moral supervenience. Either way, Blackburn's claim that only the anti-realist can offer an adequate explanation here falls flat.[15]

[15] Dreier sees clearly that Blackburn's challenge is at this point misconceived. He notes that if it were otherwise, then no realist could ever explain analytic connections among concepts (Dreier 1992: 21). McFetridge makes a similar point, though he puts it in terms of a distinction between realist and non-realist explanations of supervenience (1985: 253–4). Zangwill takes Blackburn's problem to boil down to the problem of synthetic apriority, and so thinks it is no special difficulty for moral realism (1995: 16–17). Surely the most interesting true moral supervenience theses *are* synthetic a priori. But Zangwill pays far too little attention to what precisely this means. There are many different

7

It has been argued here that attaining clarity concerning the precise sense in which the moral supervenes upon the natural yields two interrelated insights: First, that the most typical sorts of formulations of moral supervenience actually state falsehoods. Moral properties do not supervene upon the natural properties of individuals, properly so-called, any more than representational mental properties supervene upon physical properties of thinkers' bodies. Second, Blackburn's attempt to pose a problem for moral realists, by adverting to considerations concerning supervenience, fails. When one becomes clear, as Blackburn himself is not, concerning the differences between weak and strong supervenience, on the one hand, and local and global supervenience, on the other, one sees that supervenience and necessitation stand or fall together. It follows that the considerations raised concerning supervenience pose no threat to moral realism.

REFERENCES

Audi, R. (1990) "Moral Epistemology and the Supervenience of Ethical Concepts" *Southern Journal of Philosophy* 29 suppl.: 1–24.
Blackburn, S. (1973) "Moral Realism", in J. Casey (ed.), *Morality and Moral Reasoning* (London: Methuen), repr. in Blackburn (1993)—page references to reprinted version.
—— (1984) *Spreading the Word* (Oxford: Oxford University Press).
—— (1985) "Supervenience Revisited", in I. Hacking (ed.), *Exercises in Analysis* (Cambridge: Cambridge University Press), repr. in Blackburn (1993)—page references to reprinted version.
—— (1993) *Essays in Quasi-Realism* (Oxford: Oxford University Press).
Block, N. (1990) "Can the Mind Change the World?" in G. Boolos (ed.), *Meaning and Method: Essays in Honor of Hilary Putnam* (Oxford: Oxford University Press).

notions of analyticity and apriority; and Zangwill seems to share the empiricist view, which I think is false, that synthetic apriority is somehow more mysterious than analytic apriority. In any case, there is no space here to take on his wide-ranging discussion.

I believe that Shafer-Landau (1994: 148–9) takes moral supervenience to be conceptually necessary for the wrong reason. Unlike most other commentators, Shafer-Landau focuses attention on Blackburn's own, highly problematic attempt to formulate the doctrine; which crucially includes the notion of 'underlying' discussed in Section 5. This formulation claims that any natural property which once 'underlies' a moral property will always do so. But since no sense has been given to the notion of underlying distinct from 'sufficing for', or 'being correlated with'—and since these two locutions seem to be nothing more than ways of expressing a supervenience relation—Blackburn's formulation is trivial in a way in which moral supervenience proper is not. This, I believe, is what leads Shafer-Landau to claim, quite controversially, and with little apparent support, that no explanation of *psychophysical* supervenience need be or can be provided.

Brink, D. (1989) *Moral Realism and the Foundations of Ethics* (Cambridge: Cambridge University Press).

Burge, Tyler (1979) "Individualism and the Mental", in P. French, T. Uehling, and H. Wettstein (eds.), *Midwest Studies in Philosophy* 4 (Minnesota: University of Minnesota Press).

—— (1981) "Other Bodies", in A. Woodfield (ed.), *Thought and Object* (Oxford: Clarendon Press).

—— (1993) "Mind–Body Causation and Explanatory Practice", in J. Heil and A. Mele (eds.), *Mental Causation* (Oxford: Oxford University Press).

Chalmers, D. (1996) *The Conscious Mind* (Oxford: Oxford University Press).

Dancy, J. (1993) *Moral Reasons* (Oxford: Blackwell).

—— (2004) *Ethics without Principles* (Oxford: Oxford University Press).

Davidson, D. (1970) "Mental Events", in L. Foster and J. Swanson (eds.), *Experience and Theory* (Amherst: University of Massachusetts Press), repr. in his *Essays on Actions and Events* (Oxford: Oxford University Press, 1980)—page references to the reprinted version.

—— (1985) "Reply to Lewis", in B. Vermazen and M. Hintikka (eds.), *Essays on Davidson: Actions and Events* (Oxford: Oxford University Press).

—— (1993) "Thinking Causes", in J. Heil and A. Mele (eds.), *Mental Causation* (Oxford University Press).

Dreier, J. (1992) "The Supervenience Argument against Moral Realism" *Southern Journal of Philosophy* 30: 13–38.

Gibbard, A. (2003) *Thinking How to Live* (Oxford: Oxford University Press).

Grimes, T. (1995) "The Tweedledee and Tweedledum of Supervenience", in E. Savellos and Ü. Yalçin (eds.), *New Essays on Supervenience* (Cambridge: Cambridge University Press).

Hare, R. M. (1952) *The Language of Morals* (Oxford: Clarendon Press).

—— (1984) "Supervenience" *Proceedings of the Aristotelian Society* 58 suppl.: 1–16.

Heumer, M. (2005) *Ethical Intuitionism* (New York: Palgrave Macmillan).

Hooker, B., and Little, M. (2000) *Moral Particularism* (Oxford: Oxford University Press).

Horgan, T. (1982) "Supervenience and Microphysics" *Pacific Philosophical Quarterly* 63: 29–43.

Jackson, F. (1998) *From Metaphysics to Ethics* (Oxford: Oxford University Press).

Kim, J. (1984) "Concepts of Supervenience" *Philosophy and Phenomenological Research* 65: 153–76.

—— (1993*a*) "Can Supervenience and 'Non-Strict Laws' Save Anomalous Monism?" in J. Heil and A. Mele (eds.), *Mental Causation* (Oxford: Oxford University Press).

—— (1993*b*) *Supervenience and Mind* (Cambridge: Cambridge University Press).

—— (1998) *Mind in a Physical World* (Cambridge, MA: MIT Press).

Klagge, J. (1984) "An Alleged Difficulty Concerning Moral Properties" *Mind* 93: 370–80.

—— (1987) "Supervenience: Perspectives v. Possible Worlds" *Philosophical Quarterly* 37: 312–15.

Klagge, J. (1990) "Rationalism, Supervenience, and Moral Epistemology" *Southern Journal of Philosophy* 29 suppl.: 25–8.

Lewis, D. (1983) "New Work for a Theory of Universals" *Australasian Journal of Philosophy* 61: 343–77.

McFetridge, I. (1985) "Supervenience, Realism, Necessity" *Philosophical Quarterly* 35: 245–58.

McLaughlin, B., and Bennett, K. (2005) "Supervenience" *Stanford Encyclopedia of Philosophy*.

McNaughton, D., and Rawling, P. (2000) "Unprincipled Ethics", in Hooker and Little (2000).

Majors, B. (2003) "Moral Explanation and the Special Sciences" *Philosophical Studies* 113: 121–52.

—— (2005) "Moral Discourse and Descriptive Properties" *Philosophical Quarterly* 55: 475–94.

Miller, A. (2003) *An Introduction to Contemporary Metaethics* (Cambridge: Polity).

Moore, G. E. (1903) *Principia Ethica* (Cambridge: Cambridge University Press).

Paull, R., and Sider, T. (1992) "In Defense of Global Supervenience" *Philosophy and Phenomenological Research* 52: 833–54.

Petrie, B. (1987) "Global Supervenience and Reduction" *Philosophy and Phenomenological Research* 48: 119–30.

Putnam, H. (1975) "The Meaning of 'Meaning'", in his *Mind, Language and Reality: Philosophical Papers*, ii (Cambridge: Cambridge University Press).

Quine, W. V. (1985) *The Time of My Life* (Cambridge, MA: MIT Press).

Shafer-Landau, R. (1994) "Supervenience and Moral Realism" *Ratio* 7: 145–52.

—— (2003) *Moral Realism: A Defence* (Oxford: Oxford University Press).

Smith, M. (1994) *The Moral Problem* (Oxford: Blackwell).

—— (2000) "Does the Evaluative Supervene on the Natural?" in R. Crisp and B. Hooker (eds.), *Well-Being and Morality* (Oxford: Oxford University Press).

Sobel, J. H. (2001) "Blackburn's Problem: On its Not Insignificant Residue" *Philosophy and Phenomenological Research* 62: 361–83.

Sturgeon, N. (2009) "Doubts about the Supervenience of the Evaluative", in R. Shafer-Landau (ed.), *Oxford Studies in Metaethics*, iv (Oxford: Oxford University Press).

Witmer, D. Gene (1999) "Supervenience, Physicalism, and the Problem of Extras" *Southern Journal of Philosophy* 37: 315–31.

Zangwill, N. (1995) "Moral Supervenience", in P. French, T. Uehling, and H. Wettstein (eds.), *Moral Concepts*, Midwest Studies in Philosophy 20 (Notre Dame: University of Notre Dame Press).

3

Doubts about the Supervenience of the Evaluative

Nicholas L. Sturgeon

THE ISSUE

That the evaluative (or, in different versions, the ethical, the normative, or the moral) supervenes on the natural (or, again in different versions, on the non-evaluative, or on the descriptive, or on the factual) has until quite recently had the status of a commonplace among academic philosophers. Of course, with so many different accounts of what is supposed to supervene and of what it is supposed to supervene upon, there is more than one doctrine here. It will not matter to my discussion, however, which of the first four terms we use; so I shall normally just speak of the evaluative, understood broadly enough to include anything that might count as ethical, normative, or moral. By contrast, one thing I hope to show is that it turns out to matter a lot whether we speak of supervenience on the natural, the non-evaluative, the descriptive, or the factual. But until I begin to explain why I shall mostly use, as an example, the most common formulation, that the evaluative supervenes on the natural. This thesis—as

Earlier versions of this chapter were presented at the Universities of Oxford, Leeds, and Edinburgh; to the Fourth Annual Metaethics Workshop at the University of Wisconsin, Madison; and to the Creighton Club. I am grateful to Julia Markovits for helpful prepared comments in Oxford, for good discussion with others on all these occasions, and for discussion at an NYU seminar run by David Velleman and Paul Boghossian. I offer special thanks for comments from Andrew Alwood, John G. Bennett, Matti Eklund, Pekka Väyrynen, and Nick Zangwill. Work on this project has been supported by an NEH Faculty Research Award in the Humanities. Views expressed in this chapter do not necessarily represent those of the National Endowment for the Humanities.

a first approximation, that across possible situations, there cannot be an evaluative difference without a natural difference—is not by the standards of philosophy a terribly old one. To my knowledge, it is not clearly asserted before R. M. Hare's *Language of Morals*, where it is also taken to be common ground among metaethical positions—in particular, between Hare and his philosophical opponent, the ethical naturalist. To be sure, Hare assumes that his readers are familiar with the idea that, as he puts it, " 'good' and other such words are the names of 'supervenient' or 'consequential' properties."[1] And he is right that his readers would know of discussions, by G. E. Moore and Sir David Ross, of whether there is a kind of goodness that depends solely on the intrinsic properties of an object that has it. (Both think there is.) But neither discusses the question of whether all ethical or evaluative properties are supervenient.[2] The situation had certainly changed, then, when Michael Smith could write, about forty years after Hare, that "everyone agrees that it is an *a priori* truth that the moral supervenes on the natural."[3] And it did seem that everyone writing in analytic philosophy agreed on something in this neighborhood. That is presumably why Donald Davidson and Jaegwon Kim, more interested in whether the mental might supervene on the physical, chose to introduce that idea by comparing it to the familiar supervenience of the evaluative or moral on the natural.[4] It is also presumably the reason why some defenders of moral particularism, such as John McDowell and David McNaughton, were quick to reassure their readers that their doctrine is in no conflict with supervenience.[5]

---

[1] Hare (1952: 80). Hare takes it that an ethical naturalist will agree with him about the supervenience of the evaluative, but will offer a different explanation for it, an explanation Hare argues is mistaken.

[2] Moore (1959: 253–75); Ross (1930: 121–3). I explain below why the Moore of Moore (1903) should not hold that the evaluative supervenes on the *natural*. The case of Ross is complex, since he also maintains that the rightness of an act supervenes on its intrinsic nature (a position he can hold only because he counts the production of all of its consequences as part of the nature of the act: Ross 1930: 123). So he appears to hold that both rightness, and also the sort of goodness that is most important for philosophy (Ross 1930: 73), are not only supervenient, but supervenient on the intrinsic natures of their bearers. However, he has no discussion of whether other forms of goodness are supervenient—even if his view would be that they are. He is also explicit that beauty is *not* supervenient on the intrinsic nature of its bearers in this way (Ross 1930: 126–31), and he says nothing about whether it is supervenient on some broader base.

[3] Smith (1994: 22; see also 21). Smith cites Blackburn (1971) and Blackburn (1985).

[4] Davidson (1970: 214); Kim (1984: 54–5).

[5] McDowell (1981: 202); McNaughton (1988: 62). (In his (1963*b*: 18–20), Hare had introduced the term "particularism" for a view which he appears to think would have to reject supervenience.)

More recently, however, some doubts have been expressed. I note, in particular, discussions by James Griffin and Joseph Raz.[6] I have welcomed the questions these writers raise, for I have for some time been harboring doubts about supervenience theses myself, and I shall devote this chapter to explaining some of them. Despite some points of contact, however, my worries are somewhat different from theirs, and my conclusion is different. Griffin is uncertain whether the evaluative supervenes on the natural; Raz argues that it does not. By contrast, I believe that in one clear sense the evaluative does supervene on the natural. My doubts are of a different sort. There are two of them. My first doubt concerns whether there is a single doctrine about supervenience that "everyone" agrees on. My own reasons for believing in supervenience on the natural are what I shall call parochial, in that they depend on taking a particular, contested stand in metaethics. In a word, I think that the evaluative supervenes on the natural because in my view evaluative properties just are, themselves, natural properties, and because it's quite trivial that properties supervene on themselves. Of course, no philosopher who rejects ethical naturalism could believe in the supervenience of the evaluative on the natural for this reason. Might they have other reasons? My conclusion, not just about supervenience on the natural but about most of the other versions of the doctrine found in the literature, will be that, although each looks secure from some metaethical standpoint, each will also have to be rejected—or, at the very least, will look quite implausible—from other familiar standpoints, standpoints that are treated with respect in current metaethical debates. In short, I shall argue about these versions of the doctrine of the supervenience of the evaluative that they are all parochial. There is none of them that "everyone" agrees on.

About one version of the doctrine, however—that the evaluative supervenes specifically on the factual—I shall offer a slightly different argument. I shall not argue directly that there is any recognized metaethical position that must reject it. What I shall claim, instead, is that one recognized position can offer no rationale for it. (And I shall expand the coverage of my term "parochial" to cover doctrines in this position, too.) How much weaker a claim this will seem will largely depend, of course, on how important one thinks it is to a doctrine's not looking implausible, from some metaethical position, that the position be able to provide a rationale for the doctrine.

---

[6] Griffin (1996: 44–8); Raz (2000: 49–76). Michael Smith replies to Griffin in Smith (2000).

I am inspired to this pattern of argument, and to the idea that failure to provide a rationale might indeed make a doctrine look implausible, by reflection on an argument once offered by Simon Blackburn. Blackburn once claimed on behalf of his expressivist anti-realism that it can offer a clear rationale for the supervenience of the evaluative, whereas evaluative realism cannot; and he took this to count for expressivism and against realism.[7] My argument differs from his in two important ways, however. First, I claim that the problem turns out to be about expressivism, not realism (or, more generically, factualism): that realism offers an obvious justification for taking the evaluative to supervene on the factual, whereas, despite the best efforts of Blackburn and, more recently, Allan Gibbard, expressivism cannot do so. Now, for anyone who finds it obvious—as Blackburn himself appears to do—that the evaluative *does* supervene on the factual, this could of course be read as a criticism of expressivism. In this chapter, however—this is the second difference—my argument will have to leave open the possibility that, if expressivism cannot account for supervenience, the most basic problem might be, not with expressivism, but rather with supervenience. I have to allow that we may have just a further illustration of how supervenience theses that appear obvious from one metaethical standpoint can appear mistaken or (in this case) unsupported from another.

As my quotation from Smith indicates, the common view has been, not just that some thesis about the supervenience of the evaluative is true, but that it is a priori. This, too, I doubt, about the doctrines that I shall argue are parochial, precisely *because* they are parochial, and so either implausible or at least unsupported from familiar points of view. Now, I well realize that parochialism—that is, the fact that a doctrine would be rejected, or would at least look arbitrary, from some perspective with a recognized place in the philosophical debate—will not convince everyone that a doctrine is not, for all that, an a priori truth. Philosophers do accuse their respected opponents of denying, or of failing to see the rationale for, a priori truths. Still, I do see my argument as casting some doubt on the a priori status of these theses.

A second doubt about the standard view will emerge in my discussion. Some philosophers have not only thought the supervenience of the evaluative on the natural a consensus view, but have also thought it a doctrine with important consequences, that can be appealed to in defending some positions in metaethics and in criticizing others.[8] It has thus been seen as a handy dialectical weapon: universally acknowledged, yet possessed of real substance. Blackburn's argument against evaluative realism and for his expressivism is an illustration, but there are others, from other metaethical perspectives.[9] Now, as I have explained, I think it doubtful that there is any supervenience doctrine that is (or, at any rate, ought to be) universally acknowledged. But it will also emerge from my discussion that even many of the parochial versions that look plausible from some recognized philosophical perspective lack this kind of argumentative bite. This judgment applies to my own version: my reasons for holding it are not trivial but, as I shall explain below, it implies much less than writers have often supposed. Putting my two doubts together, a further main point of which I hope to persuade a reader is that it is difficult, often doubly difficult, to find a version of the doctrine of the supervenience of the evaluative that is available as a serious argumentative weapon in the dialectic of metaethics.

Since I am going to be criticizing a number of other philosophers for taking for granted something I now think is doubtful, I should make clear that what follows is in part a recantation. I am one of the writers who has appealed to a thesis about supervenience assumed both to be generally accepted and to have a useful argumentative role.[10] Fortunately, I think that the conclusions I was trying to establish by that appeal admit of other, independent, defenses, but I won't pursue that issue here.

PRELIMINARIES

There are complexities about supervenience that will not matter to my discussion, but there are some that require attention.

(1) First, supervenience is now standardly understood as I indicated briefly above, as a relation between sets of properties (where by "properties" I shall mean properties and relations, as is standard in this literature). A set of properties A is said to supervene on a set B (the supervenience base) just

---

slips into inconsistency. That would not keep supervenience doctrines from serving as useful dialectical weapons, however: much philosophical criticism takes this form.

[9] See e.g. Smith (1994: 21–4); Jackson (1998: 118–25); Railton (1995: 100–2). It would not be hard to multiply examples.

[10] Sturgeon (1985: 76 n. 22). In my own defense, I thought even at this point that the issue of supervenience is more complex than many have supposed. But the result was that I hedged my statement of the doctrine—just enough to make it harder for a reader to see my intended point, but not enough, I now think, actually to dodge the problem. I should also add that this explanation of my doubts about the supervenience of the evaluative supersedes the truncated account in my (2006*b*).

in case it is impossible for objects to differ with respect to the properties in A without differing in some way with respect to those in B. But an apparent implication of this formulation is that some philosophers, such as those anti-realists who do not believe in evaluative properties, are quickly excluded from the alleged consensus about the supervenience of the evaluative.[11] It is a mark of how well entrenched this standard account of supervenience has become that Allan Gibbard, one of these anti-realists, concedes for precisely this reason that his view cannot, strictly speaking, accommodate the supervenience of the evaluative.[12] An alternative conclusion, however (and one which Gibbard is happy to advocate, once we stop speaking quite so strictly) is to understand supervenience more broadly. Indeed, without a broader understanding we would be in the embarrassing position of having to exclude Hare, whom I have credited with first formulating the supervenience thesis, from holding it. For Hare clearly does not believe that there are evaluative properties. Supervenience, for him and for others influenced by him, is not about the relation of sets of properties, but is instead a constraint to which we are committed by some deep feature of our discourse: the constraint that we cannot think of objects as displaying A-differences without supposing them to have B-differences as well. As applied to the case that interests us, of the evaluative and the natural, this will mean that we cannot suppose two objects to differ evaluatively without taking them to differ in some natural respect as well. There is no commitment either way, in this formula, on whether supposing objects to differ evaluatively consists in attributing different properties to them, as evaluative realists might think, or whether it should receive a different account more congenial to noncognitivism. I shall follow James Klagge in calling the first understanding of supervenience "ontological" and the second "ascriptive"; and I shall speak of someone believing that the evaluative supervenes on the natural when they believe that it does so either ontologically or ascriptively.[13]

---

[11] Or else they will count as accepting it trivially, which cannot be what is intended. If there are no evaluative properties, then it will be impossible for objects to vary with respect to such properties, period, and so impossible, trivially, for them to vary with respect to such properties while not varying with respect to natural properties.

[12] Gibbard (2003: 89).

[13] For this terminology see Klagge (1988). I more or less follow Klagge in his formulation of ascriptive supervenience: "that, logically speaking, a person's judgments of a certain (supervening) kind about things cannot differ unless judgments of the other kind about the things differ" (1988: 462). He calls this a "rough" account, and I agree. One might wonder, for example, if the constraint is really violated by a thinker who judges that there is an A-difference among objects but has no view about B-differences simply because the question has never occurred to her. So we might understand the constraint to apply to any thinker who does have a view about B-differences.

I shall come back to the question of how, according to proponents of ascriptive supervenience, our discourse is supposed to commit us to this or some similar constraint. One point to note in advance, however, is that proponents uniformly think that the answer shows the constraint to be an a priori one, implicit recognition of which is required for competence with evaluative discourse. This points up an important contrast between these two characterizations of supervenience. The ontological account involves necessary covariation among properties, but says nothing about whether our knowledge of this relation is a priori. By contrast, it is built into ascriptive supervenience (at least according to its proponents, whom I shall not challenge on this point) that our knowledge of it must be a priori. If we are talking of ontological supervenience, therefore, there are, as I indicated above, separate questions as to whether it obtains and as to whether our knowledge of its obtaining is a priori. Ascriptive supervenience, by contrast, requires a priori knowledge, but may not involve relations of properties at all (though, so far as I know, all those who believe in the ascriptive supervenience of the evaluative, *and* believe that evaluations ascribe properties, also believe that our a priori knowledge is of necessary relations of these evaluative properties to a supervenience base). In what follows, I shall keep both notions of supervenience in mind, discussing them separately (sometimes in notes) where this might matter.

(2) Jaegwon Kim distinguishes what he calls weak supervenience from strong supervenience. The difference depends on whether we mean that there can be no A-differences without B-differences only within each possible world, or whether we mean for this to apply even when objects are in different possible worlds. I shall assume in what follows that we are concerned with strong supervenience. Despite some ambiguity in the metaethical literature, I believe that this fits with the implicit or explicit understanding in most discussions.[14] (So far as I can see, however, this distinction will matter very little to the argument to follow.)

Of course, in addition to philosophers with doubts about, specifically, evaluative properties, there are nominalists who reject properties altogether. But they typically argue, on behalf of their position, that there are alternative, nominalistic ways of construing any talk of properties that proves philosophically useful. Talk of supervenience as a relation between sets of properties does prove philosophically useful, so I assume they will have some way of reconstruing it.

[14] Kim defines the difference for ontological supervenience, but it seems possible to extend it to the attributive notion: the question will be whether an evaluator is constrained to believe in a B-difference whenever she accepts an A-difference across possible worlds, or only when she accepts such a difference within worlds. Hare has said that his conception of supervenience is closest to Kim's weak supervenience (1984: 4), but this fits oddly with his use of (apparently) cross-world comparisons to illustrate his views (1952: 145, 153). Blackburn appeals explicitly only to weak supervenience

(3) At one time many writers, including almost all writing about metaethics, thought that supervenience as I have defined it captured the idea that the A-properties depend on the B-properties (at least for the case in which the B-properties do not also supervene on the A-properties). It is now generally conceded that this is not so. One response has been to add to the definition I have given a clause asserting this dependence.[15] So a reader may take the additional clause as understood. Dependence does not matter to very much of my discussion, however, because almost all of my examples of views that (according to me) must reject, or cannot account for, some version of a supervenience thesis, are of views that (according to me) must reject, or cannot account for, the necessary covariation that everyone agrees is part of supervenience.[16]

(4) Finally there is the question whether supervenience precludes identity. Suppose a set of properties A is actually a nonempty subset of another set of properties B. Do the A-properties then supervene on the B-properties? (Correspondingly, is the constraint of ascriptive supervenience met if the ascriber of an A-difference believes in a B-difference, but only in one also recognized as just being an A-difference?) Standard definitions of supervenience say yes: this case, in which the supervening properties are among the properties supervened upon, is not the interesting case—the more interesting case is the one in which the supervening properties are distinct from those in the supervenience base—but it nevertheless remains a limiting case of supervenience.[17] Call this the broad understanding of supervenience. A few writers on metaethics, however, have made it part of their definition of supervenience that the supervening properties *not* be part of the supervenience base.[18] We can call this the narrow understanding. So I need to say which of these understandings I shall rely on.

in his (1971), but see his (1985: 147–8). For Kim's distinction, see his (1984: esp. 55, 57).

[15] Kim (1990: 142–9). On an ascriptive account of supervenience, this will presumably require that anyone who thinks of A-differences between objects must take this difference to depend on B-differences.

[16] It is true, however, that my reason for holding, below, that the standard ontological account of supervenience cannot account for the supervenience of the evaluative on (among other things) the supernatural, is that the standard ontological account cannot capture the intended dependence.

[17] If we understand supervenience as involving dependence, as I have just suggested, someone may wonder: can we think of properties depending on themselves? But it seems intuitive enough to think that one way for the *distribution* of the A-properties to depend on the distribution of the B-properties, is for the A-properties just to be B-properties.

[18] Blackburn (1971)—but contrast his (1985: 147); Audi (1993: 120–1); and perhaps Shafer-Landau (2003: 90). It also has seemed to me common for philosophers, in conversation, to use "supervenience" to mean supervenience-without-identity.

Obviously, this is in one way just a terminological question. I have introduced terms for both notions and my main points could be made using either one. But there is a reason why, in this discussion of whether the evaluative supervenes on the natural, we had better be using the broad understanding, according to which supervenience does not preclude the case in which the supervening properties are part of the supervenience base. For one standard metaethical position is ethical naturalism, according to which evaluative properties are themselves natural properties, and so part of the alleged supervenience base. And this means that there will be no chance at all that "everyone agrees" that the evaluative supervenes on the natural, unless we are understanding supervenience broadly. If we understand it narrowly, it turns out that ethical naturalists do not agree, and our discussion ends here.[19] So I shall understand it broadly. Importantly, I also take myself here to be following the lead of Hare, who as I have said took the supervenience of the evaluative to be common ground between himself and the ethical naturalist—though he of course took the naturalist to offer a different explanation for it, and thought that he had a proof that the naturalist's explanation was mistaken.

With this understanding in place, it should be clear why I accept the ontological supervenience of the evaluative on the natural. I take evaluative properties, themselves, to be natural properties. So, on the broad understanding of supervenience, I take them to supervene on the natural—that is, in effect, on themselves. I note three points about this commitment. First, on my understanding this thesis is, as I promised, quite insubstantial. It implies nothing about the supervenience of evaluative properties on any other properties; and because I do not tie my claim that evaluative properties are natural to any thesis about the availability of reductive definitions, either analytic or synthetic, for evaluative terms, it implies nothing about either the necessity or even the possibility of always basing our evaluative views on reasons statable in another vocabulary. Second, and even so, my own reason for believing in it is certainly not neutral, for it would be rejected by any opponent of ethical naturalism. Third, although my reasons for taking evaluative properties to be natural are not my topic here, it is worth mentioning that I do not take these reasons to be a priori: they appeal to facts about the role we appear to assign evaluative properties in explanations, to contingent facts about the apparent success of such explanations, and to the largely a posteriori plausibility of philosophical naturalism.[20] So my version of the doctrine that the evaluative supervenes

---

[19] They will reject it because it says that evaluative properties (*a*) are not natural but (*b*) necessarily vary only as natural properties vary; and of course they reject (*a*).

[20] See my (2003) and (2006*a*: 100–1).

on the natural is clearly ontological but, because it is not a priori, it is not ascriptive. I do not think it an a priori truth either that evaluative properties are natural or, as I shall make clear below, that evaluative differences vary only with natural differences.

Remembering that the standard understanding of supervenience is the broad one, we are also in position to note right away one example in which an appeal to supervenience as a dialectical weapon appears to go awry. In his discussion of David Lewis's subjectivist account of value, Mark Johnston complains that Lewis's view violates the supervenience of the evaluative on the natural.[21] This is a surprising charge. Lewis is an ethical naturalist who actually *identifies* something's being a value with its being such that we would value it under ideal conditions—where this latter circumstance is spelled out in austerely reductive terms. How could a theory that takes being a value to *be* a natural property, fail to insure the supervenience of that property on natural ones? The problem Johnston has in mind is that, on Lewis's view, if we change in our reactions over time, then the very same state of affairs may be a value at one time but not at another.[22] But, of course, it is not true that the state of affairs remains unchanged in this sort of example: it goes, for example, from being such that we value it to being such that we do not. It is surprising, and I agree implausible, that the value of something could change merely with such a change in us, but that is a characteristic implication of subjectivism, and one that Lewis appears willing to live with. I do not see any problem with Lewis's view that is profitably described as a violation of supervenience.

SUPERVENIENCE ON THE NATURAL?

Even if my own reasons for accepting the supervenience of the evaluative on the natural are parochial, and are not a priori, there might be others that

---

[21] Johnston (1989: 153). Johnston actually says "on the descriptive," but the difference is (for once) immaterial here, since Lewis's theory reduces the evaluative to the descriptive as much as to the natural.

[22] This summary is incautious. For Lewis, there is no monadic property of being a value, but only a property of being a value relative to a time (because his formula is tensed) and to a group of valuers ("we"). Nothing he says suggests that this property does not supervene on natural properties. The genuine difficulty he faces is that he must hold this: that if, changing in our reactions, we say at one time that x is a value and later that it is not, we can be right both times. This is simply an instance of a general point that Moore noticed about indexical analyses of apparently non-indexical evaluations (Moore 1912: 50–82), that they construe speakers we thought were disagreeing as instead talking past one another. Lewis discusses ways try to mitigate the implausibility of this result with respect to the first-person pronoun in his analysis (Lewis 1989: 126–9), but also appears willing to live with any residual problem.

are at least neutral and that are not implausible. So let us turn our attention now to someone who does not believe, as I do, that evaluative properties are natural. (Perhaps they are undecided, perhaps they reject this view.) How plausible should they find the view that evaluative properties supervene on natural ones?

I think that they should find this view implausible, because it ignores the difference that facts about the supernatural could make to ethics and more generally to the evaluative. To be more precise, it ignores the possibility, which I think common sense recognizes, of two situations alike in their natural features in which our obligations nevertheless differ because in one of them but not the other there is a God with certain wishes for us. (We need not be thinking here of the sort of Divine Command theory on which there is no substantive moral explanation of how God's wishes can have this effect. It might be merely that God, in virtue of her supernatural features, is supremely good in a way that merits deference from us.) Unless evaluative properties are themselves natural, then if this is a possibility, the evaluative appears not to supervene on the natural.[23]

Now, a response I anticipate at this point is that this objection ignores the broad sense in which "natural" is often used in metaethics, a sense that allows supernatural facts to count as, after all, natural.[24] This unfortunate usage seems to me simply to obscure difficulties: it requires using the term "natural" in a technical sense that requires explanation, and all the possible

---

[23] Can we really imagine a good God not communicating divine wishes, and so making some difference in the natural facts—something different on the tablets, or in the voice of conscience? I suspect that with sufficient imagination we can. But it may be easier to consider a different pair of cases: one in which God has certain wishes for us and communicates them, another in which there is no God but the natural facts are just the same. Arguably, we have in the first case an objective obligation, in the sense once explained by Richard Brandt (1959: 360–7), but not in the second. I thank David Copp for pressing this question.

[24] This appears to be part of Blackburn's very brief reply to James Klagge, who had very briefly raised this objection. (Klagge 1984: 374–5; Blackburn 1985: 146.)

There have certainly been writers on ethics who have explicitly used the term "natural" and its cognates to include the supernatural. In his (1930: 259), C. D. Broad calls a supernaturalist but reductive account of ethics "theological naturalism"; A. N. Prior uses the same term, though with what appear to be "scare quotes," in his (1949: 100). See also Hare (1952: 82), and Pigden (1991: 426). But there are also many departures from this usage, even beyond those I mention in the text. Although Griffin does not mention the supernatural, he does point out that there are substantive, narrow senses of "natural" in philosophy on which it is plausible that properties that are *not* natural can make a difference to the value of things (1996: 41–3). Frank Jackson explicitly declines to claim that the evaluative supervenes on the natural, on the grounds that the natural may be too narrow a category; this occurs in a discussion in which he also mentions views that treat the supernatural as making an evaluative difference (1998: 113, 118). (He argues instead that the evaluative supervenes on the descriptive; see below.)

explanations lead to problems I shall get to. But there is a reason for not simply rushing past this objection, which of course requires using the term in a narrower sense, more like the one it bears in other areas of philosophy.[25] For there are two ways in which a number of writers on supervenience appear in fact to commit themselves to the narrower usage, even when they are not explicit about the issue. For one thing, some introduce the notion of a natural property by alluding to Moore's account: not to his actual definition, which is by his own later admission confused, but at least to the spirit of his account.[26] (Michael Smith, for example, appeals to Moore's characterization of the natural as "the subject matter of the natural sciences, and also of psychology."[27]) But Moore, it should be noted, clearly distinguishes natural properties not just from evaluative ones but from what he calls "metaphysical" ones—that is, from supernatural properties.[28] So, for Moore, and for anyone following him in this respect, supernatural properties are not natural. And, secondly, this distinction seems reflected even in recent discussions that show little of Moore's influence. Griffin takes natural properties to be ones that figure in empirical regularities; Smith, in a reply, departing from the definition I just quoted him adapting from Moore, adds a modal element to Griffin's suggestion, making natural properties ones that are "such as" to figure in such regularities.[29] Neither of these accounts appears even to be intended, much less to be well designed, to accommodate the sorts of properties standardly ascribed to a deity; and, I claim, the thesis that the evaluative supervenes on the natural will be implausible if they do not.

Still, I should acknowledge a possible rejoinder to this objection, one that raises an interesting problem. Suppose that, in line with the characterization

[25] If a philosophical colleague were to tell you that she was working on a naturalistic account of reference, for example, I suspect that you would be surprised if she added that her view is that it is through divine mediation that our words attach to the things they do.

[26] In his (1968: 581–2), Moore says of his attempted definition of natural properties in *Principia* that it was "utterly silly and preposterous."

[27] Smith (1994: 203), quoting Moore (1903: 40). This is, in *Principia*, Moore's account of natural objects, not natural *properties*. But in his unpublished second Preface, now available in Moore (1993: 13, 15), Moore says that he should have defined a natural property as any "property with which it is the business of the natural sciences or Psychology to deal, or which can be completely defined in terms of such."

[28] Moore (1903: 38–9, 110–41). Moore says that metaphysicians "have held that their science consists in giving us such knowledge as can be supported by reasons, of that supersensible reality of which religion professes to give us a fuller knowledge, without any reasons" (1903: 112). (Moore holds that metaphysics does not in fact succeed in this aim, but he holds this only because he thinks that the term "real" should not be applied to the objects it studies.) Note that this is the reason, promised in n. 2 above, that Moore cannot believe that the evaluative supervenes just on the *natural*.

[29] Griffin (1996: 44–5); Smith (2000: 210–13).

quoted from Moore, one were to take all the properties studied by psychology to be natural ones. Now, psychology presumably studies wishes among other psychological states, so that should be enough to make the property of having a wish a natural one. And that means that it will be a natural property even when it's the property of a God. And so—if this point generalizes to all the properties of a deity that I was claiming could make an evaluative difference—I have not after all located a problem for the thesis that the evaluative supervenes on the natural: I have merely pointed out that some of the natural properties might belong to a supernatural being. It may occur to a reader, furthermore, that I cannot simply dismiss this objection, for my own view appears to imply that some properties of a supernatural being could be natural properties. For I have said that I take evaluative properties such as being good to be natural properties, and also that there might be a supremely good God.

To this rejoinder I have two quick replies and a longer one. The first reply is that it is not obvious that God's having a wish involves the same property that is studied by psychology; there is a long theological tradition, after all, of insisting that psychological terms apply to a deity only analogically. (Or, if one insists on understanding psychology so broadly as to cover both human and divine wishes, then it is this definition of natural properties, adapted from Moore, that seems wrong: for psychology turns out to study some supernatural properties along with the natural ones.) Second, even apart from this example, I think that the rejoinder does not generalize to other properties of a deity that might make an evaluative difference. I do not claim to have a good formula for saying exactly which properties count as natural and which as supernatural. But I am fairly confident in counting as supernatural such properties as omnipotence or omniscience, attributed to the deity by traditional perfect being theology; and I think that we can imagine examples in which it is, specifically, these properties that make an evaluative difference. They certainly might play a role in making a deity a distinctively appropriate object of awe, for example.

I also have a longer reply, however, that requires me to qualify some of the things I have said. For my view is that the point that I have just made about divine wishes and divine power applies also to divine goodness. That is, just as I count lesser degrees of power as natural properties but regard the kind of omnipotence that is ascribed to God as a supernatural property, so I take the sort of goodness even atheists can believe in to be a natural property, while regarding the perfect goodness ascribed to a deity as a supernatural property. My position is that if there were a God who possessed this property, then the property would arguably be a supernatural one that could only be possessed by such a being. In that case, moreover, it might also be plausible—I take no stand on this—to return even to the more mundane goodness of natural objects, seeing it as somehow derivative from God's supernatural goodness, and so in a way supernatural itself. (Robert Adams develops a theological and Platonist view of this sort in *Finite and Infinite Goods*.[30]) Of course, I do not believe any of this; but the point I am making is that my ethical naturalism depends on my atheism.

Further explanation may help. How can I say, as I do, that all evaluative properties are natural properties, if I can envisage situations in which at least some of them would be supernatural instead—and would clearly not supervene merely on the natural properties of things? My answer relies in part on a point that has sometimes been noticed concerning reasoning about what would be true if there were a God, or if there were not. For God, as conceived by orthodox theists (and also by me, when I ask what the world would be like if there were an omniscient, omnipotent, completely perfect being), would be a necessary being with many necessary properties. This means that when theists reason, as they often do, about how things would be if there were no God, or if God lacked some of these properties, they cannot see themselves as reasoning about non-actual but possible situations: they instead have to take themselves to be considering situations that are metaphysically impossible but nevertheless in some appropriate way conceivable or imaginable. A similar point applies, however, to a philosophical naturalist and atheist like me. Since I agree that a God such as orthodox theists believe in would have to be necessary, and so exist in all possible worlds, and since I believe that no such being exists in the actual world, I have to view God as not just nonexistent but impossible. And, crucially, I have to think the same about properties that only such a God could possess. Thus I, too, have to view myself as considering an impossible but appropriately conceivable or imaginable situation when I reason about how things would be if there were such a God—for example, when I allow that if there were such a God then some evaluative properties would not be natural ones.

Here, then, is how I propose to hold that evaluative properties are natural properties, and so supervene ontologically on natural properties, while granting that if there were a God some evaluative properties would not be natural properties and would not supervene just on natural properties. If we consider only metaphysically possible worlds, then, in my view, nothing in any world has any supernatural properties, and evaluative properties, being natural properties, entirely supervene on natural properties. Thus, when ontological supervenience is understood in this (quite standard) way, then I hold that the evaluative supervenes on the natural. In ethical discourse, however, both theists and atheists standardly endorse conditionals that

---

[30] Adams (1999).

attribute ethical significance to factors they have to regard as metaphysically impossible. Theists do this if they assert, for example, that if God did not exist then all things would be permitted.[31] More importantly, I do it when I allow that, if there were a God, then supernatural features of that God could make an evaluative difference. But this means that there appears to be another sense in which I, an ethical naturalist, do *not* take evaluations to supervene on the natural. There seem two ways one might try to explain this second notion of supervenience. One would involve a revision of the ontological account, appealing to features not just of possible worlds, but of a broader class of what we might call imaginable worlds, not all of them possible. Then my thesis would be that across *these* worlds evaluative differences are not always accompanied by natural ones. I confess, though, that I do not know in any detail how to spell this out. The other would be to remember that we have an ascriptive as well as an ontological conception of supervenience, as a recognized constraint on our discourse. And my thesis, which I take to be quite certainly correct, will then be that we recognize and enforce no a priori constraint against taking evaluative differences to depend on supernatural as well as on natural differences.

My conclusions about whether everyone agrees that the evaluative supervenes on the natural have thus become rather complex. To summarize: if we consider the standard ontological account of supervenience, then an ethical naturalist like me should think that the evaluative supervenes on the natural, though others should not think this.[32] On the other hand, if we consider the revised ontological account (invoking merely imaginable worlds), or if we turn to the ascriptive conception of supervenience, then neither I nor anyone else should think that the evaluative supervenes on the natural. So in any version of that thesis it is at best parochial.

DISJUNCTIONS?

At this point, someone might object as follows. If we are not to mislead by using the term "natural" so broadly as to include the supernatural;

---

[31] And they also do it if they hold, to the contrary, that even if God did not exist some acts would still be wrong.

[32] Or, perhaps, they might be philosophical naturalists who think that, so long as we confine ourselves to metaphysically possible worlds, natural properties are the only properties there are, and who think that the evaluative supervenes on the factual (that is, on all the properties there are). They will then conclude that, across such worlds, the evaluative must supervene on the natural. In that case, however, their conclusion is one for which the expressivists among them can provide no rationale: see my discussion of supervenience on the factual, below.

and if the problem for the thesis that the evaluative supervenes on the natural is then (unsurprisingly) that this ignores the evaluative difference the supernatural might make; why not just say that the evaluative supervenes on those properties that are either natural or supernatural?[33] I want to make several comments about this suggestion, some of which will carry over to other disjunctive supervenience bases that one might construct from the categories I focus on below.

I do not have an example of a recognized metaethical position that must reject this proposal. But I believe that there are considerations that should give pause to anyone who thinks that this might be the agreed-upon thesis that we are looking for. It is not certain, for one thing, that natural and supernatural properties are the only properties there are. As I have said, I think that these categories, in both popular and philosophical thought, are vague enough to leave a lot of disputable intermediate cases; and I think, for the same reason, that it is quite conceivable that the intellectually best-motivated sharpening of them would require the recognition of further categories of properties that do not supervene on these two but which could make an evaluative difference. Of course, we could avoid this problem by stipulation, by just defining the supernatural to include whatever properties are not natural. But then it would be clear that the intended proposal is really just that the evaluative supervenes on all the properties there are, a thesis that I shall examine below, as the thesis that the evaluative supervenes on the factual. (Furthermore, the objection I shall make against that thesis—namely, that there is a recognized metaethical position that can provide no rationale for it—is one that would also apply to this "disjunctive" proposal whether or not it is derived from that further one.)

A different reason for supposing the evaluative to supervene on properties that are either natural or supernatural might be found in Moore, who apparently takes natural and supernatural (or "metaphysical") properties to be all the *non-evaluative* properties there are.[34] Someone who agreed with Moore about this, and who thought (as Moore might have, though he does not address the question) that the evaluative supervenes on the non-evaluative, would then conclude that the evaluative supervenes on the union of the natural and the supernatural properties. Here again, however, the basic proposal is just that the evaluative supervenes on the

---

[33] I am grateful to Stephen Kearns and to Michael Ridge for pressing me about possible disjunctive supervenience bases.

[34] Moore appears to assume this when he argues that goodness is irreducible simply by arguing that it isn't natural and that it isn't "metaphysical" (1903: chs. 1–4). If there were some further kind of property that he also saw as non-evaluative, he would presumably have had to argue that goodness didn't fall in that category either.

non-evaluative—the suggestion I shall turn to next, and which I shall show to be parochial. Furthermore, because it is not certain that the natural and the supernatural are the only categories of non-evaluative properties, it is also not certain that the thesis that the evaluative supervenes on the disjunction of those categories really captures the intent behind the proposal.

I believe that similar points apply to other disjunctive supervenience bases one might propose, but I shall not consider any others in detail here.[35] A final point worth noting, though, is that the thesis that the evaluative requires an irreducibly disjunctive supervenience base would be a sharp departure from previous discussions. This idea is not suggested in any of the literature on the topic that I am aware of: the assumption is always that the properties in the base have something genuinely unifying in common, something covered by some familiar philosophical term. Even the stretching of the term "natural" by some writers to cover supernatural properties reflects this: it's the wrong word, but the usage surely embodies the idea that there is a real commonality among the properties that the evaluative is supposed to supervene upon. So does the often interchangeable use of "non-evaluative," "descriptive" and "factual" for the supposed base, in the proposals I shall consider below. Of course, the fact that an irreducibly disjunctive proposal would be a surprise does not prove that one could not be right, or agreeable to all. But it would be quite different from what supervenience proponents have had in mind.

THE NON-EVALUATIVE?

I am going to take it as implausible, then, for anyone except an ethical naturalist, that the evaluative supervenes on the natural, if by "natural" we mean, as I would put it, *natural*. And I have claimed (and will argue further below) that it does not help to suggest that what writers really mean by "natural" is "natural or supernatural." So what else might they have in mind?[36] I am going to focus on three suggestions that dominate in

---

[35] Michael Ridge suggested, for example, on the basis of my discussion below, that I have not identified any position that would have to reject supervenience on the non-evaluative or descriptive. A reply might draw, not just on my comments in this section on proposed disjunctive bases, but on my argument, below, that the problem for supervenience on the non-evaluative extends beyond reductive naturalism to nonreductive versions of naturalism as well.

[36] I here pass over one suggestion that Hare offers, which is merely that differences in rightness, or in goodness, must always be accompanied by some *other* difference: "The actual action couldn't have been right and the hypothetical action not right, unless there had been *some* other difference between the actions" (1952: 153; emphasis in original).

discussions of supervenience in the literature, that the evaluative supervenes on the *non-evaluative*, that it supervenes on the *descriptive*, and that it supervenes on the *factual*. It is not difficult to find writers—even those who sometimes appear to be using "natural" in a narrower sense—using these terms interchangeably.[37] I think, however, that no two of these doctrines are the same. And, having said what I think about supervenience on the natural, I now want to examine the other possibilities.

So, does the evaluative supervene on the non-evaluative? The suggestion that it does would certainly avoid the problems I have pressed concerning the supernatural. So long as we can distinguish the non-evaluative properties of the deity, such as omnipotence, from evaluative properties such as goodness, we have a thesis that applies to supernatural properties as easily as to natural ones. However, the proposal nevertheless faces a severe problem, in that it is still, to use the term I introduced, parochial. For it yields extremely implausible implications when combined with at least one recognized metaethical position, reductive naturalism. Reductive naturalists not only say that evaluative properties are natural, but offer reductive accounts of just

This formulation is in one way too strong for Hare's purposes but in another too weak. It is too strong because, as I mentioned in n. 1, he wants the doctrine of supervenience to be one on which he and the ethical naturalist agree, even though they offer different explanations for it: but the naturalist, even as portrayed by Hare, will *not* agree that the difference in, say, consequences, need be "other" than the difference with respect to rightness. It is too weak, on the other hand, because it does not rule out the possibility that the only other difference between the actions is that the first is good and the second not. One might think this precluded, since the difference in goodness must also be accompanied by some other difference: but nothing in this formula keeps that difference, and the further differences that will then be required, from being evaluative—all the way down.

[37] Jackson, Pettit, and Smith (2000: 81) speak of "*the* distinction between, on the one hand, the descriptive, non-evaluative, factual, natural, etc. and ... the evaluative, ethical, normative, moral etc." (my emphasis). Johnston cites Blackburn as having reminded us that "the supervenience of the evaluative on the descriptive is a conceptual or *a priori* matter" (Johnston 1989: 153); in the work he cites, however, what Blackburn says is that "it is widely held that moral properties are supervenient or consequential upon naturalistic ones" (Blackburn 1971: 114). Raz, who denies the doctrine, standardly talks of the evaluative supervening on the non-evaluative, but at one point equates this without warning with supervenience on the "naturalistic" (2000: 49–56, esp. 52). Intending to express agreement with Hare, Jaegwon Kim speaks within two sentences of the evaluative's supervening on "the descriptive or naturalistic details" and on "certain 'factual properties'" (1988: 235). Michael Ridge and Sean McKeever move directly from the thesis that the moral supervenes on the non-evaluative to an apparent paraphrase that has the supervenience on the descriptive (2006: 7–8). Anyone reading the metaethical literature could easily multiply examples of these terms' being used interchangeably in discussions of supervenience. (I have chosen these examples precisely because they come from habitually careful writers, moreover. Clearly, there is a widespread assumption that nothing important hangs on the differences among these terms.)

which natural properties they are. To take a couple of examples that Moore considered, they say such things as that goodness is the very same property as pleasure, or as being what we desire to desire.[38] Many philosophers have thought that Moore or his philosophical successors have shown that all such definitions must be mistaken. But reductive accounts still have their defenders, and my view, though I am not inclined to any reductive proposal, is that no one has proven reduction of the evaluative to be impossible. And recall, in any case, that it was reductive naturalism that Hare had in mind when he said that he and the naturalist agree about the supervenience of the evaluative; so it will be a serious mark against this version of the supervenience thesis, at least as an attempt to capture what Hare and others have had in mind, if the reductive naturalist has to reject it.

To see how reductive naturalism makes problems for the thesis that the evaluative supervenes on the non-evaluative, consider how the thesis would apply to a sample naturalistic reduction. To keep matters simple, assume that goodness is just pleasure. Notice that this means that, since goodness is an evaluative property—surely, the paradigm evaluative property—and pleasure is the very same property as goodness, pleasure, too, is an evaluative property. And that means, in turn, that it is not a *non*-evaluative property. So, still assuming this version of reductive naturalism, the thesis that the evaluative supervenes on the non-evaluative will imply that pleasure supervenes on non-evaluative properties that do not include pleasure among them. But this is surely doubtful—and it is even more doubtful that it is something we could know a priori. If imagination is the test, I think that I can imagine two experiences that are just alike except that one of them is pleasant and the other not, and with no further difference between the situations.[39] Insofar as I have a competing inclination to think that there must, even so, be some deeper difference between the situations that accounts for the difference with respect to pleasure, I believe that that is because I have been persuaded by philosophical argument of the thesis that the mental supervenes on the physical. But that is of course a controversial doctrine, denied by some philosophers, and often viewed even by its adherents as a paradigm of a supervenience thesis that could not be a priori. So I assume that a reductive naturalist could easily reject this version of the supervenience of the evaluative, and that it is thus not one that everyone would agree to.[40]

---

[38] Moore (1903: 15–17).

[39] Moore, too, thought that he could imagine this (1968: 588–9).

[40] So, strictly, the position I have identified that would have to reject the supervenience of the evaluative on the non-evaluative is not just a position in metaethics but the combination of a recognized position in metaethics with one about the metaphysics of

Although the problem is most easily seen with reductive naturalism, I believe that it is more general.[41] For I believe that it will afflict some nonreductive versions of naturalism (and, for that matter, of supernaturalism) as well. What makes the problem apparent for the version of reductive naturalism in my example is that we have (according to that view) a reductive formula, providing us with two terms, one evaluative and one not, for the same property. It's having the non-evaluative term ("pleasure" in the example) that reminds us that the property in question, even though it is now counted evaluative, does not obviously supervene on what we might have thought were "the rest" of the non-evaluative properties. But now think of nonreductive ethical naturalism as the view that an evaluative property is a natural property for which we lack such a reductive formula, and so lack a non-evaluative term. Even if that is so, it could easily be that the natural property in question is one that does not obviously supervene on non-evaluative properties, just as in the case of pleasure. This of course falls short of saying that *every* version of ethical naturalism will conflict with the supervenience of the evaluative on the non-evaluative; some will not. But it does mean that there is no guarantee that any given version of

mind: with respect to my example, a reductive hedonist about the good who rejects the supervenience of pleasure on the physical (or on anything else).

[41] Mark Schroeder has suggested to me that the problem may be *less* general than I have suggested, in that the plausibility of my example may depend on our thinking of pleasure as simple. For suppose our reductive naturalist were instead to identify rightness, say, with the complex property of maximizing happiness. That would take the property of maximizing happiness out of the supervenience base, but the non-evaluative properties of maximizing some quantity, and of happiness, would remain: so our evaluative property would still supervene on the non-evaluative.

I have two comments. First, it is enough for my argument that some familiar versions of reductive naturalism create the problem I have described, even if others do not: this still makes the supervenience thesis parochial. Second, some reductive identifications of evaluative properties with complex properties do create difficulties. Consider a schematic example in which our reductive naturalist identifies an evaluative property with a conjunctive natural property, that of being F and G, while maintaining that being F and being G, taken individually, are non-evaluative. Then the conjunctive evaluative property certainly supervenes on the conjuncts, and it might seem that this case raises no problem for the thesis that the evaluative supervenes on the non-evaluative. It does raise a problem, however, for on a standard, even if not uncontested, account of supervenience the supervenience base is closed under conjunction (and, more generally, under all Boolean operations: Kim 1984: 58, 65). Thus, if the conjuncts are non-evaluative, so must their conjunction be; and, by contraposition, if the conjunctive property is evaluative, as our reductive naturalist maintains, then so must be the conjuncts. And in that case, we lose our reason to suppose that the evaluative conjunctive property supervenes on the non-evaluative.

ethical naturalism, whether reductive or non-reductive, will be compatible with that doctrine.[42]

THE DESCRIPTIVE?

Where to turn, then? A suggestion that promises to avoid the problems with our previous proposals, and which is widespread in the literature, is that the evaluative supervenes on the descriptive. This distinction requires some explanation, and some comment. As it is usually understood—and as it has to be understood if it is to help with the problems we have encountered—it relies in the first instance on a distinction between two kinds of linguistic expressions (or, at least, two kinds of representations, but stick to linguistic expressions for now). These are to be sorted into the evaluative and the descriptive. Then we can distinguish, in a derivative way, between properties: evaluative properties are those ascribed by evaluative terms, descriptive properties those ascribed by descriptive terms. And the former are then claimed to supervene on the latter. (To accommodate those with qualms about evaluative properties, we can also put this supervenience claim in the ascriptive mode: anyone who evaluates two objects or situations differently is required to see them as differing in descriptive properties as well.)

There is an apparent problem with this proposal, for our purposes. The problem is that the standard explanation of the distinction between evaluative and descriptive terms, the one that motivates the use of precisely these contrasting labels, is a noncognitivist one. It says that these terms differ in function, and that what is distinctive of evaluative terms is that they are apt, not for use in stating propositions as descriptive terms are, but instead for prescribing, commending, or something of the sort. This is a problem because, if the distinction between evaluative and descriptive terms really depends on noncognitivism in this way, then so will this version of the supervenience thesis. That would make it a parochial thesis, available to noncognitivists but not to their opponents. And in that case our discussion of it could end right here.

I am of course going to argue that this proposal, that the evaluative supervenes on the descriptive, is parochial. But I don't think that it is doomed just by the fact that the terminology descends from noncognitivism.

---

[42] I am grateful to Earl Conee for helping me think about this point.

There are two ways we might avoid the difficulty. The simpler would be to understand descriptive terminology merely as terminology apt for stating propositions that are true or false, while taking no stand on the noncognitivist's contrasting account of evaluative terminology. That the evaluative supervenes on the descriptive could then be accepted by a cognitivist as well as a noncognitivist. However, this simple understanding is not quite the one that has become current among those philosophers who are not noncognitivists, but who acquiesce in calling some terms evaluative and others descriptive. (Frank Jackson, whose views I examine below, is an example, but Jackson is following many others.) For the common philosophical understanding seems to agree with noncognitivism that these are by definition contrasting categories, in that descriptive terms, or at any rate *purely* descriptive terms, cannot also be evaluative. (My simpler proposal makes no such assumption: it allows, for example, that evaluative terms may be fully descriptive, in virtue of describing—that is, stating truths about—such things as obligations and virtues.) In effect, this more common usage adds to my simpler characterization the assumption that descriptive terminology must be non-evaluative; what keeps the usage independent of noncognitivism is that there are accounts other than the noncognitivist one of what is distinctive about evaluative terminology. This further assumption is especially apparent in the usual treatment of terms like "courageous" or "brutal" that express what Bernard Williams calls "thick" evaluative concepts, and that can seem, even to a noncognitivist, to have a foot in both camps.[43] These terms, because they are partly evaluative, are standardly put on the "evaluative" list; the descriptive terms are understood to be by contrast the ones that are *purely* descriptive, where that is understood to require being not at all evaluative.

This gives us two versions of the doctrine that the evaluative supervenes on the descriptive, depending on whether we use the simpler or the more complex, and more common, account of which terms count as descriptive. In both cases, the thesis will be that the properties ascribed by the evaluative terms supervene on those represented by the purely descriptive terms (or, alternatively, that anyone who evaluates objects or situations differently is required to see them as differing in these purely descriptive properties). I do not have an argument that the first, simpler doctrine must be rejected from some recognized metaethical standpoint. However, that doctrine is very close to the thesis that the evaluative supervenes on the factual, and the argument I shall give below—that there is a recognized position that cannot account for supervenience on the factual—will apply to this simpler doctrine of supervenience on the descriptive as well. So I put it to one

[43] Williams (1985: 129).

side here. My topic in this section will instead be whether the evaluative supervenes on the purely descriptive understood in the more complex and more standard way, as those properties represented by descriptive terms that are not evaluative.

Like the proposal that the evaluative supervenes on the non-evaluative, this suggestion appears to avoid difficulties about the supernatural. We may say both evaluative and descriptive things about the supernatural, just as we do about the mundane. And this proposal also helps with the difficulty that reductive naturalism posed for the thesis that the evaluative supervenes on the non-evaluative. It helps because, even if the two lists of *terms*, the evaluative and the purely descriptive, are mutually exclusive, nothing I have said commits us either way on the question of whether some property might be represented by terms from both lists. So we may understand our reductive ethical naturalist as someone who holds that this indeed happens: to stick to our example, that the term "good," which is of course evaluative, and the purely descriptive term "pleasant," ascribe the same property. This position now poses no challenge to the supervenience of the evaluative on the descriptive. For even though it counts pleasure as an evaluative property (because it is ascribed by the term "good"), it also counts that property as descriptive (because it is also ascribed by the term "pleasant"), and so as part of the proposed supervenience base. And it is thus straightforward, even trivial, that goodness, if it is the same property as pleasure, supervenes on that base.

That is the attraction of specifying the relevant properties, the supervening ones and the ones supervened upon, indirectly, as the ones we represent in distinct ways. However, as soon as we involve our representational powers in the formulation of a supervenience thesis in this way, the plausibility of the thesis is threatened if those powers are limited. (Here I make points similar to some made by both Griffin and Raz.) Of course, this supervenience of the evaluative on the descriptive will look quite certain to anyone who holds that evaluative terms stand for descriptive properties.[44] But to anyone who is not already a "descriptivist" in this sense the doctrine can look quite implausible. I shall illustrate the difficulty with what seems to me

---

[44] This is illustrated by the example I have just used. If goodness is just pleasure (and if "pleasure" is a descriptive term), then goodness supervenes on the descriptive: that is, on properties represented by descriptive terms, of which pleasure is one. (One might of course hold that evaluative properties are descriptive without being sure which reductive account of the evaluative is correct. But so long as we understand evaluative and "purely descriptive" terms to be distinct, "descriptivism" will require that there be reductive accounts of evaluative properties, pairing evaluative with corresponding non-evaluative terms. In this it contrasts with ethical naturalism, which as I understand it does not guarantee that there are such reductions.)

an especially clear example of it. Frank Jackson takes it to be a priori (at least according to "folk moral theory") that "moral properties supervene on descriptive properties." And he is explicit that by descriptive properties he just means properties ascribable by a certain kind of non-evaluative terminology, "by language that falls on the descriptive side of the famous is–ought divide." Thus, he says: "I have to regard the purely descriptive terms as essentially given by a big list of terms that would generally be classified as such." He adds, with respect to borderline cases (such as the thick term, "honest"), that "if it is unclear whether a term is or is not purely descriptive, then we can take it off the list of the purely descriptive."[45] I see two reasons for doubting that it is even true, let alone a priori, that the evaluative will supervene on the descriptive when the categories are defined in this way. One lies in Jackson's very atheoretical way of sorting terms. He simply appeals to some philosophers' sense of which terms go where (for he thinks that some philosophers reject the distinction and cannot see the divide): and this looks to make it a contingent fact, if a fact at all, that the terms get sorted onto the right lists. Think of it this way: Even if there is *some* way of sorting terms such that the terms that end up on one list represent properties that supervene on properties represented by terms on the other, why should we be sure that this seat-of-the-pants procedure that Jackson describes for sorting will give us lists with this property?

This might be thought just a problem with Jackson's exposition, however: someone might think that there is a more principled (and non-parochial) way of sorting terms. They might even maintain that it implicitly informs even the philosophers' intuitions on which Jackson relies. So I shall put this criticism to one side and focus instead on the second. This is that there is surely room for doubt about whether descriptive properties specified in this way will include all the ones that could make an evaluative difference. Jackson's exclusion of terms expressing thick evaluative concepts from the "descriptive" list is a reminder of one way there might be a problem. For there has been a lively debate about whether we possess the resources to factor out the purely descriptive component in these thick concepts. Some philosophers have held that we lack an austerely non-evaluative vocabulary adequate to this task. Their view is controversial, but has nevertheless been

---

[45] Jackson (1998: 118–20). Jackson takes himself to be describing a procedure for finding a descriptive reduction for the evaluative. But he presents the supervenience of the evaluative on the descriptive as a principle that should look plausible—a priori, in fact—before such a reduction is found, and plausible even to those who doubt the possibility of a reduction. So his view seems subject to the difficulties I describe.

widely influential.[46] If it is true, then there are natural (or supernatural) properties for which we lack descriptive terminology, and they seem to be properties that make an evaluative difference: so the evaluative does not supervene on the descriptive. Of course, their view may be mistaken, but for the point I am making here I do not need to defend their position (even though I find it reasonable). It is enough that they represent a recognized position in metaethics, and that it is one that must deny that the evaluative supervenes on the descriptive: for that marks the thesis as parochial.

A sometime response to this difficulty is to take descriptive properties to be, not the ones for which we now have descriptive terms, but the ones for which we would have such terms in an improved language, a language tied to our "end-of-the-day" or "completed" theory of the world. The most important difficulty with this suggestion, for our purposes, is that the philosophers who think that we lack the resources to factor out the purely descriptive content in some evaluative terms pretty clearly think of this as an "in principle" problem, that would remain even on this refined understanding of the descriptive.[47] That leaves the thesis that the

[46] Williams agrees with John McDowell (1979) that we may lack the terminology: that is, that there may be natural properties that we represent only with evaluative terms (Williams 1985: 129, 140–2). Griffin writes, more recently, "Our language may often lack the vocabulary that would allow us to delineate the extension of certain value terms solely in natural predicates. That lack may sometimes not even be remediable" (Griffin 1996: 26).

I anticipate the rejoinder that we do of course have a term for, say, the purely descriptive property picked out by a thick-concept term such as "cruel": it is "the purely descriptive property picked out by 'cruel'" (or perhaps "the purely natural or supernatural property picked out by 'cruel'"). However, I doubt that proponents of this way of dividing properties will want to allow this kind of description onto the list that is supposed to define the descriptive properties. If we allow terms constructed from otherwise purely descriptive elements plus semantic or intentional notions onto that list, then "the property I am now talking about" (or "am now thinking about") will be on the list, and since I can talk and think about evaluative properties, they will all count as descriptive as well as evaluative. Even philosophers, such as Jackson, who think this conclusion correct do not think it can be established so easily. If a fuller rationale for excluding such terms is needed, it could presumably be found in the view, defended by some philosophers, that ascriptions of meaning and of intentional content are normative. Perhaps the best-known statement of the view that meaning is normative is in Kripke (1982: esp. 37). A similar view was defended by Allan Gibbard in talks at Princeton and Cornell in the early 1990s. (I do not know whether they represent his current views.) On the normativity of content attributions, see Wedgwood (2006). Of course, these views are controversial. But, as we have seen, Jackson stipulates that any term on which the verdict is unclear—as is surely the case when there is this sort of controversy—should be dropped from the list of purely descriptive terms.

[47] See e.g. the quotation from Griffin in n. 46 above.

evaluative supervenes on the descriptive still parochial, by my standards. But there are also some reasons for suspecting, with them, that the refinement would not help. As Raz notes,[48] if improving our theory of the world includes improving our evaluative account of it, that will likely involve introducing terms for newly noticed evaluative features; and, holding all else fixed, that will exacerbate rather than ameliorate the difficulty of finding an adequate descriptive supervenience base. An opponent might respond that our ethical discourse does not look as if it is converging on an end-of-the-day theory anyway, so the proposal should be more limited: just that the eventual terminology of the sciences, about which there is more room for optimism, should be our touchstone test for the descriptive. But then there seem to be two further problems. One, in my view, is that although the mature sciences seem on the whole to be approximating, in a philosophically significant way, to what appears partly for that reason to be a true account of the world, this process does not seem to involve any deceleration in conceptual and terminological innovation. I do not see anything in the history of the successful sciences that invites us to project to an imagined limit in which their vocabulary will be, or would finally be, fixed, or "completed." The other problem is that optimism about the needed sort of progress in the sciences is only rarely paired with equal optimism about theology—especially by those who are pessimistic about progress in ethics. But, as we have seen, to have an adequate descriptive supervenience base, we would need descriptive terms for all the supernatural features that could possibly (or, at least, imaginably) make a difference to the evaluative. And there are other problems besides.[49] Together, these difficulties suggest that there is at the least a considerable burden of proof on anyone who claims that the evaluative supervenes on the descriptive, where the two categories are made derivative from a linguistic distinction in this way.

---

[48] Raz (2000: 53).

[49] Some problems arise from specific proposals. Hare is one writer who suggests that, if we find ourselves lacking a descriptive term for some property, we can always introduce one: for example, if we find ourselves with only an evaluative term for some universally prized quality of a wine, we can introduce a descriptive term in addition (Hare 1963*a*: 56–9). But it is not clear, on Hare's own functional account of the distinction between descriptive and evaluative terms, that this will have the desired result: for it seems fairly easy to predict that, no matter what we say in introducing the term (e.g. "This is the term you would use even if you didn't like the quality"), it would quickly become a term of commendation—and so, by Hare's standards, evaluative, not descriptive.

A very different problem is that there can be worries about whether even an end-of-the-day theory would have enough predicates for all the properties there are (or might imaginably be). Kim takes this as a reason to formulate his supervenience theses always about properties, not about linguistic predicates (1984: 73).

And I believe that the same is true when we look beyond language to mental representations: that is, to the idea that descriptive properties are the ones that we conceive of or otherwise represent mentally in some distinctive way (or that we would conceive or represent in that way in improved circumstances). This is a distinct family of proposals, since on most views our concepts can outrun our vocabulary and on some views our representational powers can outrun our concepts. Still, these abilities are limited. Until we see some account of how an adequate supervenience base of descriptive properties could be defined in terms of them, or of some idealized development of them, I believe that we are entitled to be skeptical.

THE FACTUAL?

Thus, the thesis that the evaluative supervenes on the descriptive should look implausible except to those who already think that evaluative properties just are descriptive. In this it is like the thesis that the evaluative supervenes on the natural, which of course looks true (on one understanding) to the ethical naturalist but, I argued, ought to look implausible to everyone else. And the claim that the evaluative supervenes on the non-evaluative is also parochial. So we have not yet found any supervenience thesis that philosophers with different, recognized metaethical views can all agree on. But I have one more proposal to consider, also taken from the literature: that the evaluative supervenes on the factual. As I have said, my complaint about this proposal will be a bit different, for I shall argue not that there is any recognized position that must reject this thesis, but that there is one that can provide no rationale for it, and from which it must therefore appear arbitrary. A reader will recall that a fair bit hangs on this part of my argument, since one thing I said about proposed disjunctive supervenience bases, as well as about the simpler version of supervenience on the descriptive, is that they amount to the proposal that the evaluative supervenes on the factual.

Which properties are we to count as the factual ones? According to the spirit of the proposal, I think the answer has to be: all of them—the natural and supernatural, the non-evaluative, the descriptive, and any others there happen to be. Thus, following my discussion above of the supernatural, I am including not just possible but also merely imaginable ways that things might be. Whatever problems this may involve, I think that it is the way the category is standardly understood in metaethical discussions. Of course, philosophers disagree about what kinds of properties there are. Most importantly, for our purposes, they disagree about whether there are such things as evaluative properties. For those who deny that there are evaluative properties (and who take this to be necessary), the thesis that the evaluative supervenes on the factual will look like the thesis that the evaluative supervenes on the non-evaluative. But we should not understand "factual" just to mean "non-evaluative." For one thing, if we do, then the supervenience thesis we are considering turns out to be one I have already considered and shown to be parochial. For another, we should not let mere terminology bias us against factualist accounts of evaluative discourse. If there are evaluative properties, then there are evaluative facts (about which things have those properties), and evaluative as well as non-evaluative properties will count as factual—that is, as properties.

A PROBLEM FOR FACTUALISM?

As I have mentioned, Simon Blackburn once alleged that an evaluative realist cannot explain why there cannot be an evaluative difference without a "naturalistic difference." This objection to realism is not my main topic here: my central concern is with his accompanying claim that his expressivism *can* account for supervenience. But we can learn something from seeing what problems his argument faces. Even if we talk of factualism (which is all Blackburn appears to have in mind) rather than realism,[50] and even if we consider all the variations of this allegation—replacing "naturalistic" in turn with "non-evaluative," "descriptive," and "factual"—the objection seems misdirected. A factualist who is an ethical naturalist (or: a descriptivist) can easily explain why the evaluative supervenes, ontologically, on the natural (or: on the descriptive); a factualist who is not an ethical naturalist (or: not a descriptivist) can—and in the case of the natural, should—deny that there is this supervenience; and all should deny that the evaluative supervenes, ascriptively, on the natural. A factualist who is a reductive

---

[50] Blackburn does take the position he is targeting to hold, not just that there are moral states of affairs in virtue of which moral assertions may be true or false, but also that there is no entailment of any moral conclusion from entirely "naturalistic" premises (1971: 111–12, 116). If we generalize, we get the view that there are evaluative states of affairs in virtue of which evaluative assertions may be true or false—the view I am calling factualism—and also that there is no entailment of any evaluative conclusion from (depending on the supervenience thesis under attack) purely naturalistic, purely non-evaluative, purely descriptive, or purely factual premises. However, all of the metaethical positions I have appealed to can easily accommodate the epistemically relevant version of this latter thesis. In particular, the versions of reductive naturalism (or supernaturalism) I have mentioned can easily avoid saying that the reduction in question is a conceptual truth.

naturalist may deny that the evaluative supervenes on the non-evaluative;[51] other ethical naturalists can deny that they are committed to holding that evaluative properties supervene on non-evaluative ones. And a factualist of any variety can easily explain why the evaluative supervenes on the factual: evaluative properties supervene on factual properties because they are factual properties. Blackburn does not distinguish these positions; and, amid all the complexities, it is possible that I have overlooked a relevant doctrine that will have some problem with supervenience. But it does seem difficult to find anything here that a factualist (*a*) must maintain but (*b*) cannot account for.

Blackburn also objects, however, that a realist cannot account for the a priori status of evaluative supervenience.[52] I have already explained why I think that none of the first three doctrines I canvassed—that the evaluative supervenes on the natural, on the non-evaluative, and on the descriptive—is a priori. Each of these doctrines can be rejected from standpoints that, in my view, cannot themselves be rejected a priori: so the doctrines are not a priori. Here I anticipate resistance on behalf primarily of supervenience on the non-evaluative, from those who think that reductive naturalism and the other stances that conflict with that doctrine can be dispatched by some a priori argument inspired by Moore. I will not pursue that question here, except to repeat my disagreement, and to point out that it has not always been noticed that, if one wants to maintain that it is a priori that the evaluative supervenes on the non-evaluative, one does have to hold that some forms of reductive naturalism (and, I suggested, other naturalist and supernaturalist views) can be rejected a priori.[53]

My final candidate doctrine, supervenience on the factual, is different, because I am not claiming to have found any position that needs to reject it. Is it a priori? It might be, but I think also that it might easily appear a priori even if it is not. It of course follows by a simple and a priori step from the factualist view that evaluative properties are themselves real. Some defenders of factualism think of their arguments for that position as a priori,

---

[51] As we saw (n. 41), *some* versions of reductive naturalism (or supernaturalism) will have the evaluative supervening on the non-evaluative—but will have no difficulty in explaining why this is so. If moral rightness is just the property of maximizing happiness, there is no mystery about why it supervenes on a non-evaluative base that includes the properties of maximizing some quantity and of happiness.

[52] Here see especially Blackburn (1985).

[53] My assessment of Moore's own arguments is in Sturgeon (2003). I find it striking here that Gibbard—whose general view of Moore is that he is largely right about metaethics, once his doctrines have been translated into expressivese—dissents on the question of whether there is an all-purpose argument against naturalistic reductions. "In my own view, naturalistic reductions have to be tackled case by case; I know of no argument that proves in advance that every such definition fails" (Gibbard 2003: 35).

moreover, so are in position to hold the supervenience of the evaluative on the factual to be a priori as well. I am not in position to agree, however, for although I count myself a factualist, I don't believe that that doctrine can be established a priori.[54] The doctrine of supervenience on the factual is nevertheless in a special position, because it follows immediately not only from what factualists believe but also from what up-to-date anti-factualists say that everyone should accept most of the time, as they speak with the vulgar. It is in their view only when we stop to think with the learned that we need to remind ourselves that evaluative properties are only projected, constructed, invented, or whatever.[55] When a doctrine is endorsed in one way by factualists and in another by anti-factualists, it will not be surprising if an immediate consequence of it should come to seem very obvious.

A PROBLEM FOR EXPRESSIVISM?

Blackburn's argument that an evaluative realist or factualist cannot properly account for supervenience has received critical attention much more detailed than I have given it here. To my knowledge, there has been much less attention to his accompanying argument, that expressivism by contrast can successfully explain why supervenience holds.[56] He is discussing, specifically, moral evaluation and "naturalistic" properties, but the point is presumably meant to generalize to any kind of evaluation and properties of any sort. He is furthermore assuming, as an expressivist, that it is essential to an

---

[54] Here I sympathize with Gibbard's suggestion that his disagreement with his factualist and realist opponents, about the function of evaluative discourse, may be at bottom an empirical one (Gibbard 1990: 122 n.; 116).

[55] I have in mind of course Blackburn's and Gibbard's quasi-realism.

[56] For discussions of the anti-realist argument, see Klagge (1984); Dreier (1992); Shafer-Landau (2003: 84–8). There are brief discussions of Blackburn's argument that he, unlike the realist or factualist, can account for supervenience in Shafer-Landau (2003: 88–9), and in Zangwill (1997: 510–11).

It should be noted that Blackburn is not the first writer to propose an expressivist explanation for an ascriptive version of the supervenience of the evaluative. In his (1952: 134, 159), Hare says that we treat the evaluative as supervening because we use evaluative language to teach and express standards or principles guiding choice, something he thinks we could not do if we allowed evaluations to vary with any difference in supervenience base properties. I think that this suggestion, spelled out, would face difficulties similar to those I raise for Blackburn (see n. 58, below) and for Gibbard. But it will also be controversial to the extent it relies on Hare's distinctive understanding of the principles we teach and rely on in decision-making. For he sees these as exceptionless but indefinitely complex—so that allowing an exception to any hitherto-held principle really means adopting a new principle (1952: 65). The view that we teach or rely on such principles in moral decision-making has been widely challenged, however: see e.g. Väyrynen (2009).

evaluative judgment that it include some element of a pro- or con- attitude or choice. He writes:

There can be no question that we often choose, admire, commend, or desire, objects because of their naturalistic properties. Now it is not possible to hold an attitude to a thing because of its possessing certain properties and, at the same time, not hold that attitude to another thing that is believed to have the same properties. The nonexistence of the attitude in the second case shows that it is not because of the shared properties that I hold it in the first case.

Thus,

it is not possible to hold a moral attitude to one thing, believe a second to be exactly alike, yet at the same time not hold the same attitude to the second thing. Anybody who appears to do this is convicted of misidentifying a caprice as a moral opinion.[57]

There seem at least two difficulties with this argument. One is that even on a sympathetic reading Blackburn's principle about beliefs and attitudes seems doubtful. In real life cases are never exactly alike, but there certainly does seem to be such a thing as seeing two cases as relevantly alike, even to the point of evaluating them similarly, but finding that one has different attitudes towards them. Such cases are not of course a direct counterexample to our finding the *evaluative* to co-vary with what Blackburn will call the factual, but they seem a problem for his proposed explanation. Perhaps he will say that at least one of the attitudes in such a case is irrational, a mere caprice and no manifestation of an evaluative opinion, but that would need to be argued, not just asserted.[58] A second problem, however, is that there is

---

[57] Blackburn (1971: 122).

[58] In his (1984: 186), Blackburn offers a different explanation, appealing to the point of engaging in evaluation, which in his expressivist view is practical decision-making: evaluation not subject to the constraint of supervenience would, he thinks, be unfit for guiding choice. I think that this suggestion, like Hare's (see n. 56), will encounter a difficulty arising from the same general point that I shall raise for Gibbard, that a lot of evaluation is of situations far removed from any choices we have any chance of facing. A further question for Blackburn, however, is why he thinks that a convention on evaluation that serves this point will classify the person who flouts supervenience as a conceptually incompetent moralizer (or evaluator) rather than just as an eccentric one. Many people's intuitions support Hare's requirement of universalizability on evaluations—in effect, that proper evaluation supervenes on the universal properties of things—every bit as much as they support a requirement of supervenience. But Blackburn rejects as "Quixotic" Hare's attempt to rule those who reject universalizability out of the moral or ethical conversation: he argues that if some disputants reject universalizability we shall still "need to engage" with them and their preferences, by arguing that theirs is not "the way to find out which things are good" (Blackburn 1990: 202; Blackburn has kindly confirmed to me that the printed text, which says "we must emerge" with them, is a typographical error). Why, one may wonder, is that matter any different with a disputant who flouts supervenience?

not even a suggestion about how we are to get from Blackburn's principle, if we grant it, to the existence of all the kinds of commitments needed to make up an ascriptive supervenience relation. How, for example, does it follow that if I think of two objects' differing in value, without thinking just how, and without thinking of any catalogue of their properties, I must think *that* they differ (no matter how) in their properties? It may be that there are elements here from which a better argument could be constructed. But especially in the light of more recent expressivist discussions (including, of course, Blackburn's own) of these problems of what to make of evaluative language in unasserted contexts, what he says in this passage can seem rather perfunctory.[59]

By contrast, Allan Gibbard's recent attempt, in *Thinking How to Live*, to show how his expressivism explains the supervenience of the evaluative (or, more specifically, in his discussion, of the normative), is far more sophisticated and anything but perfunctory. (And, according to Gibbard, it also has the benefit of agreeing with Blackburn's most recent views on "normative logic."[60]) In fact, Gibbard's discussion is complex enough that I am sure not to be able to do it justice. At the same time, I think that it faces a serious difficulty.

As I explained above, Gibbard does not assume the existence of normative properties, so his will be, like Blackburn's, what we have been calling an ascriptive account of supervenience. He is assuming an expressivist account of evaluation, according to which evaluating a possible action as permissible or impermissible is a matter of accepting a conditional plan with respect to it, a plan that either positively rules it in (and so labels it permissible) or else rules it out (and so labels it impermissible). Grant this for the sake of discussion, since our interest is in seeing whether, as Gibbard claims, it can help explain the supervenience of the normative. His thesis is that any planner is committed, by requirements of consistency, to seeing differences in permissibility only where there are also differences in the facts—and also to holding such general views as that wherever there is a difference with respect to permissibility, there must be a difference in the facts as well.[61]

---

[59] For a more recent discussion of these problems by Blackburn, see his (1988).

[60] Gibbard (2003: 82–7).

[61] Gibbard gives different accounts of the intended supervenience base. Often it is the natural (where that is characterized narrowly: e.g. as part of "strict empirical science" or everyday causal explanation (2003: 32)); sometimes it is the "prosaically factual" (55, 75, 88) where "prosaic" appears to be doing duty for "non-normative." However, at one point he notes explicitly that the natural as a supervenience base has to be understood broadly, to cover features of "spooks and gods" should a planner believe in such things (p. 99); and his reason for focusing on the prosaically factual appears to be that he thinks (or, at any rate, is assuming in this discussion (p. 88)) that the prosaically factual

Gibbard's explanation makes heavy use of the notion of what he calls a hyperstate, the state of an entirely imaginary super-mind that is fully decided on every issue of what to believe and of what to do. Such a state includes a determinate belief about every question of fact (thus mirroring, as Gibbard notes, a possible world) and a determinate plan for every conceivable choice situation. Any hyperstate is understood by Gibbard to be consistent, which for beliefs means what you always thought it meant and for plans means that no alternative, in a given choice situation, is ruled both in and out, and that in every choice situation at least one alternative is permitted.[62] From the perspective of any such state, Gibbard argues, permissibility will look to supervene on the facts. He then extends the point to those of us with more fragmentary views and aims by arguing that, if we are consistent (or: on an idealization of us on which we are consistent), there will be a determinate set of hyperstates that we could come to be in (by augmenting our beliefs and plans) without changing our minds. Any claim that holds in all these hyperstates will be one that we are committed to, moreover: and since supervenience looks to hold from the perspective not just of these hyperstates but of every hyperstate, we are all committed to it.

This summary elides some elegant features of Gibbard's story, as well perhaps as some problems, but it is sufficient to bring out what I think is the main difficulty. Gibbard places key emphasis on requirements of consistency—in the hyperstates themselves, and in the requirement we must meet if the implications of our attitudes are to be explained by appealing to hyperstates consistent with them. But why is consistency so important? This may seem a strange question: don't we standardly assess what conclusions people are committed to by asking what they must do to avoid inconsistency? But notice two points. First, "inconsistent" is, for Gibbard, a descriptive term, in the narrower and more common sense. It is not evaluative, and so does not have "Boo!" built into it. And commitment, he says, is a normative notion.[63] So surely we may ask an expressivist how it comes to be that there is automatically a norm of

---

properties are the only properties there are. So it seems fair to take him, as I do, as arguing that the normative supervenes on the factual: that is, on all the properties there are. (The fact that he holds this without believing in normative facts or properties of course makes this a more interesting thesis, from him, than it is from a normative factualist.) I deliberately ignore his eventual suggestion that the supervenience is really on a narrower class, that of "recognitional" concepts (pp. 102–8). If this thesis is right, then the normative does still supervene on the factual (of which the recognitional is a proper subset); but I think that the proposal, though it faces problems of its own, is subject to the same objection I raise concerning supervenience on the factual—so doesn't require separate discussion here.

[62] Gibbard (2003: 59).   [63] Gibbard (2003: 45).

avoiding those combinations of states that are inconsistent. Second, in the case of inconsistent *beliefs* there is the beginning of a possible answer, for expressivists and non-expressivists alike, in the observation that inconsistent beliefs must some of them be false and that belief aims at truth.[64] How belief aims at truth is of course a difficult and contentious issue, but I am like many philosophers in thinking that there must be some reasonable sense in which it does so aim, with the result that recognized inconsistency in belief always presents itself as a problem. My question for Gibbard is then whether there is any comparable reason for thinking us committed to avoiding inconsistency in plans.

Gibbard does not address this question directly, but one can piece together a couple of answers from his remarks. An inconsistent plan for a situation, he says, "would preclude offering any guidance on what to do on that occasion."[65] The idea appears to be that plans have a function and that inconsistent plans cannot fulfill it. The sort of inconsistent plan he is talking about in this quotation, however, is one that rules out all alternatives; and friends of normative dilemmas will surely insist that there are situations like this in which even the best planning, the sort fully responsive to the applicable norms, does in fact offer no guidance. This view (which Gibbard does not mention) is of course controversial, but it surely deserves more than dismissal by stipulation; and it suggests that it is a substantive question how well we should expect planning to be able to carry out the function Gibbard assigns it. Dilemmas to one side, an even more obvious difficulty concerns the "wild hypotheticals" that Gibbard takes to be involved in planning.[66] Someone in a hyperstate will have plans not just for likely contingencies but for every conceivable situation, including ones certain never to arise and with no resemblance to any likely to arise. Real agents aren't in hyperstates, of course, but Gibbard insists that we can form fragments of plans for any of these fantastic situations. So why care whether our plans for such situations are consistent? Some hypothetical planning, he points out, is practice for real planning:[67] so, if inconsistency in plans is a threat to real planning, it might be a bad idea to allow it into the practice sessions. But that can hardly cover all the hypothetical plans we might have. Suppose that through make believe (as Gibbard advises[68]) I think my way into a situation in the distant past, quite unlike anything I could encounter in my life; and suppose I then

---

[64] As I was working on this topic, I was pleased to discover that this problem for Gibbard's account of supervenience had also been raised by Matthew Chrisman. See Chrisman (2005: 111–12). See also Wedgwood (2006: 47–51).

[65] Gibbard (2003: 56).   [66] Gibbard (2003: 70).

[67] Gibbard (2003: 52–3, 70).   [68] Gibbard (2003: 50 n.).

discover that, coming at the situation from different directions, I have formed inconsistent plans about what to do should it arise. Why is this a cause for alarm, or for reform in my fantastic hypothetical plans, rather than just for amusement?[69]

My conclusion about Blackburn and Gibbard, then, is that neither shows expressivism to provide a plausible basis for thinking that the evaluative supervenes on the factual. There are two directions one might go with this conclusion. One, no doubt the more natural given these writers' own intentions, would be to see this as a problem for expressivism. Blackburn, as I am reading him, alleges that a factualist cannot account for supervenience on the factual, and takes this to count against factualism. Even if he were right about factualism, it would presumably then at least neutralize that objection to show that expressivism does no better; and if, as I have argued, he is wrong about factualism as well as about expressivism, then by his own standards expressivism will come out the more problematic view. In Gibbard's case, moreover, a failure to show that the normative supervenes on the factual will ramify, threatening, for example, his discussions of factual constitution and normative causation;[70] and though difficulties there would hardly refute expressivism, they would undermine his attempt to make the view, on these topics, seem closer to opposing positions.

I cannot end, however, without at least noting another way my conclusion might be taken. One of my main themes has been that it is hard to find an uncontroversial version of the supervenience of the evaluative to serve as fixed point in debates in metaethics. That the evaluative supervenes on the natural, on the non-evaluative and on the descriptive are doctrines frequently encountered in the literature of metaethics; but each would be denied from some recognized metaethical stance, with room in each case for disagreement about whether this marks a problem with the supervenience doctrine or with the metaethical stance. To be sure, I have not located any position that must in a similar way deny the supervenience of the evaluative on the factual. Nor have I argued against this doctrine: I think, in fact, that it is true. Denying it, furthermore, would be a radical step, in that it is the weakest of the supervenience doctrines I have considered: if the

---

[69] In a passage that he says will let "us see what is wrong with inconsistency in combined belief and planning" (2003: 59), Gibbard, speaking of both plans and factual judgments as "judgments," points out that "if ... my judgments are inconsistent, there is no way I could become [fully] opinionated factually, and fully decided on a plan for living—no way that I haven't, with my judgments, already ruled out." But he says nothing about why, with respect to plans, this need be a misfortune, something "wrong." (Indeed, he says nothing *here* about why this would be a misfortune with respect even to factual beliefs.)

[70] Gibbard (2003: 94–105, 199–220).

evaluative doesn't supervene on the factual, then it doesn't supervene on anything. Still, I think an expressivist might consider whether, if she cannot account for the doctrine of supervenience on the factual, that doctrine is worth holding onto. Expressivism has looked to many of its proponents, as well as to opponents like me, like a radical doctrine that one would expect to have far-reaching implications for ethical thought; and its proponents have usually thought that there were powerful considerations in its favor, such as an argument from appraiser internalism about motivation, that would support it even on such a radical understanding. The strategy of its most prominent recent defenders has been, in "quasi-realist" fashion, to disown the radical implications. But, I have argued, the quasi-realism falls into problems, if expressivism cannot explain the supervenience of the evaluative on the factual; and, I have also argued, there is much more room for controversy about the supervenience of the evaluative than philosophers have commonly recognized. I am probably the last philosopher from whom an expressivist would take advice. But it seems to me that, in this dialectical situation, an expressivist might consider arguing that since evaluation isn't factual, it simply shouldn't be expected to supervene on the factual, either.

REFERENCES

Adams, Robert (1999) *Finite and Infinite Goods* (New York: Oxford University Press).

Audi, Robert (1993) "Ethical Naturalism and the Explanatory Power of Moral Concepts"; reprinted in *Moral Knowledge and Ethical Character* (New York: Oxford University Press, 1997).

Blackburn, Simon (1971) "Moral Realism"; reprinted in *Essays in Quasi-Realism* (New York: Oxford University Press, 1993).

—— (1984) *Spreading the Word* (Oxford: Clarendon Press).

—— (1985) "Supervenience Revisited"; reprinted in *Essays in Quasi-Realism* (New York: Oxford University Press, 1993).

—— (1988) "Attitudes and Contents"; reprinted in *Essays in Quasi-Realism* (New York: Oxford University Press, 1993).

—— (1990) "Just Causes"; reprinted in *Essays in Quasi-Realism* (New York: Oxford University Press, 1993).

Brandt, Richard (1959) *Ethical Theory* (Englewood Cliffs, NJ: Prentice-Hall).

Broad, C. D. (1930) *Five Types of Ethical Theory* (London: Routledge).

Chrisman, Matthew (2005), "Allan Gibbard: *Thinking How to Live*" review, *Ethics* 115: 406–12.

Davidson, Donald (1970) "Mental Events"; reprinted in *Essays on Actions and Events*, 2nd edn. (Oxford: Clarendon Press, 2001).

Dreier, James (1992) "The Supervenience Argument against Moral Realism" *Southern Journal of Philosophy* 30: 13–38.

Gibbard, Allan (1990) *Wise Choices, Apt Feelings* (Cambridge, MA: Harvard University Press).

—— (2003) *Thinking How to Live* (Cambridge, MA: Harvard University Press).

Griffin, James (1996) *Value Judgement* (Oxford: Clarendon Press).

Hare, R. M. (1952) *The Language of Morals* (Oxford: Clarendon Press).

—— (1963*a*) "Descriptivism"; reprinted in *Essays on the Moral Concepts* (Berkeley: University of California Press, 1972).

—— (1963*b*) *Freedom and Reason* (Oxford: Clarendon Press).

—— (1984) "Supervenience" *Proceedings of the Aristotelian Society* 58 Suppl.

Jackson, Frank (1998) *From Metaphysics to Ethics* (Oxford: Clarendon Press).

—— Phillip Pettit, and Michael Smith (2000) "Ethical Particularism and Patterns," in Brad Hooker and Margaret Olivia Little (eds.), *Moral Particularism* (Oxford: Clarendon Press), 79–99.

Johnston, Mark (1989) "Dispositional Theories of Value" *Proceedings of the Aristotelian Society* 63: 139–74.

Kim, Jaegwon (1984) "Concepts of Supervenience"; reprinted in *Supervenience and Mind* (Cambridge: Cambridge University Press, 1993).

—— (1988) "What is 'Naturalized Epistemology'?" reprinted in *Supervenience and Mind* (Cambridge: Cambridge University Press, 1993).

—— (1990) "Supervenience as a Philosophical Concept"; reprinted in *Supervenience and Mind* (Cambridge: Cambridge University Press, 1993).

Klagge, James (1984) "An Alleged Difficulty Concerning Moral Properties" *Mind* 93: 370–80.

—— (1988) "Supervenience: Ontological and Ascriptive" *Australasian Journal of Philosophy* 66: 461–70.

Kripke, Saul (1982) *Wittgenstein on Rules and Private Language* (Cambridge, MA: Harvard University Press).

Lewis, David (1989) "Dispositional Theories of Value" *Proceedings of the Aristotelian Society* 63: 113–37.

McDowell, John (1979) "Virtue and Reason"; reprinted in *Mind, Value and Reality* (Cambridge, MA: Harvard University Press, 1998).

—— (1981) "Non-Cognitivism and Rule-Following"; reprinted in *Mind, Value and Reality* (Cambridge, MA: Harvard University Press, 1998).

McKeever, Sean, and Ridge, Michael (2006) *Principled Ethics* (Oxford: Clarendon Press).

McNaughton, David (1988) *Moral Vision* (Oxford: Basil Blackwell).

Moore, G. E. (1903) *Principia Ethica* (Cambridge: Cambridge University Press).

—— (1912) *Ethics* (London: Oxford University Press).

—— (1959 [1922]) "The Conception of Intrinsic Value," in *Philosophical Studies* (Paterson, NJ: Littlefield, Adams), 253–75.

—— (1968 [1942]) "A Reply to My Critics," in Paul Arthur Schilpp (ed.), *The Philosophy of G. E. Moore* (LaSalle, IL: Open Court), 535–677.

Moore, G. E. (1993) *Principia Ethica* rev. edn., ed. Thomas Baldwin (Cambridge: Cambridge University Press).

Pigden, Charles R. (1991) "Naturalism," in Peter Singer (ed.), *A Companion to Ethics* (Oxford: Basil Blackwell), 421–31.

Prior, A. N. (1949) *Logic and the Basis of Ethics* (Oxford: Clarendon Press).

Railton, Peter (1995) "Made in the Shade: Moral Compatibilism and the Aims of Moral Theory," in Jocelyne Couture and Kai Nielson (eds.), *On the Relevance of Metaethics* (Calgary: University of Calgary Press), 79–106.

Raz, Joseph (2000) "The Truth in Particularism," in Brad Hooker and Margaret Olivia Little (eds.), *Moral Particularism* (Oxford: Clarendon Press), 48–78.

Ross, W. D (1930) *The Right and the Good* (Oxford: Clarendon Press).

Shafer-Landau, Russ (2003) *Moral Realism* (Oxford: Clarendon Press).

Smith, Michael (1994) *The Moral Problem* (Oxford: Blackwell Publishers).

—— (2000) "Does the Evaluative Supervene on the Natural?" reprinted in *Ethics and the A Priori* (Cambridge: Cambridge University Press, 2004).

Sturgeon, Nicholas L. (1985) "Moral Explanations," in David Copp and David Zimmerman (eds.), *Morality, Reason, and Truth: New Essays on the Foundations of Ethics* (Totowa, NJ: Rowman and Allanheld), 49–78.

—— (2003) "Moore on Ethical Naturalism" *Ethics* 113: 528–56.

—— (2006a) "Ethical Naturalism," in David Copp (ed.), *The Oxford Handbook of Ethical Theory* (Oxford: Oxford University Press), 91–121.

—— (2006b) "Moral Explanations Defended," in James Dreier (ed.), *Contemporary Debates in Moral Theory* (Oxford: Blackwell Publishers), 241–62.

Väyrynen, Pekka (2009) "A Theory of Hedged Moral Principles," in Russ Shafer-Landau (ed.), *Oxford Studies in Metaethics*, iv.

Wedgwood, Ralph (2006) *The Nature of Normativity* (Oxford: Clarendon Press).

Williams, Bernard (1985) *Ethics and the Limits of Philosophy* (Cambridge, MA: Harvard University Press).

Zangwill, Nick (1997) "Explaining Supervenience: Moral and Mental" *Journal of Philosophical Research* 22: 509–18.

4

A Theory of Hedged Moral Principles

Pekka Väyrynen

1 INTRODUCTION

Moral theories have explanatory aspirations. They purport not merely to tell us *which* things are right and wrong, good and bad, and just and unjust, but also to explain *why* those things have the moral features that they do. Many theorists think that explanations which help us understand or make sense of morality must in some way rely on general moral principles. Suppose, for instance, that Anna ought to help Adam who is very badly off. Views which are "generalist" in this sense hold that Anna ought to do whatever it is that she ought to do in some sense because of some moral principles with suitable content, such as that one ought to help the badly off. So, many moral theories are committed to the existence of moral principles which can contribute to explanations of the moral features of things. But it seems often to be granted that many moral generalizations might have exceptions. It might be that Anna has no duty to help Adam if he is badly off through his own fault, or doesn't deserve help, or would channel the help to some heinous end. It is far from obvious what kind of principles could reconcile these two ideas or how principles which

Material from this chapter received valuable feedback from audiences at the Fourth Annual Wisconsin Metaethics Workshop in Madison, the "Ethics without Principles" conference in Paris, and Universities of Oxford, Stockholm, and Turku. From conversations on these and other occasions, I recall particularly instructive objections or suggestions from Christian Coons, David Copp, Michael Fara, Eric Hiddleston, Brendan Jackson, Robert Johnson, Stephen Kearns, Mark Lance, Sean McKeever, Bernhard Nickel, Russ Shafer-Landau, Ian Spencer, Sarah Stroud, and Paul Teller. Michael Ridge, Connie Rosati, and a number of anonymous referees for this volume and other journals deserve special thanks for generously sacrificing their time to prepare extremely helpful comments on earlier drafts. I cannot blame these colleagues, or anyone else with whom I have discussed these issues, for the long time this paper stayed in preparation or any mistakes that still remain. I would like to express my deep gratitude to them all.

purport to do so are something that moral agents can grasp, and which can guide them.

The aim of this chapter is to show how there can be moral principles which can play the explanatory and epistemological roles required by moral theory and yet are capable of admitting exceptions. I'll argue that principles which take a certain kind of "hedged" form can be of this kind and that such principles can be used to capture not only various familiar principles which have been claimed to hold without exception but also less orthodox sorts of principles which are claimed to permit exceptions. Elsewhere I argue that these hedged principles can account for the kinds of exceptions to which moral particularists appeal in support of their view and explain how they can provide practical guidance.[1] Here I develop the account in more detail. Section 2 describes what kind of theory I seek and an important problem it must solve. Section 3 develops an account of what makes an exception permissible. Section 4 shows how this account can be used to hedge principles so as to make them tolerate exceptions and how such principles can be used to capture a wide range of principles. Section 5 gives some quick arguments to show how hedged principles can contribute to explanations of various kinds of moral facts even if they tolerate exceptions. Section 6 sketches how these principles are something that moral agents can grasp, and which can guide the moral judgments of those agents. Section 7 explains what explanatory and epistemological advantages this account of hedged principles enjoys over certain rivals.

One caveat that I cannot avoid from the start is that many of the issues raised below are extremely complex both in their own right and with respect to how various issues in metaphysics, epistemology, and the philosophy of language, science, and mind bear on them. Since I cannot address all of these issues fully here, my discussion should be understood as an outline of a theory of moral principles. But even the outline will, I think, warrant the conclusion that we should find nothing peculiarly odd or problematic about the idea of exception-tolerating and yet explanatory moral principles.

2 THE PROBLEM ABOUT PERMISSIBLE EXCEPTIONS

Moral theorists sometimes assume that substantive moral principles (henceforth 'principles') must be not only explanatory but also universally applicable and exceptionless. But such "classical" principles are hard to

---

[1] See Väyrynen (2006) and (2008). The present chapter amends my sketch of hedged principles in those articles.

find.[2] For instance, the universal generalization corresponding to 'Promises ought to be kept' is 'Any promise ought to be kept,' but counterexamples to the latter are easy to find. Sometimes you ought to break a promise because only that way can you save a life.

But often we don't seem to think that only exceptionless generalizations can be explanatory. Many think that 'Ravens are black,' 'Acids are corrosive,' and (in the sorry case of supply-side economists) 'Tax cuts create jobs' can express explanatory generalizations but that not just any counterinstance falsifies them as they would falsify the corresponding universal claims. Similarly, many think that 'Promises ought to be kept' and 'Lying is wrong' can express explanatory moral generalizations but that, again, not just any counterinstance falsifies them. Some who think that lying while playing a game of bluff isn't wrong at all, for example, don't thereby deny that 'Lying is wrong' can express a true principle. This departs from a classical picture of moral principles.

If we deny that explanatory moral principles must be exceptionless, then it becomes possible that moral principles can be the sort of generalizations which we know can be explanatory even if their truth is compatible with the existence of exceptional counterinstances. For instance, 'Lying is wrong' might express a true principle even if some lies aren't wrong to tell or there is no reason not to tell them. Another typical feature of generalizations of this kind is that there is no specific proportion of instances which must conform to them for them to be true. So, at least in principle, 'Lying is wrong' could be true even if only few lies happened in fact to be wrong.[3]

According to this alternative view, not all instances of a principle must be equally relevant to its truth. We treat albino ravens as merely apparent counterexamples to 'Ravens are black' because they are irrelevant to the truth of the kind of generic claim which this sentence is naturally read as expressing. Only *some* ravens matter to its truth, and its truth requires that *those* ravens be black. So the core idea is that a generalization may count as a principle even if its truth is properly assessed only relative to some restricted range of instances. The truth of the principle that lying is

---

[2] Classical laws of nature seem to be no less hard to find. On this general message works like *How the Laws of Physics Lie* (Cartwright 1983), *Science without Laws* (Giere 1999), and *Ethics without Principles* (Dancy 2004) agree.

[3] The features listed here are commonly attributed to "indefinite" generic sentences, such as 'Turtles are long-lived' and 'A potato contains thiamine and vitamin C,' which are often used to express non-accidental but exception-tolerating generalizations. While it is no accident that sentences like 'Lying is wrong' are naturally read as generic, my purpose here isn't to offer a syntactic or semantic analysis of any moral sentences. So, although my discussion may occasionally seem to assume a particular analysis of generics to make things concrete, my purposes here require no particular analysis. For various analyses of generics, see Carlson and Pelletier (1995), Koslicki (1999), Liebesman (Ms), and Nickel (Ms).

wrong, for instance, may require only that the relationship between lying and wrongness (or reasons not to lie, or the like) be exceptionless within some, possibly restricted, range of lies. The principle may imply only that *in all but the permissibly exceptional cases*, lying is wrong.[4]

This alternative view requires principles that can permit exceptions to have a certain kind of complex structure. But it can be applied even to ordinary principles which are often taken to be explanatory while yet admitting of exceptions. We already know that it is in general possible for sentences of a certain degree of complexity to express or convey propositions of a greater degree of complexity. Nothing seems to make the moral case exceptional. So it seems safe to assume that even utterances of such simple moral sentences as 'Lying is wrong' can, in suitable contexts, semantically or pragmatically (depending on one's views in the philosophy of language) convey moral propositions which are more complex than the simple surface form of these sentences might seem to suggest. The kinds of complexity which context can help moral utterances to convey include not only such restricting clauses as 'in all but permissibly exceptional cases' but also constituents which qualify a moral proposition as an explanatory principle. So, for instance, I'll assume that an utterance of 'Lying is wrong' can, in a suitable context, convey a principle to the effect that actions which involve lying are actions one has moral reason not to do *in virtue of* their involving lying. To keep things simple, I'll assume more specifically that principles can be expressed or conveyed by sentences of the form 'Gs are Ms' when 'G' picks out a feature that provides reasons and 'M' picks out a moral property.[5] I'll understand 'feature' loosely enough that sentences of this form include 'Promises ought to be kept,' 'Lying is wrong,' 'An action's being a lie is a reason not to do it,' and 'That an action would kill a person is a reason against doing it.'

What makes a moral generalization count as a substantive principle is controversial.[6] But everyone can agree that a generalization can play the explanatory role required by moral theory only if its content satisfies some sort of relevance constraint.[7] Principles should only specify conditions

---

[4] The general idea here can be found, in different forms, in Silverberg (1996: 215), Morreau (1997: 195), Braun (2000: 214), Fara (2005: 66), and Nickel (Ms), among other places.

[5] This is a simplifying assumption because the class of sentences that can in ordinary discourse be used to express principles is heterogeneous. It includes bare plurals, various kinds of conditionals, and more.

[6] It remains controversial even once we agree that logical tautologies which employ moral terms, infinitely long moral generalizations, and blatantly analytic moral truths don't count as substantive principles.

[7] Here is a quick example of this problem of explanatory relevance. Suppose all killings are morally wrong and all and only killers happen to have some distinctive physical mark.

which are in some sufficiently direct way relevant to the instantiation of moral properties to count as explanatory of their instantiation.[8] Moreover, since explanation is asymmetric, principles should only specify conditions on which the instantiation of moral properties depends asymmetrically.

The main task for any account of moral principles which purports to be explanatory in the above sense and yet capable of tolerating exceptions isn't to establish a distinction between instances that are relevant and those that are irrelevant to a principle's truth. Wide agreement exists, for example, that killing a person out of curiosity about how difficult it would be, or because of a bad mood, are no exceptions at all to the wrongness of killing. Wide agreement likewise exists that killing a threat in necessary self-defense is a permissible exception. So sometimes we already judge that *these ones* but not *those ones* are among the relevant instances.

The main task for any such account is, rather, to explain how principles can be explanatory if they permit exceptions and how it is that when we judge certain cases to be permissibly exceptional we needn't be just guessing, but our judgments can result from some more or less reliable ability to detect permissible exceptions. In what follows I first develop an account of what makes an exception permissible and then show how the account can answer these demands, and more.[9]

In that case 'If you were to kill someone and had a certain physical mark, then your action would be morally wrong' would give a true sufficient condition for wrongness. But this seems as much a paradigm example of a true but explanatorily defective generalization as 'If you were male and took birth control pills, you wouldn't get pregnant.' Having a physical mark seems no more relevant to the wrongness of killing than taking birth control pills is relevant to failing to get pregnant if one is male. (I don't claim that all accidental generalizations are non-explanatory; cf. Lange 2000: 16–18.)

[8] The content of this relevance constraint is also controversial. For instance, even among those who think that principles identify moral reasons for (or against) actions, policies, etc., some think that what principles thereby identify are sufficient conditions for the presence of moral reasons, whereas others think that there are different forms of moral relevance which adequate principles must reflect (e.g. being a moral reason vs. being a background condition which determines whether some other feature of an action counts in its favor, and to what degree). My account of moral principles will be neutral on this issue of how moral reasons are individuated. It is one aspect of the debate between "holism" and "atomism" in the theory of reasons. See e.g. Dancy (2004: 38–43) and Hooker (2008: 23).

[9] Related remarks concerning generics in Nickel (Ms) have aided my thinking here. I bracket two other worries as unproblematic. (1) Some worry that exception-tolerating generalizations might express no complete propositions (cf. Schiffer 1991). (2) Some worry that such generalizations might express complete propositions only with exception clauses which make them uninformative, however unobvious that may be without further analysis (cf. Pietroski and Rey 1995: 87). In ethics, Feldman (1986: 142–4) and Dancy (1999: 27), respectively, raise these worries. But neither is compelling to the extent that we already draw the distinction between relevant and irrelevant instances.

3 WHAT MAKES AN EXCEPTION PERMISSIBLE

An account of permissible exceptions can get going by observing that if something is a reason for (or against) something, then it is perfectly legitimate to ask why it is a reason, and a reason of that kind. To introduce terminology, when the fact that something would involve lying, for instance, is a reason not to do it, we can ask what is the "normative basis" of this fact's status as reason not to lie. By 'the normative basis,' I mean that factor (property, relation, condition) because of which the fact is a reason for (or against) performing the action, and which thereby explains why it is that kind of a reason in this instance. (Such analogous notions as the normative basis of a feature's status as right-making can be characterized in similar terms. I'll sometimes call reasons for doing something "positive reasons" and reasons against doing something "negative reasons.") I cannot here argue that every moral reason has a basis which makes it the kind of reason it is and explains its status as such.[10] But justification in ethics would threaten to be arbitrary unless at least generally there were an explanation of why something is a moral reason for (or against) something when it is, and why it isn't a moral reason for (or against) something when it isn't.

Thinking about exceptions in ethics in terms of this notion of a reason's normative basis turns out to have several advantages. It can be used to state a structural account of what makes an exception permissible. It can also be used to state a similarly structural account of how something gets to be a moral reason. Jointly these two will provide a satisfyingly unified account of why something is a reason for (or against) an action when it is, and why it isn't a reason for (or against) an action when it isn't. Finally, an advantage which is distinct from the previous two is that this notion of the normative basis can be used to articulate one particular form which genuinely explanatory and yet exception-tolerating moral principles could take. Or so I'll argue.

Let's begin with the account of permissible exceptions. The basic idea is that if something isn't a reason for (or against) doing something, this is a permissible exception to its status as such a reason when, and because, the normative basis of its status as such a reason is absent—when, and because, those factors fail to obtain in virtue of whose presence the feature would be a reason for (or against) doing what has it. The account is best developed through examples.

---

[10] I call this claim "the basis thesis," and give it some further support, in my (2006: 718–22).

Many who think that lying is wrong think that it can be permissible to tell a white lie about someone's appearance to bolster their self-confidence.[11] Their claim might be either that there is something wrong about such a lie but other considerations tell more strongly in favor of lying or that there is nothing at all wrong with such a lie. The former, weaker claim is no doubt preferable in many cases. But some think that the latter, stronger claim is preferable in others. Some think that there is no reason at all not to lie to a government death squad agent who is tracking down one's activist daughter.[12] Some think that there is nothing at all wrong about lying while playing the game Diplomacy, which is no fun unless the players lie rampantly. But if at least some of these cases really were permissible exceptions to the claim that something's being a lie is a reason not to do it, why might they be permissibly exceptional?

We can approach this issue by considering some toy theories about why we have reason not to lie. Let theory 1 say that an action's being a lie is a reason against it when, and because, lying contributes to undermining such beneficial social practices as trusting other people's word. And let theory 2 say that an action's being a lie is a reason against it when, and because, the addressee is owed the truth (or has a right to it, or lying violates her autonomy, or the like). Both agree that the status of this fact as a reason not to lie has a normative basis. And that is why both generate certain predictions about which exceptions to its status as a reason not to lie would be permissible. Theory 1 predicts that an action's being a lie is no reason at all against it when, and because, lying doesn't contribute to undermining a beneficial social practice (or else its contribution remains below some threshold). For example, there won't be any reason not to lie while playing Diplomacy if lying in that context has no (significant) bad spill-over effects on our trust in other people outside the context of the game. (Theory 1 also predicts that the more extensive or damaging these effects, the stronger the reason not to lie.) Theory 2 predicts that an action's being a lie is no reason at all against it when, and because, the addressee isn't owed the truth (or the like). One might hold that this is the case with Diplomacy insofar as the players have consented to playing knowing that it involves lying. And one might hold that government death squad agents have no right to information about activists' locations, given what they would do with it.

Theories 1 and 2 generate different predictions because they disagree about when and why an action's being a lie is a reason not to do it. But they agree on one thing: when an action's being a lie is a reason not to do it, its

---

[11] I owe this example to an anonymous referee.

[12] See Lance and Little (2007: 153–4). They attribute the Diplomacy example below to David McNaughton.

status as such a reason has *some* basis. According to theory 1, the proper basis for moral concern to avoid lying has to do with *sustaining beneficial social practices*. According to theory 2, it has to do with some such factor as *owing the truth to one's addressee*. They agree on another thing, too: the basis has a certain kind of structure. Each of the italicized phrases expresses a relational property which something may have if it involves lying and which may be morally significant in a way that can explain why an action's being a lie is a reason not to do it. The same structure appears in other examples. Accounts of why killing a person is wrong (or there is a moral reason not to do so, or the like) include that it *frustrates the victim's prudential interests*, that it *deprives the victim of future experiences that it would be valuable for her to have*, that it *manifests ill will*, and so on. On each of these views, the status of something's being a killing as a reason not to do it has a normative basis which explains this fact's contribution to what one has reasons to do, and each of them puts forward a candidate for what property fills that role.

These examples illustrate a general notion. When x is a lie, let "the designated normative basis" for the status of x's being a lie as a moral reason not to do x be that property P, whatever it is, such that x's being a lie is a moral reason not to do x when, and because, x instantiates P.[13] For instance, if something's being a lie is a moral reason not to do it, but not because it would *contribute to undermining a beneficial social practice*, then this letter property wouldn't qualify as the normative basis of a moral reason not to tell a particular lie even if that lie did instantiate it. If that were so, then theory 1 above would be incorrect. The designated normative basis of any other feature's contribution to some moral property can be characterized in the same way.

This is to define what sort of thing the designated normative basis is by its normative *role* in making something a reason for (or against) doing something. Schematically, an action's being G is a reason for (or against) doing it when, and because, the action, insofar as it is G, has some property which satisfies the above condition on P. A property satisfies this condition when it explains the status of the given fact as a moral reason. This definition doesn't stipulate properties into existence. It leaves open

---

[13] I take designation as a generic relation between a linguistic expression and what, if anything, it "stands for" or has as its "semantic value" (object, property, relation, function, etc.). I construe 'x instantiates P' loosely: 'x' can be satisfied by an act or its maxim or its agent, depending on P. I tried to capture the relational structure of normative bases by using the phrase 'the designated relation' in my (2006) and (2008). But this is unhelpful, and my talk of 'an action instantiating the designated relation' was sloppy. As I define 'the designated normative basis,' it typically picks out not a relation but a relational property: a role property whose realizers are the kinds of relational properties for which the italicized phrases in the text stand.

both whether something's being *G* in fact is a reason for (or against) doing it and whether that reason has a normative basis which makes it so, since 'the designated normative basis' is a definite description which may or may not be satisfied. The definition also leaves open just *which* property (if any) fills or realizes the normative basis role in the case of *being a lie* and *being a reason not to do an act*, and likewise for any other pair of features. Disputes about these issues belong to substantive moral theory. In short, then, the notion of the designated normative basis of a reason can be used to give a structural description of how something gets to be a moral reason, which can be common ground between different substantive views.

We can now state an analogous structural account of what makes an exception permissible. To ease comprehension, I state the account in terms of one of its specific instances:

(Perm) For any action *x* and any circumstances *C* such that *x* is a lie but this fact is no reason not to do *x* in *C*, *C* constitute a permissible exception to the status of something's being a lie as a moral reason not to do it when, and because, *x* fails to instantiate the designated normative basis of the status of something's being a lie as a moral reason not to do it.

If a lie fails to instantiate the relevant normative basis, this is because some feature of the circumstances operates as a "defeater" for the reason not to lie. But it counts as a defeater precisely when and because it makes the lie satisfy (Perm). So (Perm) specifies a condition because of which the circumstances are unsuitable, when they are, for the existence of a reason not to lie.

(Perm) gives the right results when plugged into theories 1 and 2 above. For example, if the relevant normative basis is the property of undermining autonomy, then (Perm) implies that a case where something's being a lie isn't a reason not to do it is a permissible exception when, and because, lying doesn't undermine autonomy. But it is important to note that we can derive specific conclusions about which cases, if any, are permissibly exceptional only once we conjoin (Perm) with some *substantive* view about what property fills the role of the designated normative basis.

(Perm) allows that a situational feature which in some other circumstances would prevent the designated normative basis from being instantiated may fail to do so in the presence of "defeaters for defeaters." These are, roughly, features which cancel the status of some other feature as a defeater that generates a permissible exception.[14] For example, if I threaten you with

---

[14] See esp. Horty (2007) for a valuable analysis of different kinds of defeaters and defeaters for defeaters.

force unless you promise not to do something that you are planning to do, this typically means that I am coercing you. Typically such cases seem to be permissible exceptions to the status of the fact that you promised not to do something as a reason for you not to do it. But coercion may still be just or permissible in some cases. Imagine someone who is planning to take another person's life or invade another country. It seems permissible to use threats of force to make them promise that they won't execute their plan.[15] In such cases, extracting a promise by threat of force needn't mean that the promise fails to instantiate the normative basis of the reason to keep promises.

It should be clear how to generalize (Perm) into a general account of permissible exceptions. All of the above points about (Perm) apply, *mutatis mutandis*, equally well to other moral reasons, to right- and wrong-making features and their normative bases, and further. They can also be accommodated by a wide range of theories of reasons, including theories which treat certain facts as "default" reasons. Moreover, nothing in this general account of permissible exceptions requires moral *principles*. Since moral particularists typically don't deny that moral facts have explanations, they can accept the above picture of moral reasons as entities which typically have a certain kind of basis and explanation. They should also be able to accept this picture of permissible exceptions as cases under which the designated normative basis of a reason fails to obtain. As we'll see, using this notion to develop an account of moral principles, as I do below, is a further move.

A caveat to (Perm) should make its compatibility with particularism clear. It seems logically possible that a property may be the normative basis of some fact's status as a reason for (or against) doing something even if the fact doesn't invariably function as a reason of that kind when the normative basis is instantiated. Suppose, for instance, that the normative basis of an action's being a lie as a reason not to do it is that being lied to undermines one's autonomy. Cases seem nonetheless possible where being lied to would undermine one's autonomy and yet the fact that the action would be a lie is no reason not to do it. One might sometimes deserve to be deceived in this way. I wish to allow that the status of a property as the designated normative basis may itself tolerate exceptions. In what follows, I'll understand this qualification to be implicit in (Perm).

This is no less a logical possibility if in many of these cases our preferred conclusion is that the property in question doesn't fill the normative basis

---

[15] See McNaughton and Rawling (2000: 270). One doesn't have to accept that in such cases threat of force would still count as coercion to accept the point that the example is meant to illustrate.

role after all. And it is a possibility we'll want to allow if we distinguish between non-derivative (ultimate, basic, primary) and derivative (subsidiary, secondary) reasons and principles.[16] For example, if the fact that you would waste another year there is a reason why you don't go back to Rockville, it would presumably be a derivative reason not to go back.[17] It would asymmetrically depend for its status as a reason on something like the longer-term harm to you from going back, which is a more basic reason not to go back. (Assume that wasting another year is something that would make you worse off.) If we draw this distinction, we should similarly distinguish derivative and non-derivative normative bases of reasons. It should be possible for factors because of which various facts count as moral reasons to be arranged in the kind of hierarchical relations in which explanations may in general be arranged. Furthermore, like definite descriptions in general, the expression 'the normative basis' is context-sensitive. So it may pick out the *most proximate* normative basis in some contexts, the *ultimate* normative basis in others, and perhaps something in between in yet others. At least the status of a property as a proximate normative basis could well be subject to permissible exceptions.[18]

The notion of the normative basis of a reason raises several yet further complications. Some of these are more usefully addressed later as concerns about my theory of moral principles. For now let me address three more immediate concerns about its role in the theory of reasons.

The first concern is that the notion of the normative basis is superfluous. Perhaps the theoretical work I assign to this notion can be done by distinctions we already have between different kinds of reasons. This might be a legitimate concern if something could serve as the normative basis of a reason only if it were itself a more basic reason from which the reason that is being explained is derived. But not all theories of reasons accept that all explanations of reasons must themselves be more basic reasons by another name. In some cases the normative basis which explains why something is a reason is better treated as just a condition for other things to be reasons.

One example is Kant's Categorical Imperative. Instead of thinking that the fact that a maxim violates the Categorical Imperative is itself a reason

[16] See e.g. McNaughton and Rawling (2000). McKeever and Ridge (2006: 130–4) argue that the distinction is a poor one. I intend my general account to be neutral on these family disputes in the theory of reasons.

[17] R.E.M., '(Don't Go Back To) Rockville' (IRS Records, 1984). For an example concerning principles, consider the discussion of "the duties of self-improvement" in Ross (1930: 21, 25–6).

[18] Such exceptions would be instances of (Perm) when the normative basis property itself provides reasons.

against acting on it, it may be more attractive to think of this as a condition for other features to count as reasons against acting on it. This move would enable Kantians to avoid the objection that they direct us to act on the wrong kind of reasons because they direct us to respond to an abstract rule instead of responding directly to the weal and woe of others. It would also allow Kantians to say that what *makes* wrong actions wrong is not their violating the Categorical Imperative but simply their being lies, killings, etc.

Another example is contractualism. It says that an act is wrong just in case any principle which permitted the act could, for that reason, reasonably be rejected (Scanlon 1998: 195). Instead of thinking that the fact that a principle permitting the act could reasonably be rejected is itself a reason against doing it, it may be more attractive to think of it as a condition for other features to count as reasons against doing it. This move would enable one to claim that the contractualist principle isn't redundant while agreeing that whenever a principle is reasonably rejectable because it permits actions which have feature F, those actions are wrong because they have F and not because their having F makes principles permitting them reasonably rejectable.[19]

I conclude that in developing a general structural account of reasons we shouldn't assume that the normative basis of something's status as a reason for (or against) doing something must itself be a more basic reason for (or against) doing it. This is a substantive assumption which is rejected by some theories which a general structural picture should accommodate. What is more, analogous assumptions in other domains are questionable. For instance, it seems better to say that the laws which relate things together as cause and effect are something in virtue of which causes have their causal powers, rather than that they must themselves be causes or parts of causes.

The second concern is that my definition of 'the designated normative basis' *trivially* entails that every moral reason has a normative basis. Suppose something's being a lie is a moral reason not to do it. Then *being an instance of lying which provides a moral reason against lying* might seem to count trivially as the normative basis of the status of something's being a lie as a moral reason not to do it. If something has this property, its being a lie is a moral reason not to do it.

It is far from clear that my definition has such trivial instances. Consider the property *being an instance of lying which provides a moral reason against lying*. Even if something's having this property entails that its being a lie is a moral reason not to do it, it is far from clear that this latter fact holds *because*

---

[19] For a related discussion of this "redundancy objection" to contractualism, see Stratton-Lake (2003).

of the former fact in any sense in which the former *explains* the latter.[20] But trivial instances might pose no real problem anyway. Substituting a property like *being an instance of killing which provides a moral reason in favor of doing it* into my definition would, as desired, typically still result in a falsehood.[21]

The third concern is that my picture of moral reasons and permissible exceptions applies generally only if every moral reason has a normative basis (non-trivially), but that this assumption leads to an infinite regress and disallows that there are any "brute" moral reasons whose status as reasons has no deeper metaphysical basis and can be given no further explanation.

No infinite regress follows, however. The normative basis of a feature's status as a reason needn't be in various senses distinct from that feature. It needn't be conceptually distinct. Some think, for instance, that it is part of the concept of cruelty that something's being cruel is a reason not to do it. In that case it would seem natural to say that the factor which explains this is some particular feature of the concept of cruelty. Nor need the normative basis of a feature's status as a reason be metaphysically distinct from it. Suppose, for instance, that the fact that something promotes well-being is a moral reason to do it. The normative basis of this reason won't be distinct from the fact in question if the property of being a moral reason is reducible to that of promoting well-being. If being a moral reason is nothing over and above promoting well-being, then one could explain why the fact that something promotes well-being is a moral reason to do it by pointing to this reduction. (The same might hold if these were one and the same property.) On this view, facts which provide moral reasons have *promoting well-being* as the normative basis of their status as moral reasons. In those cases where the fact which provides a reason to do something is, specifically, that it promotes well-being, it would seem natural to say that what grounds and explains the status of this fact as a moral reason is built into it as a matter of necessary but synthetic metaphysical truth.

It follows that a moral reason can be "basic" in one recognizable sense even if it has a normative basis: a moral reason can have an explanation even if it has no "deeper" or "further" explanation. Fundamental prima facie duties à la W. D. Ross (1930) could perhaps be analyzed as basic moral reasons in this sense. Ross appears to think that what is a fundamental prima facie duty is a feature which is intrinsically a moral reason for (or

---

[20] Even if the relevant notion of explanation allows that in some cases (cases of synthetic a posteriori property identity, perhaps) something's having one property can be explanatory of its having a differently described property that is identical with the first, these putatively trivial instances wouldn't seem to be cases of that kind.

[21] Thanks to David Copp for suggesting this point as well as the concern outlined in the previous paragraph.

against) doing what has it. For something to be intrinsically F is for it to be F solely in virtue of its intrinsic features. If, further, the relation expressed by 'in virtue of' is an explanatory one, then an action type's status as a fundamental prima facie duty can perhaps have an explanation in terms of its intrinsic features. Features which are moral reasons intrinsically may even be another case where the normative basis of a feature's status as a reason isn't distinct from that feature. In any case, it doesn't follow directly from the notion of a fundamental prima facie duty that such duties have no normative basis.

Some theorists may still insist that some moral reasons are genuinely brute in some stronger sense which does preclude their having normative bases.[22] Whether any moral reasons of this kind exist is a substantive issue not to be settled by definitional fiat. My definition of 'the designated normative basis' doesn't entail in any non-trivial way that every moral reason has a normative basis, and I don't take this to be an analytic truth on any other ground either. So here is where things stand with such theorists. On the one hand, if there are reasons which have no normative bases, then the above picture of reasons and permissible exceptions may be unable to accommodate them. But, on the other hand, those who claim that there are such reasons are to that extent unable to exploit the explanatory and epistemological advantages of this picture of reasons and permissible exceptions and the theory of moral principles which can be developed out of it.

I have argued that the notion of the normative basis of a reason can be used to state structural accounts of how something gets to be a moral reason and what makes an exception to its status as a reason permissible. It is worth noting that this account is unified in a particularly satisfying way: what explains why something is a reason for (or against) an action, when it is, is the presence of precisely that factor whose absence explains why the circumstances are permissibly exceptional, when they are, and so explains why it doesn't function as such a reason, when it doesn't.

4 AN ACCOUNT OF EXCEPTION-TOLERATING MORAL PRINCIPLES

I'll now argue that the notion of the normative basis of a reason can also be used to state an account of moral principles as a kind of "hedged" principles. Substantive principles concerning moral reasons can be captured

---

[22] Thanks to Sarah Stroud for pushing me on my response to theorists who take this kind of line.

by principles which are hedged by reference to the normative bases of those reasons.[23] For instance, if something's being a lie is a reason not to do it when it instantiates the designated normative basis for the reason not to lie, then we cannot render the implications of the generalization 'Lying is wrong' for when something's being a lie is a reason not to do it any *less* accurate if we hedge it by reference to the designated normative basis, like so:

(**Lie**) Something's being a lie is always a reason not to do it, provided that it instantiates the designated normative basis for this fact's status as moral reason not to lie.

(Lie) takes no stand on which property, if any, fills the designated normative basis role. It requires just that there be a property whose instantiation by a lie explains why its being a lie is a reason not to do it.[24] If there is no such property, then 'the designated normative basis' fails to refer, in which case (Lie) either is false or lacks truth value. So, as with (Perm), we can use (Lie) to derive conclusions about which instances of lying provide reasons not to lie, and which if any are permissibly exceptional, only once we conjoin (Lie) with some substantive view of what the relevant normative basis is. For example, if lying sometimes fails to treat someone with respect without contributing to undermining a beneficial social practice, then our toy theories from Section 3 disagree over which lies we have moral reason not to tell. But both could still accept (Lie). So (Lie) is acceptable to a variety of moral theories which make injunctions against lying.

Accordingly, the account of principles which we get by generalizing (Lie) implies no particular view about which features provide reasons for (or

---

[23] I'll focus mainly on principles which identify moral reasons to keep the discussion manageable and focused on explanatory principles. If something is a moral reason for (or against) an action, then it has got something to do with what explains the moral status of that action. But the account I'll develop will also be able to capture principles which don't directly concern moral reasons, at least on further plausible assumptions concerning the relationship between reasons and other normative properties. For example, it is often assumed that if a feature of an action is a reason for (or against) doing it, then it is right (or wrong) *pro tanto*, so far as its having that feature goes. If that is right, then principles which identify moral reasons can be used to capture principles concerning the rightness and wrongness of actions and principles which identify "right-making" and "wrong-making" factors. For, even though the reason relation and the right-making relation seem distinct (Dancy 2004: 79), it seems plausible that if, for example, something's being a lie makes it wrong, then its being a lie is a reason (for suitably situated agents) not to do it. (The converse fails: not all reasons against an action are features which make it wrong.)

[24] My earlier caveat that the status of a property as the normative basis may itself be subject to permissible exceptions applies to (Lie) as well. So I'll continue to implicitly allow the possibility that something is a lie and instantiates the relevant normative basis and yet its being a lie *permissibly* fails to be a moral reason not to do it.

against) performing actions that have them, and why. Far from aiming to supplant familiar consequentialist, deontological, and other substantive views, the account is a schema for a form that various substantive principles could take:

(HP) Any x that is G is M [e.g., x's being a lie is always a moral reason not to do x], provided that x instantiates the designated normative basis of G's contribution to M.[25]

As a mere schema, (HP) doesn't entail that there *are* true moral principles which are explanatory but can admit of exceptions. The purpose of articulating one form which such moral principles could take isn't to help us determine the truth value of particular principles of that form—at least not on its own. But, as I'll argue, the schema can be used to show how there *can be* such principles, and also to locate competing substantive moral theories in a common structural framework.

So how are principles of the form (HP) capable of tolerating exceptions? What determines whether such a principle tolerates exceptions is the property which actually fills the relevant normative basis role. But the principle doesn't say what property, if any, does so—at least not on its own. For instance, (Lie) in conjunction with (Perm) implies only that, in all but permissibly exceptional cases, something's being a lie is a moral reason not to do it. It remains possible that the set of permissibly exceptional lies is empty. If the relevant normative basis were such that every lie instantiates it, then (Lie) would tolerate no exceptions. For example, in the context of Kant's moral theory, (Lie) implies that something's being a lie is a reason not to do it when lying to a person fails to treat her as an end in itself. According to a rigorist version of Kant's theory, lying always constitutes this kind of assault on rational agency. In the context of this rigorist version of Kant's theory, (Lie) implies that its injunction against lying has no permissible exceptions. Thus (Lie) *doesn't require* the existence of permissible exceptions.

---

[25] Principles needn't ordinarily be stated using the proviso in (HP) or other hedging expressions (e.g. 'other things being equal' or 'normally') to make restrictions on their scope. Our earlier assumption that the proposition expressed may be more complex than the sentence expressing it (see Section 2) secures the possibility that propositions of the form (HP) can, in suitable contexts, be semantically or pragmatically conveyed simply by sentences of the form 'Gs are Ms.' I'll remain neutral on the precise logical form of these propositions. It affects nothing of substance whether the proviso in (HP) is to be treated as a propositional operator, part of the antecedent of a conditional, or some other kind of clause. I also cannot examine whether such non-moral generic claims as 'Turtles are long-lived' or 'Dogs are smaller than horses' can be captured by propositions of the form (HP). But my account doesn't require this.

But (Lie) *allows* the existence of permissible exceptions, since it allows the possibility that not all lies instantiate the relevant normative basis. If (Perm) is right that a permissible exception arises when, and because, a lie doesn't instantiate the relevant normative basis, and if some lies don't instantiate it, then (Lie) permits those lies as exceptions. They would be just the lies that violate the proviso in (Lie). Thus (Lie) also tells us what the exceptional lies would have in common.

To summarize: (Lie) hedges the claim that lying is wrong by reference to the normative basis of the status of something's being a lie as a moral reason not to do it. Whether (Lie) permits any exceptions depends on whether the property which actually fills the normative basis role is such that all lies instantiate it. It is because (Lie) alone takes no stand on what that property is that it allows, but doesn't require, the existence of permissible exceptions. Since (Lie) isn't special, we can generalize that principles of the form (HP) can be used to model both exceptionless and exception-tolerating principles. We can plug into such principles my account of permissible exceptions, whose particular instances will play the same role in principles of the form (HP) as (Perm) plays in (Lie). Each states a condition under which a feature's failure to provide a reason for (or against) doing what has it would be a permissible exception to the corresponding principle.

This account is the more broadly applicable, the greater the range of principles that can be construed as instances of (HP). We saw how it can model both exceptionless and exception-tolerating principles. It can also capture many other distinctions between different kinds of principles. Here I'll focus on two in particular, and address various objections to the account in the process.

One dimension of difference between principles which my account can capture concerns whether or not they are derived from other, more basic principles, and so whether or not they have independent normative weight. One can accept (Lie) irrespective of which kind of principle one takes 'Lying is wrong' to express. To illustrate, Kantians would presumably accept (Lie) only if they thought that lying to people is a way of failing to treat them as ends in themselves. Suppose they think this "Kantian property" is the normative basis of the status of something's being a lie as a moral reason not to do it. If they also thought that something's having the Kantian property is itself a reason not to do it, they would presumably think that (Lie) is derived from (End):

(End) An action's failing to treat someone as an end in itself is a reason not to do it, provided that it instantiates the designated normative basis for the status of something's having this Kantian property as a moral reason not to do it.

(End) is a hedged principle which captures the old, familiar view that the "real" reason not to lie is that lying to people is a way of failing to treat them as ends in themselves. Other possible views can also be captured on my account. One is the view that the status of something's failing to treat someone as an end in itself (or, indeed, its being a lie) as a moral reason not to do it has some such further explanation as that you cannot consistently will the maxim of such an action as a universal law. Another is the view that (End) is a non-derivative principle. This option is secured by the possibility that the Kantian property provides basic moral reasons whose normative basis isn't distinct from that property. Essentially the same menu of theoretical options will be available if we think that the wrongness of lying has something other than a Kantian explanation.

One might object that, in fact, my account has trouble capturing derivative moral principles. Letting '*DNB*' stand for the property, whatever it is, which fills the designated normative basis role, a principle of the form (HP) says that Gs are Ms, provided they are DNBs. Given what I have said about hedged principles and normative bases, such a principle seems to commit one to the following two counterfactuals concerning any action x that has G, M, and DNB:

(C1) If x had been G but not DNB, x wouldn't have been M.

(C2) If x hadn't been G but had nonetheless been DNB, x would still have been M.

The objection is that if (C1)–(C2) are true of x, then x's being G is epiphenomenal with respect to its being M. To illustrate, suppose G is the property of being a lie, M is the property of being wrong, and DNB is the property of betraying trust. If so, then it would seem that what really is wrong with lying is that it betrays trust. But shouldn't we in that case think that the corresponding principle (Lie) is false?[26] And if (Lie) is false, it cannot be rescued by treating it as a derivative principle.

This objection shows that certain hedged principles are false. Often when (C1)–(C2) are true of something, it is plausible that what makes it M isn't its being G but its being DNB. If so, then any hedged principle which purports to identify G as right or wrong making, and so implies otherwise, is false. But these are substantive claims which pose no problem for my structural account. And the objection fails to generalize in ways which would pose a real problem for my account.

---

[26] I am grateful to Robert Johnson for this objection. I should note that the objection had greater force against an earlier version of this chapter, which focused more heavily on principles that identify right- and wrong-making features.

One sort of hedged principles which escape the objection are those in whose case *DNB* isn't distinct from *G*. In that case (C1)–(C2) have impossible antecedents and hence count only as vacuously true. Another sort of hedged principles which escape the objection are those which do purport to identify *G* as a right- or wrong-making feature but in whose case *DNB* is best treated as a condition for other features to be right or wrong making. Examples include principles which would face a Euthyphro-type problem if *DNB* were treated as a feature that is itself right or wrong making. This is the sort of reason why contractualists, for example, typically deny that what *makes* wrong actions wrong is that they are permitted by a principle that could reasonably be rejected. My account does commit such a contractualist to holding that (C2) is true of an action which is *G* and wrong and has this contractualist candidate for *DNB* only if in those nearby possible worlds where the action has *DNB* and is wrong it also has some feature other than *G* which satisfies the condition set by *DNB*. But this seems not unreasonable. Nothing can have the contractualist basis property brutely, without having some other feature.

A wide range of derivative hedged principles also escape this objection. I have in mind principles which purport to identify reasons provided by features that aren't right or wrong making. What makes going back to Rockville a bad idea isn't so much that you would waste another year as that this would be a way of doing something that is bad for you. But this doesn't mean that the fact that you would waste another year doesn't count as a (derivative) reason not to go back. Something's being *G* can be a derivative reason not to do it even if (C1)–(C2) are true of it, if doing something that is *G* is a way of doing something that one has a non-derivative reason to do.[27]

---

[27] Stephen Kearns worried that, in fact, my account delivers *too many* derivative principles. Suppose I promise not to go skiing, but go anyway. One might claim that the property *breaking a promise not to go skiing* satisfies my definition of 'the designated normative basis': that something involves going skiing is a reason for me not to do it because it would break a promise not to go skiing. So my account delivers a true principle concerning each thing that one might promise to do. But such principles seem at worst false (what gives the reason isn't that I go skiing but that I break a promise) and at best wholly unnecessary. But this objection fails. If we want an account that can model both derivative and non-derivative principles and *if* some features which seem morally trivial nonetheless function as derivative moral reasons in some type of circumstances, then delivering a derivative principle which identifies those features as moral reasons just in those circumstances is hardly objectionable. I emphasize the second 'if' because the objection generalizes only under certain substantive views on reasons. It seems to require that if something's being *F* is a reason to do it and doing something that is *G* is a way of doing what is *F*, then its being *G* is a derivative reason to do it. Whether this holds generally is controversial. For instance, in certain trolley cases killing one is causally or constitutively close enough to saving five that it may count as a way of saving five. But it

Another dimension of difference between principles which my account can capture concerns their strength. For instance, 'Lying is wrong' may express either an "overall" principle that lying is wrong all things considered or a merely "contributory" principle that lying is wrong *pro tanto*, that is, so far as its being a lie goes. Something's being a lie can be a reason not to do it without determining that, overall, one ought not to do it. What one ought to do overall is some function of those factors which make some moral contribution plus the strengths of their contributions.[28]

Hedged principles capture the difference between contributory and overall principles in the strength of the normative basis role which they describe. Read as an overall principle, (Lie) entails that the designated normative basis is such that whenever lying instantiates it, one has decisive or most moral reason not to lie. Read as a contributory principle, (Lie) entails only that the designated normative basis is such that whenever lying instantiates it, one has some moral reason not to lie. These two conditions on the normative basis are distinct. The difference between them also determines whether the principle in question can permit as exceptions only lies which one ought, overall, to tell, or also lies which one has no reason at all not to tell.[29]

The distinction between overall and contributory principles is sometimes used to reconcile the appearance that principles permit exceptions with the view that genuine principles must be exceptionless. Even if sometimes lying isn't wrong overall, it might still always and invariably make some contribution to wrongness. In this way, one could claim that, although

is controversial that the fact that a certain action would involve killing someone is even in such cases a derivative reason to do it. It is similarly controversial that such seemingly trivial features as shoelace color come to function as derivative reasons when they are suitably connected to features which are agreed to give reasons. My account doesn't require views at this level of specificity concerning the individuation or derivation of reasons.

[28] I take no stand on the nature of this function here. But see e.g. the two deontic logics for modeling the calculation of "all things considered oughts" from the relevant "*prima facie* oughts" in Horty (2003). I cannot here go into the complications which arise from the possibility that some features which don't themselves count as reasons may yet intensify or diminish the strength of the reasons given by other features. See e.g. Dancy (2004: 42).

[29] An intriguing question which I cannot pursue here is whether the two types of permissible exception could be analyzed by adapting from epistemology the distinction between "rebutting" and "undermining" (or "undercutting") defeaters for evidence or reasons. See e.g. Pollock and Cruz (1999). Jonathan Vogel (in conversation) and Horty (2007: 15) suggest, to my mind plausibly, that undercutting defeat can be analyzed as a special case of rebutting defeat.

all true overall principles are false because they have exceptions, there are exceptionless contributory principles.[30]

But even if all true principles turn out, at the end of the day, to be exceptionless, a general account of principles should accommodate the possibility of contributory principles which can tolerate exceptions. Nothing seems to rule out the idea of such principles as incoherent.

This point has implications for the dialectic between moral generalists and particularists. Many particularists are moved by the thought that even putative contributory principles have exceptions. Clearly this supports particularism only on the assumption that genuine principles must be exceptionless. If this assumption is dubious, then what particularists should deny is not the possibility of true exception-tolerating principles but rather the existence of any comprehensive set of such principles or else the dependence of moral reasons on their existence (cf. Dancy 2004: 7–8).

My account of hedged principles helps us see what substantive issues are at stake in these claims. I discuss these issues in detail elsewhere (Väyrynen 2006). The only point I wish to note here is that the standard semantics for definite descriptions like 'the designated normative basis' assigns to any principle of the form (HP) the substantive commitment that it is true only if there is a *unique* property which fills the designated normative basis role.

Particularists are likely to think that what explains why something's being a lie is a reason not to do it can be one factor in some cases, another factor in other cases, and some yet different factor in yet other cases. This view is consistent with the claim that moral reasons have normative bases but it seems inconsistent with the uniqueness condition. Its availability confirms that using the notion of a reason's normative basis to state an account of moral principles is indeed a further move from the picture of reasons and permissible exceptions introduced in Section 3.

The general objection here to my account of hedged principles is that it will systematically generate false principles because it will systematically fail the uniqueness condition. So we should either reject my account of principles in favor of a better one or accept particularism.

---

[30] Ross (1930: ch. 2) is usually read as holding this view. In a later work Ross argues from cases of vicious pleasure that pleasure isn't intrinsically good, and seems to conclude that we have no prima facie duty to promote our own pleasure (Ross 1939: 272–5; cf. Stratton-Lake 2002: 130–4). Note that this seems to follow only on the assumption that a prima facie duty to promote our own pleasure couldn't permit vicious pleasures as exceptions.

To see one form of this objection, suppose there are two kinds of promises.[31] Imagine that one kind of promise gives a reason to keep it because it would be irrational to break, for no good reason, a voluntarily undertaken commitment. And imagine that the other kind of promise gives a reason to keep it because the promisee has some such right as to determine that one do what one promised or to receive the fruits of the promise. Presumably what would explain why I ought to keep my promise would be different in the two cases: perhaps something about rationality and autonomy in the first but something about the promisee's rights in the second. But then the principle that one ought to keep one's promises would seem not to designate a unique normative basis. Particularists might take this as conformation that no such true principle is to be had. Generalists might think instead that surely *this* wouldn't show that it isn't true that promises ought to be kept.

My own response is that the example involves two distinct principles of promissory obligation. The sentence 'Promises ought to be kept' can be used to express one proposition in the context of one kind of promises but another, different proposition in the context of the other kind of promises. First, if there were two different kinds of promises, then the semantic value of 'promise' would vary with context of utterance, which seems to mean that so would the principle expressed. Secondly, the two kinds of promises would also differ in their implications for when one ought to keep a promise. Two propositions are distinct if they have different implications. So if there were two different kinds of promises, then 'Promises ought to be kept' would in different contexts express different principles. Nothing in the example shows that those two principles don't each designate a unique normative basis. (*Exercising rational autonomy* might fill that role in one principle, *satisfying the promisee's right to determine what the promisor does* in the other.)

This response exploits the fact that the uniqueness implications of definite descriptions are notoriously subtle and context-sensitive to suggest that the uniqueness implications of hedged principles are going to be no different. What it offers is not an advance proof that hedged principles won't systematically fail the uniqueness condition, but rather a conceptual tool for substantive moral inquiry to use in assessing whether particular principles of the form (HP) fail it. Elsewhere I apply this idea to show how my account could approach the objection that the normative bases which hedged principles designate will be disjoint in the sense that these role properties will systematically be realized by different properties in different contexts (Väyrynen 2006: 733–4).

---

[31] Thanks to Ralph Wedgwood for pressing this example. I have changed some inessential details.

I conclude that we can capture a wide range of substantive moral principles in the kind of hedged principles introduced in this section. I also hope to have conveyed some sense of the resources this account of hedged principles can muster up for explaining whatever further distinctions we might want to draw among various kinds of moral principles. Next I'll argue that hedged principles can play the explanatory and epistemological roles required by moral theory: they can contribute to explanations of particular moral facts and moral agents can grasp and be guided by them.

5 HEDGED PRINCIPLES IN EXPLANATION

Moral theories aspire to explain various kinds of moral facts.[32] The less a moral theory helps make sense of such facts, the more epistemically imperfect state it leaves us in regarding important aspects of morality. Any account of moral principles can be expected to indicate the role which the kinds of principles that it proposes can play in explaining particular moral facts. I'll now argue that moral principles can be genuinely explanatory even if they permit exceptions.

There is a general objection to the possibility of such principles. Principles that permit exceptions tend to be compatible with the possibility that even some large proportion of their instances are permissibly exceptional. Hedged principles, for instance, don't determine what proportion of their instances instantiate the normative bases they designate because they don't themselves determine such contingent facts as how frequently lies aren't owed to the addressee, how often killings are done in necessary self-defense or just for fun instead, and so on. The objection is that principles which allow this possibility cannot be genuinely explanatory because principles can provide reliable explanatory applications only if they have some large proportion of conforming instances.[33]

---

[32] By 'explanation' I mean the content of an answer to a why-question which makes a claim that something is the case *because* something else is the case—that this something else is at least part of *why* it is the case. (I don't mean the activity of giving such an answer. What it takes to convey the content to an audience is a topic for the pragmatics of why-questions.) We may need to add that something counts as an explanation only if it also satisfies certain epistemic conditions. For example, it may be that the content of an answer to a why-question counts as an explanation only if it is (or represents) a body of information which is structured in such a way that grasping that body of information would constitute a certain kind of epistemic gain regarding what is being explained.

[33] Earman and Roberts (1999: 463) endorse effectively just this when they claim that *ceteris paribus* generalizations provide reliable applications only if the *ceteris* are *paribus* in "sufficiently many" applications of the corresponding unqualified universal generalization.

I'll argue in reply that hedged principles can be used to explain both why their conforming instances have the moral properties they do and why certain other instances are permissibly exceptional, irrespective of their proportions.[34] I wish the argument to work under reasonably neutral assumptions about explanation. In seeking an explanation we are seeking understanding and trying to make sense of things. We can agree that an explanation of a fact F contributes to these aims insofar as it is stable or robust in the sense that according to this explanation, F couldn't easily have failed to obtain. In other words, we can agree that it is a virtue in an explanation of a fact F if, according to this explanation, F is stable under some range of hypothetical changes in the circumstances and if, therefore, the explanation exhibits a pattern of counterfactual dependence.[35] We can take a generalization to inherit this explanatory virtue insofar as it plays some important role in explanations which have that virtue. And we can agree that if factor F counts as (part of) an explanation of a fact G only given some further factor H, then H plays an important kind of explanatory role. Let's say that if F explains G, then H "contributes to" this explanation if H is either part of F or some important condition for F to explain G. What I'll argue is that hedged principles can in this sense contribute to explanations of particular moral facts. The general idea will be that these moral facts stand in systematic patterns of dependence on other factors, so that the latter explain the former, only given some moral principles of the form (HP).

Hedged principles contribute to two kinds of explanations concerning their conforming instances. First, (Lie) can allow that when something is a lie, this can explain why there is a moral reason not to do it.[36] But it explains

---

[34] Sean McKeever and Michael Ridge propose that a moral principle "articulates true application conditions for a given moral concept by referring to those features of the world which explain why the concept applies when it does" but continue that "to count as a moral principle on this criterion a generalization need not explain why those considerations which are of direct relevance themselves count as having such relevance" (2006: 6). If we limit ourselves to standards for the correct application conditions for moral concepts, then our theoretical purposes don't require that principles contribute to explanations of moral reasons and permissible exceptions. But this is compatible with thinking that an account of moral principles is better if its principles also contribute to explanations of such facts.

[35] On explanatory stability, see White (2005). On explanations which exhibit systematic patterns of counterfactual dependence, see Lange (2000) and Woodward (2003). These ideas can be accommodated by the view that explanations track what makes things happen or makes something the case, insofar as these metaphysically more robust relationships imply corresponding patterns of counterfactual dependence. See Ruben (1990) and Kim (1994).

[36] My account can accommodate the claim that hedged principles, and facts to the effect that the relevant normative basis is instantiated, may enter into explanations of particular moral facts as background conditions on which those explanations rely without

this only when the instance of lying at hand instantiates the designated normative basis. Given the way (Lie) incorporates a reference to that basis, something's being a lie explains the existence of a moral reason not to lie only given a principle like (Lie). So, generalizing, hedged principles contribute to explanations of why there are moral reasons to do certain things but not others. Secondly, (Lie) implies that the fact that something's being a lie is a moral reason not to do it holds only when it instantiates the designated normative basis. But, given the way (Lie) incorporates a reference to that basis, the latter explains the former only given a principle like (Lie). So, generalizing, hedged principles contribute to explanations of why certain facts but not others have the status of moral reasons for (or against) doing various things.

The natural objection is that (Lie) is superfluous in these explanations because what in fact makes the contribution which these arguments attribute to (Lie) is the designated normative basis. Yet this is at most half correct. Facts about whether lies instantiate the relevant normative basis do contribute to these explanations. But this doesn't mean that hedged principles make no further contribution to them. The designated normative basis is just a property which particular lies instantiate or not. It exhibits systematic patterns of counterfactual dependence between whether something is a lie and whether there is a moral reason not to do it only when embedded in a generalization like (Lie). What (Lie) asserts is precisely a complex but systematic relationship of dependence between these two factors and the designated normative basis. It asserts a connection between something's being a lie and there being a moral reason not to do it which is stable under any hypothetical changes under which it still instantiates the designated normative basis, but which might not hold outside this range of conditions.[37] So the designated normative basis explains moral reasons in a systematic way only given a principle like (Lie). Hence this objection doesn't show that hedged principles fail to contribute to explanations of moral reasons.

Hedged principles also contribute to explanations of permissible exceptions. (Lie) implies that instances of lying which are permissible exceptions

constituting parts of those explanations (cf. Dancy 2000: 152). Since I can, therefore, deny that explanation requires that the explanans be sufficient for the explanandum, I can also avoid the potential objection that if a principle like 'Lying is wrong' permits exceptions, then we cannot appeal to it and the fact that you lied to explain why your action was wrong (cf. Pietroski and Rey 1995: 87).

[37] That is to say, changes in other conditions matter only to the extent that they are relevant to whether a lie instantiates the designated normative basis, and if there were a moral reason not to lie outside this range of conditions, this would be due to some other factor. Note that this sort of invariance doesn't imply exceptionlessness.

to (Lie) are permissibly exceptional because they fail to instantiate the designated normative basis. To illustrate, suppose the status of something's being a lie as a reason not to do it is based on the way in which lying contributes to undermining a beneficial social practice. If, as some writers claim, there may sometimes be no reason not to lie to a person who is going to harm innocent people, (Lie) can contribute to explaining why. If you had such a reason, then in some circumstances one could generate for you a duty not to lie simply by aiming to harm innocent people and coming to you for information one needs to achieve that aim. But a social practice which involves such a mechanism could hardly be said to be a beneficial one. Thus in lying to such a person you wouldn't be undermining a beneficial social practice. But, given the way in which (Lie) incorporates the designated normative basis, the failure of that basis to be instantiated explains why circumstances are permissibly exceptional only given a principle like (Lie). So, generalizing, hedged principles contribute to explanations of permissible exceptions.[38]

The natural objection to this argument is that the explanatory contribution it attributes to (Lie) in fact belongs to (Perm). Again, this is at most half correct. Both (Perm) and (Lie) imply that when something is a lie, its being a permissible exception to the status of its being a lie as a moral reason not to do it is invariant under any hypothetical changes under which the lie still fails to instantiate the designated normative basis. But there can be this kind of systematic pattern of counterfactual dependence for (Perm) to exhibit only if there is a systematic pattern between something's being a lie and there being a moral reason not to do it. As we just saw, (Lie) exhibits just such a pattern. So, the failure of a particular lie to instantiate the designated normative basis explains why it is a permissible exception only given a principle like (Lie). Hence this objection doesn't show that hedged principles fail to contribute to explanations of permissible exceptions.

We can now see why hedged principles contribute to explanations of permissible exceptions irrespective of the proportion of the permissibly exceptional instances. Suppose killing in necessary self-defense is a permissible exception to the wrongness of killing. According to the corresponding hedged principle, this is so when, and because, killing in necessary self-defense fails to instantiate the normative basis of killing's contribution to wrongness. But it is similarly when, and because, killing instantiates *that very same property* that it is wrong. So, the principle can be used reliably to

---

[38] Baldwin (2002: 104–6) argues from examples that principles are typically qualified in order to explain exceptions. Irwin (2000: 121) argues that Aristotle has a notion of the basis of a principle which explains exceptions. But neither provides a general account of principles to develop these claims in detail.

explain why killing is wrong, when it is. This is so even in a Mad Max world, where most killings are done in necessary self-defense, because the principle can also be used to explain why most killings are permissible exceptions in the Mad Max world.[39] Given the facts on the ground, killings in the Mad Max world couldn't easily have instantiated the normative basis of killing's contribution of wrongness.

I have argued that hedged principles make a genuine contribution to explanations of particular moral facts. Their contribution is also satisfyingly unified in character: whether we are explaining moral reasons or permissible exceptions, hedged principles exhibit stable patterns of dependence between these moral facts and the normative bases which they designate. Much more could and needs to be said about the contribution of hedged principles to explanations of particular moral facts if their contribution were assessed against different theories of explanation. But I hope that already these quick arguments are, for the present purposes, sufficient to show that hedged principles can be genuinely explanatory even if they permit exceptions.

These arguments require an obvious caveat, however. All by themselves, without further substantive assumptions about what properties fill the normative basis roles, hedged principles omit a whole lot of information concerning the actual factors because of which certain of their instances provide moral reasons and others are permissibly exceptional. Those factors are given only a relatively formal kind of role description. So, all by themselves, hedged principles make only a thin and limited contribution to explanations of moral facts. But this caveat raises no deep problem.

Since my account aims to articulate only a particular form which explanatory and yet exception-tolerating principles could take, it should be no surprise if particular principles of this form turn out to be explanatory only in the context of further substantive moral assumptions. But this is the kind of context in which we typically operate when we assess competing moral theories or when it is for some other reason important to know whether, for instance, we have a moral reason not to lie because lying betrays trust, or because it undermines a beneficial social practice, or because it fails to give the addressee something owed to them, or because of something else.

Hedged principles may also be able to contribute to explanations of particular moral facts in virtue of their general form. For instance, perhaps all that is required in some contexts to explain why something's being a lie is a moral reason not to do it is that the relationship between these two factors is stable within some range of circumstances and that we have good reason to believe that the present circumstances fall within that range. The first

---

[39] I owe the Mad Max world to Sean McKeever.

claim follows from the general form of (Lie). The second claim can at least in some contexts be supported by fairly neutral and minimal substantive assumptions which require no particular view about what property fills the normative basis role. These could concern, for instance, some implications or other identifying characteristics which we have good reason to believe to be possessed by whatever property fills the normative basis role. This sort of information is the most we often have available anyway, since we often are uncertain, ignorant, or agnostic about just what is wrong about lying, killing, and so on.

The kind of limited contribution which hedged principles can make to explanations of particular moral facts in virtue of their form can be a genuine contribution at least if hedged principles themselves can be exploited to improve our sense of the implications and other identifying characteristics of the properties which fill the relevant normative basis roles. This would improve our sense of the range of conditions under which particular moral facts hold and how those facts might have been different had the conditions been different. If hedged principles played such a role, they could help exhibit concrete patterns of dependence between particular moral facts and other factors. Hence I now turn to discuss the epistemological role of hedged principles in moral inquiry.

6 HEDGED PRINCIPLES IN MORAL INQUIRY

Moral theory would require moral principles not only to contribute to explanations of particular moral facts but also to play certain epistemological roles: they should be something that moral agents can grasp, and which can guide those agents' moral thinking. But if moral principles have exceptions, then avoiding systematic moral errors requires a reliable ability to detect both the presence of moral reasons and the presence of permissible exceptions, including in some range of novel sets of circumstances. Otherwise our moral judgments will all too easily be mistaken. So how can hedged principles guide our judgments as to whether circumstances are permissibly exceptional?[40]

My account of what makes an exception permissible suggests an account of the content of the ability to judge cases as permissibly exceptional. The idea I'll develop is that one's judgment of (say) an instance of lying as a permissible exception to the status of something's being a lie as a reason

---

[40] I address further issues about how hedged principles can provide adequate moral guidance in my (2008).

not to do it can be guided by one's *conception of* the normative basis of this reason.

The moral principles we accept symbolize our commitment to the moral ideals we care about. Thinking that lying is wrong embodies some kind of ideal of not deceiving people. Some may interpret the principle as one expression of some more fundamental ideal, such as respecting people or promoting practices which benefit them. But more typically our conception of what moral concerns or ideals underlie the principles we accept is inchoate or incomplete. This isn't changed by the plausible idea that acquiring some initial understanding of such moral concerns and ideals is part of acquiring moral concepts. Even assuming that moral knowledge is possible, it is doubtful that most of us fully grasp all the principles we accept. Actual moral outlooks are works in progress.

We have seen that hedged principles generate substantive moral conclusions only in conjunction with further assumptions about what properties realize the normative bases they designate. So they do little to guide our judgments unless we have some grasp of those properties. But the extent to which most of us probably grasp them will often leave it indeterminate just what properties they are. Jonathan Dancy, who reports that he considers freedom of expression important but has no determinate sense why, thinks this would be a problem for principles which claim to incorporate an explanation of the moral reasons they identify (Dancy 2004: 153). I disagree.

Typically our acceptance of a principle like 'Curtailing freedom of expression is [*pro tanto*] wrong' isn't brute. I would be a defective moral agent if I thought, for instance, that it is wrong for the government to censor the press or ban protests at speeches by its officials, but didn't think that there was any basis for judging such government actions to be bad. So long as I think there is some such normative basis, a hedged form of the principle that curtailing freedom of expression is wrong is available to me. And I can perfectly well accept that principle even if I have no clear sense of just which kinds of expression are those to which freedom is important (academic freedom, pornography, assertion of the Armenian genocide, denial of the Holocaust ...), or whether some restrictions on freedom to them are appropriate, or why it is important for them to be free.

The point I wish to make here is twofold. First, even if my grasp of the normative basis designated by a hedged principle to the effect that curtailing freedom of expression is wrong is incomplete, this isn't a kind of incompleteness which would leave the proposition expressed by the principle incomplete or indeterminate. The incompleteness lies mainly in one's grasp of what property realizes a normative role which is itself reasonably determinate. Secondly, even if my grasp of what property realizes the relevant normative role is inchoate or incomplete, it may still have enough content reliably to guide my judgments, at least within a certain range of cases.

This second point has several strands. Even if I am unsure about why freedom of expression is important, I may know that the designated normative basis is such that it is wrong to curtail open discussion of public policy and academic freedom. Even a grasp this limited of the implications or other identifying characteristics of the designated normative basis may be enough reliably to guide my judgment, at least within a certain range. (This can be so even if I am unsure or altogether mistaken about its implications in some other cases.) Moreover, even if I suspect that the importance of freedom of expression is connected to some further factors, such as considerations of harm or preconditions of a healthy democracy, I might not know exactly what harm is or what such preconditions are. Still, if I think that they have got something to do with such properties as the flourishing or rational autonomy of persons, my judgments may still be guided by a pretty good proxy, at least within a certain range.[41] Finally, even if I have some particular property in mind as the normative basis—such as helping people flourish or protecting their autonomy—but don't think I fully grasp it, I may still grasp it and its implications and other identifying characteristics well enough for my judgments to be reliable, again at least within a certain range.

These are some of the ways in which our judgments may be guided, at least within a certain range, by acceptance of hedged principles and a grasp of the implications and other identifying characteristics of the normative bases they designate, even if we have no particular properties in mind as those which fill the relevant normative basis roles or have only a limited understanding of those properties.[42] What explains these possibilities, according to my

---

[41] Similarly, I might not fully understand what welfare is. Still, if I think that it has got something to do with happiness, my judgments concerning permissible exceptions to various welfarist, person-affecting, or retributivist moral principles would seem to be guided by a pretty good proxy. Thanks to Connie Rosati for this example.

[42] These possibilities are general to definite descriptions. I needn't have any particular number in mind when making a *de re* utterance of 'The number of Supreme Court justices is odd.' Similarly, I needn't have any particular property in mind when making a *de re* utterance to the effect that the basis for lying's status as a reason is such-and-such. I may be speaking truly in making an attributive utterance of 'The man in the corner drinking a martini is a spy' and having James Bond in mind, even if I am uncertain or mistaken about whether he is James Bond. Similarly, I may be speaking truly in saying that the normative basis of some reason is such-and-such, even if I am uncertain or mistaken about whether whatever property I have in mind in fact does fill the relevant normative basis role.

account, is that our reliability at judging whether certain facts are moral reasons or whether the circumstances are permissibly exceptional is a function of how well we are tracking the bases of those facts' status as reasons. Since this is something that comes in degrees, hedged principles can be used to describe both the degree and the scope of the reliability of our judgments in terms of how accurate and complete a conception we have of the properties which fill the relevant normative basis roles. Even a limited grasp of those properties can help us see what the permissible exceptions have in common and so increase the reliability of our judgments, perhaps also in some novel sets of circumstances. Similarly, the better we grasp these properties, the more robustly reliable our judgments are going to be.

We can similarly explain why such interfering factors as uncertainty, ignorance, and error concerning what properties fill the normative basis roles will tend to make our judgments less reliable, or reliable only in some limited range of cases. Since what properties fill these roles is a substantive moral issue, my account correctly classifies uncertainty, ignorance, and error about moral principles and their implications as concerning substantive moral issues, such as what explains our moral reasons. Parallel points apply to moral disagreement. Disagreements about whether killing, lying, or curtailing freedom of expression are things we have moral reason not to do, and whether killing in self-defense, telling white lies for a well-meaning end, or curtailing expressions of Holocaust denial also are things we have moral reason not to do, can be explained as disagreements about what factors ground and explain whatever reasons we have in these cases. So can disagreements about whether these reasons tolerate any exceptions. For example, suppose you think that freedom of expression matters because it is crucial for healthy government whereas I think it matters because it is crucial for exercising rational autonomy. This will lead to predictable sorts of disagreement about the implications of the principle that curtailing freedom of expression is wrong.

So how to resolve uncertainty, ignorance, error, and disagreement concerning hedged principles and their implications? How can we improve our grasp of the principles we accept and our ability to detect the presence of moral reasons and permissible exceptions? Such progress will require substantive moral inquiry. To improve our grasp of when killing is wrong, for example, we need to think hard about self-defense, abortion, euthanasia, capital punishment, war, and so on. There are various ways of doing this, at least so long as conditions are generally favorable for judgment. Just how we should proceed depends on what the proper method of moral inquiry is.

To illustrate the general idea, consider what we should do if the proper method is to seek a wide reflective equilibrium among our non-moral background theories and the moral judgments and principles of various levels of generality which we accept provisionally. We should consult our moral experience and hypothetical cases to determine what our considered judgments are concerning the permissibility of killing in various contexts. We should figure out whether we accept other principles which permit killing in some circumstances. We should figure out what sorts of interests are at stake in these contexts and what biology, medicine, psychology, sociology, and other such sources would tell us about how killing someone would affect those interests. We should determine whether these sources suggest that things other than killing might have the same sort of significance for those interests. And we should organize and revise this information so that it all hangs together well.

Reasoning of this kind can no doubt improve our grasp of the principles we accept and our reliability in applying them. According to my account of hedged principles, this is because it can improve our grasp of at least the implications and other identifying characteristics of the normative bases of moral reasons. Even if such information doesn't directly identify the properties which fill these roles, it may help us determine what properties best satisfy their implications and identifying characteristics or at least rule out certain candidates. It can thereby support conclusions about what properties fill these roles via an inference to the best explanation of these facts. This kind of reasoning characterizes one sort of inquiry into what is wrong about killing, lying, and so on. The moral progress that we could make via such inquiry, even when slow and piecemeal, would still be progress. And insofar as such progress is possible, hedged moral principles are something we can grasp, and which can reliably guide our moral judgments.

One might object that hedged principles cannot adequately guide our judgments unless the restrictions on their scope can be captured in purely non-moral terms. Unless we can state their application conditions in purely non-moral terms, principles can be replaced by reasoning by cases and will fail to provide a rational basis for resolving moral disagreements (Goldman 2002: 13–16).

But I see no reason to think that hedged principles can guide our judgments only if their application conditions can be stated in purely non-moral terms. Our ordinary moral, prudential, and legal reasoning, where we commonly rely on principles employing normative terms, seem not to depend on the contingency of whether our language offers us purely non-moral vocabulary adequate for expressing moral properties. No such reduction is also required by my account of what makes an exception permissible or how we can resolve uncertainty and disagreements about principles. Whether principles provide moral insight or a rational basis for resolving moral disagreements seems not to turn on whether they offer purely non-moral starting points for moral reasoning. Descriptions which appear non-normative can be controversial; consider the famous example of 'no vehicles in the park' (Hart 1958). And claims which employ normative terms needn't pose any serious issues of disagreement; consider injunctions against torturing the innocent for no gain. I see no good reason why hedged principles could guide our judgments only if they gave us an entry to moral facts and distinctions through purely non-moral descriptions, so long as our judgments can rely on an improvable grasp of the moral concerns and ideals which underlie our acceptance of moral principles.

7 HEDGED PRINCIPLES AND RIVAL ACCOUNTS

We can usefully round out the picture of what we gain by thinking about principles and exceptions in ethics along the lines of my account of hedged principles by considering some advantages my account enjoys over some of its rivals. I'll argue that these rivals encounter difficulties which my account avoids in explaining why circumstances are permissibly exceptional when they are (or why not when not) or how our judgments about permissible exceptions can be reliably guided.

One way to make principles tolerate exceptions would be to build into them some clause simply to the effect that there are no exceptional conditions present. Call this the "quantified account":

(QA) Something's being a lie is always a moral reason not to do it, unless something occurs to prevent its being a lie from being a reason not to do it.

(QA) requires the absence of features that make a situation permissibly exceptional. So when such features are present, (QA) correctly implies that something's being a lie isn't a reason not to do it.

(QA) has an obvious problem. We know in advance of (QA) that principles imply such qualified conditionals as 'If something is a lie and nothing in the circumstances prevents its being a lie from being a reason not to do it, then its being a lie is a reason not to do it.'[43] But the quantifier

---

[43] Here I draw on the criticism of Morreau's (1997: 192–200) "fainthearted conditional" account of disposition ascriptions in Fara (2005: 56–9). The same problem plagues Hausman's (1992: 136–7) proposal that '*Ceteris paribus*, all *F*s are *G*s' is true in context *X* iff *X* picks out a property *C* such that 'Everything that is both *F* and *C* is a *G*' is true. It also plagues Braun's (2000: 215) truth conditions for "*ceteris paribus* conditionals," which can be stated in a simplified form as follows: 'If *A* then *ceteris*

clause says nothing more about what can prevent something from providing a reason for (or against) something. Thus no progress is made with respect to specifying which circumstances are permissibly exceptional, or under what condition they are so, by saying that the fact that an action is a lie is a reason not to do it unless something prevents it from being one. Although (QA) ensures *that* the circumstances are permissibly exceptional when they in fact are, it cannot be used to explain *why* they are. Nor can (QA) guide our judgments about permissible exceptions. So (QA) cannot suit principles to the explanatory and epistemological roles required by moral theory.

One alternative, the "list account," eliminates the quantifier clause in favor of its satisfiers:

(LA) Something's being a lie is always a reason not to do it, unless _____ .

The blank in (LA) is meant to stand for a complete list of permissible exceptions. What might be used to motivate (LA) is the assumption, often found in the literature on *ceteris paribus* generalizations, that hedge clauses avoid becoming catch-alls that render a generalization vacuously true only if they are shorthand for an explicit list of background provisos.[44] There are two different ways of trying to fill out such a list, corresponding to two different versions of the list account.[45] On the "merely extensional" version, the relevant list is simply a list of the conditions under which something's being a lie isn't a reason not to do it. On the "constitutive" version, the conditions on the relevant list must be ones which make it the case that something's being a lie isn't a reason not to do it. Either version of (LA) can play the explanatory and epistemological roles required by that moral theory only if the list of permissible exceptions is finite and, indeed, manageably short. We can grasp only finite principles, and they can guide our judgments only if they are cognitively manageable. The two versions of (LA) fare differently with respect to this constraint.

It seems highly unlikely that we can enumerate all the permissible exceptions to generate the kind of list which the merely extensional version of (LA) describes. Such efforts have proved unpromising outside ethics. The literature on *ceteris paribus* generalizations displays some consensus that exceptions to such generalizations rarely are finitely specifiable; it may

---

paribus B' is true at world *w*, with respect to context *c*, iff '(*A* & *N_c*) $\square\!\!\rightarrow B$' is true at *w*—where *N_c* are the conditions that would be determined by *c* to be non-exceptional with respect to the connection between *A* and *B*, and '$\square\!\!\rightarrow$' is the standard subjunctive conditional.

[44] See e.g. Hempel (1988), Schiffer (1991), and Earman and Roberts (1999).
[45] I am grateful to Sean McKeever for pressing this distinction.

even be that hedge clauses of one or another sort are needed precisely when no explicit list of background provisos is available.[46] In the absence of any a priori guarantee that morality is special, it is especially compelling that no complete list of permissible exceptions would be manageably short. But in that case any manageably short list which we might be able to generate would merely exemplify, not exhaust, the class of permissible exceptions.[47] Which conditions our incomplete list would include would be highly contingent. Since such a list could easily be unrepresentative or highly heterogeneous, it could easily fail to project appropriately to the other cases. So it seems unlikely that the merely extensional version of (LA) would reliably guide our judgments.

Even if the merely extensional version of (LA) could supply a complete but manageably short list of the permissible exceptions, it would still be both explanatorily deficient and unnecessary. It would be explanatorily deficient because to give such a list isn't yet to explain why the conditions it mentions are the ones to make the circumstances permissibly exceptional, let alone to explain why certain facts would be reasons when those conditions don't obtain.[48] A satisfactory account should do this. If the status of something as a reason permits exceptions, surely it is no accident which of its instances are permissibly exceptional and which aren't. But if we can explain these facts, the merely extensional version is unnecessary. For then we can bypass the list in favor of a condition which states when an exception is permissible and is explanatorily prior to any particular list we might happen to grasp. If our judgments concerning permissible exceptions can be guided by such a condition, then grasping any particular list of exceptions will likewise be unnecessary for guiding our judgments. So the merely extensional version of (LA) neither can nor is needed to suit

---

[46] See e.g. Fodor (1991) and Pietroski and Rey (1995) for the first point, and Smith (2007) for the second.

[47] Cf. Pettit (1999: 24) and Lange (2000: 170–4). The argument in Donagan (1977: 92–3) that the principle 'It is impermissible for anybody to break a freely made promise to do something in itself morally permissible' tolerates exceptions presupposes an extensional version of (LA). See also Shafer-Landau (1997: 593–4).

[48] A related point is that saying that something would be a reason if it occurred in some counterfactual situation isn't a satisfying account of what it is for something to be a reason in the circumstances at hand. This tells us at most how what is supposed to give the reason here would operate in a very different kind of situation (Dancy 1993: 97–8; 1999: 27; 2004: 19). Such views include: Ross's official analysis of prima facie duty (Ross 1930: 19–20); Montague's proposal that moral principles are guaranteed to hold only in "morally simple" situations where only one reason is present, whereas in morally complex situations their force is merely epistemic (Montague 1986: 646–7); and those deontic logics which assign truth conditions to principles in terms of "good-and-simple" possible worlds, in which things go as they morally ought to in the morally simple way (e.g. Asher and Bonevac 1997: 165).

moral principles to the explanatory and epistemological roles required by moral theory.

The constitutive version of (LA) is meant to avoid these problems. The list of conditions which make it the case that something isn't a reason for (or against) something is also more likely to be manageably short than a merely extensional list. Whether any particular constitutive version of (LA) in fact achieves these things depends on just what conditions it throws on the list. But my account has advantages over certain constitutive versions of (LA) independently of this issue.

In arguing this point, we should note that my account of hedged principles could be construed as one constitutive version of (LA). It specifies a condition on circumstances—namely, the presence of the relevant normative basis—whose failure to hold makes circumstances permissibly exceptional. What makes something not instantiate the relevant normative basis is some situational feature. So my account implies a condition in virtue of satisfying which a situational feature makes it the case that some feature of an action permissibly fails to provide a reason for (or against) doing it.

But now it follows that my account can subsume any version of (LA) whose list contains just the situational features which satisfy my condition. For whether something fails to instantiate the normative basis designated by a hedged principle is explanatorily prior to any such list. My account has the advantage of requiring no particular list of such conditions or that it be manageably small in number. (I am not, of course, recommending that we ignore examples of features which generate permissible exceptions. Consideration of examples is usually helpful.) The account can also unify any list given by these versions of (LA). It articulates a deeper factor which the situational features on the list have in common and in virtue of which each makes certain circumstances permissibly exceptional. The proviso requiring the instantiation of the designated normative basis presupposes no particular list of the possible ways of failing to instantiate it. So my account provides greater explanatory depth, unity, and economy than these versions of (LA).

This result has broader significance. Sean McKeever and Michael Ridge, who defend the kind of constitutive version of (LA) to which I just compared my account, claim that "the best explanation of the possibility of practical wisdom . . . entails that practical wisdom involves the internalization of a finite and manageable set of non-hedged principles" (2006: 139). (Practical wisdom is, roughly, a reliable ability to make correct moral judgments, also at least in some novel sets of circumstances.) I cannot address their extended argument for this claim. But my account suggests an explanation of the possibility of practical wisdom which is at least no worse than theirs. So, even if we can construct a finite and manageable set of true non-hedged principles to be internalized, the best explanation of the possibility of practical wisdom doesn't require this.

Both accounts explain how acceptance of moral principles can guide one's judgments concerning moral reasons and permissible exceptions and how the reliability of these judgments can be improved. But my explanation requires fewer and weaker assumptions concerning the list of permissible exceptions while providing greater explanatory depth and unity. It turns on whether, and how well, we track a condition (the presence of the relevant normative basis) whose satisfaction explains why a feature of an action is a reason for (or against) doing it and whose failure explains why certain situational features make the circumstances permissibly exceptional. McKeever and Ridge's explanation equally requires us to track these facts by grasping certain lists of features of actions and situations. But the crucial condition in my explanation gives a deeper unifying specification of what the situational features whose presence would generate permissible exceptions have in common, whereas McKeever and Ridge's doesn't. Insofar as we can track this condition, we can detect the presence of these situational features, at least within some range, without needing to grasp any particular list of features *ex ante*. On my explanation, we can also track this condition even if the situational features which generate permissible exceptions don't come in a manageably short list. Hence my explanation avoids making the possibility of practical wisdom and the reliability of our judgments hostage to what the number of these situational features happens to be.

Another rival to my account comes from Mark Lance and Margaret Little's account of defeasible moral generalizations (2007: 165). They state this "privileging account" (as I'll call it) as follows:

(PA) $P(\forall x)(Gx \ \Box\!\!\rightarrow Mx)$, where 'P' is a modal operator 'in privileged conditions' and '$\Box\!\!\rightarrow$' is the standard subjunctive conditional.

Principles of the form (PA) and the form (HP) share the implication that the connections they describe between factors such as lying and wrongness are stable or invariant under a certain range of hypothetical changes. In privileged conditions, that something is a lie will always count towards its wrongness. What explains why this contribution fails to hold, when it does, is the way the context deviates from these privileged conditions. For example, lying while playing Diplomacy isn't wrong at all because in such a context lying takes place against consensual agreements made in circumstances in which lying would have its "default" status of counting towards wrongness (Lance and Little 2006: 313–14). We can understand why circumstances are permissibly exceptional, when they are, by grasping what conditions are relevantly privileged and what implications the different kinds of deviations from those conditions would have for the connection between lying and wrongness.[49] Such an understanding should also be able to guide our judgments as to whether circumstances are permissibly exceptional. So this account agrees with mine that being reliable in these judgments requires no *ex ante* grasp of any particular list of exceptions.

The privileging account can use deviation from privileged conditions to explain why certain cases but not others are permissibly exceptional. But why are certain conditions privileged in the first place? According to Lance and Little, we are supposed to see which conditions are privileged by understanding the "defeasibly wrong-making nature" of lying, causing pain, and so on—and there the explanation stops. It is supposed to be a basic fact about what pain is, for instance, that in privileged conditions causing pain is defeasibly bad making.[50] This is a significant feature. If the nature of pain doesn't involve such explanatorily basic facts about the relevant privileged conditions, or if we don't grasp these facts, then the privileging account cannot explain how we can be reliable at judging whether circumstances are permissibly exceptional or not.

But the privileging account is unnecessary anyway, because the profile of the privileged conditions associated with a given feature needn't be treated as an explanatorily basic fact about it. The privileged status of those conditions can be accounted for by reference to the normative basis of the feature's status as a reason for (or against) doing what has it. For instance, the privileged conditions in which something's being a lie is a moral reason not to do it will be those in which it instantiates the normative basis of such a fact's status as a reason not to lie. The status of certain other conditions as non-privileged can similarly be accounted for by reference to the failure of a lie to instantiate this normative basis. Together all this makes the privileging account unnecessary at least in every case in which the normative basis of something's status as a moral reason is distinct from it (see the end of Section 3). But I suspect that in many cases what explains why something provides moral reasons isn't a part of that something or otherwise intrinsic to it. If that is right, then my account of

---

[49] Lance and Little's discussion of the different ways in which the contributions of features in non-privileged conditions may depend on their contributions in privileged conditions is subtle and insightful. But what I say here doesn't turn on the details. I detect similar ideas, but developed in a more specific Kantian context, in Schapiro (2006).

[50] Lance and Little think that true instances of (PA) involve a strong enough necessity to entitle us to say that the relevant features are "constitutively" such that in privileged conditions their instances have the specified moral character; they are "moral kinds" whose "essence" this connection characterizes. See Lance and Little (2006: 316–17) and (2007: 165–6). This seems too strong. I suspect I can fully well understand the nature of pain and many other bad-making features without understanding what the privileged conditions are in which they are bad making.

hedged principles seems to generalize better. Moreover, since the normative bases can be used to explain both why certain conditions are privileged and others are non-privileged, the explanations of moral reasons and permissible exceptions which my account provides have a satisfying unity which the privileging account seems to lack.

I conclude that my account of hedged principles compares favorably with the rivals I have considered.[51] The account shows how moral principles are something that we can grasp, and which can reliably guide our moral judgments, even if they can permit exceptions. This includes a unified account of the abilities to judge whether certain features provide moral reasons and whether the circumstances are permissibly exceptional. What supplies this account is an explanation of moral reasons and permissible exceptions which derives explanatory depth and unity from its appeal in both cases to whether or not something instantiates that factor—the designated normative basis of a moral reason—in virtue of whose presence or absence, respectively, a feature provides moral reasons or the circumstances are permissibly exceptional. While the account allows for variation in the degree and scope of the reliability of our moral judgments, it also shows how their reliability can be improved by improving our grasp of the moral ideals which explain moral reasons and permissible exceptions. The account can also explain how our judgments can be reliable irrespective of such contingencies as how frequent the permissible exceptions are and whatever particular lists of exceptions we happen to grasp *ex ante*. I know of no other account of moral principles which gives us as much if we think about exceptions in ethics along the lines that it recommends.

8 CONCLUSION

In other work, I have argued that my account of hedged principles captures many insights which are supposed to motivate moral particularism but nonetheless supports moral generalism. In this paper, I have developed this account in more detail and highlighted some of its explanatory and epistemological advantages. Although some parts of the theory remain no more than a sketch here, I think I may conclude that hedging moral principles in the way I propose shows how principles can permit exceptions while still playing the explanatory and epistemological roles required by moral theory. We should therefore find nothing peculiarly odd or problematic

---

[51] Unfortunately, space prevents me from comparing my account with the sophisticated but somewhat complicated "dispositionalist" account of exception-tolerating principles developed in Robinson (2006). But see Robinson (2008).

about the possibility of exception-tolerating and yet genuinely explanatory generalizations in morality.

My parting observation is that thinking about moral principles along the lines I have recommended directs us to such questions as: What is it about censoring the press that makes it wrong? Why is it that well-being matters to what our moral obligations are? What is so bad about killing a person as to make it wrong? Why might it be all right to tell someone a white lie to bolster their confidence? Since these are just the sorts of questions which exercise moral theorists, perhaps something like the hedged principles I have articulated already are an implicit part of their kit.

REFERENCES

Asher, Nicholas, and Bonevac, Daniel (1997) 'Common Sense Obligation,' in D. Nute (ed.), *Defeasible Deontic Logic* (Dordrecht: Kluwer).

Baldwin, Thomas (2002) 'The Three Phases of Intuitionism,' in P. Stratton-Lake (ed.), *Ethical Intuitionism: Re-evaluations* (Oxford: Clarendon Press).

Braun, David (2000) 'Russellianism and Psychological Generalizations' *Nous* 34: 203–36.

Carlson, Gregory N., and Pelletier, Francis Jeffry (eds.) (1995) *The Generic Book* (Chicago: University of Chicago Press).

Cartwright, Nancy (1983) *How the Laws of Physics Lie* (Oxford: Clarendon Press).

Dancy, Jonathan (1993) *Moral Reasons* (Oxford: Basil Blackwell).

—— (1999) 'Defending Particularism' *Metaphilosophy* 30: 25–32.

—— (2000) 'The Particularist's Progress,' in B. Hooker and M. O. Little (eds.), *Moral Particularism* (Oxford: Clarendon Press).

—— (2004) *Ethics without Principles* (Oxford: Clarendon Press).

Donagan, Alan (1977) *The Theory of Morality* (Chicago: University of Chicago Press).

Earman, John, and Roberts, John (1999) '*Ceteris Paribus*, There Is No Problem of Provisos' *Synthese* 118: 439–78.

Fara, Michael (2005) 'Dispositions and Habituals' *Nous* 39: 43–82.

Feldman, Fred (1986) *Doing the Best We Can* (Dordrecht: D. Reidel).

Fodor, Jerry A. (1991) 'You Can Fool Some of The People All of The Time, Everything Else Being Equal; Hedged Laws and Psychological Explanations' *Mind* 100: 19–34.

Giere, Ronald (1999) *Science without Laws* (Chicago: University of Chicago Press).

Goldman, Alan H. (2002) *Practical Rules: When We Need Them and When We Don't* (Cambridge: Cambridge University Press).

Hart, H. L. A. (1958) 'Positivism and the Separation of Law and Morals' *Harvard Law Review* 71: 593–629.

Hausman, Daniel M. (1992) *The Inexact and Separate Science of Economics* (Cambridge: Cambridge University Press).

Hempel, Carl G. (1988) 'Provisos: A Problem Concerning the Inferential Function of Scientific Theories' *Erkenntnis* 28: 147–64.

Hooker, Brad (2008) 'Particularism and the Real World,' in M. Potrc, V. Strahovnik, and M. Lance (eds.), *Challenging Moral Particularism* (London: Routledge).

Horty, John F. (2003) 'Reasoning with Moral Conflicts,' *Nous* 37: 557–605.

—— (2007) 'Reasons as Defaults' *Philosophers' Imprint* 7(3), http://www.philosophersimprint.org/007003/.

Irwin, T. H. (2000) 'Ethics as an Inexact Science: Aristotle's Ambitions for Moral Theory,' in B. Hooker and M. O. Little (eds.), *Moral Particularism* (Oxford: Clarendon Press).

Kim, Jaegwon (1994) 'Explanatory Knowledge and Metaphysical Dependence' *Philosophical Issues* 5: 51–69.

Koslicki, Kathrin (1999) 'Genericity and Logical Form' *Mind and Language* 14: 441–67.

Lance Mark, and Little, Margaret (2006) 'Defending Moral Particularism,' in J. Dreier (ed.), *Contemporary Debates in Moral Theory* (Oxford: Blackwell Publishers).

—— (2007) 'Where the Laws Are,' in R. Shafer-Landau (ed.), *Oxford Studies in Metaethics*, ii (Oxford: Oxford University Press).

Lange, Marc (2000) *Natural Laws in Scientific Practice* (Oxford: Oxford University Press).

Liebesman, David (Ms) 'Simple Generics.' Unpublished.

Little, Margaret O. (2000) 'Moral Generalities Revisited,' in B. Hooker and M. O. Little (eds.), *Moral Particularism* (Oxford: Clarendon Press).

McKeever, Sean, and Ridge, Michael (2006) *Principled Ethics: Generalism as a Regulative Ideal* (Oxford: Clarendon Press).

McNaughton, David, and Rawling, Piers (2000) 'Unprincipled Ethics,' in B. Hooker and M. O. Little (eds.), *Moral Particularism* (Oxford: Clarendon Press).

Montague, Phillip (1986) 'In Defense of Moral Principles' *Philosophy and Phenomenological Research* 46: 643–54.

Morreau, Michael (1997) 'Fainthearted Conditionals' *Journal of Philosophy* 94: 187–211.

Nickel, Bernhard (Ms) 'Processes in the Interpretation of Generics and CP-Laws.' Unpublished.

Pettit, Philip (1999) 'A Theory of Normal and Ideal Conditions' *Philosophical Studies* 96: 21–44.

Pietroski, Paul, and Rey, Georges (1995) 'When Other Things Aren't Equal: Saving Ceteris Paribus Laws from Vacuity' *British Journal for the Philosophy of Science* 46: 81–110.

Pollock, John L., and Cruz, Joseph (1999) *Contemporary Theories of Knowledge*, 2nd edn (Lanham, MD: Rowman & Littlefield).

Robinson, Luke (2006) 'Moral Holism, Moral Generalism, and Moral Dispositionalism' *Mind* 115: 331–60.

—— (2008) 'Moral Principles Are Not Moral Laws' *Journal of Ethics and Social Philosophy* 2(3), http://www.jesp.org.

Ross, W. D. (1930) *The Right and the Good* (Oxford: Clarendon Press).

—— (1939) *The Foundations of Ethics* (Oxford: Clarendon Press).

Ruben, David-Hillel (1990) *Explaining Explanation* (London: Routledge).

Scanlon, T. M. (1998) *What We Owe to Each Other* (Cambridge, MA.: Harvard University Press).

Schapiro, Tamar (2006) 'Kantian Rigorism and Mitigating Circumstances' *Ethics* 117: 32–57.

Schiffer, Stephen (1991) 'Ceteris Paribus Laws' *Mind* 100: 1–17.

Shafer-Landau, Russ (1997) 'Moral Rules' *Ethics* 107: 584–611.

Silverberg, Arnold (1996) 'Psychological Laws and Non-Monotonic Logic' *Erkenntnis* 44: 199–224.

Smith, Martin (2007) 'Ceteris Paribus Conditionals and Comparative Normalcy' *Journal of Philosophical Logic* 36: 97–121.

Stratton-Lake, Philip (2002) 'Pleasure and Reflection in Ross's Intuitionism,' in P. Stratton-Lake (ed.), *Ethical Intuitionism: Re-evaluations* (Oxford: Clarendon Press).

—— (2003) 'Scanlon's Contractualism and the Redundancy Objection' *Analysis* 63: 70–6.

Väyrynen, Pekka (2006) 'Moral Generalism: Enjoy in Moderation' *Ethics* 116: 707–41.

—— (2008) 'Usable Moral Principles,' in M. Potrc, V. Strahovnik, and M. Lance (eds.), *Challenging Moral Particularism* (London: Routledge).

White, Roger (2005) 'Explanation as a Guide to Induction' *Philosophers' Imprint* 5 (2), www.philosophersimprint.org/005002/.

Woodward, James (2003) *Making Things Happen* (Oxford: Oxford University Press).

5

Ethical Neo-Expressivism

Dorit Bar-On and Matthew Chrisman

A standard way to explain the connection between ethical claims and motivation is to say that these claims express motivational attitudes. Unless this connection is taken to be merely a matter of contingent psychological regularity, it may seem that there are only two options for understanding it. Either we can treat ethical claims as expressing propositions that entail something about the speaker's motivational attitudes (subjectivism), or we can treat ethical claims as nonpropositional and as having their semantic content constituted by the motivational attitudes they directly express (noncognitivism). In this chapter, we argue that there is another option, which can be recognized once we see that there is no need to build the expression relation between ethical claims and motivational states of mind into the *semantic content* of ethical claims.

In articulating the third option, we try to capture what we think is worth preserving about the classical expressivist idea that ethical claims directly express motivational states, and separate it from the wrong semantic ideas with which it has traditionally been caught up. Doing so requires arguing for and deploying a distinction between claims considered as products—such as sentences—and claims considered as linguistic acts—such as utterances. In our view, the former are properly seen as standing in an expression relation to propositions, whereas the latter are properly seen as standing in an expression relation to mental states.

In the first section below, we use this act/product distinction to defend a "neo-expressivist" view of the way in which ethical claims express

For helpful feedback on earlier versions of this chapter, we'd like to thank the audience at the fourth annual metaethics workshop in Madison, Wisconsin (especially Daniel Boisvert, David Copp, Matthew Kramer, Stephen Finlay, Joshua Glasgow, and Mark Schroeder), the 2006 metaethics reading group at UNC-Chapel Hill (especially Ben Bramble, Geoffrey Sayre-McCord, and Teemu Toppinen), Collin Allen, Simon Blackburn, Peter Hanks, Grant Goodrich, Mitchell Green, Andrew McAninch, Ram Neta, Dean Pettit, Michael Ridge, and Carol Voeller.

motivational states. The core idea is to argue that ethical claims considered as acts of claim-making should be seen as expressing motivational states of mind, since this best serves the point and purpose of ethical thought and discourse. However, we insist that this idea should be kept separate from any thesis about the semantic content of ethical claims considered as products. We maintain that it is best to think of the products of ethical claims as expressing propositions. In addition to presenting a defensible version of expressivism, ethical neo-expressivism, we argue, also gives foundation to a new (and in our opinion highly plausible) form of internalism. In the second section below, we discuss another family of views that deny that the connection between ethical claims and motivational states is a matter of the literal semantic content of ethical claims (in the sense of being part of what such claims *say*). In opposition to the classical subjectivists, who maintain that ethical claims express propositions that ascribe motivational states to their speakers as part of their semantic content, Copp (2001) and Finlay (2004, 2005) have separately argued that we should instead see such propositions as only implicated, rather than directly asserted, by ethical claims—either conventionally (Copp) or conversationally (Finlay). We consider these "neo-subjectivist" views (as we call them) to be the principal competitors to neo-expressivism, and so we offer reasons for favoring neo-expressivism. In the final section below, we flesh out ethical neo-expressivism by addressing a number of potential objections.

NEO-EXPRESSIVISM

On a popular Humean view of motivation, being motivated to act is never merely a matter of having certain beliefs but also always requires the presence of some conative attitude. Given this account of motivation, if we are to regard an agent's ethical claim as internally connected to her motivation, we have to see it as somehow 'betraying' the presence of conative attitudes. Perhaps Humeanism is the wrong view of the psychology of motivation (more on this in the final section below); but assuming that it isn't, every view of moral discourse will want to capture at least *some* sense in which ethical claims betray conative attitudes.

Classical subjectivism offers one way to do this. The subjectivist argues that ethical claims *report* that the speaker has the relevant conative attitude. According to subjectivism, this is a feature of their semantic content. For example, on a crude form of subjectivism, "Tolerance is a virtue" just means that I (the speaker) approve of tolerance.

One of the original motivations for expressivism was to capture what is right about this view without succumbing to the obvious problem with it.

What the expressivist thinks is right is that sincerely made ethical claims betray the speaker's conative attitudes. The obvious problem is that, if they do so by reporting that the speaker has the relevant attitude, then it is wildly unclear how ethical disagreement is possible. Or, to put the point differently, it seems that we could only disagree with someone's ethical claim by saying "You don't feel that way." But this seems implausible. Whatever problems we may have with others' ethical views, that they are an instance of self-deception is not usually one of them. The expressivist's leading idea for avoiding this problem is to construe the way in which ethical claims betray a conative attitude not as a matter of reporting its presence but as a matter of *directly expressing* it.

Here is Ayer on the difference:

if I say, "Tolerance is a virtue," and someone answers, "You don't approve of it," he would, on the ordinary subjectivist theory, be contradicting me. On our theory, he would not be contradicting me, because, in saying that tolerance was a virtue, I should not be making any statement about my own feelings or about anything else. I should simply be evincing my feelings, which is not at all the same thing as saying that I have them.   (1936/46: 109)

The subjectivist can, in a sense, agree with Ayer that conative attitudes are evinced by ethical claims. But he'll have to see this as, so to speak, an indirect consequence of what he thinks ethical claims assert; and it is precisely the subjectivist view of what ethical claims assert that gets the subjectivist into trouble. Ayer writes,

The distinction between the expression of feeling and the assertion of feeling is complicated by the fact that the assertion that one has a certain feeling often accompanies the expression of that feeling ... [However,] even if the assertion that one has a certain feeling always involves the expression of that feeling, the expression of a feeling assuredly does not always involve the assertion that one has it. And this is the important point to grasp in considering the distinction between our theory and the ordinary subjectivist theory. For whereas the subjectivist holds that ethical statements actually assert the existence of certain feelings, we hold that ethical statements are expressions ... of feelings which do not necessarily involve any assertions.   (1936/46: 109–10)

We think there remains something of promise in Ayer's strategy for divorcing the way in which ethical claims express conative attitudes from what ethical claims assert. But it was precisely his view that (genuine and pure) ethical claims do not involve *any assertion at all* that led him to deny that (genuine and pure) ethical claims are truth-apt and to insist on a radically noncognitivist semantics for them, according to which their meaning, much like the meaning of expletives, is just a matter of what conative attitudes they express. In ordinary discourse, however, ethical claims exhibit undeniable semantic continuities with ordinary descriptive claims. We often say things like "It's true that tolerance is a virtue, but it's also true that some things are over the line." Moreover, we embed ethical claims in force-stripping contexts, e.g.: "If tolerance is a virtue, then one's children should be raised to be tolerant" and "Either tolerance is a virtue or the doctrine of 'turn the other cheek' is a farce." Ayer, it seems, is simply forced to explain away these appearances; and many philosophers have taken his (and others') failure to do so to be the major stumbling block for ethical expressivism.

However, we think that contrasting Ayer's noncognitivist semantics for ethical claims with the subjectivist's implicitly reflexive semantics has encouraged a conflation in this debate that makes the expressivist's leading idea seem much more problematic than it really is. To see this, it is helpful to consider a recent expressivist view in a different domain that is explicitly not a view about the semantic content of claims in that domain. This is the 'neo-expressivist' view of avowals defended in Bar-On (2004). Avowals—that is, ordinary first-person present-tense ascriptions of mental states, such as "I'm feeling anxious," "I'm hoping that you'll come to the party"—are distinctive for their security. It is usually misplaced to challenge an avowal or ask for the speaker's reasons for thinking that it is true. However, avowals manifest undeniable semantic continuities with ordinary descriptive statements, such as "I am bleeding," or "I am walking down the street." We treat avowals as truth-evaluable, saying things such as "It's true that I am feeling anxious, but I'll pull through." And we embed avowals in force-stripping contexts, saying things such as "If I am feeling anxious, you should be concerned."

This may seem to militate against treating avowals as directly expressive of the underlying mental states they ascribe; however, that appearance rests on a conflation of different senses of 'express.' The first sense is:

(a-expression)   the *action* sense: a *person* expresses *a mental state* by intentionally doing something.

For example, when I give you a hug, or say: "It's so great to see you," I express, in the action sense, joy at seeing you. In this sense, one can express dis/approval of *x* by saying (to others or to oneself): "I don't/like *x*," as well as by using a dis/approving verbal epithet for *x* or displaying nonverbal dis/approving behavior toward it, just as one can express dis/agreement with *p* by saying: "I dis/agree that *p*" as well as by saying simply "(not) *p*" or by nodding in dis/agreement. It is important to note that a-expression is a relation between a person and *a mental state*. It is also worth noting that the notion of a-expression requires that a person do *something* intentionally. It does not require that what one does intentionally is *express*. Though one *can* intentionally express a mental state—for example, by deciding and setting out to give vent to a present emotion, instead of suppressing it, it seems that the more basic case is one in which a person gives spontaneous expression to a present state of hers by performing some intentional act, such as giving a hug or uttering a sentence, that doesn't have expression as its intentional aim. The second sense of 'express' is:

(**s-expression**) the *semantic* sense: for example, a *sentence* expresses an abstract proposition by being a (conventional) representation of it.

Thus the sentence "It's raining outside" expresses in the semantic sense the proposition that it is raining at time t outside place p. This is what this English sentence has in common with its counterpart in other languages, such that they mean the same thing. (A speaker who utters this sentence will typically be a-expressing the belief that it's raining at the time and place of her utterance.) We can also speak of a thought-token as expressing a proposition (and a thinker who produces the token will typically be a-expressing the relevant belief).[1] The important thing to bear in mind is that s-expression is a semantic relation, holding between linguistic expressions (and their analogues in thought) and their meanings, whereas a-expression is a relation between subjects and mental states.

The distinction between a-expression and s-expression lines up with a further distinction between the *act* of making a claim and the *product* of this act. The act of making a claim a-expresses certain mental states, whereas the product of this act s-expresses a particular proposition. And these distinctions can be applied to claims made both in language and in thought. An act of saying "This painting is interesting" produces a sentence token, whereas a mental act of thinking it has as its product a thought token, where both tokens s-express the proposition that a designated painting is interesting. In producing these tokens, a person may (only) be a-expressing her state of believing that the painting is interesting. She may (also) be a-expressing her state of feeling intrigued by the painting (or whatever).

---

[1] The distinction between expression in the action vs. semantic sense is due to Sellars (1969: 506–27). Sellars identifies a third sense of 'express': in the *causal* sense, an *utterance* or piece of outward behavior expresses an internal episode by being the culmination of a causal process beginning with that episode. For example, one's unintentional grimace or trembling hands may express, in the causal sense, one's feeling pain or nervousness, respectively. We will set aside expression in the causal sense in what follows. Bar-On (2004: chs. 6–8) makes extensive use of the threefold distinction, in order to capture the distinctive security of avowals. Kalderon (2005: 64) also deploys a distinction between conveying and expressing, which is similar to the distinction between what we are calling a-expression and s-expression when arguing that proponents of noncognitivist semantics are guilty of what he terms the 'pragmatic fallacy,' which is, in essence, the mistake of confusing s-expression and a-expression.

It is often uncritically assumed that what we are calling a-expression requires engaging in a *communicative* act, even if not speech. But we think this is wrong. Given the definition of a-expression, it seems to us that one can a-express one's affection to a beloved one by caressing her photo in the solitude of one's room, one can cuss to oneself without making a sound, one can think "This room is a mess!" as one walks into a child's room, giving (silent) vent to one's annoyance while suppressing both vocal and facial expressions, and one can reflect on the steps of an argument, expressing one's thoughts to oneself all along the way. In all of these cases, the a-expression/s-expression distinction applies since there is both an expressive act and a product of this act. For example, the thought: "This room is a mess!" s-expresses the proposition that the room is a mess, but for all that, in the act of thinking it, one may be a-expressing one's annoyance at the mess.[2]

Properly understood, the a/s-expression and the act/product distinctions can be accommodated by any number of views on the relationship between sentence meaning and mental states. In particular, suppose one adopts a roughly Gricean view of meaning. Using our terminology, the Gricean view is that we should explain what a sentence in a public language s-expresses in terms of what mental state one expresses with sincere utterances of this sentence. For instance, and roughly, the sentence "Grass is green" on this view, would be taken to s-express the proposition that grass is green in virtue of the fact that one conventionally a-expresses one's belief that grass is green with an utterance of this sentence. This may appear to collapse the distinction between s-expression and a-expression, by reducing the former to the latter. But this is a mistake. The Gricean account must presuppose, rather than reduce away, the notion of s-expression *as it applies to mental states*. So *at best* it would allow us to reduce s-expression *as it applies to items in a public language* to a-expression of items endowed with powers of s-expression all on their own. Moreover, even setting aside this point, it seems clear that a viable Gricean view would have to (and should be able to) accommodate the s/a-expression distinction. Take for example a declarative sentence in a public language—"There's a thief in the yard"—that, on the Gricean account, is linked by convention to the expression of a belief state with the relevant content. On a given occasion, a speaker may utter the sentence intentionally and comprehendingly while failing to have the relevant belief—say, if she is lying, or dissimulating. In such a case, we might say, the speaker expresses the belief that there's a thief in the yard without expressing *her* belief to that effect. (The distinction between expressing *a*

---

[2] For relevant discussion and further examples, see Bar-On (2004: esp. chs. 6 and 7) and Green (2007).

mental state and expressing *one's mental state* can then be seen as a first approximation to a Gricean equivalent of the distinction between s- and a-expression.[3])

Now, consider a simple expressivist account of avowals, according to which an avowal such as "I am in pain" is just like a natural expression of it (say, a wince, or a grimace) in that it does not serve to *ascribe* pain to the subject who avows; it serves *only* directly to express the feeling of pain itself. This view is often thought to explain the distinctive security of avowals but at the cost of disrespecting the obvious semantic continuity between avowals and other mentalistic ascriptions. However, if we apply the act/product distinction here, we can generate a highly plausible explanation of the distinctive security of avowals that has the explanatory advantages of simple expressivism without its disadvantages. As acts, avowals, like acts of natural expression (such as wincing, or smiling) directly a-express the mental state avowed. Consequently, avowals, like natural expressions, enjoy protection from epistemic criticism (we would not challenge a sigh of relief, ask for reasons for it, etc.); however, unlike acts of natural expression, avowals have as their products sentence- (or thought-) tokens with genuine truth-conditions.

Here is not the place to explore further the neo-expressivist view of avowals.[4] Our point in bringing it up is rather this: it seems as though a parallel neo-expressivist treatment of ethical claims promises to retain Ayer's leading idea for understanding the way in which ethical claims betray their speakers' motivational attitudes without going in for the dubious noncognitivist semantics and the denial of semantic continuity that it entails. The key is that we can separate what speakers (or thinkers) a-express through their acts from what the products of these acts s-express. This makes room for a view about what mental states are a-expressed by a claim (act) that does not imply any particular view about the appropriate semantics for that claim (product). In the case of avowals, we saw that one can issue a claim that s-expresses a proposition about the avower ("I feel excited") but where what the avower a-expresses is the self-ascribed state

---

[3] For relevant discussion of some of these points, see Bar-On (1995). And for a recent comprehensive development of the Gricean approach that would accommodate our distinctions, see Davis (2003). Thanks to Michael Ridge for prompting us to make the clarification in this paragraph. (For more on the Gricean account in relation to ours, see n. 5 below.) Since we do not take ourselves to be providing an account of the meaning of ethical claims, we will not take a stand here on the appropriate semantic theory for ethical sentences. Suffice it to say that the Lockean/Gricean approach is not without viable rivals in this as in other cases. One well-known alternative is the Davidsonian view. (And see Chrisman (2008) for the beginnings of an inferential role approach to the meaning of ethical claims.)

[4] The view is developed in Bar-On (2004; see esp. chs. 6–8).

itself (excitement), rather than, or perhaps in addition to, her self-ascriptive belief. One can also a-express a mental state (feeling joy at seeing one's addressee, or feeling intrigued by a painting) that *isn't* self-ascribed by the proposition that one's utterance s-expresses ("It is great to see you," "This painting is interesting," respectively).[5] Similarly, we can distinguish between the act of making an ethical claim and the product of this act. An ethical claim considered as a product—that is, a sentence- (or thought-) token that essentially employs ethical terms (or concepts)—can be said to s-express a proposition. It is this feature of ethical claims considered as products that can be used to explain their semantic continuity with ordinary, non-problematic descriptive claims.

However, as with avowals, the issue of what is s-expressed by an ethical claim shouldn't be taken to prejudice the issue of what mental state one who makes the claim characteristically a-expresses by it. Here, independently of any more specific view about the semantics of the products, we want to suggest that the original expressivist idea about what someone making an ethical claim a-expresses is, at least within a Humean framework, quite plausible. It's plausible precisely because it provides an explanation of the apparently 'internal' connection between sincerely making an ethical claim and having certain conative attitudes. On the expressivist view, people who issue ethical utterances characteristically a-express the very same states whose presence is required for understanding the necessary connection of such utterances to motivation. But they do so without their token sentences or thoughts s-expressing propositions that *self-ascribe* those states. Thus, as long as we're talking about expressive acts and working within a Humean framework, we can agree with Ayer that ethical claims betray conative

---

[5] What if one were to insist (along the lines of the Gricean approach mentioned earlier) that what the sentence "It is great to see you" s-expresses must be given in terms of the mental state one a-expresses (perhaps in context) by uttering it? We think there are powerful (Frege–Geach style) considerations that would require us to give at least *a* meaning assignment to the sentence that was a straight function of its compositional semantics (capitalizing on the rules governing "great," "see," "you," etc.). Moreover, we think that our understanding of what mental state a speaker a-expresses when uttering the sentence is partly parasitic on this meaning, rather than the other way around. (This could remain so even if one thought that the rational reconstruction of how the sentence *came* to have the linguistic meaning that it has requires reference to the mental states that speakers of the language have somehow converged on a-expressing. For relevant discussion, see Lewis (1970) and (1975), and see our earlier distinction between expressing a mental state and expressing *one's* mental state.) However, our present point can be taken to be the more modest one: that once we have the a/s-expression and the act/product distinctions in place we at least *can* separate what a given sentence 'linguistically says' or 'means' (= s-expresses) from what mental state a speaker uses the sentence to express (= a-expresses) on a given occasion. (See above, n. 3.)

attitudes, not because they report them, but because speakers who make the claims express them directly. However, given the distinction between a-expression and s-expression, accepting this does not force us to agree with Ayer's noncognitivist account of the meaning of ethical claims. For it seems open to us to maintain that ethical claims, considered as products, s-express truth-evaluable propositions.

Since it is modeled on the neo-expressivist view of avowals, we shall call this view of ethical claims *ethical neo-expressivism*. A bit more carefully stated, the view's two main tenets are these:

(*a*) Ethical claims understood as *products* are semantically continuous with ordinary descriptive claims in being truth-evaluable, embeddable in conditionals, negation, logical inferences, etc. This is because ethical claims *s*-express true or false propositions.

(*b*) Ethical claims understood as *acts* are different from ordinary descriptive claims in that an agent who felicitously makes an ethical claim (in speech or in thought) essentially *a*-expresses a motivational state—a state whose presence is normally required for the explanation of the agent's relevant actions. This—rather than any semantic feature of the propositions speakers communicate when making ethical claims—is what allows us to explain the 'internal' connection between making an ethical claim and being motivated to act in accordance with it.

Before moving on, it may prove helpful to elucidate each of these claims a bit further.

In our view, ethical claims can be made in speech or in thought; the notion of a-expression applies to expressive acts, and we see no reason to presume that all expressive acts have speech as their medium. Because of this, the neo-expressivist view of ethical claims, like the neo-expressivist view of avowals, is not a view about acts made exclusively in *speech*. The view is that agents who make ethical claims in speech *or* in thought produce sentence-tokens (in speech) or thought-tokens (without speech) that possess truth-evaluable content and thus s-express propositions. What propositions? For present purposes, the proposition s-expressed by an ethical claim can be specified disquotationally. For example, the claim: "Murder is wrong" (understood as product) can be taken to s-express the proposition that murder is wrong. In saying this, we're not committing to a disquotational theory of the *truth* of ethical (or other) claims. We're just prescinding from any paraphrastic semantic analysis thereof. Moreover, we are not suggesting that the meaning of *every* sentence is to be specified disquotationally. Many sentences (including ones that use ethical vocabulary) are semantically complex and do admit of semantic analysis. What we are resisting, however, is the idea that all ethical sentences must admit of such analysis.[6]

We think that to say that ethical claims s-express propositions is to make a logico-semantic point concerning ethical discourse and reflection, which does not have any automatic implications regarding moral psychology or the nature of moral reality. Consider a nonmoral sentence (or thought): "John loves Mary." Within a broadly Davidsonian semantic framework, the sentence (or thought) has as its truth-condition *that John loves Mary.* By contrast, "John and Jason love Mary" will have a non-disquotational truth-condition—to the effect that John loves Mary *and* Jason loves Mary. But assigning this truth-condition is consistent with any number of views on the nature of love and the worldly conditions that constitute John's loving Mary. (Perhaps, indeed, there is no such thing as love; so "John loves Mary" will always be false.) This assignment of truth-conditions is also silent on the characteristic psychological states of those who go in for the use of the vocabulary of love. It may be interesting to speculate on the reasons human beings have come to possess the concept of love, or the role this concept plays in the cognitive economy and lives of creatures like us. But it's very unclear how to translate the results of such investigation into an analysis of the literal meaning of sentences containing the word "love," or the semantic content for propositions involving the concept. (For another case, consider a well-known metaphysically problematic case: sentences of the form 'X caused Y,' whose Davidsonian truth-conditions, even if not disquotational, will still not serve to unpack the meaning of 'cause.')

To be sure, if one thought that a proposition is true just in case it corresponds with a fact, and one thought that some (positive atomic) ethical sentences are correct because they express true propositions, then the neo-expressivist view would combine with these commitments to yield the realist view that there are ethical facts. However, we take the commitment to the correspondence account of truth and to the success-theory of ethical sentences to be open to debate within the philosophy of language and the metaphysics of morals, respectively. So, strictly speaking, neo-expressivism is neutral on those debates. We see this as an advantage of the view.

Crucially, unlike traditional expressivism, neo-expressivism does *not* offer a *meaning analysis* of ethical sentences in terms of the attitudes they express. Nonetheless, we think that our account can capture a suitable sense in which there is an internal connection between ethical claims and motivation to

---

[6] We discuss this issue further in our concluding section. Fodor (1998) offers powerful considerations in support of the view that very few, if any, atomic sentences admit of semantic analysis.

act. The connection is captured by maintaining that what is distinctive about *acts* of making ethical claims (in speech or in thought) lies precisely in their expressive import: such acts are essentially linked to the expression of motivational attitudes. The precise characterization of the link is a delicate matter to which we now turn.[7]

Although an ethical claim, considered as product, does not s-express a proposition that ascribes a motivational state or attitude to the person making the claim, we think that for a person to make a genuine ethical claim is for her to a-express such a state or attitude. (Insofar as one accepts the Humean explanation of motivation, this encourages the view that ethical claims a-express conative states.) In other words, if we want to locate an internal connection between ethical claims and motivation, we should look to the nature of acts of making ethical claims and the character of a-expression. Consider again the case of avowals. On the neo-expressivist account, there's a difference between a person who *avows* and a person who simply *reports* feeling disappointed. Though they may both say (or think) the same thing, namely: "I'm feeling disappointed," the person who avows is engaging in an act whose point is to express (vent, give voice to, show) the very state whose presence would make the avowal true, namely, the feeling of disappointment. By contrast, the reporter is only giving voice to her *belief* that she is disappointed. This characterization gives us a way of separating genuine avowals from non-avowing acts of self-ascription—notably, self-reports—*not* in terms of semantic content but rather in terms of the kind of act performed. We want to carry over this idea to the ethical case. We suggest that the connection to motivation that is thought by internalists to be an essential characteristic of ethical claims should be located in the kind of acts performed when making ethical claims rather than in their semantic content. The suggestion is that *for a person to make a genuinely ethical claim is for her to a-express a motivational state or attitude*, and so *having* this attitude is a condition on *properly issuing the claim.* Notice that, given the distinction between a-expressing a mental state M and a-expressing *one's* M, it *is* possible for one to make a genuine ethical claim and thereby a-express a motivational state *without* having this motivational state; however, our suggestion is that it is not possible to do so without violating one of the *propriety conditions* on making ethical claims. In such a case, one will be giving voice to a motivational state or attitude that one doesn't have, which, on the present suggestion, stands in the way of *properly* making an ethical claim.

[7] We wish to thank Dan Boisvert, Stephen Finlay, Josh Glasgow, Matthew Kramer, Mark Schroeder, and an anonymous editor for correspondence and discussion that helped us to clarify the characterization of our version of internalism that follows.

Denying that the connection to motivation is forged in the semantic content of ethical claims makes room for the following conceptual possibility: a person could issue a claim such as "Torturing cats is wrong," or "It is good to rescue a drowning person" sincerely and while understanding what it says, yet without being motivated to act in accordance with it. Making theoretical room for this possibility is important, not only because it seems to be conceptually possible, but also because various cases that are thought to undermine motivational internalism—of psychopathic, or extremely lethargic, or satanic individuals—may well provide actual illustrations of this possibility. It seems to us implausible to legislate, along the lines of a strong motivational internalism, that such individuals are either insincere or fail to have mastered the semantic rules governing the sentences they use. On the other hand, we don't believe that acknowledging this requires us to agree with a strong motivational externalism that holds that such individuals are *only* psychologically abnormal and/or morally deficient. We think that the neo-expressivist framework is attractive because it affords a more nuanced picture of the relationship between ethical claims and motivational states than is afforded by *either* subjectivism and classical expressivism, on the one hand, *or* externalist views, on the other. This framework also allows us to capture intuitive differences between the ways the link to motivation can be broken.

To see this, notice that on the neo-expressivist view we are proposing, the connection to motivation is forged in the character of ethical claims understood as acts (made in speech or in thought), rather than in the semantic content of ethical claims understood as products. As we saw, the neo-expressivist about avowals proposes that what is distinctive about avowals is that a person who avows does not *report* the presence of an occurrent mental state of hers, but rather is supposed to give vent, air, share, or give voice to the relevant mental state using an articulate linguistic (or language-like) vehicle that self-ascribes that mental state. This is not simply a generalization about what happens when people avow; rather it is a characterization of a certain category of acts, avowals, in terms of the *point* of avowing, which distinguishes it from other kinds of acts that may be performed using mental self-ascriptions, and has implications for their *proper* performance. Somewhat similarly, ethical neo-expressivism makes room for the following internalist claim: that what is distinctive about ethical claims—what renders them *ethical* claims—is the fact that a person who issues an ethical claim is supposed to give voice to a (type of) motivational state using a linguistic (or language-like) vehicle that involves ethical terms or concepts. This too is not offered simply as a generalization about what regularly happens when people issue ethical claims; rather it is a characterization of a certain category of acts—acts of making ethical claims—in terms of their point, which distinguishes them from other kinds of claim-making acts, and has implications for their proper performance.

Issuing a claim is an intentional act; issuing an ethical claim, according to ethical neo-expressivism, is issuing a claim whose point is in part to give voice to a motivational state. But, unlike traditional expressivism and subjectivism, ethical neo-expressivism allows that the *vehicle* of expression—the sentence (or sentence-like) token used to express the motivational state—has truth-conditions and is not itself a *self-ascription* of the motivational state. (As we mentioned, the view is neutral on what *satisfies* the truth-conditions.) Of course, intentional acts can fail, and expressive acts are no exception. We think that one advantage of locating the expressive import of ethical claims in their character as acts is that we can recognize a varied range of *expressive failures*, where an (apparently) ethical claim can be issued in the absence of the relevant motivational states. This, we believe, is the key to articulating a more nuanced view of the connection between ethical claims and motivation than is afforded by either an implausibly strong internalism or an equally implausibly strong externalism.

It is agreed on all hands that the possibility of issuing ethical claims insincerely does not refute internalism. That a person can insincerely say "It's good to help the poor" while lacking all motivation to help the poor does not show that there is no internal connection between making an ethical claim and being at least somewhat motivated to act in accordance with it. But why not? The answer can't be that the insincere person says what she believes to be false. For one thing, traditional expressivists deny that ethical claims express beliefs in the first place; they locate the internal connection to motivation precisely in the fact that ethical claims express conative states rather than cognitive (belief-like) states. But then what is the expressivist to make of the failure of insincere ethical claims to express the relevant conative states?

We'd like to suggest that a better way to understand insincere ethical claims, one that could accommodate noncognitivist as well as cognitivist construals of such claims, is along the lines of a certain model of insincere promises. The person who says insincerely "I promise to take you to dinner" isn't typically thought to have said what she believes to be false. Rather, she is thought to have made an *empty* promise, as we say. This is because she has failed to fulfill a *different* propriety condition on making promises, namely, having the intention to do as the promise says. Her promise fails to 'come from' the relevant intention. To the extent that the promise comes from the *wrong* intention—to mislead, for example—her act may still be criticizable. And there may be good reasons to insist that she *ought* to do as the promise says. But we can still recognize the act as disingenuous. Similarly, we could think of the insincere person who says "It's good to help the poor" as having *failed to properly make an ethical claim*, not because she doesn't believe (or understand) what she has said, but rather because she (knowingly) fails to meet another propriety condition on making such claims, namely having the appropriate motivational state.

The case of avowals offers a similar model for understanding expressive mismatches that result in a failure to meet the propriety conditions for a specific kind of expressive act. A person can say insincerely "I feel awful" without feeling awful, perhaps just to gain sympathy. Such a person, we may suppose, understands what she has said, and the sentence she utters is a genuine self-ascription of a mental state. But given the description just given, it is reasonable to maintain that this person has failed properly to issue an avowal (indeed, it may even be suggested that she's only issued a *pretend-* or *mock*-avowal) though she has said of herself that she feels awful, she hasn't 'spoken from' the relevant mental state. But now consider a different case. Having undergone psychoanalysis, a person may conclude: "I feel intimidated by my sister." The self-ascription in this case is sincere—it represents the person's belief about her state, one she has acquired on the basis of her therapist's testimony. Here it seems very reasonable simply to deny that this person has issued a genuine avowal at all. What the person has issued is an evidential self-report, albeit using a sentence that could have been used in issuing an avowal.

We have seen that the possibility of saying "I promise" without the right intention doesn't show that there isn't an internal connection between making a promise and having an intention to do as the promise says. We have also seen that the possibility of saying "I am in M" without expressing M doesn't show that there isn't an internal connection between avowing and expressing the avowed state. We now want to argue that the possibility of issuing a claim such as "It's wrong to torture cats" in the absence of the relevant motivational state, even when done sincerely, doesn't show that there isn't an internal connection between making an ethical claim and a-expressing such a state. It is open to the internalist to maintain that the person in such a case fails to be *properly* making an ethical claim *because she fails to a-express the relevant motivational state of hers*, since a-expressing one's motivational state is a condition on proper performance of acts of making ethical claims.

So the idea is that one of the norms governing the proper performance of acts of making ethical claims is that a person making such a claim is giving voice to the relevant motivational state. If a person says something such as "Stealing is wrong" but lacks the relevant motivational state, she may be sincerely and comprehendingly issuing a claim with the same semantic content as an ethical claim. But, on our view, she should not be counted as properly making an ethical claim. This could be because she fails to recognize the point of making ethical claims, which need not mean that she has failed to master the relevant ethical concepts—she may be as adept as anyone at tracking the extensions of such concepts. (This may be a reasonable diagnosis of at least some versions of the case of the psychopath.) Or it could be because, though she recognizes the point of making ethical claims, she suffers some psychological impairment that stands in her way of a-expressing *her* motivation state (as may be the case with the lethargic). In these sorts of cases, the person issues a claim with the *semantic content* of an ethical claim in the absence of the right motivational state. And we may accept that she is issuing an ethical claim all right. But it is still open to the internalist to insist that she cannot be regarded as making the ethical claim *properly*, since she violates one of the propriety conditions governing the making of such claims.

The satanic case is interestingly different. In this sort of case, the person supposedly does recognize the point of making ethical claims, but she appears to be out to subvert it or deliberately flout it. Depending on the details of the case, we may want to assimilate it to the case of insincerely making an ethical claim or instead to one of the foregoing cases. Either way, the internalist can insist that the satanic issuer of an ethical claim fails to make such a claim *properly*.

The above diagnosis allows us to respect the internalist intuition that the psychopathic, lethargic, satanic, etc. are more than just psychologically and/or morally deviant. However, unlike the strong internalist, we do not regard this as failure to have mastered the semantic rules for the application of ethical terms/concepts or the semantic conventions underlying ethical language. On the neo-expressivist construal of the internal connection between making an ethical claim and being appropriately motivated, the link is not merely a matter of contingent psychological regularity, nor is it simply a condition on being a morally virtuous agent. At the same time, the view does not build the link into the *semantic content* of individual ethical claims, considered as products, nor does it portray it as a pre-condition on the very mastery of ethical concepts. Rather than exposing the internal link to motivation by offering a revealing, paraphrastic analysis of the *meaning* of individual ethical sentences, the neo-expressivist account proposes investigating the conditions on properly performed acts of making ethical claims. Since the general sort of link we are pointing to has some analogs, it will be useful to consider them.

One kind of example comes from the use of color vocabulary. Color concepts and predicates have extensions that can be tracked in a variety of ways. Suppose we come across an individual who is able to track the extension of the predicate "looks blue" as well as any of us, but who lacks our ability to track colors through vision. In other words, such an individual systematically fails to have the sorts of visual experiences that underwrite the normal use of color concepts among us. Arguably, such an individual is not a full participant in our color discourse. If she utters: "This piece of paper looks blue" when asked for the color of a piece of paper in front of her, then even if we are willing to credit her with deploying the concept *looks blue*, we can still recognize her utterance as infelicitous or inappropriate. She has successfully identified an item within the extension of "looks blue." But although she has managed to *say* (and think) truly *that the piece of paper looks blue*, she did not—indeed could not—properly issue a *visual report* about the color of the paper. There may be good reasons for crediting her with having mastered and mobilized the relevant color concepts. Still, arguably, *properly making* a *visual* color report (using the 'looks' locution) requires making it on the strength of a visual experience. Consequently, a person who under ordinary circumstances issues a claim about what color something looks to be in the absence of the relevant visual experience will be guilty of an impropriety, even if she issued the claim sincerely, and even if what she claimed (the product) is correct.

Perhaps a closer kind of example comes from acts of producing a gesture, facial expression, or turn of phrase that are conventionally associated with the expression of certain sentiments (e.g. shaking hands, tipping one's hat, showing the 'thumbs up,' rolling one's eyes, saying "Have a nice day," "Pleased to meet you," or "Sorry!"). It seems uncontroversial that there are conventional rules connecting the use of these diverse expressive vehicles with certain sentiments; the *point* of using them is to express the relevant sentiments. (In these cases, however, the relevant products—the utterances, gestures, or facial expressions—do not all s-express propositions that are *about* those sentiments. Gestures and facial expressions do not s-express anything. And "This is great!" is not *about* the expressed sentiment. Nor does it seem plausible that producing such expressions contextually *implies that* the speaker has the relevant sentiment, courtesy of the speaker's intention to communicate that information.) That there are such rules is of course no guarantee that one could *only* use the relevant expressions when one has the relevant sentiments. Tipping one's hat is used to express respect; but it may fail to express *my* respect. One can deliberately tip one's hat to deceive or mislead one's audience into thinking that one feels respect. But under deviant circumstances, one may tip one's hat sincerely and *still* fail to express *one's own* feeling of respect (just as one may sincerely emit "Ouch!" without actually feeling pain when primed to anticipate pain). It thus seems that the best way to think of the conventions as laying down norms for *proper* acts of producing the gestures, utterances, etc. Given the conventional link, the actual presence of the relevant sentiments is required for the act to be *proper*. Thus, one who says: "Pleased to meet you" without feeling at all pleased to meet her addressee, or "Sorry" while having absolutely no regret for what she is apologizing about, is guilty of a certain kind of impropriety. And total absence of the correct sentiments will make it difficult to view someone as having full mastery of the point of the discourse in question.

Finally, consider someone's saying: "That's ugly" pointing to a sofa in a furniture store. The product of this act (the sentence token) ostensibly ascribes an aesthetic property (being ugly) to a certain item (an ostended sofa). But for all that, it is compelling to take the speaker (or thinker) who produces the sentence token to be giving voice to a (negative) aesthetic attitude. Suppose she proceeded to purchase the sofa, put it in her living room, proudly show it to her friends, or even added: "I really like it"; in other words, suppose it became amply evident that she felt no aesthetic repulsion toward the sofa whatsoever. Then even if we came to think of her original pronouncement as sincerely made, we would question its propriety. The sofa may well *be* ugly (whatever makes that the case), our speaker may well be very good at tracking ugly things and separating them from the non-ugly ones, so she may be credited with mastery of the relevant aesthetic concepts, and may also have no intention to deceive anyone when saying "That's ugly." Nonetheless, given the absence of any negative aesthetic attitude or sentiment it seems that 'she has no business' *using* the epithet 'ugly.' Her act seems not unlike that of someone who *puts on* a smile or a sad face.[8]

The neo-expressivist view invokes a similar sort of expressive failure by way of explaining the internal link between ethical claims and motivational states. When it comes to *ethical* discourse and thought, absence of the appropriate motivational state is presumably connected with *more* than just failure to be a fully competent participant in the discourse. It will often also attest to criticizable moral failures and/or lamentable psychological failures of various sorts. But the expressive failure is what matters to capturing an internal connection between ethical claims and motivational states. On the present proposal, the internal link to motivation is to be captured through the appeal to the requirements on proper engagement in ethical discourse and reflection. A person *could* sincerely say (or think) that, for example, it would be morally wrong not to help someone in trouble on a given occasion, and yet not feel in the least inclined to offer the needed help. This may not be conceptually impossible; nor can a proponent of the neo-expressivist

---

[8] Or, consider someone like Star Trek's Data, incapable of normal human affective states, who learns to classify correctly some jokes as *funny* without ever feeling amused.

view insist that such a person cannot possibly understand what she is saying. Still, the person who says/thinks "This is the morally good thing to do" without any motivation to act accordingly will fail to properly issue an ethical claim just as the person who says "Congratulations!" without feeling in the least pleased for the addressee will fail to properly issue a congratulation or the person who says "This is beautiful" but has no positive aesthetic attitude toward the relevant item will fail to properly issue an aesthetic claim. For, in keeping with the version of internalism we have articulated here, the norms governing ethical discourse as well as reflection dictate that issuing genuine ethical claims (whether in speech or in thought) involves a-expressing motivational states or attitudes, and thus *properly* issuing such a claim requires the speaker (or thinker) to *have* the relevant state or attitude.

NEO-EXPRESSIVISM VS. NEO-SUBJECTIVISM

The strategy we have pursued for saving the expressivist insight while avoiding the core problem for noncognitivist semantics is, in effect, to enforce a separation between the semantic content of a claim considered as a product and the mental state that gets expressed by the person who makes the claim. There is, however, a more familiar distinction in the philosophy of language that might seem to be put to similar use. This is the distinction between asserted and implicated content. Often we can distinguish between the asserted content of what someone said and the content of what, due to linguistic conventions or conversational dynamics, they implicate. For one familiar example, a professor writing "Mr. Smith has good handwriting" in a letter of recommendation might be thought of as having asserted the proposition that Mr. Smith's handwriting is good and implicated the proposition that Mr. Smith is not a good student. And, it has been suggested that, when someone says, for example: "The krauts are at it again" she might be thought to have asserted the proposition that the Germans are gearing up for war again and implicated the proposition that the speaker dislikes the Germans.

This distinction provides the basis for a rival strategy for capturing the internal connection between ethical claims and motivations to action. The basic idea is subjectivist, but not in the traditional sense. Traditional subjectivists capture the way in which ethical claims are expressively loaded and, in turn, the internal connection between ethical claims and motivations to action by taking ethical claims to have something like *I dis/approve of x* as their asserted content. The proposal presently under discussion utilizes the distinction between asserted and implicated content to suggest that ethical claims do not assert propositions such as *I dis/approve of x* but rather implicate them. Because we take this ethical neo-subjectivism (as we might provocatively label it) to be the main rival to ethical neo-expressivism, we will consider it more carefully in this section and argue for the superiority of neo-expressivism.[9]

There are two ways to deploy the notion of implicature to develop a neo-subjectivist account. These are distinguished by two different kinds of implicature—conventional and conversational. In defense of the conventional-implicature view, David Copp writes:

> it seems plausible to me that the term "morally wrong" has a coloring such that, other things being equal, a person who asserts that an action is "morally wrong," using the term literally in asserting a moral proposition, *conventionally* implicates that she subscribes to a standard that prohibits the action ... This is explained by the fact that the use of "morally wrong" is governed by expressive linguistic conventions of the kind I have described.   (2001: 36–7)

Since he sees subscription to a moral standard as a conative mental state, there is a sense in which, on Copp's view, ethical claims express a conative mental state. He writes, "it is matter of linguistic convention that in asserting a basic moral proposition by uttering a sentence in which a moral term is used, a speaker 'expresses' a relevant conative state of mind, other things being equal" (2001: 14–15). However, this is not the direct sort of expression of a mental state that seems plausible in the case of avowals and that we used as our model in developing the neo-expressivist view of ethical claims above. Rather, it's an indirect sort of expression which Copp defines as "Frege-expression": "a speaker's use of a term Frege-expresses a state of mind just in case it is a matter of linguistic convention governing the use of the term that other things being equal, if a speaker asserts a simple isolated subject-predicate sentence in which the term is used literally, the fact that the speaker used the term conveys that the speaker is in the state of mind" (2001: 20). The important point is that, unlike expressivists who think that a conative mental state is *directly* expressed by an ethical claim, Copp thinks that the conative state is conveyed courtesy of the fact that an ethical claim, due to the linguistic conventions of moral language, *implicates* the self-ascriptive proposition *I (the speaker) subscribe to such-and-such moral standards.*

---

[9] In what follows, we discuss Copp's view as it's presented in Copp (2001). In his contribution to this volume, which is in part a response to an earlier draft of our chapter, Copp clarifies and amends the account offered in the earlier paper, and addresses some of the difficulties we raise below (as well as ones raised by Finlay (2004, 2005), which we also briefly discuss below). For obvious reasons, we cannot here undertake a detailed response to Copp's more recent paper (but see n. 14 below).

Stephen Finlay (2004, 2005) defends a similar view, but he uses the device of *conversational* implicature to explain "the fact that a speaker's uttering 'T is good' is a sign *by itself,* independent of extra-linguistic information about social values, human motivational nature, etc., that she possesses (and expresses) corresponding motivational attitude" (2004: 222). Finlay's view is that it is in virtue of the dynamics of conversations in which an ethical term occurs, rather than the linguistic conventions surrounding the term, that this internal connection between ethical claims and motivation should be explained. More specifically, he thinks that value terms such as 'good' are always indexed to interests or ends, but this index is often omitted in normal conversation because speaker and audience both typically know what the index is. He writes, "We are conversationally licensed to omit constituents of our assertions precisely when their presence and identity can be presupposed by our audience. Nonexplicitly indexed value judgments are thus conversationally appropriate just when the audience can be relied upon to presuppose or identify the desire-index without verbal directives" (2004: 217). So it is due to the conversational dynamics whereby we omit what can be assumed that Finlay thinks value claims can convey that their speaker has a particular motivational state. He writes,

> In some paradigm contexts ... of value judgement, when speakers neglect to specify the relevant interests, their audiences are conversationally justified in assuming them to be motivated by the interests their speech acts presuppose ... They therefore express pragmatically that they are relevantly motivated, hence that they approve of T, which they judge to satisfy those interests.   (2004: 219)

Again, the conative mental state is not directly expressed; rather it is expressed because the proposition (roughly) *I (the speaker) am in this conative state* is, due to the conversational dynamics, implicated.

What then is the proposition *asserted* on the neo-subjectivist view? Copp and Finlay take different lines. For a sentence such as 'A is good' Copp seems to think that the asserted content is (roughly) that the relevantly justified moral standard M positively values A, which he takes to be compatible with many different views (relativist and objectivist) of what the relevantly justified moral standard is. Finlay, on the other hand, argues for a relational analysis on which such a claim would assert (roughly) that moral standard M positively values A-ing, where the value of M is context-dependent (2004: 11–13).

Whatever their views on the propositional content of ethical claims, Finlay has an argument for why his way of working out the neo-subjectivist view of the connection between ethical claims and motivational states in terms of conversational implicature is superior to Copp's way of doing it in terms of conventional implicature. Briefly, Finlay notes that a key feature of conversational as opposed to conventional implicatures is that they are *cancelable*. And, as many examples typically used to argue against internalism suggest, what is implicated by ethical claims *is* cancelable. For instance, when Satan says, "Evil be thou my good," arguably he cancels any implication that he is motivated to do what is good and avoid doing what is evil. If he were to go on and say, "Torturing babies is evil," with a satanic grin, we wouldn't suppose him to be implicating that he dislikes the torture of babies. And, more generally, Finlay argues that there are clear cases where we adopt another's point of view in making value claims, and in so doing we cancel the implication that we have the relevant conative attitude. For example, one might be discussing a new Pope and his plans for the church, and, given an implicit understanding of his interests and convictions, when the question of gays in the clergy comes up, one might say, "Letting gays into the clergy would be a very bad thing." Here it seems that the conversational setting cancels the implicature that the speaker is motivated to adhere to a moral standard that forbids letting gays into the clergy. For the speaker is presumably speaking from the point of view of the Pope.

Perhaps Copp can reply to this argument, but what is important to notice for our immediate purposes is that, if Finlay is right, this represents a major drawback of the neo-subjectivist strategy as compared to our neo-expressivist strategy. For conversational implicature typically requires a *conversation*, which means that Finlay's view can explain only the way that ethical claims made *in conversation* are expressively loaded. Yet the expressive character of ethical claims and the attendant internal connection between making ethical claims and being motivated to act appears to cross the speech–thought divide. We don't have to be engaged in a conversation with someone to express our ethical commendation or condemnation of some action; indeed, we don't even have to be talking out loud. We can just *think* "Stealing is wrong," and it seems that there will be just the same sort of internal connection to motivations not to steal. On our neo-expressivist view, the notion that ethical claims directly express underlying motivational states applies both to ethical discourse and to ethical reflection. And this, we think, represents an advantage of our view over Finlay's. Of course, Finlay might argue that even in thought we can conceive of ourselves as, so to speak, conversing with ourselves or with an imaginary audience; and it is for the benefit of this audience that we conversationally implicate things in thought. However, though we don't doubt that this happens, we do doubt that this is the normal case of thinking, namely making claims in thought.

Since conventional implicature clearly occurs in thought as well as speech, this may provide fodder for Copp to argue that the notion of conventional implicature is a better way to work out the neo-subjectivist view after all. Moreover, perhaps, *pace* Finlay, cancelabity does *not* speak in favor of the conversational-implicature view. Copp argues that the implicature carried by ethical claims is *not* cancelable in the strong sense adumbrated by Grice (1989: 44) and deployed in Finlay's argument.[10] However, he suggests that it is cancelable in a weaker sense that is consistent with conventional implicature. This is the sense in which one can use a statement *intelligibly* even when the implicature carried by the use of a contained term is canceled either explicitly or contextually, so "[i]t would not be self-contradictory, and it would be fully intelligible as an assertion despite the nonstandard use of the term" (2001: 18). What he seems to have in mind are cases where there is some recognizable conversational point to using the term, which typically triggers the implicature, in a nonstandard way, which on this occasion does not trigger the implication. For instance (to use Copp's own type of example involving 'coloring'), an American who feels no particular contempt for the English might mock his Australian friends by saying, "You can't stand the Pommies, and you love beating them at cricket. But at the end of the day you all are very similar; you play all of the same sports." Here, the contempt implicated by the standard use of the colored term 'Pommie' is canceled by the context.[11]

Does this provide a plausible explanation of the cases of the amoralist, Satan, or anyone who apparently sincerely and comprehendingly makes ethical claims while lacking the relevant motivational state? The idea would be to argue that these individuals use ethical terms in a nonstandard way that is nonetheless intelligible, given the conversational point of so doing. For instance, this seems to be a plausible account of the case where Satan says, "Torturing babies is evil" with a satanic grin. We remain unsure whether this move can be generalized to save the conventional implicature way of working out the neo-subjectivist view. But what is worth noticing is that, even if it does, this move *too* trades on features of *conversation*, thus exposing Copp's view to the difficulty we pressed above against Finlay's view. For, given that the amoralist, Satan, and others can make (even if not completely felicitously) ethical claims *in speech* without having the relevant motivational state, it seems that they should be equally well able to make such claims *in thought*. However, in thought there are not the same sorts of conversational points which may make nonstandard uses of a

---

[10] For Finlay's response see his (2005: 13–17).

[11] We're here following Copp in supposing that the phenomenon of coloring is properly explained through implicature. This is not obvious to us, however. It may well be that the use of derogatory or approbatory terms is *also* better explained within a neo-expressivist framework. But we cannot explore this issue here.

term intelligible. So, again, a view which captures the expressive character of ethical claims in a unified way across speech and thought is preferable. And the neo-expressivist strategy of construing ethical claims, whether made in speech or thought, as directly expressing a motivational state does just that.

Perhaps there is a way for Copp to meet this worry by just insisting that the implicature carried by ethical claims is not really cancelable.[12] We are sympathetic to something like this idea because we think that making ethical claims while failing to be in the relevant motivational state represents an impropriety: one cannot sincerely and *properly* make an ethical claim while failing to be in the relevant motivational state. However, we want to argue that, even if there is some way to save Copp's view from the criticisms pressed so far, the neo-expressivist view still has a distinctive advantage over neo-subjectivist views (of whatever kind).

This advantage traces back to the original debate between subjectivists and expressivists. In this debate, virtually everyone agreed that subjectivism is faulty because it cannot explain why saying "No, you don't dislike torture"—as opposed to "No it isn't wrong"—is not a cogent way to disagree with someone who says, "Torture is wrong." Expressivism was thought to be superior to subjectivism precisely because it can explain this. According to expressivism, in saying "Torture is wrong" one doesn't report a negative attitude towards torture; one directly expresses it. To disagree, one must express an attitude that conflicts with the negative attitude; that's why one's conversant says something like "No, it isn't wrong."

Now, it would seem that the neo-subjectivist view, which has it that the asserted content of an ethical claim is (roughly):

Action A conforms (or doesn't conform) to moral standard M[13]

avoids this problem with traditional subjectivism. For this proposition doesn't have anything to do with the speaker's attitudes, so to respond to a claim that asserts this proposition with "No, you don't" is clearly inappropriate. Moreover, this account of the asserted content of ethical claims provides for a clear sense in which someone who responds to "Torture is wrong" with "No, it isn't wrong" is disagreeing. The first claim asserts the proposition that torture doesn't conform to some moral standard M, while the second claim asserts the proposition that torture does conform to M. These are contradictory propositions.

---

[12] This seems to be his current view. See Copp's contribution to this volume (Ch. 6).

[13] Again, as we said above, there are several available accounts of what determines the value of this M. Copp suggests that it is a matter of the "relevantly justified standards," which is meant to be vague and neutral between many different accounts. Finlay suggests that it is a matter of the conversational dynamics in which the sentence is uttered.

However, in our view, this can only be a special case of disagreement between ethical claims and it is unclear whether it constitutes genuinely *ethical* disagreement at all. To see this, recall the example of talking about the Pope and his policies. There is surely a genuine question about whether it is bad according to Catholicism to allow gays in the clergy. You may think that it is, and I may think that it isn't. Where we are discussing things from the Pope's point of view, we might then disagree by saying, "Letting gays into the clergy would be very bad" and "No, it wouldn't be very bad." But that is no *ethical* disagreement; it's rather a straightforward factual disagreement about what is good or bad *according to the moral standard of Catholicism*, which standard *we may both reject*.

A genuinely ethical disagreement or, at least, the more standard sort of disagreement we encounter in ethical discourse is one where we accept different ethical standards (or moral principles) and because of this evaluate some action differently. For instance, the committed pacifist says "War is always wrong" and the skeptical hawk says "No, it's not always wrong." Here, in order to capture disagreement, the neo-subjectivist would say that what the pacifist is asserting is that war never conforms with some moral standard M, whereas the hawk is asserting that war does sometimes conform to M. But this is surely implausible. Rather, if we follow neo-subjectivists in thinking that the asserted propositions are of the form:

Action A conforms (or doesn't conform) to moral standard M

we should say that the pacifist is asserting that war doesn't conform to moral standard P and the hawk is asserting that war sometimes conforms to moral standard H. However, there's no disagreement in that. Nor is there disagreement in the putatively implicated propositions, respectively, that the one speaker is motivated to adhere to P and that the other is motivated to adhere to H. We've lost the apparent disagreement.

So neo-subjectivism appears to be subject to the same sort of difficulty that has beset classical subjectivism—the difficulty of explaining the full range of genuine ethical disagreement. By contrast, neo-expressivism has two avenues for locating potential disagreement. Like the neo-subjectivist, the neo-expressivist thinks that ethical sentences s-express propositions, and it is surely possible to use sentences which s-express contradictory propositions. But the neo-expressivist is not committed to construing ethical propositions as descriptive of ethical standards or codes. It is open to other construals, which would make it possible to have disagreement even between individuals who agree on what a given ethical standard prescribes. Moreover, for the neo-expressivist, there are also the motivational attitudes that are directly a-expressed by one who uses ethical sentences to make ethical claims. These attitudes can stand in conflict, which represents a different sort of disagreement.[14]

[14] Strictly speaking, Copp's view about the proposition implicated by ethical claims could be neutral with respect to the proposition s-expressed by moral sentences. So, for instance, he could allow that moral claims about something being wrong express the proposition not that some action is forbidden by standard M, but that some action has the *sui generis* nonnatural property of wrongness. Or, he could adopt our disquotational tack from above and say that these claims express the proposition that the action in question is wrong. In either case, he could then claim to explain what we are calling genuine ethical disagreement at the level of asserted content rather than at the level of implicated proposition. However, insofar as his account is supposed to remain neutral about the proposition expressed by ethical claims, it won't yet explain the appearance of disagreement. Indeed, in his contribution to the present volume, Copp explicitly embraces this sort of neutrality, and retracts the epithet *"realist* expressivism" in favor of *"cognitivist* expressivism." But note, first, that this would allow him to accommodate 'cognitive' disagreement only on *some* construals of the content of ethical sentences; there will remain those construals (e.g. *A is forbidden by contextually determined standards M*) that will still not afford *ethical* disagreement. And, secondly, it looks as though cognitivist expressivism could at best accommodate the appearance of one sort of disagreement. For note that, on the amended view, it is still the case that the proposition implicated by an ethical claim (or rather, 'simplicated,' to use Copp's now-preferred term) is a self-ascriptive subjective proposition—a proposition about what one's motivational attitude is. But such propositions, viz. "I don't approve of murder" (s)implicated by one person vs. "I approve of murder" (s)implicated by another do *not* conflict. By contrast, the neo-expressivist view can still explain the appearance of conflict between e.g. "Murder is wrong" and "Murder is not wrong" along traditional expressivist lines, in terms of the *mental states a-expressed* by those making the ethical claims, *regardless* of how one construes the proposition s-expressed by these sentences.

The source of the remaining difficulty, as we see it, is that Copp is still working within a subjectivist framework insofar as the link he wishes to forge between ethical claims and motivation is made via a proposition *about the speaker's own mental states*, which the speaker communicates (albeit indirectly, by 'simplicating' it). We are told that the speaker who says "Murder is wrong" indirectly conveys the information ('simplicates') that she disapproves of murder whereas the one who says "Murder is not wrong" conveys that she doesn't disapprove of it. But from an expressivist perspective such as Ayer's (see quotation above p. 135), this does nothing to explain the disagreement in attitude *unless* we add that in conveying this information the two speakers directly *express conflicting attitudes* (as they would if, for example, they were to *avow* their attitudes in self-ascribing them). Copp helps himself to this idea by defining "Frege-expression" in such a way as to collapse Ayer's distinction between a speaker directly expressing a state of mind and asserting or even (s)implicating, *that* she has it. (To wit: "a speaker's use of a term Frege-*expresses a state of mind* just in case it is a matter of linguistic convention ... that the fact that the speaker used the term *conveys that* the speaker is in the state of mind" (2001: 20, emphasis added). In the contribution to the present volume, it is amply evident that Copp thinks we can move freely between the idea of a speaker expressing her disapproval and her conveying the information *that* she disapproves. However, it is not clear to us how simply appealing to the fact that speakers convey information about their motivational states *indirectly* (by 'simplicating' it), as opposed to directly stating it (as subjectivists would have it) helps capture the kind of ethical disagreement Ayer points to. Moreover (and relatedly), it is also not clear to us how Copp's 'cognitivist

So, in sum, we suspect that there are problems for either way of developing the neo-subjectivist view having to do with its dependence on *conversation* to explain the internal connection between ethical claims and motivation. However, even if these can be overcome, we think that the neo-subjectivist will still have problems accounting for the full range of ethical disagreement.

SUMMARY, OBJECTIONS, AND REPLIES

Ethical neo-expressivism is motivated by a desire to recognize the semantic continuities between ethical and nonethical claims while capitalizing on the expressivist explanation of the connection ethical claims bear to motivation. Semantic continuity can be preserved as long as ethical claims *qua products* are taken to s-express truth-evaluable propositions. The connection to motivation, on the other hand, is accommodated by considering ethical claims *qua acts* and supposing that when making such claims we a-express motivational attitudes. We think the view is sufficiently broad and neutral that it should be acceptable to opposing parties of many central debates in ethics and metaethics.

One standardly central issue we have elided is the question of what sort of mental states play the requisite motivational role in creatures like us. As far as we're concerned, there is an interesting and substantive debate here concerning *moral psychology*, a debate that is not to be automatically settled by one's views about what ethical claims regarded as products s-express. Much of this debate has proceeded as though Humeanism is true. If that's right, then the relevant states cannot be purely cognitive states such as beliefs, in which case it may very well be true that when making ethical claims we a-express *conative* states. These are the kind of states whose presence (in combination with the presence of beliefs) is invoked by the Humean in explanations of actions.[15] However, the important point is that, whatever one's account of moral motivation is, it need not rule out the possibility that the products of acts of making ethical claims still have propositional character and possess truth-evaluable content.

We have allowed that these products, ethical sentence- (or thought-) tokens, may not admit of any illuminating paraphrastic analysis, that ethical propositions may have any number of different kinds of 'truth-makers'

---

expressivism' can genuinely claim to do justice to the internalist link that the expressivist seeks to capture. However, spelling out these concerns goes beyond what we can do in this chapter.

[15] These explanations are the sort pursued in action theory, rather than the sort we might want from a fully physicalistic theory or from a social-political theory.

(or none), and that in acts of making ethical claims, speakers may a-express either cognitive or noncognitive states (or both). Thus the account of ethical claims that we have presented purports to remain relatively neutral on the nature of the *meaning* of ethical claims, of their *metaphysics*, and of the nature of the *motivational states* they express. How could a substantive (and successful) account of the connection between ethical claims and motivation remain neutral on these key issues? In the remainder of this section, we try to answer this question by addressing a few potential objections to the alleged neutrality of our account.

Ethical claims, we have said, should be taken to s-express truth-evaluable propositions. But which propositions do they express? What *do* ethical sentences say or mean? We think that decades of trying to offer revealing meaning analyses of ethical sentences should have taught us that the attempt may be futile. Indeed, if there's a clear lesson to be learned from Moore's (1903) Open Question argument, it is that there's little hope for reconstructing the meaning of ethical sentences *in other terms* (whether normative *or* nonnormative). Here we are in agreement with Blackburn who writes, "Moore's negative argument against identifying moral propositions in different terms remains convincing. I believe he was absolutely correct about the content of the moral proposition. It is what it is, and not another thing" (1998: 86). That is, there is not much to be said here as far as the *semantics of English* (or any other language) is concerned, at least not by way of offering a response to the question: what do competent speakers mean when they say (or think): "Murdering innocent people is morally wrong," "Helping the poor is morally good," "One ought not to torture animals," "Taxing the rich so little is unfair" (or their translations into other languages). Ethical sentences, however, are not unique in this regard. There is not much hope for a paraphrastic meaning analysis of "John loves Mary," or "Tom is a handsome fellow," "Grass is green," and even of "Energy equals mass times speed of light squared," "The wreckage was caused by the explosion," or "Whales are mammals." Even if we deny that there can be such an analysis, we can still point to conceptual or inferential connections between the relevant sentences and other sentences. So we are not left without things to say about the meaning of the relevant sentences. However, we *are* giving up on the possibility of *saying in other words* what a sentence in the given class is used to say. This is what we had in mind when suggesting that the proposition an ethical claim s-expresses should be specified disquotationally; that, for example, "Tolerance is a virtue" s-expresses the proposition that, well, tolerance is a virtue.

We do not maintain that meaning can be assigned disquotationally to *any* syntactically well-formed sentence (what with sentences such as "Colorless green ideas sleep furiously" or "'Twas brillig and the slithy toves did gyre and gimble" around). To say that we should assign meaning disquotationally is *not* to say that for a sentence to *have* meaning it is *sufficient* that it be possible to disquote it. Meaning*fulness* requires much more than that; but we would deny that it requires the possibility of providing a synonymous sentence, analytic paraphrase, or translation. Obviously more could be said here about deep issues in the philosophy of language; but we must leave further discussion for another occasion.

In addition to semantic neutrality, we want to allow that it makes sense to speak of an ethical sentence expressing a proposition prior to settling on the correct metaphysics for ethical discourse. Thus, we are assuming that it can make sense to say that by "Tolerance is a virtue" we mean *that* tolerance is a virtue, even though we may not (yet) know what, if anything, constitutes the nature or essence of tolerance, or virtue. We realize, however, that on some views of meaning, if there is *no* property for "tolerance" or "virtue" to denote, sentences involving these terms will lack all meaning (so there will be no proposition expressed by them and no thoughts they can properly be said to articulate). We find comfort in the fact that this view of meaning is controversial and will face great difficulties even outside the ethical context. We trust that if the difficulty with assigning meaning to "Phlogiston is combustible," given the (perhaps necessary) non-existence of phlogiston, can be overcome, so can the difficulty with "Tolerance is a virtue."

We think that a virtue of the view we are proposing is that it locates the link between ethical discourse and motivation in *acts* of making ethical claims rather than either in any aspect of their semantic content *or* in their truth-makers. This is what saves us from the traditional dilemma of either subscribing to non-cognitivist semantics, which Geach argued is hopeless, or embracing necessarily motivating properties, which Mackie argued is queer.

This brings us to another worry. If the point of making ethical claims is indeed as the neo-expressivist maintains, and if, moreover, it is allowed that there are no facts that make ethical claims true, why is it that ethical claims need to be understood as s-expressing propositions at all? Why not go back to Ayer's expressivism? Put differently, if we begin with the (anti-realist) metaphysical assumption that there are no ethical facts for us to describe, then, even granting that ethical claims exhibit propositional form, why should we suppose that this form is anything more than merely superficial?

Of course, on one way of understanding the classic Frege–Geach problem, it's necessary to see ethical sentences as s-expressing propositions in the same way as any other indicative sentence does in order to explain the logical interaction between the sentences that form *inter alia* valid *modus ponens* inferences. However, we think it is important to note here that the issue of the propositionality of ethical sentences is orthogonal to the issue of what someone who utters these sentences a-expresses. For compare: utterances of "Yuck!" typically serve to a-express an utterer's state of disgust. "Yuck," it seems, is not a descriptive term whose function is to denote an observed property of things. For all that, "Yuck" can be replaced by utterances that have propositional form: "This is yucky!"[16] Now, having recognized the roots of "This is yucky" in the purely expressive "Yuck," couldn't we leave it at that, notwithstanding the semantic continuity of this sentence with sentences such as "This is 5 feet long"? Must we insist that it has to s-express a truth-evaluable proposition, especially given how implausible it is to think of the world as furnished with the property of yuckiness? Or think of other sentences whose characteristic use is to give voice to present states of mind: "It's nice to meet you," "I'm much obliged." These too exhibit semantic continuity with ordinary descriptive claims such as "It's hard to pick up this suitcase," and "I'm walking down Franklin Street." Despite their expressive function and origin, once possessed of propositional dress, they admit of significant negation, and can presumably be embedded in conditionals and other propositional contexts (including logical inferences).

But this just seems to be grist to our mill. Reflection on these other clear cases of *purely* expressive uses of language suggests that semantic continuity (and the features that give rise to most statements of the Frege–Geach problem) comes with acquired propositional form, and does not require descriptive origins or grounding in objective facts.[17] This is all the more reason why we should have recourse to a relatively innocuous notion of a proposition, one that does not require analytic paraphrase and does not commit us to 'robust' truth-makers. It is precisely this notion that we invoked when claiming that ethical claims s-express propositions, by way

---

[16] This replacement process seems to be very productive. And the expressive term need not always be replaced by an adjective; it can be replaced by a noun. One hears parents saying things like: "Do you have an owie?" In this context, it is also instructive to consider utterances such as: "This is so *funny*!" "*Great* to see you!" "I *hate* you!" "This is *gorgeous*!", and so on, which can be thought as replacements of non-propositional expressions (and which, moreover, have distinctively expressive uses in thought, and not just in conversation).

[17] Although we don't have space to discuss it fully here, we would say something similar about the sort of worry pressed by Dorr (2002) about the nature of the mental states involved in accepting an ethical claim. Dorr argues that one must agree that these states are belief-like states on pain of otherwise endorsing bad forms of inference such as wishful-thinking. However, even if they must be counted as beliefs in the sense that they are the proper kinds of mental states to reason to and from, this doesn't imply that they have to be beliefs in the sense of being mental states that aim to represent/describe the objective features of the world. We can similarly reason to and from states of accepting propositions of the form 'This is yucky.'

of avoiding the difficulties posed by semantic continuity for traditional expressivism.

This is not to deny that there may be an interesting story yet to be told about the emergence of ethical propositional content, *if one denies* that ethical terms/concepts are genuinely descriptive and serve to pick out objective properties of things (or even just 'response-dependent' properties). Here's one way such a 'genetic' story might go. In keeping with the idea that ethical language and thought have their origins in expressive behavior, we can perhaps think of ethical terms such as "good/bad," "right/wrong" as initially serving as verbal replacements for 'reactive' verbal emissions of the "Yum/Yuck" or "Boo/Hurray" variety.[18] We have seen that even an uncontroversially expressive term such as "Yuck" can acquire adjectival form and work its way into indicative sentences, much like color terms (which, at least on some views, begin their lives as externalizations of human visual responses). What could be the point of endowing an expressive term with a grammatical form that allows it to be used predicatively? Speculation: doing so affords what we may call 'discursive negotiation.' When we move from "Yuck" to "Yucky," and thereafter to "X is yucky," we are poised to draw others' attention and attend ourselves to features of X relevant to our yuck-reactions; and our own 'yuck' reactions become ripe for intersubjective give-and-take. (Something like this may happen when terms like "ought" and "should" come to replace verbal "Do/Don't" injunctions.)

In the case of "yuck" it may, however, be argued that the gain is purely verbal. Nothing will be lost if we gave up on the advantages of being able to say/think: "X is yucky." This is not completely clear, since it seems as if we can, once they have taken on a propositional guise, embed our claims about what is yucky in complex logical constructions. Still, we recognize the intuition that moral discourse involves more than trade in subjective reactions. However, a neo-expressivist account can respect that intuition. For an expressivist may be able to locate a relevant difference between ethical discourse and yuckiness discourse in the function of the very states of mind to which (she claims) we initially give voice when using ethical terms. Ethical terms are, arguably, not merely associated with approbation

---

[18] For a story of this sort concerning the expressive character of avowals, see Bar-On (2004: ch. 7). For 'quasi-genetic' stories in the ethical case, see Gibbard (1990: ch. 3) and Blackburn (1998: ch. 3). Bar-On (1995) briefly discusses the philosophical status of such stories in connection with a 'genetic' interpretation of Grice's account of nonnatural meaning. Whichever way one wants to spell out the details, we could imagine a stage at which ethical terms were introduced into language to replace specific sorts of expressive verbal emissions (in the style of Sellars' (1956) "Myth of Jones"). We should emphasize that we are not ourselves committed to this particular story. We are here offering it only by way of forestalling objections to our claim that the neo-expressivist account can remain neutral in the ways we have indicated.

and disapprobation *tout court*, but with *commendation* and *condemnation*. Perhaps, then, we should think of the initial states of mind to which the use of these terms serves to give voice as rather more complex than states of disgust, enjoyment, dis/pleasure, etc. Expressing such states does not just play the role of displaying merely subjective reactions but rather serves to display reactions and behavioral tendencies that one expects others to share. Perhaps, for example, they are states that incorporate a person's perception or apprehension of potential more or less immediate consequences of a perceived act or conduct, and involve a person's desire for herself or others to alter the perceived situation or conduct, to promote or prevent them.[19] If so, then this may give rise to a difference in what happens at the predicative stage. Whereas "X is yucky" can (perhaps) continue to be interchanged with the purely expressive "Yuck" with no appreciable loss, arguably, "X is good/bad; right/wrong" and "You ought/not to do A" may not. Whereas gustatory discourse could remain at (or return to) a primitive emotive stage without much loss, ethical discourse has additional point and purpose, which is only fully served by a propositional discourse.[20]

Obviously, a lot more needs to be said. We think that we have said enough, however, to indicate in broad outline the kind of 'genetic' story one could try to tell to explain why ethical discourse naturally takes on propositional form while remaining expressive in its function. What is important for us as neo-expressivists is to insist that, even if one wants to tell such a story about ethical discourse, there is no reason to expect that we should be able to read the story off the *semantic* behavior of ethical sentences. Instead, we should locate whatever 'traces' are left by the 'genesis' of ethical discourse in the account of what those who make ethical claims a-express rather than in what the claims s-express.

Perhaps there are other views concerning the expressive character of ethical claims yet to be articulated. However, we think that the neo-expressivist view we have outlined here has considerable advantages over traditional forms of expressivism and subjectivism as well as over the neo-subjectivist views that have been defended in more recent years. The relative neutrality of ethical neo-expressivism allows it to avoid some of the main difficulties that beset other views of ethical discourse and thought. And this very same neutrality, we believe, should make it acceptable to members of otherwise opposing camps in the contemporary metaethical debate.

---

[19] This is in line with Gibbard (2003: 65), who argues that disagreement is key. You can't disagree with a state of disgust, but you can disagree with a moral commitment.

[20] The above suggestion was couched in terms of *discourse* that affords intersubjective negotiation. A fully adequate story would need to show us how to extend the notion of discursive negotiation from the intersubjective case of ethical discourse to the intrasubjective case of ethical thinking.

REFERENCES

Austin, John (1962) *How to Do Things with Words* (Cambridge, MA: Harvard University Press).

Ayer, A. J. (1936/1946) *Language, Truth and Logic* (London: Gollancz).

Bar-On, Dorit (1995) 'Reconstructing "Meaning": Grice and the Naturalization of Semantics' *Pacific Philosophical Quarterly* 76: 83–116.

—— (2004) *Speaking My Mind: Expression and Self-Knowledge* (Oxford: Clarendon Press).

Blackburn, Simon (1984) *Spreading the Word: Groundings in the Philosophy of Language* (Oxford: Clarendon Press).

—— (1998) *Ruling Passions: A Theory of Practical Reasoning* (Oxford: Clarendon Press).

Chrisman, Matthew (2008) 'Expressivism, Inferentialism, and Saving the Debate' *Philosophy and Phenomenological Research* 77(2).

—— (Ms) 'Normative Thought and Inference'.

Copp, David (2001) 'Realist-Expressivism: A Neglected Option for Moral Realism' *Social Philosophy and Policy* 18: 1–43.

Davidson, Donald (1967) 'The Logical Form of Action Sentences,' in Nicholas Rescher (ed.), *The Logic of Decision and Action* (Pittsburgh: University of Pittsburgh Press).

Davis, Wayne (2003) *Meaning, Expression and Thought* (Cambridge: Cambridge University Press).

Dorr, Cian (2002) 'Non-Cognitivism and Wishful Thinking' *Nous* 36: 97–103.

Finlay, Stephen (2004) 'The Conversational Practicality of Value Judgement' *Journal of Ethics* 8: 205–23.

—— (2005) 'Value and Implicature' *Philosophers' Imprint* 5: 1–20.

Fodor, Jerry (1998) *Concepts: Where Cognitive Science Went Wrong* (New York: Oxford University Press).

Geach, P. T. (1965) 'Assertion' *Philosophical Review* 74: 449–65.

Gibbard, Allan (1990) *Wise Choices, Apt Feelings: A Theory of Normative Judgment* (Cambridge, MA: Harvard University Press).

—— (2003) *Thinking How to Live* (Cambridge, MA: Harvard University Press).

Grice, H. P. (1989) *Studies in the Way of Words* (Cambridge, MA: Harvard University Press).

Green, Mitch. (2007) *Self-Expression* (Oxford: Oxford University Press).

Kalderon, Mark (2005) *Moral Fictionalism* (Oxford: Clarendon Press).

Lewis, David (1970) 'General Semantics' *Synthese* 22: 18–67.

—— (1975) 'Languages and Language,' in Keith Gunderstone (ed.), *Minnesota Studies in the Philosophy of Science* (Minneapolis: University of Minnesota Press).

Moore, G. E. (1903) *Principia Ethica* (Cambridge: Cambridge University Press).

Ridge, Michael (2006) 'Ecumenical Expressivism: Finessing Frege' *Ethics* 116(2): 302–36.

Sellars, Wilfrid (1956) *Empiricism and the Philosophy of Mind* (Indianapolis: Bobbs-Merrill).

——(1969) 'Language as Thought and as Communication' *Philosophy and Phenomenological Research* 29: 506–27.

Stevenson, Charles L. (1937) 'Emotive Meaning of Moral Terms' *Mind* 46: 14–31.

6

Realist-Expressivism and Conventional Implicature

David Copp

Anna says that capital punishment is morally wrong, yet whenever she hears that a criminal is about to be executed, she seems indifferent. There is never any indication that she disapproves of capital punishment, other than the fact that she says it is wrong. When we challenge her, she continues to insist that capital punishment is wrong, but she agrees that she has no negative attitude toward it. She denies that she disapproves of it. Something appears to be amiss. Her assertion seems to be at odds with the indifference that she displays and avows. Perhaps she does not really believe that capital punishment is wrong. Perhaps she does not know her own mind, or perhaps she is being insincere. Or perhaps she does not have a thorough understanding of what she is saying, in saying capital punishment is wrong. Perhaps she thinks she is merely categorizing capital punishment—bringing it under a descriptive category—in saying it is wrong.

Some would argue that a fundamental misunderstanding of this latter kind underlies all versions of moral realism. Allan Gibbard claims, for instance, that "the special element that makes normative thought and language normative" is that "it involves a kind of endorsement—an endorsement that any descriptivistic analysis treats inadequately" (1990: 33).[1] According to *noncognitivist-expressivism*, the states of mind we describe as

In working on this chapter, I received helpful comments and suggestions from many people. In particular I would like to thank Dorit Bar-On, Andrew Alwood, Matthew Chrisman, Michael Glanzberg, Christopher Hom, Michael Jubien, Robert May, Mark van Roojen, Jon Tresan, Pekka Väyrynen, and two anonymous readers. I am especially grateful to Kent Bach, Stephen Finlay, and Mark Schroeder for extensive and detailed criticisms of my views. A version of the chapter was presented to the Department of Philosophy at the University of California, Davis. I am grateful to the audience on that occasion for a useful discussion.

[1] See also Blackburn (1988).

moral "beliefs" are not actually cognitive states, but are instead conative or motivational states, and our moral judgments express these states. On this view, then, there is more than merely an oddity in Anna's saying that capital punishment is morally wrong but then denying that she disapproves or has any other relevant conative attitude. There is a kind of pragmatic contradiction involved. For according to noncognitivist-expressivism, in saying that capital punishment is wrong, Anna is expressing disapproval (or some other relevant conative attitude). In denying that she disapproves, she is undercutting the sincerity of her claim that capital punishment is wrong.[2]

Realist-expressivism seeks to accommodate intuitions that underlie non-cognitivism, such as the intuition that moral discourse involves a kind of endorsement, and the intuition that there is something like a pragmatic contradiction in making a moral assertion while denying that one has any relevant conative attitude. It seeks to do this, however, while also accommodating the intuitions that underlie moral realism, such as the intuition that moral beliefs are, straightforwardly, beliefs. It aims to achieve these goals, moreover, without adopting the subjectivist view that moral claims *report* our attitudes. It holds that moral assertions *express* relevant conative attitudes such as approval and disapproval and that they also express moral beliefs. According to realist-expressivism, in claiming that capital punishment is morally wrong, Anna expresses both a belief and a relevant conative attitude, presumably a kind of disapproval.

Realist-expressivism is therefore a hybrid view. As a kind of moral cognitivism, it accepts the *cognitivist thesis*. That is, our moral thoughts are beliefs, properly so-called—they are cognitive states that represent moral states of affairs and that can be accurate or inaccurate to those states of affairs; moreover, in making a moral assertion, we express a moral belief. As a kind of expressivism, realist-expressivism also accepts the *expressivist thesis*. That is, in making moral assertions, we express certain characteristic conative states of mind. Realist-expressivism is a kind of expressivism that is compatible with any plausible realist account of the truth conditions of moral beliefs.

In this chapter, as I did in the paper where I introduced the idea of realist-expressivism (Copp 2001), I take moral realism as given, and I also take as given the intuitions that underlie the expressivist thesis. My central goal is to show that moral realism is compatible with the expressivist thesis and the intuitions that underlie it. In Copp (2001), I took these intuitions

---

[2] For the notion of a pragmatic contradiction, see Bach (1999: 364). Bach says a similar pragmatic contradiction would be involved in asserting a proposition but then denying that one believes it, as illustrated by Moore's paradox (p. 364 n. 39).

to support the *semantic thesis*, the thesis that the meaning of the moral predicates ensures that a person making a moral assertion using a moral predicate expresses a suitable conative attitude. I took pejorative predicates as my model, predicates such as "wop." To explain how such predicates work, I invoked Paul Grice's idea of "conventional implicature" (Grice 1989).[3] Accordingly, I suggested that the meaning of the moral predicates is such that a person making a moral assertion *conventionally implicates* that she has a suitable conative attitude. This is the conventional implicature version of realist-expressivism. In Copp (2001), I also had the goal of showing that the version of moral realism that I initially defended in Copp (1995) can be combined with realist-expressivism, and that it suggests a specific view about the nature of the conative attitudes we express in making moral assertions. My overall view therefore is a complex package. For present purposes, however, I set much of this aside in order to focus on defending the conventional implicature version of realist-expressivism.

The conventional implicature version of realist-expressivism has been criticized for a variety of reasons. In this chapter, I aim to respond to the main criticisms. In Section 1, I explain the sense in which realist-expressivism is an ecumenical view. In Section 2, I discuss the idea of expression. In Section 3, I outline the conventional implicature version of realist-expressivism. In Section 4, I discuss Kent Bach's arguments that there is no such thing as conventional implicature properly so-called (Bach 1999). Fortunately, nothing in my position requires me to disagree with Bach, for, I believe, his arguments do not show that there is no such thing as the kind of phenomenon I had in mind. Hence, in Sections 5 and 6, I define and explain "conventional simplicature," which is a close relative of conventional implicature. The view I want to defend, then, is the "conventional *simplicature* version" of realist-expressivism. In Sections 7 and 8, I discuss objections to the conventional simplicature view, especially those of Stephen Finlay (2005). I argue that the objections are unsuccessful. I conclude that the conventional simplicature version of realist-expressivism appears to be defensible.

1. AN ECUMENICAL VIEW

Realist-expressivism initially might seem a surprising view. Pejorative terms illustrate the basic idea. In the usage I have in mind, to say that someone is a "wop" is to say that the person is Italian while also expressing contempt

---

[3] Others have done so as well. See Davis (2005: 148); Williamson (forthcoming).

for Italians. If Betty says, "Leonardo is a wop," she expresses the belief that Leonardo is Italian and also expresses contempt for Italians. One version of realist-expressivism would claim that typical moral predicates, such as "morally right," are similar to pejorative terms in that their use can both ascribe a property and express a relevant conative attitude. The idea would be that, in asserting that capital punishment is morally wrong, Anna expresses the belief that capital punishment has the property of being wrong and also expresses disapproval of (or some other relevant conative attitude toward) actions that have the property of being wrong.

Realist-expressivism as such is, however, an ecumenical view. On the cognitivist side, it is compatible with any plausible version of moral realism.[4] It holds that the contribution made by a predicate such as "morally wrong" to the propositions semantically expressed by sentences in which it occurs is relevantly similar to the contribution made by a nonmoral 'descriptive' predicate to the propositions semantically expressed by sentences in which it occurs. The semantics of "morally wrong" in the sentence "Lying is morally wrong" is relevantly similar to the semantics of "widespread" in the sentence "Lying is widespread." Beyond this, realist-expressivism is neutral on a wide range of questions. It takes no position on the truth conditions of moral beliefs. It is neutral regarding the disagreement between moral naturalism and nonnaturalism. Indeed it is neutral in the debate between realists and cognitivist anti-realists, or error theorists or fictionalists. Perhaps, for this reason, I should have called it "cognitivist-expressivism" rather than "realist-expressivism," but I don't want to cause confusion by changing terminology at this point.

Similarly, on the expressivist side, realist-expressivism is ecumenical. First, it is compatible with a variety of views regarding the nature of the conative attitudes that are expressed by persons in making moral assertions. Any plausible version would hold that a person who said that lying is morally wrong would thereby express some kind of disapproval of lying and that a person who said that honesty is a virtue would thereby express approval of honesty. Different versions of realist-expressivism might nevertheless provide different accounts of the nature of moral approval or disapproval.[5]

---

[4] Realist-expressivism is logically independent of the naturalistic moral realism that I initially proposed in Copp (1995). A criticism of the latter is not a criticism of realist-expressivism. This is a partial response to Bar-On and Chrisman (2009).

[5] One could perhaps take a cognitivist view of moral attitudes, holding, for instance, that moral disapproval of lying is just the belief that lying is wrong. On such a view, it is trivial that in expressing the belief that lying is wrong one expresses disapproval of lying. This is not a version of realist-expressivism. According to realist-expressivism, a person who asserts that lying is wrong thereby expresses a relevant *conative* attitude.

Second, different versions of realist-expressivism would propose different accounts of the sense in which moral assertions 'express' conative attitudes, or different explanations of the (putative) expressivist fact that, in making moral assertions using moral terms, we express relevant conative attitudes. Realist-expressivism as such is not committed to taking pejorative terms as the model of how this works. Moreover, realist-expressivism is not committed to the semantic thesis, according to which the expressivist fact has an explanation in the semantics of the moral predicates. One might hold instead, as I once did myself, that the expressivist fact is explained by the fact that a person making a moral assertion typically *conversationally implicates* that she has an appropriate attitude.[6] I think that a stronger, semantic explanation can be defended, but realist-expressivism as such is neutral on this issue. Moreover, even if one accepts the semantic thesis, realist-expressivism can be developed in various ways. The conventional implicature version is only one kind of realist-expressivism.[7]

It is perhaps worth mentioning that realist-expressivism is not the only way to hybridize cognitivism with expressivism. There are also anti-realist or noncognitivist hybrid views. For example, a noncognitivist semantics for moral predicates, according to which their meaning is such that moral utterances are essentially expressive of conative attitudes, and according to which these predicates do not ascribe moral properties, could be combined with a view of the pragmatics of moral assertion according to which a person making a moral assertion also typically expresses a belief. Such a view would differ from realist-expressivism, for it would deny that the semantics of the moral predicates is such that moral assertions express *moral* beliefs that are true only if relevant *moral facts* obtain. There are different views of this kind just as there are different kinds of realist-expressivism.[8]

---

[6] See Copp (1995: 35). See Finlay (2004).

[7] Dan Boisvert (2008) proposes a view he calls "expressive-assertivism," which appears to be a version of realist-expressivism. Bar-On and Chrisman also seem to propose a version of realist-expressivism, a position they call "ethical neo-expressivism" (2009).

[8] R. M. Hare says, for example, that moral terms have "descriptive meaning" as well as "evaluative meaning." In commending things, we apply standards of evaluation. If a speaker's standards are well known, Hare says, we can infer that she would attribute certain descriptive characteristics to the things she evaluates. "If a parson says of a girl that she is a good girl, we can form a shrewd idea, of what description she is; we may expect her to go to church, for example." This is "part of what the *parson* means," says Hare. Hare says, however, that the "descriptive meaning" of "good" is "secondary to the evaluative." See Hare (1952: 146). For other examples of anti-realist hybrid views, see Blackburn (1988), Gibbard (1990), Barker (2000), Ridge (2006).

2. VARIETIES OF EXPRESSION

It is not clear how to understand the thesis that a person making a moral assertion *expresses* a conative attitude. The word "express" is here being used in a technical sense. There is a usage in which the word is used to refer to a semantic relation between a declarative sentence and a proposition. In this usage, a sentence would be said to "express" a proposition.[9] But we are here interested in the use of "express" to refer to a relation between a person making a speech act and a state of mind.[10] A person who assertorically utters the sentence "Leonardo is a wop," would 'express' the belief that Leonardo is Italian and also 'express' contempt for Italians. But there are different expression relations. Without claiming to be exhaustive, I briefly discuss four.

First, "expression" in some cases refers to a relation of 'evincing' or 'venting' a state of mind. For example, in crying, I may be evincing sadness. If I injure myself and say spontaneously, "It hurts," I am evincing my pain. I take it that evincing a state of mind is a matter of manifesting a state of mind by exhibiting behavior that is a spontaneous effect of one's being in that state of mind, although one could perhaps modify the behavior or inhibit it. A person might not be evincing pain in saying "It hurts." She might be answering a question about how it feels to undergo a certain kind of dental procedure. She might be asserting that it hurts, and doing so deliberately, rather than as a spontaneous uninhibited effect of believing it. Assertion is not generally a matter of evincing a belief.

It is not in general true that a person making a moral assertion evinces a conative attitude, although in special cases someone might. Suppose a person recoils in horror on seeing someone torturing a cat and blurts, "That's wrong." This response might qualify as evincing disapproval. But a person who says, "That's wrong," could be answering a question about a complicated public policy proposal. In a typical case of this kind, her utterance would not evince disapproval, even if it would express disapproval,

---

[9] For simplicity, throughout this chapter I ignore sentences containing indexicals and other context sensitive expressions.

[10] To be more exact, relations of the kind at issue hold between a person, a speech-act property (such as the property of asserting that *p*) and a state-of-mind property (such as the property of believing-that-*p* or the property of having-contempt-for-Italians) when, in performing a given speech act, a person expresses a given state of mind. (There might be additional parameters as well, including a contextual parameter.) I thank Michael Jubien for helpful discussion.

for it would be a deliberate utterance rather than a spontaneous uninhibited effect of her disapproval.

Second, one might propose that speakers 'express' conative attitudes in making moral assertions in the sense that an assertion counts as a genuine ethical claim only if the speaker has a relevant conative attitude that she thereby manifests. Dorit Bar-On and Matthew Chrisman defend a proposal of this kind on the basis that, they say, the *point* of making an ethical claim is to manifest a relevant attitude (2009). There are cases, however, in which a person makes a claim that we would intuitively take to be a moral claim where the point of making the claim is not to manifest a conative attitude. Suppose Anna says, "Capital punishment is wrong," hoping that her audience will focus on the fate of the people on death row and not be distracted by thoughts about her attitudes. In this case, intuitively, the point of Anna's assertion is not to display her attitude of disapproval. It is to communicate a proposition or a position. Moreover, she might not actually disapprove. One might reply that, if not, then Anna does not qualify as making an ethical claim. But this reply seems intuitively implausible, for Anna would be contradicted by someone who shouted from the audience that capital punishment is right, thereby plainly expressing approval of capital punishment and uncontroversially making an ethical claim. Moreover, as I will explain, I think that amoralists can make genuine ethical claims even though they do not have the relevant conative attitudes.

Third, in some cases "expression" refers to the relation between a person performing a speech act and the psychological state having which is the 'sincerity condition' of that speech act. In this sense, for example, an apology can be said to express regret and an assertion to express a belief. Of course, a person can assert something without believing it. A person who asserts that p expresses the belief that p in that, roughly, if she is sincere in what she says, and if she knows her own mind and knows the meaning of the sentence she utters, she believes that p. More generally, a person performing a speech act thereby "sincerity-expresses" a state of mind just in case, if she is sincere in what she says, and if she knows her own mind and knows the meaning of the sentence she utters, she is in that state of mind.

One might propose that a person making a moral assertion thereby sincerity-expresses a relevant conative attitude (see Gibbard 1990: 84). I think this is not so. Suppose Anna says capital punishment is morally wrong. I think she could know her own mind, know the meaning of the sentence she utters, and be sincere in asserting that capital punishment is wrong, even if she does not actually disapprove of capital punishment. If so, she does not sincerity-express disapproval. Perhaps, as Michael Smith suggests, a failure to disapprove of capital punishment would "cast serious doubt" on her sincerity (1994: 7), but this does not mean that she must actually *be* insincere. There need not be any deceit or pretense on her part. She might be convinced capital punishment is wrong and be honestly expressing her belief it is wrong even if her feelings are at odds with her belief. She might agree that it is perverse of her not to feel disapproval. So I think her assertion need not be insincere. If she does express disapproval in saying capital punishment is wrong, it seems that this is not a matter of sincerity-expression.

Fourth, "expression" can refer to the relation between a person who uses a pejorative term in saying something and the relevant pejorative attitude. In my 2001 paper, I used the term "Frege-expression" to refer to this relation because pejorative terms seem to be "colored" in Frege's sense.[11] I say, for instance, that a person Frege-expresses contempt for Italians in calling someone a wop.

Frege-expression is different from the other kinds of expression. In some cases, the use of a pejorative would *evince* or *vent* a pejorative attitude, but this need not be so. In some cases the point of using a pejorative term is to convey a pejorative attitude, but this also need not be so. Moreover, pejoratives do not *sincerity-express* pejorative attitudes. Suppose that Betty says Leonardo is a wop. She expresses contempt for Italians, but she might not actually have contempt even if she speaks sincerely, knows her own mind, and knows the meaning of the sentence she utters. Perhaps her intention is simply to communicate that Leonardo is an Italian. Perhaps "wop" is the only term people use in her community to speak of Italians. If she does not want to draw attention to herself, she might use the term "wop," hoping that no Italians will overhear her and hoping that no one will be misled. In this case, there need not be any deceit or pretense on her part. She might be speaking sincerely. If so, then Frege-expression is not a kind of sincerity-expression. Perhaps we can say that an utterance of a sentence Frege-expresses a state of mind if the linguistic appropriateness of the utterance depends on the speaker's actually being in that state of mind.

There is an apparent parallel between pejorative terms and moral predicates. It seems plausible that, for example, if Betty says, "Leonardo is a

---

[11] Nothing in my paper depends on whether this reading of Frege is correct. Frege thought that the term "cur" is colored, for instance. He said that there is no difference in the "thoughts" expressed by the sentences "This mongrel dog howled all night" and "This cur howled all night," but there is a difference in the "contents" of the sentences. Frege (1979: 197–8; also 140–1).

wop," she thereby Frege-expresses contempt for Italians, and it seems that she is able to express contempt in this way because of the meaning of the term "wop." Similarly, in the moral case, it seems to me that a person who makes a moral claim using a typical moral predicate thereby Frege-expresses a relevant attitude such as approval or disapproval and that she is able to do this because of the meaning of the moral predicate she uses. For example, when Anna asserts, "Capital punishment is morally wrong," it seems plausible that she Frege-expresses disapproval of capital punishment. It seems that she is able to do this because of the meaning of the predicate "morally wrong."

I had two goals in this section. First, I wanted to make it clear that there are different expression relations and that, because of this, realist-expressivism can be developed in different ways. Second, I wanted to draw attention to the idea of Frege-expression and to the apparent parallel between pejorative terms and moral predicates. Both kinds of terms can be used in utterances that express relevant conative attitudes, and this plausibly is due to their meanings.

3. THE CONVENTIONAL IMPLICATURE VIEW

In Copp (2001), I used the idea of conventional implicature to explicate Frege-expression. My proposal was that a person who makes a moral assertion using a moral predicate normally thereby expresses a conative attitude *in that* she *conventionally implicates* that she has such an attitude. Given plausible assumptions, this position implies, for instance, that in asserting that capital punishment is wrong, Anna conventionally implicates that she disapproves of capital punishment. When we look closely, however, it turns out that the phenomenon I described as conventional implicature is not strictly speaking a kind of implicature. It is, nevertheless, a close relative of implicature.

Grice introduced the idea of an implicature, saying that he would use "implicate" as a technical term for a family of verbs that includes "imply," "suggest," and "mean."[12] Arguably, someone implies, suggests, or means something only if she intends to convey it, so I assume that implicatures are part of what speakers intend to communicate.[13] Implicatures are part

---

[12] Grice (1989: 24–5); in Saul (2002: 239). I follow Bach and Jennifer Saul in interpreting Grice (1989). See Bach and Harnish (1979), Bach (1999 and 2006*b*), and Saul (2002). I am grateful to Bach for helpful correspondence.

[13] See e.g. Bach (2006*a*: 494). The assumption is questioned by Saul (2002: 237–40).

of speaker meaning (Saul 2002: 228). Grice specifies, moreover, that what a speaker implicates is not part of what she says (Saul 2002: 228). An implicature therefore is a proposition that is part of what a speaker means to communicate in saying something without being part of what she actually says.

Conversational implicatures are determined, as Grice says, by what the audience must "assume the speaker to think in order to preserve the assumption that she is following the Cooperative Principle"—that she is saying something that is relevant in the context—and that she is otherwise following the "conversational maxims."[14] That is, conversational implicatures are "calculable" (Bach 1999: 329). What is implicated can be worked out (Potts 2005: 27). Consider a familiar kind of example. Suppose I am writing a letter of reference for a student who is applying for an academic position. I mean to communicate that he should not be hired, but I do not want to say this, so I write only that he talks often on the telephone. In this case, I have not said that the student should not be hired, but it appears that, in order to understand me to be saying something relevant to the context, the hiring committee must assume that I think the student should not be hired. If so, I have conversationally implicated this.

Conventional implicatures are supposed to be determined by the linguistic meaning of the words a person uses.[15] Suppose Betty says, "Leonardo is a wop," intending to communicate that he is Italian and that she has contempt for Italians. In this case, assuming that she implicates that she has contempt for Italians, and given that the implicature is due to the meaning of "wop," she would be thought to have conventionally implicated that she has contempt for Italians.

Christopher Potts has suggested that conversational implicatures, unlike conventional implicatures, tend to be "reinforceable without redundancy" (2007: 669–70). For example, if my letter of reference initially says merely that my student talks often on the telephone, I can add without redundancy that I think he should not be hired. But it would be redundant for Betty to say "Leonardo is a wop" and then add "I have contempt for Italians." Similarly, I think, there would be a sense of redundancy if Anna were to say "Capital punishment is morally wrong and I disapprove of capital punishment." Grice proposed various more familiar tests to distinguish

[14] Grice (1989: 86). Grice formulates the Cooperative Principle as follows: "make your conversational contribution such as is required, at the stage at which it occurs, by the accepted purpose or direction of the talk exchange in which you are engaged" (1989: 26). For discussion, see Saul (2002: 233–5).

[15] Saul (2002: 229). For discussion, see Potts (2005: 8–11, 26–30).

between conventional and conversational implicatures, which I discuss below, in Section 7.[16]

I can now explain the first, technical problem with the conventional implicature view. The problem is that the phenomenon of interest—the phenomenon that seems to be illustrated by pejorative terms and, I say, by moral terms—appears not to be a kind of implicature, properly so-called, for it is not always an aspect of speaker-meaning.

Begin with pejorative terms. Betty says, "Leonardo is a wop." Suppose, however, that she merely wants to communicate that Leonardo is Italian and suppose that she does not actually have contempt for Italians. She says Leonardo is a "wop" only because her audience always uses the term "wop" to refer to Italians and because she doesn't want to draw attention to herself. She hopes desperately that no one will think she has contempt for Italians.[17] As Bach might say, she does not *mean* that she has contempt for Italians (2006a: 494). But if not, then, on the standard conception of implicature, Betty has not implicated that she has contempt for Italians, so she has not conventionally implicated this. Despite this, she has conveyed that she has contempt for Italians in just the way that, I think, a person who makes a moral assertion might convey that she has a relevant conative attitude.

Now turn to moral assertions. Suppose that Anna says, "Capital punishment is wrong," meaning to communicate that capital punishment is morally wrong, but not meaning to convey anything about her conative attitudes. She does not mean that she has any particular attitudes. She does not want her audience to have thoughts about her attitudes. She wants them to be thinking of the people on death row, and not to be distracted by thoughts about her. But if she does not intend to convey anything about her attitudes, then, on the standard conception, Anna has not implicated that she disapproves of capital punishment, so she has not conventionally implicated this. Despite this, I think, she has conveyed that she disapproves, and she has conveyed this in exactly the way that I aim to capture.

The same example undermines, incidentally, the thesis that Anna would *conversationally* implicate that she disapproves of capital punishment in saying what she does. For, in the example, Anna does not implicate this, so she neither conversationally nor conventionally implicates it.

This problem, the 'intentionality problem,' shows that, for a technical reason, the phenomenon of interest is not strictly speaking a kind of implicature. As we will see, however, we can define a close relative of

---

[16] (1989: 44, 39). For a useful summary, see Potts (2007: 669–70).
[17] For a similar example, see Saul (2002: 238).

implicature, which I will call "simplicature." The phenomenon of interest is a kind of *simplicature*.

4. BACH AND "THE MYTH OF CONVENTIONAL IMPLICATURE"

Kent Bach argues that the phenomena that have been described as involving conventional implicature are all "instances of something else," that there is no such thing as conventional implicature (Bach 1999: 327). This is not a substantive objection to the conventional implicature version of realist-expressivism, however, as I think Bach would agree.[18] For we can define a close relative of conventional implicature—conventional "simplicature." The phenomenon of interest is conventional *simplicature*, and Bach's arguments do not show that there is no such thing as conventional simplicature. The conventional *implicature* view was my proposed way to explicate realist-expressivism. It turns out that it needs to be replaced with the conventional *simplicature* view.

Bach's target is the "conventional implicature (CI-) thesis," the thesis that "there are certain locutions which do not contribute to what is said and do not affect the truth or falsity of what is said and yet, by virtue of their conventional meanings, generate implicatures" (Bach 1999: 329). An example is the word "but," the use of which is generally said to implicate that there is a contrast of a relevant kind in the offing. If Kent says "Shaq is huge but agile," he seems to implicate that there is some kind of contrast between being huge and being agile. Intuitively, however, the proposition that there is such a contrast is in addition to what Kent says, and what Kent says may be true even if there is no such contrast. Bach calls "but" and similar locutions "alleged conventional implicature devices," or "ACIDs" (p. 333).

Bach's argument turns on the idea of "what is said." He claims, basically, that in cases in which it is intuitively plausible that extra propositions are communicated in virtue of the meanings of ACIDs that are used by speakers, these extra propositions are part of what is said. Call this the "inclusionary thesis." Bach seems to be thinking that if it is the *meaning* of an ACID used by a speaker that generates an alleged implicature, then the content thereby communicated must be part of what the speaker said. The meaning of "but," for example, is, roughly, "and, by contrast."[19] If this is

---

[18] Judging from what he said in corresponding with me about these issues.
[19] Compare the first entry for "but" in *American Heritage Dictionary* (New York: Houghton Mifflin, 1992).

right, then the sentence "Shaq is huge but agile" means, roughly, "Shaq is huge and, by contrast, agile." But then, if Kent says "Shaq is huge but agile," he will have said that there is a contrast between Shaq's being huge and his being agile.

The best evidence for the inclusionary thesis, Bach suggests, is that ACIDs "can occur straightforwardly in indirect quotation" (p. 328). Suppose Kent says "Shaq is huge but agile." We might then report, "Kent said that Shaq is huge but agile." Our report would be less than fully accurate if we replaced "but" with "and." This and other examples suggest that ACIDs are part of what is said in such cases, and this suggests in turn that the extra propositions communicated by means of ACIDs are also part of what is said. If so, these propositions are not *implicated*, for an implicature is a proposition that is communicated without being part of what is said. And if they are not implicated, they are not *conventionally* implicated.

Bach agrees that in such cases a speaker communicates multiple propositions (pp. 345–7). One of these is more prominent than the others, and we take its truth or falsity to settle the truth or falsity of what is said by the speaker (pp. 350–6). This is the "primary proposition" communicated by the speaker. A proposition communicated due to a speaker's use of an ACID is "secondary," in that its truth value intuitively does not affect the truth value of what is said (p. 346).[20] According to Bach's inclusionary thesis, however, the secondary proposition is part of what is said. In saying "Shaq is huge but agile," for instance, Kent communicates both the primary proposition that Shaq is huge and agile and the secondary proposition that there is some relevant contrast between being huge and being agile. Both are part of what Kent says, Bach argues, so the secondary proposition is not merely implicated.

The indirect quotation test clearly poses a challenge to defenders of the CI thesis, and Bach might be correct about "but" and about the other examples he considers. But I am not convinced.

My chief worry is that the indirect quotation test seems not to show what Bach needs it to show. In the cases of interest, I agree it is plausible that the ACID used by a speaker needs to be included in an accurate report of what the speaker said. Bach seems to think this means that the secondary *proposition* that is communicated by the speaker due to her use of the ACID is also part of what is said. The problem is that, in the cases of interest, as Bach agrees, it would be inaccurate to report what the speaker said by using a sentence that explicitly expressed this proposition (pp. 347–8). For example, if Kent says "Shaq is huge but agile," it would be inaccurate to

---

[20] Hence, Bach holds, the speaker does not assert the *conjunction* of the primary and secondary propositions.

report "Kent said that Shaq is huge and agile and that there is some kind of contrast between being huge and being agile" (p. 347). But if this is right, then, despite what Bach claims, the indirect quotation test actually supports the idea that the secondary proposition is *not* part of what is said.

Bach is therefore in an awkward position. If a secondary proposition is communicated in such cases and if it is included in what is said, then it is puzzling that it would be inaccurate to report what is said by using a sentence that *explicitly* expresses that proposition. Bach says that a sentence that explicitly expressed the secondary proposition as well as the primary proposition in a case of the kind at issue would fail to meet the constraints that Grice places on reports of what is said (pp. 335–8). It would have too many conjuncts (pp. 347–8). But then, again, it seems that the indirect quotation test implies that the secondary proposition is *not* part of what is said.

In the cases of interest, I agree with Bach that an ACID may be used in providing an accurate report of what a speaker said, so I agree that in this sense an ACID "contributes to what is said" (p. 340). But the intuition lying behind the indirect quotation test is that what is said by a person in making an utterance—at least, what is said "in the sense of propositional content" (p. 340)—is the proposition (or propositions) expressed explicitly by the 'that'-clause in an accurate and complete indirect quotation of the utterance. As Bach says, "the 'that'-clause in an indirect quotation specifies what is said in the utterance being reported" (p. 339). On this test, the secondary proposition in the cases of interest is not included in what is said.

Part of the problem is that the indirect quotation test is not a test simply of what is said "in the sense of propositional content" (p. 340). Suppose that I say "Anna is a bitch." In this case, obviously, it is important that I used the word "bitch" and, for many purposes, we would view a report of what I said as inaccurate if it did not itself use that word. This case illustrates the fact that indirect quotation is not used simply to communicate what was said in the sense of propositional content. In some cases, it is used also to capture certain aspects of *how* the speaker communicated this content. Because of this, a friend of conventional implicature can agree that an ACID used by a speaker belongs in an indirect speech report of what she said because it shows how the secondary proposition was communicated. This is compatible with denying that the secondary proposition is part of what is said "in the sense of propositional content."

To be clear, I do not *need* to disagree with Bach about the examples he considers. I agree that there is something puzzling about the CI thesis as applied to ACIDs like "but." In these cases, the semantic content or "core meaning" of the ACID seems to be responsible for the fact that a speaker using the ACID communicates both a primary and a secondary proposition.

I am interested, however, in cases in which, instead, a kind of semantic *usage rule* associated with an ACID is responsible for the fact that the use of the ACID may communicate both a primary and a secondary proposition. I will explain this more fully in the following sections of the chapter.

Pejoratives seem to illustrate the phenomenon. The term "wop" arguably is governed by a semantic usage rule according to which one is not to call someone a "wop" unless one has contempt for Italians.[21] This is why, if I am correct, when Betty says, "Leonardo is a wop," she simplicates that she has contempt for Italians. Or consider the word "tu," the second person singular pronoun in French. It is governed by a semantic usage rule according to which, roughly, one is not to address someone as "tu" unless one has a relevant kind of relationship with the person.[22] This is why, if I am correct, when Christophe says, "Tu es belle," he typically simplicates that he has a relevant relationship with the person he is addressing. Of course he does not *say* that he has such a relationship with her, and whether he actually has such a relationship with her is irrelevant to whether what he said about her is true. So "tu" seems to give rise to conventional simplicatures because of a semantic usage rule that governs its use.

Bach's inclusionary thesis is implausible in cases of these kinds. Suppose that Christophe says, "Tu es belle," and suppose that he thereby conveys that he has a relevant relationship with the person he is addressing. On the inclusionary thesis, this proposition is part of what he said. But this is implausible, for it would be inaccurate to report Christophe as saying that he has a relevant relationship with this person. He does not *say* any such thing. Moreover, on the inclusionary thesis, it would be self-contradictory for Christophe to say, "Tu es belle," and then straightaway to deny that he and the person he is addressing stand in a relevant relationship. On the inclusionary thesis, this would be for him to say *inter alia* that he has a relevant relationship with the person and then to deny that he has a relevant relationship with the person. Intuitively, however, there would be no contradiction in this case.[23] I think, then, that we should reject the inclusionary thesis for examples of this kind.

---

[21] The rule is semantic, or a matter of "meaning," since it is underwritten by linguistic conventions and since a person who did not know the rule would not be linguistically competent in using the word. But nothing substantive in my argument turns on these admittedly broad uses of "semantic" and "meaning."

[22] Bach discusses "tu" and argues that its use does not produce a conventional implicature (1999: 332 n. 8). His argument leaves it open whether the use of "tu" produces a conventional simplicature. Where I speak of "usage rules," Bach speaks of "conditions of appropriate use."

[23] Bach might suggest that Christophe would be guilty of a pragmatic contradiction (1999: 364). But the inclusionary thesis would commit us to holding him guilty of a logical contradiction.

Our interest in the accuracy of an indirect quotation is mixed. We are interested in knowing what proposition was communicated, but often we are also interested in knowing how it was communicated. Despite this, however, in the next section I will define conventional simplicature by means of an indirect quotation test of what a speaker says *explicitly*. In the cases that interest me, the test can be used to show that a secondary proposition that is communicated by a speaker is not part of what is said explicitly.

5. A PROPOSED DEFINITION OF CONVENTIONAL SIMPLICATURE

A speaker can communicate a proposition in saying what she says even if she does not assert it explicitly, and even if the proposition is not logically entailed by what she says. In saying what she says, that is, a speaker can communicate that p without actually *saying* that p, even if p is not a logical consequence of what she says. This is the phenomenon we are interested in. It builds on an idea of inexplicit communication.

To capture this idea, I will introduce a test based on Bach's indirect quotation test. I stipulate that

> A proposition is part of "what is said explicitly" by a person in assertorically uttering a sentence just in case a sentence that expresses exactly that proposition would be part of the 'that'-clause in a complete and accurate indirect quotation of the utterance.[24]

Call this the "said-explicitly test." I now propose stipulative definitions of *simplicature* and of *conventional* simplicature by building on the said-explicitly test.

To begin, I stipulate that

> A person *simplicates* that p in assertorically uttering a sentence just in case, (*a*) in assertorically uttering the sentence, the speaker communicates that p (whether intentionally or not), but (*b*) the proposition that p is not part of what is said explicitly by the speaker in uttering the sentence, so that (*c*) the falsity of p is compatible with the truth of what is said explicitly by the speaker.[25]

---

[24] The proposal is intended for the case of complete sentences that do not contain indexicals and other context sensitive expressions. I intend the test to be applied in accord with Bach's restrictions on his IQ test (1999: 340).

[25] This definition is based on Bach's definition of conventional implicature (1999: 331).

We could define an implicature as a simplicature that the speaker intends to communicate. *Conventional* simplicature is a kind of simplicature. Before I explain this, however, I need to clarify how the definition is to be understood.

Begin with clause (*a*). Bach objects that the definition will be too inclusive if it allows propositions that are communicated *unintentionally* to count as simplicatures.[26] Suppose that Kent is overheard absent-mindedly talking to himself. Suppose he says, despondently, "It's raining again." In saying this, Kent might unintentionally communicate to his audience both that it is raining and that he is disappointed in the weather. Of course, my definition does not count him as simplicating that it is raining since he said this explicitly. But it might count him as simplicating that he is disappointed in the weather given that clauses (*b*) and (*c*) are satisfied. It appears, then, that the definition may be too inclusive since it may count a speaker as simplicating anything that she happens to convey, provided she doesn't say it explicitly. This does not matter for my purposes, however. My interest is in *conventional* simplicature, and as will become evident, Kent would not count as conventionally simplicating his disappointment in the weather. Neither would he count as *conversationally* simplicating his disappointment.

It might nevertheless be useful to provide a somewhat more restrictive reading of the definition. To that end, I propose that, in interpreting clause (*a*), we should count a speaker as 'communicating' that *p* in saying something just in case either she intends to convey that *p*, or, given the meaning of the sentence she uses and the 'conversational' situation, it would be reasonable to take her to intend to convey that *p*.[27] In the above example, Kent is talking to himself, and it would not be reasonable to take him to intend to convey that he is disappointed in the weather, so he does not count as 'communicating' his disappointment. In the relevant sense, a speaker can communicate a proposition she does not intend to communicate, but only if the surrounding linguistic phenomena make it reasonable to think she intends to communicate it.

Turn now to clauses (*b*) and (*c*). Bach notes that utterances of "yes," and "no" intuitively do not make explicit the propositions they communicate in relevant contexts, but he claims that these propositions are not merely (conventionally) implicated (1999: 331). Given clauses (*b*) and (*c*) of my

---

[26] In personal communication.

[27] I do not attempt to provide a precise formulation of the proposal. The basic idea was suggested by Bach in personal communication and in Bach (2006b: § 7). See also Saul's suggestion that, in implicating, speakers "make information available" (2002: 244–5).

definition, they also are not simplicated. Suppose I say "Tebow is fast" and Kent responds, "Yes." If we were asked what Kent said, it would be accurate to report him as having said that Tebow is fast, and so, on the said-explicitly test, Kent counts as having said explicitly that Tebow is fast. Given clause (*b*) of the definition, then, Kent does not merely simplicate that Tebow is fast.[28] Similarly, if Kent says "Château Margaux" when asked to name his favorite wine (Bach 1999: 335–6), it would be accurate to report him as having said that his favorite wine is Château Margaux. Hence, given clause (*b*), he does not merely simplicate this.

I now stipulate that[29]

> A speaker *conventionally simplicates* that *p* in assertorically uttering a sentence just in case (*a*) in assertorically uttering the sentence, the speaker communicates that *p* (whether intentionally or not), and (*b*) the fact that the speaker thereby communicates the proposition *p* is determined by the (or a) conventional meaning of some particular linguistic device in the sentence,[30] but (*c*) the proposition that *p* is not part of what is said explicitly by the speaker in uttering the sentence, so that (*d*) the falsity of *p* is compatible with the truth of what is said explicitly by the speaker.

So understood, "conventional simplicature" turns out to be conventional, given clause (*b*), and it turns out to be simplicature, given clauses (*a*), (*c*), and (*d*).[31]

The key clause in the definition is clause (*b*), which requires that what a speaker conventionally simplicates, if anything, be determined by the

---

[28] Intuitively, it might be objected, Kent does not communicate any proposition *explicitly* merely in saying "Yes." But the said-explicitly test is not intended to capture our intuitions about explicit communication. Moreover, if Kent does not communicate any proposition explicitly in the example, then nothing is compatible with the truth of 'what he said explicitly,' so clause (*c*) of the definition is not satisfied.

[29] The following is derived from Bach's definition of conventional implicature (1999: 331).

[30] Bach's definition says that "which proposition that is depends upon the (or a) conventional meaning of some particular linguistic device" (1999: 331). But "depends upon" is too weak, for even conversational simplicatures *depend upon* the meaning of the sentence uttered. See Bach (2006*b*: § 1). Unfortunately, "is determined by" might be too strong given the important role of context. The following formulation might be an improvement: "the fact that it is the proposition *p* that the speaker thereby communicates is determined by the (or a) conventional meaning of some particular linguistic device in the sentence together with what the speaker says explicitly in uttering the sentence in the given context."

[31] Dan Boisvert pointed out in correspondence that nonassertive utterances can have 'simplicatures.' For example, a person who asks whether Leonardo is a wop plausibly would simplicate that she has contempt for Italians. The definition would need to be amended to allow for such cases.

meaning of some linguistic device that she uses. We can illustrate how this clause works with an example we have already discussed. Suppose Christophe says to someone, "Tu es belle." Assume that he intends to convey that he has a relevant relationship with the person he is addressing. Or assume at least that the conversational situation is such that, given the meaning of the sentence he utters, it would be reasonable to take him to intend to convey this. On either of these assumptions, he simplicates that he has a relevant relationship with this person. But this is not part of what he says *explicitly*, for it would be inaccurate to report him as having said that he has a relevant relationship with this person. Moreover, the falsity of this proposition is compatible with the truth of what he says explicitly, namely that the person he is addressing is beautiful. So clauses (*a*), (*c*), and (*d*) of the definition are satisfied. And finally, clause (*b*) is satisfied. The fact that Christophe simplicates that he has a relevant relationship with the person he is addressing is determined by the conventional meaning of the term "tu." I conclude that he *conventionally* simplicates this.

It is important to understand that Bach's arguments do not undermine the claim that there is such a thing as conventional *simplicature*. Bach thought that, in the cases he considered, the indirect quotation test reveals that the secondary propositions that are communicated do not qualify as implicatures because they are part of what is said. For my purposes, the key point is that, in the examples that interest me, the extra propositions are not part of what is said *explicitly*, according to the said-explicitly test. If I am correct, they are cases of conventional *simplicature*.

6. PEJORATIVE TERMS AND MORAL TERMS

Given my goals in this chapter, I need to focus on the case of pejorative terms and to explain how uses of these expressions give rise to conventional simplicatures. If I am correct, moral predicates work in a similar way.

I shall distinguish between the "core meaning" of a term and semantic properties of a term that may underwrite conventional simplicatures. For convenience, I call these properties the term's "simplicature meaning."[32] Assuming that the semantic properties of expressions are determined by linguistic conventions, we need then to distinguish between core-meaning conventions and simplicature-meaning conventions. Pejorative terms and, I think, moral predicates, are "double-aspect terms" that have

---

[32] I introduced the term "core meaning" in Copp (2001). Potts distinguishes between "at-issue meaning" and "CI meaning" (2005: 48, 82–4).

both simplicature meaning and core meaning.[33] Not all expressions are double-aspect, of course, and some cases of conventional simplicature may not involve a double-aspect term.[34]

The *core meaning* of an expression determines the contribution that the expression makes to the primary propositions that are semantically expressed by sentences in which it occurs.[35] For example, in virtue of the core-meaning convention governing its use, the predicate "wop" refers to Italians, so it would be false to say that Leonardo is a "wop" unless he is Italian. I do not want to assume that every pejorative term has a non-pejorative equivalent.[36] But I believe that the core meaning of "wop" is the same as the core meaning of "Italian."

If an expression has *simplicature meaning*, then its simplicature meaning is what determines (*inter alia*) which proposition it is that is conventionally simplicated, if any, by an utterance in which the expression is used. In the case of pejoratives, I take it, their simplicature meaning is a function of semantic (non-core) *usage rules* that govern their appropriate use. For example, I believe, it is semantically inappropriate to use the term "wop" unless one has contempt for Italians. In virtue of the convention establishing this rule, it would be, in Grice's terms, a "semantic offense," or a violation of "semantic proprieties" of some kind not "touching truth value," to call Leonardo a "wop" if one does not have contempt for Italians.[37] Because of this, if Betty calls Leonardo a "wop," she communicates that she has contempt for Italians. If she intends to communicate this, she simplicates it. She does not say it explicitly, and the truth of what she does say explicitly does not depend on whether she has contempt for Italians. Moreover, the fact that she simplicates this is due to the usage rule for "wop." She therefore conventionally simplicates that she has contempt for Italians.

There are subtle questions about semantic usage rules that I cannot explore here. Different pejoratives are presumably associated with different usage rules, for although some pejoratives are offensive in all uses, some are not. Not all uses of the term "jerk" are offensive, for example. If the rule

---

[33] Potts says there are no lexical items that contribute both "an at-issue and a CI meaning" (2005: 48, 82–4). Pejorative terms appear to be a counter-example. See also Bach (2006a: 494).

[34] There are examples in Potts (2005: 13–16, 32).

[35] Again, I set aside indexicals and other context sensitive expressions.

[36] Robert May has suggested that "untouchable" is a pejorative term that does not have a non-pejorative equivalent. There could be cases in which a pejorative predicate "P" and a non-pejorative predicate "N" are extensionally equivalent but where it is not analytic that "Ns are Ps."

[37] These are Grice's words (1989: 362, 365). One might worry that the usage rules for a term of the kind I have in mind are not a matter of the term's meaning. But they are a matter of its meaning in a broad sense of "meaning." See above, n. 21.

for "wop" says not to *use* the word unless one has contempt for Italians, the rule for "jerk" presumably says not to *call* anyone a jerk unless one has contempt for that person. I may simplicate that I have contempt for Italians in saying, "She thinks you are a wop," but I do not simplicate that I have contempt for anyone in saying, "She thinks you are a jerk."

Uses of a double-aspect expression that deviate from its core meaning have a different significance from uses that deviate from its simplicature meaning. If a person uses a term in a way that is nonstandard given its core meaning, her assertion likely will not be understood. If Betty says that Leonardo is a wop but denies that he is Italian, she contradicts herself, and it will not be clear what proposition she is attempting to express. But if a person uses a term in a way that is nonstandard given its simplicature meaning, her assertion might well be understood for it might be clear what proposition she means to express. If Betty says that Leonardo is a wop but then denies that she has contempt for Italians, she will not have contradicted herself and she likely would manage to express the belief that Leonardo is Italian. Even so, it will not be clear why she expressed her belief in this way. Her usage will call for explanation. In general, if a speaker violates a semantic (non-core) usage rule in uttering a sentence, and if she understands the meaning of the sentence, she should recognize that her utterance is linguistically inappropriate.

Consider now the moral predicate "morally wrong." According to the conventional simplicature version of realist-expressivism, this term has a core meaning in virtue of which it expresses the property moral wrongness.[38] It also has a simplicature meaning, which I think is determined by a semantic usage rule. In particular, I assume, it is semantically inappropriate to use the term in making a moral judgment unless one disapproves of actions that have the property of being wrong.[39] In virtue of the convention establishing this rule, in saying that capital punishment is wrong, Anna conventionally simplicates that she disapproves of wrong actions, so she simplicates that she disapproves of capital punishment.

There is, I think, an important difference between the usage rule for "wop" and the rule for "morally wrong." The rule for "wop" seems to be that one is not to *use* the term unless one has contempt for Italians. The rule for "morally wrong" seems to be that one is not to use the term *in making a moral judgment* unless one disapproves of actions that are wrong. This explains why a speaker who says, "Betty believes Leonardo is a wop," simplicates that she has contempt for Italians but a speaker who says, "Anna believes capital punishment is wrong," does not simplicate that

---

[38] I provide an account of what this property is in Copp (1995) and (2001).
[39] I thank Mark Schroeder for helpful discussion of this idea.

she disapproves of capital punishment. A person with no moral attitudes who says, "Anna believes capital punishment is wrong," does not violate the usage rule for "wrong" since she does not thereby make a moral judgment. A full account of the usage rules for pejoratives and for moral predicates would have to work out details that are beyond the scope of this chapter.

One might wonder why there is no familiar predicate that stands to "wrong" as "Italian" stands to "wop." Why is there no familiar term with the same core meaning as "wrong" but without its simplicature meaning?[40] I can only speculate that there would be little use for such a predicate, perhaps because people who do not disapprove of actions that are wrong would only rarely have an interest in ascribing the property wrongness. They might occasionally have reason to categorize things morally in order not to appear amoral, but then they would not worry about violating the usage rule. They might have reason to talk about other people's beliefs about which actions are wrong, but on my view they would not thereby violate the usage rule. Of course, even though there is no familiar term that is a neutral equivalent for "wrong," there are neutral equivalent *phrases*, such as "has the property called 'wrongness.'" Because of this, people who do not disapprove of wrong actions can ascribe the property without being forced to violate the usage rule for "wrong."

A complete and fully general semantic theory would need to include a theory of simplicature meaning as well as a theory of core meaning and it would need to include an account of the relation between the two. It is beyond the scope of this chapter to provide such a theory, but Potts has made sophisticated progress in this direction (2005).[41]

I should stress that my defense of the conventional simplicature version of realist-expressivism does not depend on whether my account of pejorative terms is correct. The conventional simplicature account of pejoratives is a model for the kind of account I want to propose for moral predicates. If it is correct, then my account of moral predicates is not unprecedented, so there is one less reason to worry about it. However, I discuss pejoratives mainly because they illustrate the kind of account I want to propose for

---

[40] I thank Kent Bach for pressing this worry.

[41] Potts does not provide a definition of "conventional implicature" in a form that facilitates comparison with my definition of "conventional simplicature." His definition deploys, in effect, the distinction between the primary and secondary propositions expressed by a person while mine deploys the distinction between explicit and inexplicit content. I believe he is trying to capture a different notion from the one I am trying to capture, so our accounts should not be viewed as competitors. Potts allows for a "rich ontology" of diverse "means for invoking non-at-issue content" (2005: 44) and for various notions that are close relatives of the notion that interests him (pp. 211–18).

moral predicates and because the conventional simplicature account of how they work is intuitively plausible.[42]

7. THE CONVENTIONAL SIMPLICATURE VIEW AND CONVERSATIONAL MAXIMS

On any plausible version of realist-expressivism, in asserting that capital punishment is morally wrong, Anna expresses some kind of disapproval. The semantic thesis seeks to explain this on the basis of the semantics of the expression "wrong." According to the conventional simplicature version of realist-expressivism, the semantics of typical moral predicates is such that a person making a moral assertion using a moral term *conventionally simplicates* that she has a relevant attitude. This is the sense in which she expresses such an attitude.

Stephen Finlay has proposed instead that a person making a moral assertion characteristically would *conversationally* implicate that she has a relevant conative attitude. He thinks a conversational implicature version of realist-expressivism would be more plausible than my conventional implicature version (Finlay 2005).

For a technical reason I have already mentioned, I think Finlay's thesis is best understood to be that, as he puts it, "attitudinal content" is conversationally *simplicated* rather than that it is conversationally *implicated*. Furthermore, Finlay's arguments do not turn on the technical differences between implicature and simplicature, so I will read them as directed against the conventional simplicature view.

---

[42] A variety of objections to the model have been raised by Christopher Hom (2008). I will briefly discuss two of his objections. First, consider the sentence (I), "Italians are wops." If "wop" and "Italian" have the same core meaning, then (I) is analytic, but, Hom would object, it would be intelligible for a person who understands the meaning of (I) to refuse to admit that (I) is true. I agree, but the reason this would be intelligible, I think, is that to agree that (I) is true would be to express what one would express in uttering (I). It would be to express contempt for Italians, which one might not want to do. Second, Hom would object that there are contexts in which a person uses "wop," for example, but does not express contempt. This should not be possible because conventional simplicatures are not "cancellable," as I will explain. Hom gives several problematic examples. Consider the sentence (W), "It is wrong to treat Italians as wops," which one can utter without expressing contempt. I believe I can account for this. A person uttering (W) would plausibly be understood to assert that it is wrong to treat Italians with contempt. Her utterance could not be understood literally since, on my view, the core meaning of (W) is the same as the core meaning of the sentence (W′), "It is wrong to treat Italians as Italians," which is infelicitous. Unlike (W′), (W) can be used to assert that it is wrong to treat Italians with contempt because of the simplicature meaning of "wop." A fuller discussion of this example would need to invoke a general account of nonliteral usage.

The dispute between Finlay's conversational simplicature view and my conventional simplicature view is not merely technical. The conventional simplicature view can explain, for example, why it might seem that the expression of a suitable conative attitude is *internal* to the making of a moral judgment in moral terms, or why it might seem to be a *conceptual* truth that the making of such a judgment involves the expression of a suitable attitude. Finlay's conversational view cannot accommodate this intuition. For on the conversational view, the fact that moral assertions characteristically implicate that the speaker has a relevant attitude is merely a contingent fact having to do with the pragmatics of assertions made in certain kinds of context and with the characteristic purposes of moral discourse.[43] So, if Finlay is correct, the intuition that the expression of an attitude is internal to moral assertions made in moral terms must be denied or explained in some other away.

Finlay offers three basic arguments against the conventional simplicature view: the "redundancy argument," the "Gricean tests argument," and the "silencing argument."

The Redundancy Argument

Finlay argues that the kind of semantics he and I both favor for moral utterances can explain the "attitudinal content" of moral assertions "as a conversational implicature, rendering the alleged conventional implicature redundant" (2005: 2, 10). This argument relies on Finlay's "standard-relational property theory," or "relational theory" (p. 9), according to which the sentences standardly used in making moral assertions implicitly refer to moral standards. Different utterances of such a sentence can semantically express different propositions, depending on which standard is relevant in the context.[44] Given such a theory, Finlay claims, a person making a moral assertion *conversationally* simplicates that she has a relevant attitude. In light of this, he claims, there is no need to suppose that moral

---

[43] There is a complication. One could claim it is a conceptual truth that in making a moral judgment a speaker expresses a suitable attitude. One might propose combining this supposed conceptual truth with Finlay's conversational simplicature account. On the resulting view, a person does not count as making a moral judgment unless she conversationally simplicates a relevant attitude. Suppose Betty says, "Capital punishment is morally right," and Anna says, "Capital punishment is morally wrong." Intuitively, each has made a moral judgment and their judgments are contradictory. But on the view we are considering, one of these judgments might not be a moral judgment. For example, if Anna denies that she disapproves of capital punishment, thereby cancelling any conversational simplicature that she disapproves, she does not count as making a moral judgment. This is a counter-intuitive implication of the view.

[44] I proposed a theory of this kind (Copp 1995: 9–36, 218–24).

predicates have simplicature meanings that would support *conventional* simplicatures. I see two major problems with this argument, even setting aside the worry that the relational theory is controversial.

First, we need to explain more than simply the fact that moral assertions simplicate attitudinal content. We also need to explain or accommodate widely shared intuitions about these simplicatures. There is, first, the intuition I mentioned before that the expression of a relevant conative attitude is internal to moral assertions made in moral terms, or that it is a conceptual truth that such assertions involve the expression of suitable attitudes. I think that this intuition is robust and widespread. On the conversational view, however, even if a "ubiquitous conversational feature of moral assertion" explains the simplicatures, as Finlay suggests (2005: 11; also Finlay 2004), it is not a conceptual truth that this feature is ubiquitous, and there will be contexts in which it is absent. So on the conversational view, the expression of conative attitudes is not internal to moral assertion in any interesting way. On the conventional view, however, since it is the *meaning* of the typical moral predicates that underwrites the relevant simplicatures, conative expression is internal to moral assertion in a way that answers to the intuition. There are also, second, intuitions about linguistic misuses of terms. I think that it intuitively would be linguistically odd or inappropriate to use a moral predicate in making a moral assertion unless one has a relevant attitude. This is evidence that a relevant convention governs the use of the word. Unlike Finlay's view, my conventional simplicature view can accommodate this intuition.

Second, it is not clear how Finlay can support his thesis that a person making a moral assertion conversationally simplicates that she has a relevant attitude. Conversational implicatures, properly so-called, are calculable, and the same goes for conversational *simplicatures*, as I am using the term. They "exist in virtue of the maxims and the cooperative principle" (Potts 2005: 26). A person making a moral assertion conversationally simplicates that she has a relevant conative attitude only if the audience must assume that she has such an attitude in order to sustain the assumption that she is following the cooperative principle and the conversational maxims (Grice 1989: 26, 86). We need to ask how Finlay proposes to show that this necessary condition is met (see Saul 2002: 231).

It is true that much moral discourse takes place in a "context of decision," where the speaker aims to reach a decision about what to do. In such a context, it is plausible that the audience must suppose that the speaker is motivated to do what she says ought to be done. Otherwise, what she says would be of doubtful relevance. This suggests that a person saying that something ought to be done in a context of decision would conversationally simplicate that she is motivated appropriately (Copp 2001: 31–3; Finlay

2005: 10). But this argument does not work for other kinds of context. If we are discussing a remote historical event, for example, the audience may have no need to suppose that a speaker has any particular conative attitude in order to see her as a cooperative participant in the discussion.

One might think that the simplicatures in question are "generalized" conversational simplicatures, simplicatures that do not depend, other things being equal, on contextual details. I argued for such a position in my 2001 paper (pp. 31–3). I suggested that moral discourse has the practical significance it has because there is a tendency for our moral beliefs generally to be accompanied by an appropriate motivating attitude. Given this, and given how participants in moral discourse understand what they are doing, we generally expect those who make moral assertions to have relevant attitudes, and, because of this, it is typically misleading to make a moral assertion if one does not have a relevant attitude. I argued on this basis that, other things being equal, a person making a moral assertion conversationally implicates that she has such an attitude. Finlay agrees (2005: 10).

Unfortunately my argument was too quick. It did not pay close enough attention to the question of what audiences need to assume in order to understand speakers to be following the cooperative principle and the conversational maxims. Even generalized conversational implicatures, properly so-called, are calculable on the basis of the maxims and the cooperative principle.[45] The fact than an audience can reasonably infer something about a speaker, given its background knowledge and what the speaker says, does not show that the speaker conversationally implicates it (Bach 2006*b*: § 6). If someone approaches me at a bus stop and says "The buses are not running," I can reasonably infer that she speaks English. She would have misled me if she were just practicing her pronunciation. But she neither conversationally implicates nor simplicates that she speaks English.

It does not help to invoke the relational theory. On this theory, a moral assertion expresses a proposition only if a relevant moral standard is specified, whether explicitly or not. Similarly, an assertion to the effect that some action is lawful expresses a proposition only if a relevant legal system is specified; lawfulness is a relation between kinds of action and legal systems. In the moral case, since speakers typically do not refer explicitly to the relevant standard, on the relational theory audience members cannot understand what a speaker is saying unless they make an assumption about which standard is the relevant one. Whatever standard they assume to

---

[45] Potts (2007: 670; 2005: 26–7). Wayne Davis has a view of "generalized implicatures" according to which they seem to have a great deal in common with conventional implicatures (2005: 148–9). This would not be a problem for my position.

be relevant, Finlay argues, they will reasonably assume that the speaker subscribes to it. Hence, he concludes, "in most contexts, a speaker in uttering an unrelativized moral sentence conversationally [simplicates] that she subscribes to that standard" (2005: 12). The problem with this reasoning is that although the audience must assume that the speaker has some standard in mind, and even if the audience would reasonably assume that the speaker subscribes to the standard, it does not follow that the speaker conversational simplicates that she subscribes. To show that she does, Finlay needs to show that the audience must assume that she subscribes in order to understand her to be following the cooperative principle and the conversational maxims.

I conclude, then, that Finlay's redundancy argument is inconclusive. Even if we assume that the relational theory is correct, the conversational view appears unable to explain how it is that moral assertions simplicate attitudinal content in all the cases in which the conventional view would explain this. This means we have not been shown that it would be redundant to invoke the expressive linguistic conventions that are postulated by the conventional view.

The Gricean Tests Argument

Finlay's most persuasive argument rests on Grice's account of the characteristics that distinguish conversational implicatures from conventional implicatures. Grice proposes that conventional implicatures are "detachable" but not "cancellable" and that conversational implicatures are "cancellable" but not "detachable" (1989: 44, 39). Since nothing here turns on the technical differences between implicature and simplicature, we can carry on as if Grice's tests were intended to distinguish kinds of simplicatures. Finlay claims that the attitudinal content simplicated by moral assertions is cancellable but not detachable so that the simplicatures in question are conversational.

Begin with the detachability test (Grice 1989: 39, 43–4). Suppose Betty says, "Leonardo is a wop," thereby simplicating that she has contempt for Italians. This simplicature is "detachable" since Betty could have asserted the same proposition about Leonardo without simplicating that she has contempt for Italians by uttering the sentence, "Leonardo is Italian." In general, if a person utters a sentence S, thereby asserting that p and simplicating that q, the simplicature is "detachable" just in case there is a sentence S' such that the person would have asserted that p without simplicating that q if she had uttered S' instead of S, where S and S' are identical except that an expression E that occurs in the former has been replaced in the latter by an expression E' with the same core meaning. In the above example, Betty's simplicature is detachable, which is evidence that it is *conventional* since it is evidence that clause (*b*) in my definition of conventional simplicature is satisfied. It is evidence that the simplicature is due to the meaning of "wop."

Conversational simplicatures are usually not detachable.[46] In the letter of reference example, I write only that my student talks often on the telephone. In this case, I have conversationally simplicated that I think my student should not be hired. No matter what sentence I had written, if it expressed exactly the same proposition as the sentence I actually wrote, I would have simplicated that the person should not be hired.

Finlay argues that the attitudinal content simplicated by moral assertions is not detachable. There are no predicates in common use that can be substituted for moral terms in moral assertions to eliminate the relevant simplicature without changing the proposition that is thereby semantically expressed. Even if this is correct, however, it is not clear what significance it has. It is a contingent matter whether there is a word that has the same core meaning as some other term. English does not have a familiar neutral equivalent for the term "morally obligatory" but it *could* have such a term. Moreover, English is flexible enough that we can usually find ways to say what we need to say. Even if there are no familiar terms that are neutral equivalents for the moral predicates, we can construct neutral equivalent phrases.

There are descriptions that could be substituted for moral terms in moral assertions where the result would be to eliminate the simplicatures. Anna says, "Capital punishment is morally wrong," thereby simplicating that she disapproves of wrong actions. If she had said, instead, "Capital punishment has the property that would be ascribed by saying it is 'morally wrong,'" then, at least arguably, she would not thereby simplicate that she disapproves. Elsewhere I suggested (or meant to suggest) that we could stipulate that a moral term placed in 'scare-quotes' is to have a meaning of the kind we need.[47] We could stipulate that a moral term and its twin in scare-quotes have exactly the same core meaning but the twin lacks any simplicature meaning. Finlay objects that this suggestion is "glib" since it "strains the sense of 'different but coextensive terms'" (2005: 14). The important point, however, is that the suggestion provides a way of testing whether clause (*b*) in my definition of conventional simplicature is satisfied. The coherence of the suggested stipulation provides evidence that the fact

---

[46] Bach points out that conversational simplicatures are detachable if they work by exploiting the maxim of manner (1999: 330).

[47] Copp (2001: 35). Finlay seems to take me to have been claiming that scare-quotes are actually used in English to remove simplicatures (2005: 14).

that moral assertions simplicate attitudinal content is due to the meaning of a moral predicate used in making the assertion.[48]

Turn now to the cancellability test. Grice said the simplicature that *p* is "explicitly cancellable" if it would be "admissible to add *but not p*, or *but I do not mean to imply that p*." It is "contextually cancellable if one can find situations in which the utterance of the form of words would simply not carry the implicature" (1989: 44, 39) Suppose Betty says, "Leonardo is a wop, but I do not mean to convey contempt for Italians." It would be odd for her to say this because doing so would involve a nonstandard use of "wop." In this sense it would *not* be *admissible* for her to say this, so she cannot in this way cancel the simplicature of contempt. Grice holds in general that conventional simplicatures are not cancellable.

Conversational simplicatures *are* cancellable, however. Suppose again that I am writing a letter of reference for a job candidate, and suppose that I write only, "He talks often on the telephone." We can find contexts in which an utterance of this sentence would not simplicate that the person referred to should not be hired, so the simplicature is contextually cancellable.

In my 2001 paper, I perhaps confused matters by using the term "cancellability" to talk about a different, although related notion. I ought to have used a different term, such as "chancellability." My idea was that there is a sense in which conventional simplicatures are 'chancellable' even if they are not cancellable in Grice's sense. There are two points here. First, if Betty said, "Leonardo is a wop, but I do not mean to convey contempt for Italians," we would have no difficulty determining what proposition she had asserted, despite her nonstandard use of the term "wop," assuming she was using the term in accord with its core meaning. Second, if Betty said this, she would not count as simplicating that she has contempt for Italians. Implicatures must be meant or intended, as we saw. Hence Betty would not *implicate* contempt if it is true that, as she said, she did not *mean* to convey contempt. Moreover, given what she said, it would not be reasonable to take her to intend to convey contempt. Therefore, if it is true that she did not mean to convey contempt, she also would not *simplicate* contempt despite her use of the word "wop." It remains true, however, that in saying what she does Betty would not *cancel* the simplication in Grice's sense, for it would remain true that what she said was not 'admissible.' She misused

---

[48] The evidence is not conclusive since conversational simplicatures that work by "exploiting the maxim of manner" are detachable (Bach 1999: 330). Because of this, we need to rule out the possibility that the maxim of manner is at work before we conclude that a detachable simplicature is conventional. But compare Finlay (2005: 14).

the word "wop" and her usage calls for explanation. The simplicature is chancellable but not cancellable in Grice's sense.

Finlay asks us to consider the moral assertions of an amoralist, someone who "sincerely makes assertions about the moral value of things but ... doesn't express approval (etc.) by her moral speech acts." Finlay suggests that the amoralist can explicitly cancel any simplicature that she has relevant moral attitudes merely by explaining that she is an amoralist. Moreover, he suggests that any such simplicature would be contextually cancelled "if her audience already knows of her amoralism" (2005: 15). The important point, however, is whether the amoralist is successfully *cancelling* the simplicature that she has relevant attitudes or whether she is instead *chancelling* the simplicature. Finlay says that it seems clear to him that the simplicature is cancelled (pp. 14–15). He says, "moral assertions do not seem to be rendered ... linguistically inappropriate" when they are supplemented by a denial that the speaker has any relevant moral attitude. It appears that Finlay and I have different intuitions about this case. I think it plausibly is linguistically inappropriate, for example, for Anna to say, "Capital punishment is morally wrong," if she does not disapprove of capital punishment. Finlay sees no inappropriateness, but the disagreement might be more apparent than real.

To understand this, it is important to bear four things in mind. First, in the case Finlay describes, the amoralist would not simplicate that she has the relevant moral attitudes for she would not intend to convey this and, given what she says, it would not be reasonable to take her to intend to convey this. As I explained before, however, this does not mean that she has cancelled the simplicature in Grice's sense, since, if I am correct, her usage is non-standard.

Second, there is a distinction between a misuse of a term relative to its core meaning and relative to its simplicature meaning. Finlay appears to think that both kinds of misuse would make a person's utterance "not fully intelligible" or "not understood" (2005: 19). However, misuses of a term relative to its simplicature meaning need not result in a lack of full intelligibility, as I explained before. For Grice, a simplicature that *p* is not "explicitly cancellable" if it would not be *admissible* to add that one does not mean to convey that *p*. I do not see Grice as suggesting here that it would be less than fully intelligible to add this. The point rather is the addition would make the overall utterance linguistically nonstandard.

Given this, third, I can agree with Finlay that an amoralist would make a moral judgment in saying, "Capital punishment is morally wrong." On my view, the proposition that the amoralist asserts in assertorically uttering a sentence such as "Capital punishment is wrong" is the same proposition that anyone would assert in assertorically uttering the sentence in the same context, assuming of course that she is using the moral terms with their standard core meaning.

Finally, recall that people sometimes develop nonstandard dialects. If a group of English speakers does not have contempt for Italians, for example, it might develop a dialect in which the term "wop" does not have the standard simplicature meaning. Similarly, an amoralist might have a nonstandard idiolect in which moral terms lack simplicature meaning. Audiences can understand this. Hence, even if the amoralist uses moral language in a nonstandard way relative to simplicature meanings, she presumably uses it in a standard way relative to core meanings, and she uses it appropriately in her own idiolect. Accordingly, she is able to make moral assertions.

This completes my response to Finlay's Gricean Tests Argument. I have argued that the simplicatures in question are detachable but are not cancellable in Grice's sense. Despite this, although a person who lacks moral attitudes uses moral language in a nonstandard way when she makes a moral assertion using standard moral vocabulary, she does assert a moral proposition. The amoralist is able to make moral assertions.

The Silencing Argument

Finlay's final argument is that the conventional simplicature view is committed to postulating linguistic conventions that "would be unsustainable" since they would limit the expression of information. They would in effect "silence" the amoralist (2005: 19). There are four steps in the argument. First, it would be contrary to the "natural dynamic" of language if conventions were to develop that restrict our ability to communicate (p. 18). Because of this, second, if a convention were to develop that restricted the proper use of certain terms to those who have relevant accompanying attitudes, it would be "unsustainable" unless there were some other term in the language with the same core meaning that could be used by a person who lacked the accompanying attitudes. For unless there were some such term, a person who lacked the relevant accompanying attitudes would have no way to express her beliefs except by using the available term, and, knowing this, audiences would not be puzzled by her choice of words (p. 19). But third, we have no familiar neutral equivalents for moral terms. Fourth, the amoralist therefore would use the usual moral vocabulary to express her moral beliefs, and since this would be "the easiest and most natural way for her to do so," audiences would not be puzzled by her choice of words. Hence, Finlay concludes, the conventional simplicature view must be false. "There cannot be a linguistic convention" requiring speakers to have relevant conative attitudes as a condition of the proper use of moral vocabulary in making moral assertions (p. 19).

I have already answered this argument, in effect. I agree that there are no familiar neutral equivalents for moral terms. But I have argued despite this that the attitudinal content simplicated by the use of moral expressions is detachable. The amoralist need not use moral vocabulary in the standard way to express her moral beliefs. She could say that capital punishment has the property standardly ascribed by the predicate "morally wrong." Or she could introduce a term into her idiolect, a term that, by stipulation, has the same core meaning as a given moral term but without its simplicature meaning. Or she could simply carry on to use moral vocabulary as if it lacked simplicature meaning. The result might be that her audience would come to understand that, in her idiolect, the moral terms lack simplicature meaning. Even if the amoralist would misuse moral terms relative to their simplicature meaning, this would not prevent her from being seen to use them correctly relative to their core meaning, in making moral assertions. The fact that the moral terms have simplicature meaning need not silence the amoralist.

It could be, moreover, that a language or dialect simply fails to have a neutral equivalent for a double-aspect term.[49] Bigotry against homosexuals could be so deeply entrenched and widespread in a group, for instance, that the group's language has no non-pejorative term with the core meaning of our term "homosexual." This would make it difficult for anyone who is not a bigot to speak about homosexuals, but such a person would not be "silenced." To be sure, if she uses the local pejorative term to refer to homosexuals, her usage can be challenged as nonstandard if it emerges that she has no contempt. But instead she can introduce a new term to refer to homosexuals and stipulate that it lacks any pejorative simplicature meaning, or she can simply use the local pejorative term and chancel the simplicature of contempt. So it seems to me that the fact that there are not terms in common use that have the same core meaning as the moral terms but lack their simplicature meaning is not an objection to my position.

I conclude, then, that Finlay's silencing argument against the conventional simplicature view is unsuccessful. And I have argued that his other two arguments are also unsuccessful.

8. CONCLUSION: ADDITIONAL PROBLEMS

I have been defending the conventional simplicature version of realist-expressivism against a series of objections. I first considered Kent Bach's

---

[49] Robert May has suggested that "untouchable" might be an actual example.

argument that there is no such thing as conventional implicature. In response, I defined a notion of conventional *simplicature* and I argued that Bach's argument does not show that there is no such thing as conventional simplicature. I then considered a series of arguments by Stephen Finlay against the idea that moral assertions conventionally simplicate attitudinal content. I believe I have shown that Finlay's arguments are inconclusive at best.

I have here taken the intuitive plausibility of the expressivist thesis as a given. I have simply assumed that there are widespread and robust intuitions that support the thesis that a person making a moral assertion thereby expresses an appropriate conative attitude. I have also assumed that there are widespread robust intuitions that support the semantic thesis that it is the meanings of the moral predicates that explain how we manage to express conative attitudes in making moral assertions. Finlay challenges these assumptions, but I do not need to defend them in order to achieve my limited goal in this project, which is to show that the intuitions that support the semantic expressivist thesis are compatible with moral realism. To achieve this goal, I need only to show that the conventional simplicature version of realist-expressivism is defensible and that it accommodates the expressivist intuitions.

It would be worrisome, however, if there were robust and widespread intuitions that are not accommodated by the conventional simplicature view. I will briefly point out two lines of argument that challenge the view from this direction.

First, it might seem intuitively plausible that a person who says that lying is wrong expresses disapproval of lying in the direct and immediate way that, in saying, "Lying is widespread," she would express her belief that lying is widespread, or in saying, "It is so sad," she would express her sadness. Intuitively, it might seem, a person speaking sincerely directly reveals her beliefs and attitudes in conversation. She does not merely simplicate *that* she has them. The worry, then, is that the conventional simplicature view does not capture the direct nature of attitudinal expression.[50]

There is nothing in the conventional simplicature view that rules out these claims, or that is incompatible with the idea that we 'directly' reveal our attitudes in moral discourse. The conventional simplicature view is intended to explain what communicative resources we can use in expressing our moral beliefs and attitudes. We express the belief that lying is widespread in uttering "Lying is widespread" due to the meaning of the sentence. Similarly, we express sadness in uttering, "It is so sad," due to the meaning of that sentence. On the conventional simplicature view, we

---

[50] See Bar-On and Chrisman (2009). Bach (2006*a*: 494).

express attitudes such as moral disapproval in making moral claims due to the semantic usage rules for moral terms.

Second, it might seem intuitively plausible that conative attitudes such as approval and disapproval are "internal" to moral beliefs. Gibbard claims that "normative thought" involves "a kind of endorsement—an endorsement that any descriptivistic analysis treats inadequately" (1990, 33). Realist-expressivism implies that moral *discourse* involves a kind of endorsement, but it does not imply that moral *thought* also involves a kind of endorsement. According to realist-expressivism, a person's believing that, say, lying is wrong consists in the person's having the familiar cognitive attitude to a moral proposition, and a person can have this very attitude to a moral proposition whether or not she has a suitable conative attitude. Nevertheless, attitudes of approval and disapproval might be involved in moral thought, as I shall explain.

There is an intuitive difference, it seems, between thinking that Leonardo is a "wop" and thinking that he is an "Italian."[51] This suggests that our thoughts can be linguistically organized. It suggests that a person who has an occurrent belief might 'entertain' a sentence she could use to express it, even if she does not actually utter the sentence. This is also suggested by the fact that when we vocalize a thought we normally are able straightaway to assert it without needing to search for the words. If our thoughts can be linguistically organized in the way I have in mind, then a person with an occurrent moral belief might entertain a sentence she could use to express this belief. And the realist-expressivist can hold that a person who has a moral belief might thereby in effect be affirming a moral sentence in a way that commits her to having an appropriate corresponding conative attitude. This would extend realist-expressivism to explain the element of "endorsement" in moral thought.[52]

I began by discussing an example in which a person says capital punishment is wrong but then straightaway denies that she disapproves of capital punishment. According to noncognitivist expressivism, I suggested, there is a kind of pragmatic contradiction involved in cases of this kind. For in saying capital punishment is wrong, the person is expressing a kind of disapproval, but she then denies that she has any such attitude. According to the version of realist-expressivism I want to defend, the person would be conventionally simplicating that she disapproves of capital punishment. In going on to deny that she has any such attitude, she would be undercutting the felicity of her utterance. She would be revealing that her utterance was nonstandard. This would indeed be a kind of pragmatic contradiction. It

---

[51] Bach raised this point in correspondence.
[52] See Williamson (forthcoming).

appears, then, that realist-expressivism can explain the expressivist intuitions that have been invoked in support of noncognitivism. It can do so in a way that is compatible with any plausible version of moral realism.

REFERENCES

Bar-On, Dorit, and Chrisman, Matthew (2009) 'Ethical Neo-Expressivism,' in Russ Shafer-Landau (ed.), *Oxford Studies in Metaethics*, iv.

Bach, Kent (1999) 'The Myth of Conventional Implicature' *Linguistics and Philosophy* 22(4): 327–66.

——— (2006*a*) Review of Christopher Potts, *The Logic of Conventional Implicatures*, *Journal of Linguistics* 42: 490–5.

——— (2006*b*) 'The Top 10 Misconceptions about Implicature,' in Betty Birner and Gregory Ward (eds.), *Drawing the Boundaries of Meaning* (Amsterdam: John Benjamins), 21–30.

——— and Harnish, Robert M. (1979) *Linguistic Communication and Speech Acts* (Cambridge, MA: MIT Press).

Barker, Stephen J. (2000) 'Is Value Content a Component of Conventional Implicature?' *Analysis* 60: 268–79.

Blackburn, Simon (1988) 'How to Be an Ethical Antirealist' *Midwest Studies in Philosophy* 12: 361–75.

Boisvert, Daniel (2008) 'Expressive-Assertivism' *Pacific Philosophical Quarterly* 89: 169–203.

Copp, David (1995) *Morality, Normativity, and Society* (New York: Oxford University Press).

——— (2001) 'Realist-Expressivism: A Neglected Option for Moral Realism' *Social Philosophy and Policy* 18: 1–43. Reprinted in David Copp, *Morality in a Natural World* (Cambridge: Cambridge University Press, 2007).

Davis, Wayne (2005) *Nondescriptive Meaning and Reference: An Ideational Semantics* (Oxford: Clarendon Press).

Finlay, Stephen (2004) 'The Conversational Practicality of Value Judgement' *Journal of Ethics* 8: 205–23.

——— (2005) 'Value and Implicature' *Philosophers' Imprint* 5(4): 1–20. Accessed at www.philosophersimprint.org/005004/.

Frege, Gottlob (1979) *Posthumous Writings*, ed. Hans Hermes, Friedrich Kambartel, and Friedrich Kaulbach, trans. Peter Long and Roger White (Chicago: University of Chicago Press).

Gibbard, Allan (1990) *Wise Choices, Apt Feelings* (Cambridge, MA: Harvard University Press).

Grice, H. Paul (1989) *Studies in the Way of Words* (Cambridge, MA: Harvard University Press).

Hare, R. M. (1952) *The Language of Morals* (Oxford: Oxford University Press).

Hom, Christopher (2008) 'The Semantics of Racial Epithets' *Journal of Philosophy* 105: 416–40.

Potts, Christopher (2005) *The Logic of Conventional Implicatures* (New York: Oxford University Press).

—— (2007) 'Into the Conventional-Implicature Dimension' *Philosophy Compass* 2: 665–79.

Ridge, Michael (2006) 'Ecumenical Expressivism: Finessing Frege' *Ethics* 116: 302–36.

Saul, Jennifer (2002) 'Speaker Meaning, What is Said, and What is Implicated' *Nous* 36: 228–48.

Schroeder, Mark (2008) 'Expression for Expressivists' *Philosophy and Phenomenological Research* 76: 86–116.

Smith, Michael (1994). *The Moral Problem* (Oxford: Blackwell Publishers).

Williamson, Timothy (forthcoming) 'Reference, Inference, and the Semantics of Pejoratives,' in J. Almog and P. Leonardi (eds.), *The Life and Work of David Kaplan* (Oxford: Oxford University Press). Accessed at http://www.philosophy.ox.ac.uk/faculty/members/docs/Reference.pdf.

7

Guilt-Free Morality

Gilbert Harman

How essential is the complex emotion of guilt to morality? Can we define moral standards, in contrast with other sorts of standards, as those standards it is appropriate to feel guilt for violating? Is it essential to being a moral person to be disposed to feel guilt if one takes oneself to have acted morally wrongly?

1. PROPOSED CONNECTIONS BETWEEN MORALITY AND GUILT FEELINGS

Here are some of the ways in which some philosophers and psychologists have taken the emotion of guilt to be essential to morality.

One relatively central idea is that guilt feelings are *warranted* if an agent knows that he or she has acted morally wrongly. It might be said that in such a case the agent has a strong *reason* to feel guilt, that the agent *ought* to have guilt feelings, that the agent is *justified* in having guilt feelings and *unjustified* in not having guilt feelings. It might be said that it would be *immoral* of an agent not to have feelings of guilt after realizing that he or she has acted morally wrongly or that only an agent with *bad character* would not have such feelings.

Some think that there is a *definitional* connection between morality and guilt feelings. In one version of this idea, moral standards are by definition those standards that a person is warranted in feeling guilty for violating. Or, it might be said that a particular agent's moral principles are by definition those principles the agent *would feel guilty* for violating. Alternatively, an

I am indebted to my colleagues Philip Johnson-Laird and Eldar Shafir and students in our course, PSY 237/PHI 237, "The Psychology and Philosophy of Rationalit." I have benefited from discussion with David Velleman and from comments by Charles Starkey, Elizabeth Harman, and two anonymous readers.

agent's moral principles might be distinguished from other principles as those principles for the violation of which the agent takes guilt *to be warranted*.

Another thought is that all *normal* adults are susceptible to guilt feelings. In this view, children who do not acquire such a susceptibility to guilt feelings will not acquire a moral sense. Psychopaths are adults who, among other things, have no such moral sense and are not susceptible to guilt.

A further thought is that moral motivation is at least in part motivation to avoid guilt feelings for acting immorally. This thought might explain the previous idea, because it would imply that someone not susceptible to guilt feelings would not be susceptible to moral motivation and would therefore lack a moral sense.

Are guilt feelings central to morality in any of these ways? In order to answer this question, we need to consider what are to count as guilt feelings.

2. GUILT FEELINGS

Consider amoral psychopathic Mary. While she believes that it is morally wrong to steal a book from the library, that consideration does not motivate her at all and she steals a book without regret or concern. She has no guilt feelings about her action even though she *feels that* she is guilty of stealing and so in that respect *feels as if* she is guilty. It appears to Mary that she is guilty of acting wrongly.[1]

If that were enough for Mary to have guilt feelings, many but not all of the views mentioned in the previous section of this chapter would be trivially true. Moral principles are trivially principles that one is guilty of violating if one violates them. If one knows one has acted wrongly, one is trivially warranted in feeling that one is guilty of having acted wrongly.

Obviously, psychopaths like Mary would be trivially susceptible to guilt feelings of this sort as long as they were able in this sense to feel that they were guilty of doing something morally wrong.

So, let us assume that guilt feelings are not simply feeling that one is guilty of something, but involve something more. What more?

Nontrivial guilt feelings have to be real feelings—with affect—indeed, with negative affect. To feel guilt is to feel bad.

They may involve agent regret, but that by itself is not enough for guilt. One regrets many things one has done without feeling guilty about them.

---

[1] Greenspan (1992) identifies guilt feelings with feeling as if one is guilty. Darwall (2007) endorses this identification.

For example, one may regret having moved one's queen to a particular square in a game of chess.

And it is not enough for feeling nontrivial guilt that one regrets having done something morally wrong. Psychopathic Mary can have such regret even though she has no guilt feelings. (I consider nonpsychopathic examples below.)

One conception of guilt feelings identifies them with feelings of remorse, involving deep regret, painful humiliation, distress, self-punishment, and/or self-flagellation. Some theorists suggest that guilt feelings also involve anxiety (e.g. Freud 1962) and perhaps the thought that one deserves punishment (e.g. Kaufmann 1973).

Given this more serious understanding of guilt feelings, the alleged connections between morality and guilt feelings mentioned in the previous section may seem to have some plausibility without being trivial. Perhaps it is true that guilt feelings in this sense are warranted if one acts wrongly; but on the other hand, it might be argued that such feelings are never warranted. Maybe there is a definitional connection between morality and guilt feelings in this sense, but maybe not. It may or may not be true that normal nonpsychopathic adults are susceptible to guilt feelings in this sense and that children who fail to acquire a susceptibility to such feelings will not develop a moral sense. And maybe moral motivation is motivation to avoid such guilt feelings, or maybe not.

Are there good reasons to believe in any or all of the suggested connections between morality and guilt feelings, so understood?

3. ARE THERE GOOD REASONS TO THINK NONTRIVIAL GUILT FEELINGS ARE CENTRAL TO MORALITY?

Two sorts of reasons have been offered for thinking guilt feelings are central to morality: empirical psychological reasons and more speculative conceptual reasons.

Empirical Psychological Reasons

Relevant empirical psychological research includes studies of psychopaths and studies of certain aspects of moral development in children. There are also studies indicating that sometimes guilt can be a better motivator of other-regarding action than empathy.

To begin our discussion of allegedly relevant psychological research, consider that lack of susceptibility to nontrivial guilt feelings is standardly taken to be one of the defining criteria of psychopathy (Hare 1993). It would of course be rash to conclude that all normal nonpsychopathic adults are susceptible to guilt feelings. From the fact that *all* psychopaths lack susceptibility to guilt feelings, it does not follow that *only* psychopaths lack guilt feelings. By itself, the point about psychopaths is compatible with the existence of moral adults who are not susceptible to guilt feelings.

Similarly, children born with certain brain deficits, or who suffer certain brain injuries, lack susceptibility to guilt and are unable to acquire morality. It would be a mistake to conclude from this that normal children without such deficits who do acquire morality must be susceptible to guilt feelings. By itself, the relevant evidence about brain deficits or injuries in children is obviously compatible with the existence of children who acquire morality without becoming susceptible to guilt feelings. Such abnormalities or injuries affect other emotions and capacities in addition to guilt that are needed for acquiring morality (Damasio 2003: 152–5). Indeed there appears to be no evidence at all for the claim that children cannot become moral beings without being susceptible to guilt.

In the following section of this chapter, we will consider anecdotal evidence that there are normal moral adults who are not and perhaps never have been susceptible to guilt. But before we get to that, let us consider also an example from psychological research that indicates a respect in which guilt is a better motivator of other-regarding action than empathy or sympathy.[2] Carlsmith and Gross (1969) studied subjects' motivation to help

(1) someone to whom they have caused distress,

(2) someone to whom they have seen someone else cause distress, and

(3) someone who has witnessed them cause someone else distress.

The very interesting result was that subjects tended to be more inclined to help in case (3) than in the other cases!

Notice, however, that this experiment does not address the question whether moral acts are motivated by the goal of avoiding guilt feelings. It is concerned with the question whether feeling guilt can make people more likely to be helpful to others whom they have not treated wrongly.

Furthermore, the sense in which subjects "feel guilt" in this experiment is the first quite weak sense considered above: *feeling that one is guilty.* People who are thinking that they have just been guilty of causing distress to someone X are more likely than otherwise to help someone else Y.

So, this sort of experiment is actually irrelevant to the concerns of the present chapter.

---

[2] Charles Starkey called this research to my attention.

Relatively Speculative More Philosophical and Conceptual Reasons

Philosophers often suppose that a connection to guilt feelings is obviously definitive of or essential to morality, without the need for any evidence or argument.

For example, Brandt (1967) takes the following to be definitive of a person's thinking sincerely that any action of kind F is wrong:

> If he thinks he has just performed an F-action, he feels guilty or remorseful or uncomfortable about it, unless he thinks he has some excuse—unless, for instance, he knows that at the time of action he did not think his action would be an F-action. "Guilt" (etc.) is not to be understood as implying some special origin such as interiorization of parental prohibitions, or as being a vestige of anxiety about punishment. It is left open that it might be an unlearned emotional response to the thought of being the cause of the suffering of another person. Any feeling that must be viewed simply as anxiety about anticipated consequences, for one's self or a person to whom one is attached, is not however, to count as a "guilt" feeling.

Brandt later (1979: 164–70) develops the same point, saying for example that a person's "moral code is evidenced by his autonomous guilt feelings—those arising from failure to act in accord with his own moral motivation" (p. 167). When I objected to this in a review of Brandt's book (Harman 1982), he wrote to me, "I think a moral system does need guilt-feelings" (letter of December 18, 1983). And Brandt (1992) continues to insist that "a person's morality consists of intrinsic aversions to some types of actions and corresponding dispositions to feel guilty and to disapprove of others and to think these attitudes are justified in some way" (p. 7).

Similarly, Williams (1985) says as if the point is obvious, needing no further evidence or argument, perhaps as definitive of morality or of being a moral agent: "if an agent never felt [remorse or self-reproach or guilt], he would not belong to the morality system or be a full moral agent in its terms" (p. 177).

According to Gibbard (1992) it is definitive of moral standards that, "if an agent violates [them] because of inadequate motivation to abide by them, guilt is warranted on his part, and resentment on the part of others" (p. 202), where the relevant sort of guilt consists in "agonized" feelings of "self blame" (p. 201).

And Greenspan (1995) offers a subtle account of the teaching of "ought" in terms of anticipatory guilt, by getting a child to feel guilt for acting in certain ways. In her view, the distinctive motivational force of moral considerations arises from this connection with anticipatory guilt.

As far as I can tell, however, the proposed necessary connections between morality and guilt are arrived at through introspection and are accepted merely because they seem plausible to the authors, presumably because of their own experiences of guilt. The authors may expect their proposed necessary connections to seem plausible to their readers also, but that is just speculation on their part and they offer no evidence that it is so. In fact the suggestion that such connections are necessary will not seem plausible to *all* their readers. They do not seem plausible to me, for example, presumably because my own experience has been different. In any event, the issue is not whether such necessary connections seem plausible but whether they are in fact necessary aspects of morality.

4. REASONS TO THINK GUILT FEELINGS ARE NOT CENTRAL TO MORALITY

It cannot be an a priori definitional truth that an agent can have moral principles only if the person is susceptible to nontrivial guilt feelings, nor can it be an a priori definitional truth that all moral agents are susceptible to such guilt feelings. It is easy at least to *imagine* a moral person with moral principles who is not susceptible to the relevant sort of guilt feelings. Choose someone A you take to be a highly moral person. Then imagine another person B who acts and reacts in the same way as A, with the (possible) exception of not being susceptible to guilt for doing something wrong. B regrets wrong actions and is determined to do better, but does not suffer remorse, feel agony, or engage in self-punishment. Clearly, this imagined agent can nevertheless be quite moral and can have moral principles.[3]

Furthermore, there seem actually to be many moral people with moral principles but no susceptibility to nontrivial guilt feelings. To mention one example, as far as I can tell, I am not susceptible to nontrivial guilt feelings, yet I have moral principles and seem (at least to myself) to be a relatively moral person. When I have discussed this topic with various colleagues, many of them say they too do not feel nontrivial guilt. Some say that they, like me, have never experienced guilt. Others say that they used to feel guilt but have in one or another way been able to get over being susceptible to guilt.

I do not find that the moral quality of people I know varies with their susceptibility to nontrivial guilt. Some of those who seem capable of great

[3] Aristotle's (1985) fully virtuous person and Nietzsche's (1966) overman are also possible examples.

guilt feelings seem to me to be not very moral at all and some who seem not to be susceptible to nontrivial guilt seem very moral.

Moral Motivation

How can one acquire morality and moral motivation if not by developing a susceptibility to feel guilt for doing something wrong?

To some extent one picks up the local morality from the people around. This is not necessarily by instruction. Exposure to others may be enough.

One does not always come to accept exactly the moral standards one has been exposed to. Adam Smith (1976) and others observe that one tends to pick up an idealized version of the morality one is exposed to when young. One may start out more idealistic than other people and even end up with a very personal morality that one does not take oneself to share with other people.

How do people tell what is right or wrong in particular cases? Sometimes they react emotionally. For some, thinking of a particular course of action produces an anticipatory feeling of guilt. This tells them that such a course of action would be wrong. But other emotional reactions can play an important role, for example, empathy with others and concern for moral principle.

In Adam Smith's version, one acquires morality by developing a habit of imagining how an impartial sympathetic spectator would react to one's actions. One does this by pretending to be such a spectator and seeing how one reacts. As this pretense becomes habitual, one acquires the sympathetic emotional responses of such a spectator and so comes to care more or less directly about other people and about following moral principles.[4]

Even without any prospect of agonized guilt for failing to do what is right, one might do the right thing anyway out of concern for the people affected, or for other reasons such as concern for principle, not because one would feel bad for not doing what is right.

There is of course an issue here about how motivation works. Some theorists take psychological hedonism (Moore 2004) seriously. That is the view that motivation is simply a matter of aiming at things one expects will give one "positive affect," and avoiding things that will give one "negative affect." Psychological hedonism implies that people do not care directly about others, that they care about others only to the extent that they think it is likely they themselves will probably benefit from what happens. But it seems to me that I do care directly about many people, including my

---

[4] For more about this see Harman (1986).

wife and children, friends, colleagues, neighbors, and many others. I have
trouble believing that the reason I want to do something for my children,
for example, is that I will feel good for doing that, since it seems to me that
I do not care as much about my feeling good as I care about their feeling
good.[5]

Desirability of Guilt?

Of course, the fact that there are moral agents with moral standards who
are not susceptible to guilt (if this is a fact), does not establish that it is
not reasonable or desirable or warranted to be subject to guilt. Indeed, one
might argue as follows.

> When somebody violates the moral code, others may get angry at them
> and that anger is sometimes warranted or reasonable. So, isn't one
> reasonable and warranted in getting angry with oneself for violating the
> moral code? And isn't that to have the relevant sort of guilt?[6]

Now, on the one hand, it can be useful for people to have a disposition to
get angry at wrongdoers. Such a disposition can serve as a useful deterrent
of wrongful behavior. It does not follow that it is equally useful to be
susceptible to guilt. If there are people who have adequate motivation to
act morally without being susceptible to nontrivial guilt feelings, which
there seem to be, guilt does not have to be reasonable for them even if
having a disposition to outrage and anger at others for their wrongful acts
is reasonable.

Appropriate or Warranted Guilt?

Gibbard (2006), says,

Here is something we may perhaps accept as truistic, as not in need of debate and
discussion: Guilt over something one has done is warranted just in case outrage over
it is warranted on the part of impartial observers.

I say, on the contrary, that we cannot accept this "as truistic, as not in need
of debate and discussion."

Of course, an attitude is sometimes appropriate or warranted even if, all
things considered, it would be undesirable to have that attitude. A certain
belief might be warranted by one's evidence even though it would be better,
all things considered, not to have that belief and to believe the opposite.
So, the fact that feeling guilt would not be useful on a given occasion

---

[5] See Feinberg (1984).   [6] Here I am indebted to Philip Johnson-Laird.

cannot by itself establish that one is not warranted in feeling guilt on that occasion.[7] Whether one is *warranted* in feeling guilt for doing something wrong is of course a normative issue and my normative view is that guilt is not reasonable, appropriate, or warranted for people who have adequate motivation to act morally without being susceptible to guilt feelings.

Social Function of Guilt and Fairness

A possible worry about a morally good person who is not susceptible to nontrivial guilt feelings is that other people often expect one to feel guilt for doing something wrong. If one does not, they may get even angrier at one than they would otherwise. One's showing guilt can allow others to be less angry with one, because one takes on some of the anger oneself. This is connected with what is sometimes referred to as "the social function of guilt" (Baumeister et al. 1994).

The admirable people I have in mind feel regret about moral mistakes, but not guilt. In order not to incur the wrath of others, they can apologize, say that they are sorry for what they have done, try to make amends, and sincerely promise not to do it again. Furthermore, as moral people, they will not pretend to feel guilt and pretend to beat themselves up about it, since that would involve wrongfully misrepresenting themselves.

Guilt and Fairness

A possibly related further worry is that it can be unfair for someone to go unpunished for a wrongful act.[8] So, it might be argued that, in the absence of external punishment, it is fairer for the wrongful agent to feel punishing guilt than not and certainly not enough for the wrongful agent just to pretend to feel guilt!

I suggest that morally good people with no disposition to feel guilt will not want to benefit from any wrongful acts and so will try to make amends in some other way than by feeling or pretending to feel guilt.

5. WHY IT IS BETTER NOT TO BE SUSCEPTIBLE TO GUILT

Non-trivial guilt is of course a negative experience that can make people miserable. It might be worth paying this price if susceptibility to guilt made

---

[7] Here I am indebted to Nicholas Sturgeon and Elizabeth Harman.
[8] Here I am indebted to Eldar Shafir.

people act better. But there is no evidence that susceptibility to nontrivial guilt is needed to make people act morally.

As noted above, some psychological studies (Carlsmith and Gross 1969) can be described as showing that guilt better motivates moral behavior than mere altruism. But, as already noted, these studies did not explicitly discuss nontrivial guilt. They showed certain effects of feeling that one is guilty of a moral infraction. Furthermore, as discussed, the studies were not concerned with motivation to avoid an act for which an agent might feel guilt. They were concerned with how feeling that one is guilty of acting wrongly toward *A* can lead one to help someone else *B*.

Furthermore, consider the question whether those otherwise normal nonpsychopathic people who are not subject to nontrivial guilt feelings act more wrongly than other people who are subject to nontrivial guilt feelings. I see no reason to think the otherwise normal people not subject to guilt are as a group less moral than those who are subject to guilt.

Punishment versus Reward

How can children be brought up to be morally good without being susceptible to guilt? Perhaps it is enough for loving parents to refrain from punishment while helping children to develop sympathy and empathy with others. The thought is that children will internalize punishment only as a way of anticipating and avoiding external punishment.

It may seem hard to believe that setting a good example for one's children and praising their morally good actions would be sufficient for them to develop into good moral agents rather than spoiled brats. Clearly, when children are punished for acting wrongly, they tend not to repeat the wrong act the next time. On the other hand, children who are praised for doing the right thing, tend not to act so well in the future.

But it is a fallacy to treat this observation as an argument that punishment is needed and praise is ineffective, the fallacy of ignoring the statistical phenomenon of *regression toward the mean*. Quite apart from the actual merits of punishment and reward, exceptionally bad actions are likely to be followed by less bad actions and exceptionally good actions are likely to be followed by less good actions.

Unfortunately, people tend not to understand the purely statistical explanation of the fact that extreme behaviors tend to be followed by less extreme behaviors.[9]

---

[9] The point has been famously discussed by Kahneman and Tversky (1973: 250–1).

Gotcha!

Consider the plight of those morally good people I am addressing who are susceptible to feelings of guilt when they perceive that they have transgressed against the moral code. Having absorbed my argument here, the next time they violate the moral code, they feel guilty about it and then, remembering my arguments, they feel guilty for feeling guilty![10]

6. CONCLUSION

I have argued that guilt is not essential to morality. There are morally excellent people who are not subject to guilt. I am inclined to think that it is even within the realm of possibility that anyone could be brought up without such a disposition to feel guilt.

I agree of course that many moral people are susceptible to guilt. While I think that is a defect in them, I agree that they may be in other respects morally good.

It is widely believed that susceptibility to guilt is necessary for moral motivation. While I agree that susceptibility to guilt can serve in this way as a moral motivation, I say it is possible and better not to need that motivation.

I have been objecting to the sort of guilt that involves internalized self-punishment, the sort of guilt that many take to provide an important motive for moral actions. I find that there are morally good people not susceptible to such guilt. I conclude that susceptibility to such guilt is not needed for moral motivation, that it is incorrect to define moral standards as those standards it is appropriate to feel guilt for violating, that people can lack susceptibility to guilt without being psychopaths, that it would be a good thing to try to bring up children in such a way that they are not susceptible to such guilt, and that it would be a good thing for those moral people who feel guilt to try to eliminate it.

REFERENCES

Aristotle (1985) *Nicomachean Ethics*, translated by Terence Irwin (Indianapolis: Hackett).

Baumeister, R. F., Stillwell, A. M., and Hetherton, T. F. (1994) "Guilt: An Interpersonal Approach" *Psychological Bulletin* 115(2): 243–67.

---

[10] Philip Johnson-Laird noted this possibility.

Brandt, R. B. (1967) "Some Merits of One Form of Rule-Utilitarianism" *University of Colorado Studies, Series in Philosophy*, no. 3.

—— (1979) *A Theory of the Good and the Right* (Oxford: Clarendon Press).

—— (1992) "Introductory Comments," in *Morality, Utilitarianism, and Rights* (Cambridge: Cambridge University Press).

Carlsmith, M., and Gross, A. E. (1969). "Some Effects of Guilt on Compliance" *Journal of Personality and Social Psychology* 11: 232–9.

Damasio, A. (2003) *Looking for Spinoza* (Orlando, FL: Harcourt).

Darwall, S. (2007) "Moral Obligation and Accountability," in R. Shafer-Landau (ed.), *Oxford Studies in Metaethics*, ii: 111–32.

Feinberg, J. (1984) "Psychological Egoism," in S. Cahn, P. Kitcher, and G. Sher (eds.), *Reason at Work* (San Diego: Harcourt, Brace, and Jovanovich), 25–35.

Freud, S. (1962) *Civilization and its Discontents*. Translated and edited by James Strachey (New York: Norton).

Gibbard, A. (1992) "Moral Concepts: Substance and Sentiment" Philosophical Perspectives, 6, *Ethics*.

—— (2006) "Moral Feelings and Moral Concepts," in R. Shafer-Landau (ed.), *Oxford Studies in Metaethics*, i (Oxford: Oxford University Press).

Greenspan, P. S. (1992) "Subjective Guilt and Responsibility" *Mind* 101: 287–303.

—— (1995) *Practical Guilt: Moral Dilemmas, Emotions, and Social Norms* (New York: Oxford University Press).

Hare, R. D. (1993) *Without Conscience: The Disturbing World of the Psychopaths among Us* (New York: Pocket Books).

Harman, G. (1982) Critical Review: Richard B. Brandt, *A Theory of the Good and the Right*. In *Philosophical Studies* 42: 119–39.

—— (1986) "Moral Agent and Impartial Spectator," Lindley Lecture (Lawrence: University of Kansas). Reprinted in Harman (2000).

—— (2000) *Explaining Value* (Oxford: Clarendon Press).

Kahneman, D., and Tversky, A. (1973) "On the Psychology of Prediction" *Psychological Review* 80: 237–51.

Kaufmann, W. (1973) *Without Guilt and Justice: From Decidophobia to Autonomy* (New York: Peter Wyden).

Moore, A. (2004) "Hedonism," in E. N. Zalta (ed.), *Stanford Encyclopedia of Philosophy* (summer 2004 edn), http://plato.stanford.edu/archives/sum2004/entries/hedonism/.

Nietzsche, F. (1966) *Thus Spoke Zarathustra: A Book for All and None*, translated by W. Kaufmann (New York: Viking Press).

Smith, A. (1976) *Theory of Moral Sentiments* (Glasgow Edition) (Oxford: Oxford University Press).

Williams, B. (1985). *Ethics and the Limits of Philosophy* (Cambridge, MA: Harvard University Press).

8

Reasons as Evidence

Stephen Kearns and Daniel Star

Normative reasons are strange beasts. On the one hand, we are all intimately familiar with them. We couldn't live for long without the guidance they continually offer us when we are trying to work out what to believe and what to do. At the same time, they seem to resist being analyzed in other terms. We can say that they "count in favor of..." (acts, beliefs, intentions, desires, emotions, etc.), and some have thought that this rather uninformative characterization is pretty much all we will ever be able to come up with when attempting to answer the question, what are reasons? (Scanlon 1998: 17; Parfit 2007).

Philosophers have distinguished between species of reasons in a number of ways (moral/prudential/aesthetic, practical/theoretical etc.), but it is commonly thought that no unified and informative analysis of the genus is possible.[1] Some think *reasons for action* can be analyzed in terms of (ideal) desires, but most of the very same philosophers would be unhappy with the idea that *reasons for belief* could also be analyzed in terms of desires (ideal or otherwise). No unified analysis of reasons seems possible.

We would like to thank the many participants at the *Fourth Annual Metaethics Workshop* who helped us with their comments, as well as a number of people who offered us similarly excellent comments elsewhere. In particular, we appreciate the feedback we received from Wylie Breckenridge, John Broome, Krister Bykvist, Fabrizio Cariani, David Chalmers, Roger Crisp, Terence Cuneo, James Dreier, Andy Egan, Geoffrey Ferrari, Peter Graham, Gilbert Harman, Karen Jones, Clayton Littlejohn, Errol Lord, Ofra Magidor, Julia Markovits, Elinor Mason, Sean McKeever, James Morauta, Adam Pautz, Wlodek Rabinowicz, Andrew Reisner, Jacob Ross, Jonathan Schaffer, Mark Schroeder, Wolfgang Schwarz, Russ Shafer-Landau, Michael Smith, Nicholas Southwood, Ralph Wedgwood, and two anonymous referees for *Oxford Studies in Metaethics*.

[1] The 'counting in favor of' account of reasons subscribed to by Scanlon and Parfit might be thought to be unified, but it is not informative, since these authors deny that it is possible to provide an analysis in other terms of what it is to be a reason. Other accounts of reasons are informative, but not unified.

The purpose of the present chapter is to suggest that despair on this front is premature. We believe it is possible to give an informative and unified analysis of reasons. A reason to ϕ is simply evidence that one ought to ϕ, where ϕ is either a belief or an action.[2] Of course, this will seem far from obvious to many readers, especially in the case of reasons for action. We are fortunate that this is the case, because it provides us with a good rationale for trying to convince readers that our analysis is correct. In the last part of the chapter, we consider the views of opponents (real and imagined). Our main claim may seem obviously true to some other readers. If so, we are also fortunate that this is the case, because we think our view is intuitively appealing, and because we need all the allies we can get.

The chapter has three main parts. To begin with, we quickly run through our new analysis of what it is to be a reason, without providing any substantive arguments for this analysis. We discuss both reasons for belief and reasons for action, but the most controversial of the principles we provide in the first part of the chapter is a principle connecting reasons for action and evidence. In the second part of the chapter, we provide arguments for this principle, and in the last part of the chapter we examine some important objections to it.

1. REASONS

Here are several principles, each of which specifies necessary and sufficient conditions for being a reason of a particular kind (or for being a reason of the most general kind, in the first case):

Reasons

R Necessarily, a fact F is a reason for an agent A to ϕ **iff** F is evidence that A ought to ϕ (where ϕ is either a belief or an action).

Reasons for Belief

RB Necessarily, a fact F is a reason for an agent A to believe that P **iff** F is evidence that A ought to believe that P.

Reasons for Action

RA Necessarily, a fact F is a reason for an agent A to ϕ **iff** F is evidence that A ought to ϕ (where ϕ is an action).

---

[2] We believe this analysis can be extended to reasons to intend, to desire, etc., but we will not discuss such reasons.

Epistemic Reasons for Belief

ER Necessarily, a fact F is an *epistemic* reason for an agent A to believe that P **iff** F is evidence that A ought to believe that P, and F is evidence that A ought to believe that P because F is evidence that P.

Pragmatic Reasons for Belief

PR Necessarily, a fact F is a *pragmatic* reason for an agent A to believe that P **iff** F is evidence that A ought to believe that P, and this is not just because F is evidence that P (and it may be the case that F is not evidence that P).

R is our main claim. It says that a fact F is a reason just in case it is evidence that one ought to ϕ, for some particular ϕ, where this ϕ is either a belief or an action. RB and RA are belief-specific and action-specific versions of R. The reader should note that it is *not* a feature of our account of reasons that we collapse the distinction between reasons for belief and reasons for action, or attempt to reduce one kind of reason to the other kind of reason. We have found this to be a common misunderstanding of our view. There is nothing in our general view that rules out the possibility that the oughts that govern belief are very different than the oughts that govern action.

In the case of reasons for belief, we claim that a fact F is a reason to believe a proposition P just in case F is evidence that one ought to believe P. ER and PR are both versions of RB, which we have provided simply in order to demonstrate that our account of reasons leaves room for there to be both epistemic reasons for belief and pragmatic reasons for belief.[3] We claim that in the case of epistemic reasons for belief, the very same fact F that is evidence that one ought to believe a particular proposition P is itself evidence for the truth of this proposition, and it is *because* it is evidence that P that the fact F is evidence that one ought to believe P. In the case of pragmatic reasons for belief, on the other hand, the fact F that is evidence that one ought to believe a proposition P is evidence that one ought to believe P in a way that is not merely explained by F being evidence for the truth of P, and F may well completely fail to be evidence that P.[4]

---

[3] It is an interesting feature of our account of reasons that it seems evidentialist in one sense, but non-evidentialist in another sense. Our account clearly has an evidentialist flavor about it because we say that all reasons to believe rest on evidence, but our account also leaves open a possibility that is typically taken to be incompatible with evidentialism, i.e. the possibility that some reasons to believe are pragmatic, rather than epistemic.

[4] Why do we say that "F *may* fail to be evidence that P," rather than the simpler "F fails to be evidence that P"? In most cases of pragmatic reasons to believe that one might ordinarily consider, the pragmatic reasons to believe are not also epistemic reasons to

It might seem to be a substantial objection to RB that there is a simpler account of what it is to be a reason for belief readily available to us. Perhaps a reason to believe a proposition just *is* evidence for the truth of that proposition (in all cases). This would either rule out pragmatic reasons to believe altogether, or make all reasons to believe pragmatic in nature (assuming one could provide a plausible pragmatist account of evidence). Nonetheless, it might be thought that this simpler claim still has an advantage over our claim that a reason to believe a proposition is evidence that one ought to believe that proposition, just because it is more simple, or because it does not contain any mention of oughts. In any case, we believe this objection to RB can be largely defused merely by pointing out that it can still be true on our account that:

EE Necessarily, for all agents A, F is an epistemic reason for A to believe P **iff** F is evidence that P.

EE is not inconsistent with any of the principles listed above. In fact, EE follows from ER in conjunction with two very reasonable principles:

EO Necessarily, for all agents A, **if** F is evidence that P **then** F is evidence that A ought to believe P.

EC Necessarily, for all agents A, F is evidence that A ought to believe P and (F is evidence that A ought to believe P because F is evidence that P) **iff** F is evidence that A ought to believe P and F is evidence that P.

If the reader happens to feel compelled to deny that there are any pragmatic reasons to believe, he or she should still be happy with ER and EE and may feel free to scratch out the word "epistemic" (not because its inclusion makes either of these principles false, but rather because it will then play no important role).

The attentive reader who compares RB and EE may well wonder which statement is more fundamental. This raises an important issue that we do not intend to resolve here. All of the claims we have listed above are *if and*

---

believe, so the relevant F does fail to be evidence for the truth of the relevant P. However, it seems that one and the same fact can be both a pragmatic reason for belief and an epistemic reason for belief, assuming one accepts that there are any pragmatic reasons for belief at all (and it doesn't really matter to us, so far as the main arguments in this paper are concerned, if the reader doesn't accept that there are such reasons). Consider the complex fact that *water is thirst-quenching and believing that water is thirst-quenching will make my life go much better than if I don't believe that water is thirst-quenching.* This complex fact seems to be both a pragmatic reason for belief and an epistemic reason for belief. It is evidence that I ought to believe water is thirst-quenching, but this is not only because it is evidence that water is thirst-quenching, for the same fact is also evidence that I ought to believe water is thirst-quenching in virtue of the good practical consequences that will follow from doing so.

only if claims. As such, they are weaker than identity claims, and are only analyses in a *broad* sense of the term. We have found it easier to argue for the truth of these *if and only if* claims than to argue for corresponding claims that state that the properties of being a reason and being evidence of an ought are identical. We will be more than satisfied if the reader accepts our arguments for the *if and only if* principles alone. Nonetheless, we also believe that the *best* explanation of the truth of all these principles is that the property of being a reason and the property of being evidence of an ought are identical.

Although we have described R as our main claim, we will actually spend most of this chapter discussing RA. This is because we take RA to be the most controversial of the claims listed above, RA and RB together entail R, R is not true if RA is not true, and perhaps the best thing that can be said for R (apart from what can be said for RA) is that it provides the basis for a *unified* account of reasons for belief and reasons for action.

2. ARGUMENTS FOR RA

We will present six arguments for RA. Two of the arguments take the form of an inference to the best explanation, one argument is based on induction, and three of the arguments are deductively valid. Each argument on its own *might* be considered only weakly persuasive; in combination, the six arguments provide us with a strong case for the new analysis of reasons.

2.1. The Simplicity Argument

The first argument runs as follows:

(1) Epistemic and practical reasons are of a kind.
(2) RA provides the only plausible account of reasons according to which (1) is so.
(3) Therefore, RA is true (*inference to the best explanation*).

Let us consider premises (1) and (2) in turn. The first premise simply states the position that we consider to be the natural *default* position concerning the relationship between epistemic reasons (i.e. epistemic reasons for belief) and practical reasons (i.e. reasons for action and pragmatic reasons for belief). Epistemic and practical reasons should be thought of as being of the same basic kind prior to the presentation of good arguments to the contrary.

What entitles us to think of (1) as stating a default position? We believe we are entitled to do so on the basis of linguistic evidence. Here are three relevant linguistic observations. First, and most obviously, the same word, "reason," is used when people talk about epistemic reasons for belief as when people talk about reasons for action. If epistemic reasons for belief alone concern evidence and reasons for action alone concern right-makers and wrong-makers (for instance), then it is surprising that we use the word "reason" in cases involving evidence as well as cases involving right-makers or wrong-makers. One might have thought we would have different words for these different kinds of entities. It is certainly difficult to detect any ambiguity in our ordinary normative reasons talk.

Secondly, the word "reason" behaves the same way, grammatically speaking, in both reasons for action and reasons for belief talk, so long as we restrict our attention to normative reasons. We talk about there being a "reason *to* act" when concerned with a normative reason for action, and we similarly talk about there being a "reason *to* believe" when concerned with a normative epistemic reason to believe. Of course, it is true that there are also non-normative uses of "reason" in English, but it is interesting to note that "reason" does not normally take the infinitive when used in a non-normative fashion. We say "the reason *that* it is raining is because the clouds are heavy," or "the reason *why* it is raining is that the clouds are heavy," but we do not say "the reason *to* it is raining is because the clouds are heavy."

Thirdly, it is possible to construct grammatically correct sentences of the following form: F is a reason to believe P and to ϕ (where ϕ is an action). An example of a sentence that has this form is: "That the ground is wet is a reason to believe it is raining and to take an umbrella." Note that the word "reason" only appears once in this well-formed sentence. One would not expect this sentence to be grammatically correct if epistemic reasons for belief and reasons for action were reasons of two very different kinds. Of course, one *can* say "That the ground is wet is a reason to believe it is raining and a reason to take an umbrella" but the second occurrence of "a reason" seems unnecessary.

Apart from these reasons to accept that (1) states a position that should be considered to be the default position, and to accept that (1) is true, there are additional reasons to accept (1). Most notably, it seems that we can weigh up reasons to act and epistemic reasons to believe against each other. This would not be possible if they were not of a kind. Here is an example of what we have in mind: imagine a professional high-jumper who must jump higher and higher every time he jumps in a particular prestigious competition if he is to succeed in winning a medal. The high-jumper is aware that he could think carefully about the height of the jump on each occasion he jumps and thus come to form a well-justified belief about whether or not he is going to succeed on each particular occasion. However, he is also aware that paying attention to this kind of reason for belief may be something that will guarantee that he fails to successfully make certain jumps. He has a reason to ignore the evidence concerning whether or not the high-jump is too high for him, given his track-record, and this is the reason he has to win the competition. A reason for action trumps a reason for belief, over and over again.

Similarly, a distraught mother might ignore evidence that her kidnapped child has been murdered, and continue searching for him, and this extra effort might actually be required if she is to find her child. Her reason to believe that continuing to search for her child is futile would be outweighed by the very weighty reason that speaks in favor of continuing to search for her child.

The second premise says that RA provides the only plausible account of reasons according to which epistemic and practical reasons are of a kind.[5] Being an epistemic reason for belief is simply being evidence for something. (On the simplest view, an epistemic reason for P is evidence that P. On our view, an epistemic reason for P is both evidence that P and that one ought to believe that P.) Epistemic reasons for belief are the same kind of thing as reasons for action (and pragmatic reasons for belief). Therefore, one very natural view is that reasons for action are also evidence for something. Evidence for what, however? Given that practical reasons ultimately concern what one ought to do (or believe), then we should infer that practical reasons are evidence for propositions concerning what one ought to do (or believe). In short, we extend a plausible analysis of epistemic reasons to all normative reasons.

In order to capture the idea that epistemic reasons and practical reasons are of a kind, other analyses of reasons must find something else that they have in common. If we should not analyze practical reasons in terms of evidence, then how should we analyze them (keeping in mind that epistemic reasons should be so analyzed)? One view is that reasons of both kinds 'count in favor' of beliefs or actions. This is no *analysis*, since the notion of counting in favor is one that cannot be understood separately from the notion of being a reason (as we have already noted).

One might think that reasons for action and reasons for belief are both types of explanations. John Broome argues that normative reasons for action are (parts of) explanations of why one ought (or ought not) to perform actions (see Broome 2004 and Kearns and Star 2008). However, epistemic

---

[5] Thank you to Sean McKeever for the written comments that helped us improve this section of the chapter.

reasons are not explanations, but evidence. (This can be brought out with the following case. A piece of undiscovered evidence, such as the fact that Bob's fingerprints are on the murder weapon, is a reason to believe that Bob is the murderer. It is not any part of an explanation concerning what we ought to believe, however, because we do not *have* this evidence/reason.[6]) If epistemic reasons are to be analyzed in terms of evidence and nothing more, and if epistemic and practical reasons are of a kind, then practical reasons must also be analyzed in the same way.

2.2. The Standard Cases Argument

Our second argument is fairly straightforward. It runs as follows:

(1) Standard cases of practical reasons to ϕ are cases of evidence that one ought to ϕ, and vice versa.

(2) Therefore, RA is true (*argument from induction*).

In order to provide support for (1) we could catalogue a very large number of examples, but we hope the reader will in fact be content to be provided with just a couple of carefully chosen examples. It should be apparent from the general features of these examples that not much work would be required to generate many more suitable cases.

Here is a fairly simple case to start with. Imagine that I (Stephen or Daniel) am passing by my friend John's house and I find him standing in the street next to his car. He is wincing and crying out for help. I notice his foot is stuck under his car wheel. I see, or at least infer, that he is in pain. Clearly, the fact that John is in pain is a reason to help him and to believe that I ought to help him. It is also evidence that I ought to help him. Perhaps I had promised to meet another friend in two minutes' time for a conversation about his new metaethics paper. I remember that fact as I rush over to the car to find a way to help John, and I feel a touch of guilt that I may not get to fulfill my promise. I ask myself (even as I try lifting the car), ought I to be helping John? After all, the fact that I promised to meet my other friend very soon is a reason to rush to meet the other friend. It is also evidence that I should now be rushing to meet the other friend. Clearly John's pain provides much stronger evidence that I ought

---

[6] It might be objected that there are cases where one ought to believe a proposition even though one doesn't *have* evidence for that proposition. Such cases always seem to involve some form or other of epistemic irresponsibility on the part of the relevant believer which explains why it is that they ought to believe a particular proposition (since they ought to *have* the evidence that is readily available to them). Thus we merely need to stipulate that the above example involves no epistemic irresponsibility.

to be doing exactly what I am now doing (by now, I am attempting to lift the car off his foot using a crowbar). The pain also provides a reason to help John that is much stronger than the reason I have to meet the other friend (i.e. the reason that springs from the fact that I have promised to meet him).

This first case involved moral reasons. Let us now consider a case that concerns prudential reasons for action. Jack works hard for a good charity relief organization during the day. He lives alone. In the evenings he likes to either carefully read excellent science books, in order to come to a better understanding of the world, or simply relax in front of his television. He generally finds that he is unable to enjoy the relatively petty shows on television any evening when he has been reading one of his books, and he is unable to concentrate on reading one of his books any evening when he has already watched some television, due to its mind-numbing properties. One night after arriving home he is wondering what to do (sometimes he doesn't bother wondering what to do, but sometimes he does), having already determined that he wants to do one of these two things. The fact that reading a particular book would help him better understand the world is a reason for him to read that book. The same fact is evidence that he ought to read the book. The fact that watching television would give him a lot of pleasure (certainly much more than he would get from reading the book) is a reason for him to watch television. The same fact is evidence that he ought to watch television. He weighs these reasons against each other, and judges that he ought to read a book on the basis of these considerations. This is, on our view, just another way of saying that he weighs the evidence that he ought to read a book against the evidence that he ought to watch television, and judges that he ought to read a book on this basis. However, even if you do not accept the last claim, it seems that you should accept that the normative reasons that figure in this case correspond, on a one-to-one basis, to examples of evidence that he ought to act in the ways he is considering acting.

Cases such as these seem to be examples where it is not controversial to claim that the facts that provide practical reasons to ϕ also provide evidence that one ought to ϕ. They are examples where the relevant facts are transparent to the agent, that is, where there are no false beliefs playing any role in deliberation and there is no misleading evidence around clouding the water. As such, they are *standard* cases, for we all encounter such cases over and over again during the course of a day.

However, it must be admitted that examples that lack the transparency or simplicity of these cases may well be thought to tell against RA. Consider a case of someone who is thirsty and who, in a state of ignorance (which he is in through no fault of his own), is about to drink from a glass that contains deadly poison. It is far from uncontroversial to say that this person has a normative reason to drink from the glass, even though he clearly has evidence that he ought to drink from the glass (e.g. it looks like it contains an ordinary thirst-quenching liquid). Niko Kolodny (2005) has argued that such a person has no real reason to drink the liquid he has the option of drinking, although it may well be rational for him to form an intention to do so. We will not be assessing Kolodny's interesting arguments here, but we wish to note that basic intuitions concerning the matter of whether or not such an unlucky person has a reason to drink from such a glass seem to differ from philosopher to philosopher (Kolodny himself does not claim otherwise). We return to supposed counterexamples to RA below, in the third part of the chapter.

2.3. The Deliberation Argument

The third of our arguments is deductively valid. We have split it up into an argument for the left to right of RA (i.e. the claim that reasons to ϕ are evidence that one ought to ϕ) and the right to left of RA (i.e. the claim that evidence that one ought to ϕ is a reason to ϕ). We will consider the former first. The argument runs as follows:

(1) Practical reasons to ϕ can play an important role in reliable practical reasoning concerning whether or not one ought to ϕ.

(2) If practical reasons to ϕ are not evidence that one ought to ϕ then they cannot play this important role in reliable practical reasoning.

(3) Therefore, reasons to ϕ are evidence that one ought to ϕ.[7]

By "reliable practical reasoning" we mean practical reasoning that is generally successful in terms of issuing in correct judgments concerning what it is one ought to do (or, at least, judgments that get as close to being correct as is normally possible). Bearing this in mind, the first premise seems true. It may even be true by definition, because there is clearly a very tight connection between reasons and reasoning. It is plausible to suppose that, whatever else they are, reasons are facts that can be correctly used in reasoning about what to do or believe. This is suggested by the fact that the words "reason" and "reasoning" have a similar etymology. In any case, (1) seems obvious as a matter of empirical fact. Over and over

---

[7] This conclusion may seem to be stating the strong identity thesis that we said we would not directly argue for in this chapter. However, this conclusion does not state that the *property* of being a reason is identical to the property of being evidence of an ought. All it says is that facts that are reasons are evidence of oughts. Similar considerations apply to similarly worded conclusions below.

again, we each consider practical reasons when we are engaged in practical reasoning.

Premise (2) also seems true, although it is by no means as obvious as (1). Why do we think (2) is true? Reasons are often successfully used by rational people to determine what they ought to do, but we think this would be *miraculous* if such reasons are not evidence. Consider a person who is trying to work out what it is she ought to do. It seems natural to describe her as aiming to hit a target. Being a sensible person, she realizes that she may fail to hit the target, that is, despite her best efforts, she might fail to do what it is she really ought to do. Being a reasonable person, she will try her best to hit the target, given relevant time constraints (and, for all we say on the topic, it may be reasonable for her to be content with getting very close to hitting the target). Now, ask yourself: how could the person we are considering ever properly aim to hit the target, or, indeed, ever succeed in hitting the target (other than through sheer luck), if reasons to ϕ are *not* evidence that one ought to ϕ? On the other hand, if reasons to ϕ are evidence that one ought to ϕ, then it is possible to see how agents are able to reliably engage in practical reasoning, in order to work out what they ought to do. We can conclude that (3) reasons to ϕ are evidence that one ought to ϕ.

Let us now turn to the right to left direction of RA, which the following argument is designed to defend:

(4) If a fact F is evidence that one ought to ϕ, then F can play an appropriate role in one's reliably concluding that one ought to ϕ.

(5) If a fact F can play this role, then F is a reason to ϕ.

(6) Therefore, evidence that one ought to ϕ is a reason to ϕ.

Again, this argument is valid. Let us now assess premises (4) and (5).

Premise (4) says that evidence that an agent ought to ϕ can help this agent conclude that she ought to ϕ. The plausibility of this idea stems from the very notion of what it is for a fact to be evidence for something. We use evidence precisely to work out which propositions are true. If a fact is evidence that one ought to ϕ, then such a fact is able to help an agent conclude that she ought to ϕ. This fact *raises the probability* of the proposition that she ought to ϕ (see Section 2.6 below for more details). If the agent is reasoning well, she can use this fact to conclude that she ought to ϕ on those occasions she ought to ϕ.

Premise (5) says that if a fact can play an appropriate role in an agent's reliably concluding that she ought to ϕ, then this fact is a reason to ϕ. This follows from the idea that it is sufficient for a fact to be a reason that it plays such a role in reasoning. Practical reasons simply *are* whatever facts are used in reasoning in this way. Reasons are facts that can help us determine what we ought to do. Reasons to ϕ are facts that can help us determine that we ought to ϕ.

One way to show that premise (5) is true to assume it is false. On the assumption that (5) is false, it is possible that a person may come to know what she ought to do without considering or even knowing any of the reasons she has for acting. Thus, if there is a fact that is evidence that one ought to ϕ without being a reason to ϕ, then one may use this evidence to work out that one ought to ϕ without being aware of any reason to ϕ at all. This result is unattractive as it implies that reasons need not play any important role in our deliberations about what we ought to do. (We expand upon this point in our paper 'Reasons: Explanations or Evidence?' 2008.)

We conclude, then, that reasons to ϕ are evidence that one ought to ϕ and that evidence that one ought to ϕ is a reason to ϕ. This is equivalent to RA. Because a fact's being able to play a certain important role in practical reasoning is both necessary and sufficient for this fact to be a reason and for it to be evidence, we conclude that reasons are evidence.

2.4. The Public Role Argument

Our fourth argument complements the third argument. Again, we have split it up into a defense of the left to right of RA and the right to left of RA. Here is the argument for the left to right of RA:

(1) Practical reasons to ϕ can play an important public role in rationally convincing people (by providing justifications) that they ought to ϕ, and rationally convincing people that when one ϕ-ed one did what one ought to have done.

(2) If practical reasons to ϕ are not evidence that one ought to ϕ then (1) is not true.

(3) Therefore, reasons to ϕ are evidence that one ought to ϕ.

Consider premise (1) to begin with. When asked why one did something, there is a vast difference between a reply that offers up a causal reason (e.g. "I was pushed onto you") and a reply that offers up a justifying reason (e.g. "I realized that pushing you out of the way of the bus would be the only way to save your life"). In cases where one is *only* causally explaining what happened one is typically implicitly admitting that one had insufficient justification for what one did, or that one was failing to respond appropriately to reasons at all (as might be the case if one had lost control of one's body due to having been pushed by someone else). In contrast, when one appeals to normative reasons, one can justify (or at least partly justify) one's actions. Similarly, one can appeal to normative reasons in order to rationally convince others about what they ought to do.

Now consider premise (2). When considering how we go about convincing others to act one way or the other, or convincing them that we were right to have acted one way or the other, people generally recognize that there is all the difference in the world between efforts to convince others that depend on violence or propaganda (subtle or otherwise), and efforts that consist in providing evidence. But if practical reasons to ϕ are not evidence that one ought to ϕ then this distinction effectively collapses and there is no genuine trading in rational justifications to be had, so (1) is not true. In this context, it is worth reminding ourselves of an important and common criticism of Ayer and Stevenson's simple versions of non-cognitivism. It is often said that Ayer and Stevenson effectively collapse the distinction between providing a normative reason and causing to believe, and our view both endorses this objection to simple non-cognitivism and further explains the basis of the objection. It is only because (3) reasons to ϕ are evidence that one ought to ϕ that we are able to rationally and reasonably persuade each other that there are various things that we ought to do.

The argument for the right-to-left reading of RA runs as follows.

(4) If a fact F is evidence that someone ought to ϕ, then F can play an appropriate public role in rationally convincing that person that she ought to ϕ and in rationally convincing other people that she ought to ϕ.

(5) If a fact F can play this role, then F is a reason to ϕ.

(6) Therefore, evidence that one ought to ϕ is a reason to ϕ.

Again, it should be clear how this argument parallels that given in Section 2.3 above. Our defense of these premises also parallels our defense of the related premises in Section 2.3. If a fact is evidence that one ought to ϕ, then this fact can be used to justify one's own ϕ-ing. If a fact is evidence that someone ought to ϕ, informing them of this fact can rationally convince this person that she ought to ϕ. Thus premise (4) is true. Furthermore, this role that facts can play is sufficient to ensure that such facts are reasons. It is the *reasons* one has to ϕ which one appeals to in order to justify one's own ϕ-ing. It is the *reasons* to ϕ to which one appeals in order to convince others that they ought to ϕ. Thus premise (5) is true. We conclude, therefore, that RA is true.

2.5. The Normative Principles Argument

In this section, we present another argument for RA. The basic argument runs as follows:

(1) A fact F is a reason to ϕ if and only if it is normally the case that if a fact relevantly similar to F obtains, then one ought to do something relevantly similar to ϕ-ing.

(2) A fact F is evidence that one ought to ϕ if and only if it is normally the case that if a fact relevantly similar to F obtains, then one ought to do something relevantly similar to ϕ-ing.

(3) Therefore, a fact F is a reason to ϕ if and only if F is evidence that one ought to ϕ (that is, RA is true).

It should be clear why the conclusion follows from (1) and (2).[8] We shall now discuss each premise in turn.

The first premise says that a fact is a reason to perform a certain action if and only if it is normally the case that if something like this fact obtains, then one ought to perform something like this action. In order to see why we should accept this premise, consider the following typical fact that can act as a reason to perform an action: John is in pain. This fact is, like most typical reasons, a non-normative fact that simply describes how the world is. Such a fact can, however, act as a normative reason to try to help John.

Thus we have, on the one hand, the non-normative fact that John is in pain and, on the other, we have the normative fact that one should try to help John. How are the two linked? A natural answer to this is that there is a (hedged) normative principle that states that, if someone is in pain, then one ought to try to help that person. That is, it is generally the case that if a certain type of fact obtains (e.g. a fact of the form 'x is in pain'), then a certain type of normative fact obtains (e.g. a fact of the form 'one ought to

---

[8] One might worry that what counts as *relevantly similar* to F and to ϕ-ing is something different in the first premise than what it is in the second (i.e. what counts as relevantly similar with regards to reasons is different from what counts as relevantly similar with regards to evidence), in which case the argument would not be valid. In fact, we intend the occurrences of the phrase 'relevantly similar' not to be read with reference to the notions of evidence or reason. We think it is straightforwardly true that, for instance, it is normally the case that if a fact relevantly similar to the proposition that John is in pain obtains, then one ought to do something relevantly similar to helping John. The phrase 'relevantly similar' is simply meant to ensure that, whatever similarity the pertinent fact has to F, the associated action has a relevant similarity to ϕ-ing, and vice versa. Thank you to Elinor Mason for prompting us to think carefully about this matter.

help x'). Thus the fact that John is in pain is a reason to help John because, normally, when relevantly similar facts obtain (e.g. 'Mary is in pain,' 'Henry is in pain'), then one ought to perform relevantly similar actions (e.g. help Mary, or help Henry). What bridges the gap between non-normative facts and unconditional normative facts are conditional normative principles that state, in effect, that if something like this non-normative fact obtains, then so does something like the unconditional normative fact.

A slightly different account of the link between the fact that John is in pain and the fact that one ought to try to help him is that the former *explains* the latter (see Broome 2004). That is, one ought to try to help John *because* he is pain. But what makes *this* true? Why does John's being in pain explain why one ought to help him? The most natural answer to this question is again that there is a (hedged) normative principle that says that if someone is in pain, then one ought to try to help that person. It is in virtue of this principle that we may truly say that one ought to help John because he is in pain.

A non-normative fact is a reason to perform a certain action, then, whenever there is a normative principle that says that if a relevantly similar fact obtains, then one ought to perform a relevantly similar action. Such a principle need not be strict or necessary. It can be hedged and contingent. However, such a principle needs to be more robust that a simple material conditional. It is not sufficient for F to be a reason to ϕ that the material conditional 'if a fact relevantly similar to F obtains, then one ought to do something relevantly similar to ϕ-ing' is true. Such a material conditional would be true if it simply happened that its consequent were true. The normative principle expressed in (1) needs, at the very least, to be a generic truth that links F-like facts to relevant normative facts. If the normative principle is true, it does not simply *happen* to be the case that if a fact relevantly similar to F obtains, then one ought to do something relevantly similar to ϕ-ing. Rather, this is *normally* the case. Such a principle links non-normative facts to unconditional normative facts.

The second premise is very similar to the first. It says that a fact is evidence that one ought to ϕ if and only if it is normally the case that if a relevantly similar fact obtains, then one ought to do something relevantly similar to ϕ-ing. To see why this is true, again consider the fact that John is in pain. When this fact is evidence that one ought to help John, as it surely often is, what makes it evidence?

An initially plausible answer to this question is that the fact that John is in pain is evidence that one ought to help John if and only if this fact *reliably indicates* that one ought to help John. Though we think something like this is correct, it is too simple as it stands. A generalization of this idea would produce the following principle. A fact is evidence for a proposition if and only if this fact reliably indicates this proposition. If this were right, then there could be no misleading evidence for necessarily false propositions, as no fact could reliably indicate something necessarily false. Consider also the following case: a normally reliable telephone book says that John's number is 123456. As it happens, the book is wrong. The fact that the book says that John's number is 123456 does not reliably indicate that John's number is 123456. Still, the fact that the book says John's number is 123456 is still *evidence* that his number is 123456. Therefore, a fact can be evidence for a proposition without reliably indicating this proposition.

The obvious fix for this problem is to say that, though the fact that the book says John's number is 123456 does not reliably indicate that his number is 123456, there are many relevantly similar facts that do reliably indicate relevantly similar propositions (e.g. the book does reliably give the correct numbers for Mary and Henry and many others). We may therefore conclude that a fact is evidence for a proposition if and only if relevantly similar facts reliably indicate relevantly similar propositions. In the normative case, then, we can say that a fact F is evidence that one ought to ϕ if and only if facts relevantly similar to F reliably indicate propositions relevantly similar to the proposition that one ought to ϕ. Furthermore, if facts relevantly similar to F reliably indicate propositions relevantly similar to the proposition that one ought to ϕ, then it is normally the case that if a fact relevantly similar to F obtains, then one ought to perform an action relevantly similar to ϕ-ing. That is, a generic conditional is true whenever the antecedent of this conditional reliably indicates the consequent. From these ideas, premise (2) follows. From (1) and (2), RA follows.

In short, the argument presented in this section is the following. A fact, F, is a *reason* to perform a certain action if and only if a principle holds that links F to the proposition that one ought to perform this action. A fact, F, is *evidence* that one ought to ϕ if and only if this same principle holds. Therefore, F is a reason to ϕ if and only if it is evidence that one ought to ϕ.

2.6. The Strength of Reasons Argument

In this section we present a final argument for RA. This argument goes as follows:

(1) Reasons can have different strengths.

(2) RA is the best explanation of how this is possible.

(3) Therefore, RA is true. (*inference to the best explanation*).

This argument takes the form of an inference to the best explanation. Such an inference may not be deductively valid, but it provides good reason to believe RA. Let us examine each of the premises of the argument.

Premise (1) is uncontroversial. Some reasons are stronger than others. If John is in excruciating pain, then this is a strong reason to help him. If he offers you five pounds to help him, this is a less strong reason to help him. Reasons can outweigh other reasons. If Mary offers you five pounds not to help John, this reason not to help John is outweighed by the fact that John is in excruciating pain. Reasons can combine their strengths. The fact that John is in excruciating pain and the fact that he offers you five pounds to help him combine to make an even stronger reason to help him. All these facts need explaining. What exactly does it mean to say that one reason is stronger than another? How do reasons outweigh other reasons? How do reasons combine their strengths?

Premise (2) says that RA suggests very attractive answers to these questions. Evidence also comes in different strengths. If John is in excruciating pain, then this is strong evidence that one ought to help him. If he offers you five pounds to help him, this is weaker evidence that one ought to help him. Evidence can outweigh other evidence. If Mary offers you five pounds not to help John, this evidence that one ought not to help him is outweighed by the fact that John is in excruciating pain. Pieces of evidence can combine their strengths. The fact that John is in excruciating pain and the fact that he offers you five pounds to help him combine to form stronger evidence that one ought to help him.

These parallels between reasons and evidence are suggestive enough in themselves to give us good reason to believe RA. Furthermore, these parallels provide us with an explanation of what the strength of a reason comes to. Without appealing to RA, the strength of reasons is somewhat mysterious. Some who appeal to a primitive 'counts in favor of' relation between a reason and an action may say that one reason is stronger than another when this reason counts more strongly in favor of this action, where such a relation is also primitive. This is not very satisfying.[9]

When we appeal to RA, however, accounting for the strength of reasons is unproblematic. We have a good grasp of the idea of the strength of evidence. The strength of a piece of evidence E for a proposition P depends on the

---

[9] John Broome (2004) appeals to the notion of a weighted explanation to explain the way in which the strengths of reasons can be compared. We criticize this idea, as well as his general account of reasons, in a separate paper that compares his account of reasons with our own, 'Reasons: Explanations or Evidence?' (2008).

degree to which E increases the probability of P.[10] The more probable P is given E, the stronger evidence E is that P is true. E is stronger evidence than another piece of evidence E* for P if and only if E makes P more probable than E* makes P. E outweighs a piece of evidence E* if and only if E is evidence for P, E* is evidence for ~P and E makes P more probable than E* makes ~P. Two pieces of evidence, E and E* can combine to form stronger evidence if the probability of P given the conjunction of E and E* is greater than both the probability of P given E and the probability of P given E*. The strength of evidence for the truth of a proposition, then, can be accounted for in terms of the probability of the proposition being true given this evidence.

This idea translates very nicely into an account of the strength of a reason. The strength of a reason to ϕ, R, depends on the degree to which R increases the probability that one ought to ϕ. The more probable it is that one ought to ϕ given R, the stronger reason to ϕ R is. R is a stronger reason to ϕ than another reason R* if and only if R makes the proposition that one ought to ϕ more probable than R* makes it. R outweighs R* if and only if R is a reason to ϕ, R* is a reason not to ϕ, and R makes the proposition that one ought to ϕ more probable than R* makes the proposition that one ought not to ϕ. Two reasons R and R* can combine to create a stronger reason to ϕ if the probability that one ought to ϕ given the conjunction of R and R* is greater than the probability that one ought to ϕ given R and the probability of the same proposition given R*. The strength of a reason to perform an action can be accounted for in exactly the same way as the strength of evidence can.

We claim, then, that if we understand normative reasons to be evidence for oughts, we are able to give a very attractive account of what it is for such reasons to have strengths. A reason to ϕ makes the proposition that one ought to ϕ more probable. The stronger the reason is, the more probable it is that one ought to ϕ. RA best explains how reasons can have strengths.

[10] This raises two questions. First, what kind of probability is increased by evidence? It is evidential or epistemic probability. For an extended discussion of this see Timothy Williamson (2002: ch. 10). Second, what is the probability increased relative to? There are two natural answers to this that are not quite right. One is that evidence increases the probability of the truth of a proposition from a position of total ignorance. This is not correct because a fact's being evidence for a proposition can sometimes depend on the existence of other evidence. The other is that evidence increases the probability of the truth of a proposition given one's entire body of other evidence. This is not correct because it is possible for a fact to be evidence for a proposition even if one's entire body of other evidence already makes the probability of this proposition equal to 1 (one's evidence may be overdetermined). The correct answer is that evidence increases the probability of a proposition relative to some salient relevant subset of one's total body of evidence. Thank you to Jacob Ross for prompting us to address this point.

3. OBJECTIONS TO RA

3.1

In this part of the chapter, we consider various objections to RA and furnish replies. The first objection is that there are counterexamples to the thesis that all pieces of evidence that one ought to ϕ are reasons to ϕ. Consider the following example. A newspaper says that there are people starving in Africa.[11] This is evidence that one ought to give money to Oxfam. However, the fact that the newspaper says that people are starving in Africa is not a *reason* to send money to Oxfam. This may seem most obvious when the newspaper (which is, on the whole, reliable) actually incorrectly reports that there are people starving in Africa. Rather, it is the fact (if it is a fact) that there are people starving in Africa that is a reason to send money to Oxfam. Thus it seems possible for a fact to be evidence that one ought to ϕ without being a reason to ϕ.

Why exactly might one think that the fact that the newspaper says that there are people starving in Africa is not a reason to send money to Oxfam? A plausible diagnosis is that such a fact, though evidence that one ought to send money to Oxfam, does not *make it right* to send money to Oxfam. What makes it right to send the money is that there are people starving in Africa. Evidence that one ought to ϕ may not be a reason to ϕ if this evidence is not a right-maker for ϕ-ing. Given that there are cases in which a fact is evidence for a normative proposition but where this fact does not make this proposition true, not all evidence that one ought to do something is a reason to do it.

How should we reply? First, it is plausible that a fact can act as a right-maker for an action simply by being good evidence that one ought to perform this action. The newspaper case can illustrate this point. Let us say that, in fact, though the newspaper is extremely reliable, in this case they got it wrong. Still, someone who reads this newspaper may be acting immorally if they do not send money to Oxfam (or do something similar). The fact that the newspaper says that people are starving in Africa may in itself be enough to create an obligation to send money to Oxfam.

Secondly, those who reject the idea that the fact that the newspaper says there are people starving in Africa is a reason to send money to Oxfam may also need to reject the idea that the fact that there are people starving in Africa is a reason to send money to Oxfam. After all, the fact that people

[11] James Morauta may have been the first to suggest that cases like this might be construed as counterexamples.

are starving *need* not mean that they are badly off. In some distant possible worlds, starving might be extremely pleasant and not life threatening at all. Being starving certainly *indicates* that a person is badly off, but this is just to say that it is evidence that one ought to send money to Oxfam. Indeed, *most* of the facts we cite as reasons merely indicate what we ought to do. Therefore, unless one wishes to deny that most facts that we think of as reasons really are reasons, the fact that the newspaper says there are people starving in Africa is really a reason to send money to Oxfam.

3.2

A second objection attacks the claim that if F is a reason to ϕ, it is evidence that one ought to ϕ. Consider the following case. There is a time-bomb in a building in which John resides. This time-bomb is counting down and, when it explodes, it will destroy the building and kill everyone in it. It seems, then, that John has a reason (a very good reason) to flee the building. This reason is that there is a time-bomb in the building. However, John has no evidence whatsoever that there is a time-bomb in the building. It is extremely well hidden. Therefore, it seems that the fact that there is a time-bomb in the building is a reason for John to flee the building, but it is not *evidence* that John ought to flee the building, as he (and, we may assume, everyone else) is oblivious to this fact. Therefore, RA is false.

This objection relies on two claims. The fact that there is a time-bomb in the building is a reason for John to flee. The fact that there is a time-bomb in the building is not evidence that John should flee. Both of these claims are controversial. If John really has *no idea* that there is a time-bomb in the building, does he really have a reason to flee? And isn't it possible that a fact could be evidence even if no one is aware of this fact (how could we look for evidence if all the evidence we have is known to us)? It seems that in some moods we think that the fact that there is a time-bomb in the building is a reason to flee even when no one knows this fact, while in some moods we do not. Similarly, in some moods we think that the fact that there is a time-bomb in the building is evidence that one ought to flee even when no one knows this fact, while in some moods we do not.

We think that to account for this, it is necessary to distinguish there *being* a reason/evidence from someone's *having* this reason/evidence. The fact that there is a time-bomb in the building is indeed a reason for John to flee the building. However, John does not *have* this reason. It is in this sense that John has no reason to flee the building. Similarly, the fact that there is a time-bomb in the building is indeed evidence that John ought to flee the building. However, John does not have this evidence. It is in this sense that John has no evidence that he ought to flee. Once this distinction is pointed out, the objection to RA loses its force. The above case is not one in which a fact is a reason to ϕ without being evidence that one ought to ϕ. It is simply a case in which a fact is a reason to ϕ without anyone *having* it as evidence that one ought to ϕ. This is perfectly consistent with RA.

Not only is the distinction between there *being* a reason/evidence and *having* a reason/evidence a distinction that provides us with a response to the above objection; it is also a distinction that provides us with additional evidence for our view. That is to say, we take it that one thing that speaks in favor of our view is precisely the fact that the being/having distinction in the case of reasons maps very nicely onto the being/having distinction in the case of evidence. To say that there *is* evidence that one ought to do something in particular is to say that there *is* a reason to do that thing, while to say that one *has* evidence that one ought to do something in particular is to say that one *has* a reason to do that thing.[12]

3.3

The third objection is simple. If F is a reason for an agent A to ϕ, then A *can* ϕ. However, it is not the case that if F is evidence that A ought to ϕ then A can ϕ. Therefore RA is false. In short, 'reason' implies 'can,' while 'evidence' does not.

We certainly admit that, even if a fact is evidence that one ought to ϕ, it need not be the case that one can ϕ. Therefore, we must reject the idea that 'reason' implies 'can.' This idea is obviously derived from the more familiar thesis that 'ought' implies 'can.' Some philosophers reject this thesis. Such philosophers will have little sympathy with 'reason' implies 'can.' What about those people who accept 'ought' implies 'can'?

RA does retain some connection between reasons to ϕ and the ability to ϕ. If it is true that a person ought to ϕ only if she can ϕ, then it is also true that she has *conclusive* reason to ϕ only if she can ϕ. This is because a person who has conclusive reason to ϕ has conclusive evidence that she ought to ϕ. Furthermore, if someone has conclusive evidence that she ought to ϕ,

---

[12] We could thus list principles that concern *having* reasons, in order to complement our original list of principles. For instance, RA* would correspond to RA.

RA* Necessarily, F is a reason for an agent A to ϕ and A has this reason to ϕ iff F is evidence that A ought to ϕ and A has this evidence that he/she ought to ϕ.

then she ought to ϕ. RA, then, does not break the link between 'reason' and 'can' completely.

Still, in those cases in which a person cannot ϕ, but has (non-conclusive) evidence that she ought to ϕ, RA claims that she has a (non-conclusive) reason to ϕ. This is a rather weak principle. Consider a surgeon who, unbeknownst to her, is performing surgery on someone whom she cannot save. After her patient dies, she realizes this. Would it be right of this surgeon to conclude that she had no reason at all to save her patient? That absolutely nothing counted in favor of her saving the patient? It seems not. She had a reason to save the patient, but she was simply unable to do so.

3.4

Another objection runs as follows. One has reason to perform supererogatory actions. One does not have evidence that one ought to perform supererogatory actions, since supererogatory actions are essentially actions that are beyond the call of duty. Therefore not all reasons for action are evidence that one ought to perform these actions. Of course, this objection depends on there really being supererogatory actions. While the "beyond the call of duty" thought is present in moral common sense, it has proven notoriously difficult to provide an account of supererogatory actions that succeeds in making good sense of their existence. Either as a result of this, or for other reasons, many moral philosophers doubt that there are any supererogatory actions.

One way to understand supererogatory actions is to depend on a distinction that is sometimes made between obligations and oughts and claim that supererogatory actions ought to be done but are not obligatory (though this need not be thought of as a sufficient condition for an action to be supererogatory). This is suggested by the phrase "beyond the call of *duty*." It should be obvious that this conception of the supererogatory is entirely compatible with our reasons as evidence thesis.

However, it might be claimed that this is an incorrect conception of the supererogatory (perhaps because there is no relevant distinction to be made between obligations and oughts). An alternative interpretation of "beyond the call of duty" is the view that it is not the case that one ought to perform supererogatory acts (this certainly isn't a sufficient condition). This conception seems to conflict with RA. However, we have three responses available to us at this point. First, we could simply accept this view but deny that we have reasons to perform supererogatory actions. Though it may be good, kind, or nice to perform such actions, one really has no reason to perform them and there is thus no evidence that one ought to perform them. Secondly, we could instead claim that there are reasons to perform supererogatory actions and also evidence that one ought to perform these actions, albeit evidence that is always *misleading*. Finally, one could modify RA in the following way:

> Necessarily, F is a reason for an agent A to ϕ **iff** F is evidence that A ought to ϕ or F is evidence that is supererogatory for A to ϕ.

This is our least favorite solution to the problem, but is still one that is very much in the spirit of the account of reasons defended in this chapter.

3.5

We sometimes receive the following objection to RA. One fact F can be both a reason to ϕ and a reason not to ϕ, but no fact can be both evidence for P and evidence for not P. Therefore, not all reasons to ϕ are evidence that one ought to ϕ. Consider the following example, provided by Andy Egan when pressing this objection.[13] A runner in a competition realizes that if he sticks his leg out at a particular time he will trip over his main competitor without others observing him do so. The fact that if he were to do this his main competitor would trip over is a reason to stick his leg out (because it will increase his chances of winning the race) *and* it is a reason not to stick his leg out (either because it would provide an unfair advantage, or because it would be likely to injure the other person). However, this fact is *not* both evidence that he ought to stick his leg out and evidence that it is not the case that he ought to stick his leg out. This is because it is impossible for a fact F to be both evidence that P and evidence that not P. After all, no fact can increase the probability that P and increase the probability that not P. Therefore, RA is false.

This objection relies on conflating two distinct notions—that of evidence that one ought not to ϕ and that of evidence that it is not the case that one ought to ϕ. Look carefully at RA. There is no negation before any ought. According to RA, a reason to ϕ is evidence that one ought to ϕ and a reason not to ϕ is evidence that one ought not to ϕ (rather than evidence that it is not the case that one ought to ϕ). It should be uncontroversial that if a fact is evidence that one ought not to ϕ this does not entail that this fact is evidence that it is not the case one ought to ϕ.[14] To see that this is so, just consider any fact that is evidence that an action is not merely

---

[13] The same objection was pressed on us by James Dreier, who provided his own colorful example.

[14] To be fair to our critics, it should be said that their worries may have sprung from the highly plausible thought that any true proposition that one ought not to ϕ will entail a true proposition that it is not the case that one ought to ϕ (this seems correct, on the plausible assumption that there are no deontic conflicts). This is a different claim and we

permissible. Such a fact increases the probability both of the truth of the proposition that one ought to ϕ and of the truth of the proposition that one ought not to ϕ.[15] It will not increase the probability of the truth of the proposition that it is not the case that one ought to ϕ. Thus, evidence that one ought to not ϕ is not always evidence that it is not the case that one ought to ϕ.

In the above example, then, the fact that if the runner were to stick his leg out, it would trip his main competitor is both evidence that he ought to do so, and evidence that he ought not to do so. It is not, however, evidence that it is not the case that he ought to do so. It is not the case, then, that on the view that reasons are evidence, we must accept the implausible idea that one fact can be both evidence for a proposition and evidence against the same proposition.

3.6

The following objection was suggested by Ralph Wedgwood. Consider Buridan's Ass. An ass stands between two equidistant identical bales of hay. There is reason for him to eat the left bale (e.g. it is nutritious) and there is reason for him to eat the right bale (it is just as nutritious). However, there is no evidence that the ass *ought* to eat the left bale or that he *ought* to eat the right bale. After all, there is absolutely nothing to choose between the two bales. It is thus simply obvious that it is not the case that he ought to eat the left bale and that it is not the case that he ought to eat the right bale. Rather, he ought to eat one or the other, but which one he eats does not matter. Therefore, there are reasons that are not evidence. RA is false.

We have two mutually incompatible replies to this objection. We wish to remain agnostic as to which reply is correct. First, it is not obvious to us that the ass lacks evidence that he ought to eat the left bale of hay. The left bale of hay is, after all, nutritious. Is this not then evidence that he ought to eat it? Of course, this evidence is not conclusive, but it is no part of our

---

are not opposed to it. The example that follows establishes that evidence is not closed under this entailment.

[15] To see why this must be so, notice that the relevant probability space can be completely divided into three non-overlapping sectors: the probability of the truth of the proposition that the action is merely permissible, the probability of the truth of the proposition that one ought to do the act, and the probability of the truth of the proposition that one ought not to do the act. These three probabilities must add up to one, so when the first probability decreases, as it does when one receives new evidence that the act is not merely permissible, then the other two probabilities must both increase (assuming this new evidence is not also evidence that the act is obligatory or evidence that it is forbidden).

view that reasons must be conclusive evidence for oughts. Secondly, it is not obvious to us that the ass has a reason to eat the left bale of hay. The ass has a reason to eat either the left bale of hay or the right bale of hay, but does he have a reason to eat the left bale in particular? It is not clear.

Though we are undecided on these matters, we are committed to the idea that *if* the ass has a reason to eat the left bale then he has evidence that he ought to eat the left bale. In light of the fact that intuitions about this case are not firm, RA is not threatened.

3.7

Suppose you are a good person and you trust yourself to make good decisions.[16] You know that at a future point in time you will do a particular act. The fact that you will do this act is evidence that you ought to do it (because you are a person who makes good decisions), but it doesn't seem like a reason to do it. How could the fact that you will do something be a reason to do it?

How should we respond to this objection? There are two kinds of case that would fit the preceding description: there are cases where one is aware one will do a particular act and one is aware of possessing sufficient reasons for performing the act that are separate from the fact that one will do the act; and there are cases where one is aware one will do a particular act but one is not aware of (sufficient) reasons for performing the act that are separate from the fact that one will do the act. About each kind of case we wish to say different things. If one is aware of the sufficient reasons of the standard kind to do an act, then the fact that one will do the act in the future is not evidence that one can *have*, even though it *is* evidence that one ought to perform the act, and (thus) the fact that one will do the act in the future is not a reason that one can *have*, even though it *is* a reason to perform the act. On the other hand, if one is not aware of having sufficient reasons of the standard kind that one will do an act, then the fact that one will do the act in the future is evidence that one can *have*, and (thus) the fact that one will do the act in the future is a reason that one can *have*.

A different example that will quickly illustrate why one should accept this view is a case where you provide your name (John, say) to another person then hear that person utter your name soon afterwards. Clearly the later uttering of the name is evidence that you are John and it is a reason for a bystander who has never met you to believe that you are John. Would you

---

[16] We owe this example to Peter Graham. The objection that follows was also pressed upon us, in one form or another, by a number of other people with other examples. Adam Pautz was the first to raise an objection of this kind.

take it to be a reason to believe you are John? Not ordinarily. Ordinarily, your particular epistemic state of knowing to a high degree of certainty that your name is John would stand in the way of being able to think of the utterance of your name as evidence for yourself (i.e. evidence that you only now *have*) that your name is John, or as a new reason to believe that your name is John. A situation in which you could accept this utterance as new evidence and a new reason to believe is one where you are suffering from amnesia. What explains why it is not possible to have evidence/a reason in one case, but it is possible to have evidence/a reason in the other case? We believe it is the apparent *independence* of pieces of evidence in one case and not in the other. If a person immediately repeats your own name to you without anything strange having happened to your memory in the interim, the relevant utterance is blocked from being considered as a reason because it is not viewed as evidence independent of evidence that you already possess.

If we now return to the original example we can see that the very same story that we just told about reasons for belief can be told about reasons for action. If one is aware of the ordinary reasons on the basis of which one will do a particular act at some point in the future, then the mere fact that one will do this act is not in itself evidence concerning what one ought to do that one can *have*, and it is (therefore) not a reason that one can *have*. It is still a reason to act. Is this a bullet that we are biting? That this question should be answered in the negative becomes clear if one imagines a situation where one suddenly forgets all the ordinary reasons that speak in favor of doing a particular act but where one does not give up an intention to do that act and hence still believes that one will do it. Remember that we are assuming that one believes oneself to be trustworthy (if this is not granted, then there is no reason to accept that the fact that one will do a particular act is evidence that one ought to do it). It seems quite right that one would therefore take the fact that one is going to do a particular act as evidence that one ought to do the act, and as a reason to do the act, and we hope that the reader will share this judgment on reflection.[17]

3.8

Sean McKeever and Michael Ridge effectively deny RA. They argue that "For a fact to be a reason for action cannot plausibly be understood in

---

[17] Consider the following advice: Do what the virtuous person would do in your situation. The fact that a virtuous person would do a certain act is in fact a reason to do this act. This is similar to what is going on in the above case. If one knows oneself to be virtuous, then the fact that one will do a certain act is a reason to do it.

terms of that fact's reliably *indicating* anything, not even reliably indicating that the action ought to be done" (McKeever and Ridge 2006: 127), and they take it that this implies that reasons for action are fundamentally different from reasons for belief, because they can not be understood in terms of evidence. They provide an example that is meant to establish this conclusion (also from McKeever and Ridge 2006: 127):

> Let us suppose that the fact that an action would give someone pleasure is typically a reason in favour of the action. This in no way entails that the fact that an action would give someone pleasure reliably indicates the rightness of the action. To see that this entailment does not hold, simply imagine a world in which whenever one person gives another person some pleasure a perverse demon causes (and is known to cause) great pain to some innocent person. Here we have an illustration of how being a reason for action and being a reliable indication of the rightness of an action can dramatically come apart.

The example is supposed to work like this. In a certain possible world, an action, ϕ-ing, would give somebody pleasure. This is a reason to ϕ. However, it is not evidence that one ought to ϕ in this world because it does not reliably indicate that one ought to ϕ. This is because whenever someone gives another person pleasure, a demon causes someone else great pain. Thus it is never the case in this world that one ought to give someone pleasure. Therefore, the fact that ϕ-ing would give someone pleasure does not reliably indicate that one ought to ϕ.

We have two responses to this objection. The first point has been mentioned before. McKeever and Ridge's argument relies on the idea that a fact is evidence for the truth of a (contingent?) proposition only if it reliably indicates this proposition. In our discussion of the Normative Principles Argument, however, we mentioned that a fact can be evidence for the truth of a proposition even if this fact does not reliably indicate this proposition. Even McKeever and Ridge say that "the only obvious and serious difficulty here is with reasons for believing necessary truths, which arguably are equally well reliably indicated by everything" (2006: 127). As we have seen above, facts can be evidence even for contingent propositions without reliably indicating these propositions. The phonebook case is such an example. We thus reject this premise of their argument.

McKeever and Ridge's argument also relies on the idea that the fact that ϕ-ing would cause pleasure is a reason to ϕ. However, one may dispute this. As McKeever and Ridge say, this is merely 'typically' a reason to ϕ. This implies that it is merely contingently a reason to ϕ. But if it is merely contingently a reason to ϕ, then surely the demon world is one world at least in which it is no reason at all to ϕ (if not that world, which?). We conclude, therefore, that McKeever and Ridge's argument fails.

This brings our discussion of arguments against RA to an end. We hope to have persuaded you that RA and R are plausible statements of how reasons and evidence are related. Like many other philosophers, McKeever and Ridge believe that no unified account of reasons for action and reasons for belief can be provided. They claim that while it is fine to view the world as containing a very large number of reasons for belief, it would be very odd to think that we are surrounded by a similarly large number of reasons for action (2006: 124–37). We do not think this is odd at all.[18] Rather, we think it is very odd that the idea that there may be an underlying unity to reasons for action and reasons for belief—a unity that is capable of being analyzed (and seems to us to be best explained by the thesis that reasons *are* evidence)—has not been given more of a run for its money.

REFERENCES

Broome, John (2004) 'Reasons,' in J. Wallace, M. Smith, S. Scheffler, and P. Pettit (eds.), *Reason and Value: Themes from the Moral Philosophy of Joseph Raz* (Oxford: Oxford University Press), 28–55.

Kearns, Stephen, and Star, Daniel (2008) 'Reasons: Explanations or Evidence?' *Ethics* 119(1).

Kolodny, Niko (2005) 'Why be Rational?' *Mind* 114: 509–63.

McKeever, Sean, and Ridge, Michael (2006) *Principled Ethics* (Oxford: Oxford University Press).

Parfit, Derek (2007) *Climbing the Mountain,* unpublished MS.

Scanlon, T. M. (1998) *What We Owe to Each Other* (Cambridge, MA: Harvard University Press).

Star, Daniel (2007) 'Review of S. McKeever and M. Ridge, *Principled Ethics*' *Notre Dame Philosophical Reviews,* http://ndpr.nd.edu/review.cfm?id=9203.

Williamson, Timothy (2002) *Knowledge and its Limits* (Oxford: Oxford University Press).

[18] The view that this claim is not really that odd is discussed in Star (2007).

9

How to be a Cognitivist about Practical Reason

Jacob Ross

Cognitivism about practical reason is the view that intentions involve beliefs, and that the rational requirements on intentions can be explained in terms of the rational requirements on the beliefs that figure in intentions. In particular, cognitivists about practical reason have sought to provide cognitive explanations of two basic requirements of practical rationality: a *consistency* requirement, according to which it is rationally impermissible to have intentions that are jointly inconsistent with one's beliefs, and a *means–end coherence* requirement, according to which, to a first approximation, it is rationally impermissible to intend an end while failing to intend what one regards as a necessary means to this end. In order for the cognitivist to explain these requirements, she must arrive at an account of the beliefs that figure in intentions, on the basis of which she can show that any agent who violates these requirements of pratical rationality must have beliefs that violate the requirements of theoretical rationality. Providing such an account, however, turns out to be no easy task.

This chapter will be divided into three parts. In the first, I will lay out some general constraints that a theory of intentions must satisfy if it is to figure in a cognitivist explanation of the requirements of intention consistency and means–end coherence. In the second part, I will consider the standard cognitivist account of intentions, according to which the intention to ϕ involves the belief that one will ϕ because of that very intention. I will show that this account of intention faces a number of serious problems. And in

I am grateful for very helpful comments on an earlier draft of this chapter from Stephen Finlay and from Gideon Yaffe. I have also benefited greatly from discussions with Jeff King and David Manley, from the students in my Practical Reason seminar, held at the University of Southern California in the spring of 2007, and from participants in the 4th Annual Metaethics Workshop. My greatest debt is to Mark Schroeder, for countless extremely illuminating discussions.

the third part, I will discuss an account according to which the beliefs that figure in intentions must be defined not only in terms of their content, but also in terms of the other attitudes on which they are based. I will argue that this is the kind of account of intentions that the cognitivist about practical reason should adopt.

1. GENERAL CONSTRAINTS ON A COGNITIVIST ACCOUNT OF INTENTIONS

1.1. The Intention Consistency Requirement and the Strong Belief Thesis

Some cognitivists hold that intentions are *identical* with a certain kind of belief. Minimally, cognitivists hold that intentions *involve* beliefs. And generally, cognitivists maintain that the intention to ϕ involves the belief that one will ϕ. We may call this latter claim the *Strong Belief Thesis*.[1] One of the primary motivations for the Strong Belief Thesis is that it allows for a cognitivist explanation of the consistency requirement on intentions. This is the requirement that one's intentions be logically consistent not only with one another but also with the totality of one's beliefs.

In order to state this requirement precisely, it will be useful to introduce a term. When someone intends to ϕ, let us say that the *propositional content* of her intention is the proposition that she ϕs. We can now state the requirement of *Intention Consistency* as follows:

> One ought rationally to be such that the set consisting of all propositional contents of one's beliefs, as well as all the propositional contents of one's intentions, is logically consistent.

We can easily provide a cognitivist explanation of this requirement so long as we assume the Strong Belief Thesis. For this thesis implies that believing that p is a necessary condition for having an intention whose propositional content is p. And it is widely accepted that there is a requirement of *Belief Consistency*, which can be stated thus:

> One ought rationally to be such the set of all the propositions one believes is logically consistent.

---

[1] See Michael Bratman, "Intention, Belief, Practical, Theoretical," forthcoming in Jens Timmerman, John Skorupski, and Simon Robertson, eds., *Spheres of Reason*. Bratman calls this thesis the "strong belief requirement," though I will reserve the latter expression for a normative principle, which I will discuss below.

But if believing that p is a necessary condition for having an intention whose propositional content is p, then any proposition that is the content of one's intentions will also be the content of one's beliefs. Therefore the set that includes all the propositions that one believes will be identical with the set that includes all the propositions that are the contents either of one's intentions or of one's beliefs. And so, if it is rationally required that the former set be logically consistent, then it is likewise rationally required that the latter set be logically consistent.

Furthermore, it does not appear to be possible to provide a purely cognitivist explanation of the consistency requirement on intentions on the basis of any assumption that is weaker than the Strong Belief Thesis. For if the necessary condition for intending that p is having some doxastic attitude that is weaker than belief in p, then the doxastic attitudes involved in having inconsistent intentions may themselves be fully consistent. There is no inconsistency, after all, in having a high degree of confidence in each proposition in a set of jointly inconsistent propositions, as the lottery paradox illustrates. Thus, it seems that in order to explain the consistency requirement on intentions in terms of a demand of cognitive consistency, the doxastic attitude involved in intention can be nothing weaker than all-out belief. One might still hold that in order to intend that p, one need not believe *that* p, but that it is instead sufficient to believe some weaker proposition. Jay Wallace, for instance, has proposed a cognitivist theory according to which the belief involved in intending to ϕ is the belief that is, in some relevant sense, possible that one ϕs.[2] However, if the belief involved in intending that p is weaker than the belief that p, then it is possible to have inconsistent intentions without having inconsistent beliefs.[3]

For suppose the content of the belief constitutive of intending to ϕ is weaker than the proposition that one will ϕ, and suppose the content of the belief constitutive of intending not to ϕ is weaker than the proposition that one will not ϕ. Let p be the proposition that one will ϕ, and let q be the weaker proposition that is the content of the intention constitutive of intending to ϕ. Since q is weaker than p, q is equivalent to (p or (q and not p)). Hence, the belief constitutive of intending to ϕ will be the belief that (p or (q and not p)). But since (p or (q and not p)) is consistent with (not p), one can consistently have the belief constitutive of intending

---

[2] Jay Wallace, "Normativity, Commitment, and Instrumental Reason" *Philosophers' Imprint* 1(3) (December 2001).

[3] The following argument is a generalization of an argument Bratman makes in "Intention, Belief, Practical, Theoretical."

to ϕ while believing that not p. A fortiori, since we are assuming that the belief constitutive of intending not to ϕ is weaker than the belief that not p, (p or (q and not p)) is consistent with the belief constitutive of intending not to ϕ. Hence, it follows from our assumptions that one can intend to ϕ, and intend not to ϕ, without having inconsistent beliefs. And so, on these assumptions, a violation of intention consistency need not involve any cognitive inconsistency. And so, if the cognitivist is to explain the consistency requirement, he must not hold that the belief constitutive of intending an action is weaker than the belief that one will perform this action.

One might hold that the cognitivist could explain the Belief Consistency Requirement not on the basis of the Strong Belief *Thesis*, but instead on the basis of *Strong Belief Requirement*:

> One ought rationally to be such that (if one intends to do something, one believes one will do it).

While the Strong Belief Thesis is a metaphysical principle, according to which believing one will ϕ is a necessary condition for intending to ϕ, the Strong Belief Requirement is a normative principle, according to which intending to ϕ without believing that one will ϕ, though metaphysically possible, is irrational. On the basis of the Strong Belief Requirement, we can give a straightforward explanation of the Consistency Requirement. For if rationality requires that one believes one will do whatever one intends to do, then rationality will require that the set of propositional contents of one's intentions be a subset of the set of propositions one believes. Hence, if rationality requires that the set of propositions one believes be logically consistent, then rationality will also require that the propositional contents of one's intentions be consistent with one's beliefs. Hence, from the Belief Consistency Requirement, together with the Strong Belief Requirement, we can derive the Intention Consistency Requirement.

Thus, we might explain the Consistency Requirement by appealing not to the Strong Belief Thesis, but instead to the Strong Belief Requirement. This strategy, however, is not available to the cognitivist about practical reason. For the cognitivist about practical reason aims to explain certain requirements of practical rationality, including the Consistency Requirement, purely on the basis of requirements of theoretical rationality. And while the Strong Belief Requirement may be a requirement of rationality, one cannot plausibly hold that it is a requirement of *theoretical* rationality. For intending to ϕ without believing that one will ϕ, if it is indeed possible, would not seem necessarily to involve any irrationality in one's beliefs. If, for example, one does not believe that ϕ will ϕ because one has compelling evidence that one will not ϕ, and yet one intends to ϕ

nonetheless, then it will be one's intentions, and not one's beliefs, that are irrational. Thus, violations of the Strong Belief Requirement, if they can occur at all, needn't involve theoretical irrationality.

Hence, since the cognitivist aims to explain the Intention Consistency Requirement in terms of the requirement of theoretical rationality, it seems she has no choice but to accept the Strong Belief Thesis. In the next section, I will raise what appears to be a serious problem for this thesis, and I will indicate how I believe the cognitivist should respond.

1.2. A Problem for the Strong Belief Thesis, and How the Cognitivist Should Respond

Suppose you are an unlucky train passenger. On a thousand past occasions, a strange sequence of events have occurred: you have been the only passenger onboard a train, the train has been approaching an oncoming train, and the conductor has suddenly died of cardiac arrest, forcing you to take control of the train in order to avoid a collision. On each of these occasions, you have arrived at a junction prior to colliding with the oncoming train, and you have had the options of turning the train you are on either to the left or to the right. On five hundred of these past occasions, you chose to turn the train to the left, and on the remaining five hundred occasions you chose to turn it to the right. There has not, however, been any discernible pattern within this sequence of choices. And so you form the justified belief that you choose at random, and that you have an equal propensity to send the train to the left or to send it to the right.

Today you are once again the only passenger onboard a train, whose conductor is Casey Jones. You are very familiar with Casey, and with this particular route: you know that at River Junction, Casey either turns the train to the left or to the right, and that he turns in both directions with equal frequency, and without any discernible pattern. Hence, on this particular occasion, you are 50 percent confident in the following proposition:

R The train will turn to the right at River Junction

Today Casey appears to be in poor health, and so you think it quite possible that he will die during today's voyage. Moreover, because of your unfortunate track record, you regard the following proposition as a genuine epistemic possibility:

D Casey dies right before the train reaches River Junction, at which point there is another train approaching, and there are only two equally good ways to avoid a fatal collision, namely to turn the train to the left or to turn the train to the right.

In this case, conditional on D, how confident should you be in R? Since you justifiedly believe that you have an equal propensity to send the train to the left or to the right in the kind of circumstance under consideration, you should believe that if D were true, you would have a 50 percent chance of sending the train to the left, and a 50 percent chance of sending it to the right. Hence, by the Principal Principle, your credence in R conditional on D should be one-half. And so your credence in R conditional on D should be equal to your unconditional credence in R.

Now according to a plausible evidentialist view of reasons for belief, only something that makes it more likely that p is true (relative to a given agent's epistemic situation) can be a reason for this agent to believe that p is true. But in the situation under consideration, D does not make it any more likely that R is true. Hence, it seems that D is not a reason to believe R.

We can arrive at a similar conclusion by another route. For, plausibly, a rational agent updates her beliefs by conditionalizing on her total evidence. Hence, when one learns, and learns only, that D is true, one should conditionalize on D, and so one's new credence in R should be equal to one's prior credence in R conditional on D. In other words, upon learning that D is true, and in the absence of any further evidence, one's credence in R should remain one half. And so one's credence in R should not be anything close to unity. But if, in response to learning that D is true, one's credence in R should be one half rather than unity, then it seems that D cannot be a sufficient reason to believe that R is true.

However, R is a sufficient reason to turn the train to the right at River Junction (just as it is also a sufficient reason to turn the train to the left at River Junction). But assuming one can only turn the train to the right at River Junction if one intends to do so, it seems that R must also be a sufficient reason to intend to turn the train to the right at River Junction. Now suppose that the strong belief thesis were true. In this case, the belief that one will turn the train to the right at River Junction is a constituent of the intention to turn the train to the right at River Junction. Hence, any sufficient reason to intend to turn the train to the right at River Junction must also be a sufficient reason to believe that one will turn the train to the right at River Junction. But any sufficient reason to believe that one will turn the train to the right at River Junction must also be a sufficient reason to believe that the train will turn to the right at River Junction. Hence, if the Strong Belief Thesis is true, then D must be a sufficient reason to believe that the train will turn to the right at River Junction, that is, to believe R. We have seen, however, that there is strong reason to deny that

D is a sufficient reason to believe R. Hence, there is strong reason to deny the Strong Belief Thesis.

How should the cognitivist respond to this objection? I believe she should take issue with the following inference:

(1) R is a sufficient reason to turn the train to the right.
(2) One can only turn the train to the right by intending to turn the train to the right.
(3) R is a sufficient reason to intend to turn the train to the right.

This inference seems to rely on the following principle:

> If X is sufficient reason to ϕ, and one can only ϕ by ψ-ing, then X is a sufficient reason to ψ.

But the above principle only applies to actions. It does not apply to things that are not subject to the will. Suppose, for example, that the fact that it is a beautiful Sunday afternoon is a sufficient reason to go for a walk. And suppose that I can only go for a walk if I do so by converting glucose into adenosine triphosphate. We cannot conclude that the fact that it is a sunny day is a sufficient reason to convert glucose into adenosine triphosphate. Indeed, the fact that it is a beautiful Sunday afternoon could not be a reason for me to convert glucose into adenosine triphosphate, since the latter process is not an action.

But if the above principle applies only to actions, then we cannot apply it to intentions unless we regard intentions as actions. And since the cognitivist holds that intentions involve beliefs, and since there is good reason to deny that beliefs are actions, the cognitivist has good reason to deny that intentions are actions, and hence that the above principle applies to intentions. So the cognitivist has good reason to deny the inference from (1) and (2) to (3).

Thus, the counterargument to the Strong Belief Thesis that we have considered in this section relies on a principle which the cognitivist can reasonably reject. There are, however, other objections to the Strong Belief Thesis. And since, as I have argued above, the cognitivist has little choice but to accept the Strong Belief Thesis, anyone who is persuaded by these objections should reject cognitivism, at least in its pure form. There may, however, be interesting views in the neighborhood of pure cognitivism that do not involve the Strong Belief Thesis. In Appendix A, I discuss one such view, a view according to which intending to ϕ involves not believing that one will ϕ, but rather accepting that one will ϕ from the practical point of view.

1.3. Means–End Coherence and the Non-Cognitive Conditions of Intention

The simplest formulation of the means–end coherence requirement, which we may call the *Strong Means–End Coherence Requirement*, is this:

SME   One ought rationally to be such that (if one intends to ψ and one believes that ϕ-ing is a necessary means to ψ-ing, then one intends to ϕ).

In other words, it states that anyone who intends to ψ and believes that ϕ-ing is a necessary means to ψ-ing is thereby rationally required to intend to ϕ. Now in order to explain the consistency requirement on intentions, it is sufficient to find a *necessary* condition for intention, such as the condition that anyone who intends to ϕ must believe that she will ϕ. However, in order to explain the means–end coherence requirement, we must also find a sufficient condition for intention. For if all we knew were a necessary condition for intending to ϕ, then although we might be able to show that a belief–intention pair rationally requires the satisfaction of this necessary condition, this would not amount to showing that this pair of attitudes rationally requires intending to ϕ.

(A note on terminology: for brevity, I will say that an agent is *rationally required* to A whenever she has a set, S, of attitudes such that she could not rationally fail to A while retaining this set of attitudes. Thus, in saying that an agent is rationally required to A, I do not mean to imply that the agent in question could not rationally fail to A *simpliciter*, but only that she could not rationally fail to A while keeping her other attitudes constant.)

Although cognitivists must hold that intentions involve beliefs, and some cognitivists maintain that intentions are *identical* with a certain kind of belief, cognitivists needn't make this stronger claim, since they may hold that intentions also involve a non-cognitive component, such as a desire or disposition. However, there are significant constraints on the type of non-cognitive component the cognitivist can posit. In particular, the cognitivist must hold that the non-cognitive component of the intention to ϕ is a condition that is present whenever one is required, by the means–end coherence requirement, to intend to ϕ—let us call such a condition a *non-cognitive background condition* of the intention to ϕ. For suppose the cognitivist denies this. Then she must hold that someone could violate the means–end coherence requirement purely in virtue of failing to have the non-cognitive component of the required intention. That is, she must hold that there could be a case in which someone intends to ψ, believes that ϕ-ing is a necessary means to ψ-ing, and has the belief-component of the intention to ϕ, but fails to intend to ϕ because she lacks the non-cognitive component of the intention to ϕ. Since such an agent would violate the means–end coherence requirement, any cognitivist explanation of this requirement would need to imply that any such agent would violate a requirement of theoretical rationality. But this implication is implausible. For while the requirements of theoretical rationality may require that an agent who has certain beliefs, or other attitudes, have certain beliefs, but such a requirement does not require that an agent who has certain belief or other attitudes have certain non-cognitive attitudes, dispositions, or the like. Hence, if it is possible for an agent to be required, by means–end coherence, to intend to ϕ, and yet to lack the non-cognitive component of the intention to ϕ, then it will be impossible to give a cognitivist explanation of the means–end coherence requirement. Therefore, the cognitivist must deny that this is possible, and so she must claim that the non-cognitive component of the intention to ϕ is what I have called a background condition.

But if the non-cognitive component of the intention to ϕ is a background condition in this sense, then the belief component of the intention to ϕ cannot be simply the belief that one will ϕ. For it is possible to satisfy any background conditions of the intention to ϕ, and to believe that one will ϕ, without intending to ϕ.

Consider the following case. Barry the banker has received a shipment of a million dollars. Right now the money is on the counter where any thief could easily take it. Barry intends to protect the money, and he believes that locking the money in the safe is a necessary means to doing so. Normally, at this point in the day, he would engage in some simple instrumental reasoning, and form the intention to lock the money in the safe. But today, before he does so, Robbie the robber enters, disguised as Marvin the Martian. Robbie declares "I have come from the twenty-third-and-a-half century to give you a copy of your biography." Barry is very keen to read his biography, and he immediately turns to today's date, where he reads "Barry locks the money in the safe." Being the gullible individual he is, he believes every word that he reads, and thus believes that he will lock the money in the safe. And yet, enthralled in reading about his own future, he doesn't make any intentions, and in particular, he doesn't form the intention to lock the money in the safe. And while Barry is engrossed in his biography, Robbie makes off with the money.

Surely this sort of case is possible. And in this case, though Barry does not intend to lock the money in the bank, he does believe that he will, and he satisfies the background conditions for intending to lock the money in the safe (since these are present whenever one is required by means–end coherence to intend to lock the money in the safe). Thus, more is involved in the intention to ϕ than the belief that one will ϕ plus the non-cognitive background conditions of this intention. And since, as we have seen, the cognitivist must hold that the only non-cognitive condition of the intention to ϕ is a background condition, it follows that the cognitivist must hold that the intention to ϕ involves some cognitive condition beyond the belief that one will ϕ. And, as we will now see, there are tight constraints on what this cognitive condition can plausibly be held to be.

1.4. The Problem of Mere Recognition

In the simplest kind of instrumental reasoning, we begin in a state in which we intend some end, to ψ, and in which we believe that ϕ-ing is a necessary means to ψ-ing, and we then form the intention to ϕ. Thus, we begin in a situation in which we have other attitudes which require, by means–end coherence, a further intention that we lack, and we then form this required intention. I might, for example, intend to drink a beer, and believe that going to the fridge is a necessary means to drinking a beer. Since I am required, by means–end coherence, to intend to go to the fridge, I must satisfy the non-cognitive background conditions of this intention. And so it follows that when, at the outset of the process of instrumental reasoning, I have not yet formed the intention to go to the fridge, I must lack only the cognitive component of this intention. And so my forming this intention requires, and requires only, that I form this cognitive component. More generally, the cognitivist must hold that, in the simplest cases of instrumental reasoning, forming the instrumental intention consists entirely in forming the belief component of this intention.

And suppose that, at time t, I intend to drink a beer, and I believe that going to the fridge is a necessary means to doing so, and hence I satisfy the non-cognitive background conditions for this intention. Let p be the propositional content of the belief component of the intention to go to the fridge. And suppose that, at t, I have compelling reason to believe that p is true, and I form the belief that p purely on the basis of this compelling evidence. In this case, my belief that p would have been formed in a rational manner. But in my situation, my forming the belief that p is tantamount to forming the intention to go to the fridge. Hence, if I can rationally form the belief that p on the basis of compelling evidence, then I can rationally form the intention to go to the fridge on the basis of this same evidence. Now at least in the case where p is true, to come to believe that p on the basis of compelling evidence is to *recognize* that p. And so, if it is possible to form the belief constitutive of intending to ϕ on the basis of compelling evidence that p is true, then it will be possible for a mere process of recognition to constitute practical reasoning. But it would seem that mere recognition can never constitute practical reasoning. Certainly, recognition can play an important role in practical reasoning, since very often one of the things we do in reasoning our way to the intention to ϕ is to recognize practical reasons to ϕ. But as cases of akrasia illustrate, the recognition of these reasons is only part of practical reasoning, and the formation of the intention to ϕ, though causally influenced by such recognition, is a distinct event from this recognition. The formation of intentions, it seems, is not a matter of merely recognizing that something is true, but rather of resolving to make something true.

Since, therefore, the cognitivist must hold that, at least in the simplest cases of instrumental reasoning, forming the instrumental intention consists entirely in forming the belief component of this intention, it follows that, in order to avoid the conclusion that practical reasoning can consist in mere recognition, the cognitivist must hold that the belief component of the instrumental intention cannot be formed on the basis of compelling evidence. And so it seems that if the belief component of the intention to go to the fridge is the belief that p, the cognitivist must hold that p is a proposition that one cannot come to believe on the basis of compelling evidence.

One possibility is that p could be a proposition for which there can never be compelling evidence. The problem with this view, however, is that while there are many propositions for which there could never be compelling evidence (e.g. "Caesar did and did not cross the Rubicon") it is doubtful that any such proposition can be rationally believed, and if a proposition cannot be rationally believed, then it cannot be a component of a rational intention. One might hold that there are certain propositions for which the evidence can be at most merely sufficient, but can never be compelling. But if there were any such propositions, then it would seem that belief in them would be, at most, rationally permissible, and never rationally required, and hence, having formed the belief in such a proposition, one would always be at liberty to subsequently withhold one's assent. And so if practical reasoning consisted in the formation of beliefs for which there could be sufficient evidence, but for which there could never be compelling evidence, then it would seem that, having formed an intention on the basis of practical reasoning, one would always be at liberty to rationally withdraw the belief component of the intention, thereby withdrawing the intention.[4]

---

[4] One might object that I am here assuming a form of evidentialism which no cognitivist would accept: I am assuming that the only reasons for belief are evidential reasons. But so long as one understands a reason for belief a consideration that can figure in the reasoning whereby this belief is formed, this is a very reasonable assumption. So-called practical reasons for a belief, such as the fact that having the belief in question would serve one's interests, can figure in reasoning whereby one forms the intention to

Fortunately, in order to maintain that the belief component of an intention cannot be formed on the basis of compelling evidence, the cognitivist needn't hold that the belief in question is the belief in a proposition for which there can never be compelling evidence. For she might instead maintain that although one can have compelling evidence for the belief that constitutes intention, one cannot form this belief on the basis of compelling evidence, since one never has this evidence *prior to the existence of the belief in question.* And the way this might be true is that the propositional content of the belief in question might entail that one has this very belief. For, arguably, someone who lacks a given belief can never have compelling evidence for a proposition that entails that she has this belief. Although one might have plenty of evidence for the claim that believes that *p* even if one does not, it is arguable that such evidence can never be decisive. After all, one can always ask oneself whether *p* is true, and if one answers negatively, or suspends judgment, then one can be fairly confident that one does not believe that *p*, however much other evidence there may be for the claim that one does so believe. Hence, if the content of the belief-component of a given intention is a proposition that entails that one believes this very proposition, then, at least arguably, this belief could never be formed on the basis of compelling evidence. But once one has formed this belief, one may then have compelling evidence that the proposition believed is true, and so one may then have good reason to retain this belief.

It seems, therefore, that the cognitivist has strong reason to adopt the *Self-Referential Belief Thesis*:

Every intention involves a belief that entails that one has this very belief.

For this thesis enables her to maintain both that the formation of intentions can never consist entirely in the formation of a belief on the basis of compelling evidence, and that, having formed an intention, one may have good reason to retain this intention. And many cognitivists have indeed proposed accounts of intention that entail the Self-Referential Belief Thesis. So let us now turn our attention to these accounts.

2. SELF-REFERENTIAL BELIEF ACCOUNTS OF INTENTION

In his seminal paper "Practical Reasoning," Gilbert Harman proposed that the intention to ϕ involves the belief that one will ϕ because of that very

---

acquire the belief in question, but they cannot figure in reasoning whereby one forms the belief in question.

intention. Similarly, in "Cognitivism about Instrumental Reason," Kieran Setiya argues that an intention to ϕ is a belief that can be expressed thus: "I will ϕ in part because of this very intention."[5] And David Velleman, in *Practical Reflection*, provides several alternative characterizations of the content of the beliefs that constitute intentions, all of which involve such direct self-reference. Sometimes he characterizes the intention to ϕ as a belief that can be expressed simply as "I'll ϕ *herewith*," while on other occasions he identifies this intention with a more complicated belief, expressed, for instance, as "because I have such and such motives for getting myself to ϕ, and I know that I have such motives, I am *hereby* reinforcing these predispositions to the point where I'll ϕ."[6]

On these views of intention, intentions involve beliefs that refer to themselves, or to the intentions of which they are essential constituents, directly, so that their proper expression involves indexicals or demonstratives such as "*hereby*," "*herewith*," or "*this* very intention." Hence these views entail not only the Self-Referential Belief Thesis, but more specifically the *Direct Self-Reference Thesis*:

> Every intention involves a belief that refers to itself directly, in the sense that its expression requires an indexical or demonstrative that refers directly to the belief in question, or to the intention in which it figures.

In the next section, I will show that the Direct Self-Reference Thesis faces a number of serious difficulties, but that many of these difficulties can be avoided if we move to an indirect version of the Self-Reference Thesis. Later I will show that there are further problems that are faced by both versions of the Direct Self-Reference Thesis.

2.1. Direct and Indirect Self-Reference Accounts of Intention

There are several problems with the view that intentions involve directly self-referential beliefs. For one thing, it is questionable whether there are any such beliefs. For it is plausible that anything that can be believed can be doubted, and hence that at any time, one can believe a given proposition only if one could alternately suspend judgment concerning this proposition. Now let B_p be any directly self-referential belief, and let p be its content. It follows that p involves direct reference to B_p. Hence, at the time at which

[5] Kieran Setiya, "Cognitivism about Instrumental Reason" (forthcoming in *Ethics*); see also *Reasons without Rationalism* (Princeton: Princeton University Press, 2007).

[6] See J. David Velleman, *Practical Reflection* (Princeton: Princeton University Press, 1989), 86–8.

one first believes p, one could not have any attitude toward p unless B_p exists. And so at this time, one could only suspend judgment concerning p if one simultaneously believed that p, which is impossible. Thus, if it were possible, at this time, to believe that p, then it would be possible to believe something which one could not possibly doubt, which contradicts our initial assumption.

A further reason for doubting that there are such things as directly self-referential beliefs is that it is hard to see how such beliefs could be assigned identity conditions. For if someone has a belief B_1 at one time, and a belief B_2 at a later time, then a necessary condition for these being numerically the same belief is that they have the same content. Thus, we can only specify the identity conditions for a belief if we can independently specify the belief's content. But if a belief involves direct reference then we can only specify the content of this belief if we can independently specify the identity conditions of the objects to which it directly refers. Therefore, if a belief involves direct reference to itself, then we can only specify its content if we can independently specify its own identity conditions. But since we can only specify its identity conditions if we can independently specify its content, it follows that we cannot specify its identity conditions. Hence, if there were such things as directly self-referential beliefs, then either they must lack identity conditions, or they must have identity conditions that are ineffable. And neither of these possibilities appears to be very plausible.

Moreover, even if directly self-referential beliefs were possible, they could not be formed by any valid inference. For a conclusion that involves direct reference to a given object, x, can only follow from premises that likewise involve direct reference to x. Thus, if the belief B makes direct reference to itself, then it can follow only from premises that likewise make direct reference to B. But this is possible only if B already exists at the time when one believes the premises. And if B cannot follow from any premises that precede its existence, then B cannot be formed by any valid inference.

The cognitivist need not regard this last argument as a decisive objection to the view that intentions consist in directly self-referential beliefs, for the cognitivist may hold that practical reasoning does not consist in valid inferences. Indeed, Harman, Velleman, and Setiya all reject the view that practical reasoning can be expressed in the form of a logical inference. Still, if there is to be such a thing as practical reasoning, then it must be possible to have reasons for forming intentions. And hence if intentions are directly self-referential beliefs, then it must be possible to have reasons for acquiring such beliefs. It seems, however, that there can be no such reasons.

For, in general, one can only have reason to A if one can consider the question as to whether to A, and can hence see various considerations as bearing on this question. And one can have reason to acquire a directly self-referential belief only if there is some proposition, p, such that one can have reason to come to believe that p, and such that, in coming to believe that p in an appropriate manner, one would thereby acquire a self-referential belief. It follows that one can have reason to acquire a directly self-referential belief only if there is some proposition, p, such that one can consider the question as to whether to come to believe that p, and such that, in coming to believe that p in an appropriate manner, one would thereby form a directly self-referential belief. But it will only be true that, in coming to believe that p in an appropriate manner, one forms a directly self-referential belief, if p is a proposition that refers directly to the belief that one would thereby form. Yet prior to having formed a belief, there is no proposition one can consider that refers directly to this belief. Therefore, prior to forming a self-referential belief, there will be no proposition that one could consider coming to believe, such that in coming to believe this proposition in an appropriate manner one would thereby acquire a self-referential belief. Therefore, there can be no reason for acquiring a directly self-referential belief. And so if intentions involve directly self-referential beliefs, there can be no reason to form an intention. Hence, it will be impossible to reason one's way to an intention.

Fortunately, however, we can solve all these problems if we modify the account of intention under consideration. On what we may call the *indirect self reference account*, intentions involve beliefs that refer to themselves not indexically, but by means of descriptions.[7] On a simple version of such an account, the intention to ϕ involves a belief that can be expressed thus: "I will ϕ because of my current intention to ϕ." For the sake of simplicity, I will focus, in what follows, on this simple version of the indirect self-reference account of intentions, though my arguments apply more generally.

Any account of the intention to ϕ as involving a belief of the form "I will ϕ because of my intention to ϕ" clearly involves circularity. Hence, it can hardly qualify as a reductive analysis of intention. Such an account is no more circular, however, than Setiya's account according to which to intend to ϕ is to have a belief that can be expressed as "*I will ϕ because of this very intention.*" Further, such circularity is not a serious problem for the cognitivist. For the ultimate aim of the cognitivist is not to elucidate the concept of intention, but rather to explain the rational requirements

---

[7] In "Intentions and Self-referential Content" (*Philosophical Papers* 24 (1995), 151–66), Tomis Kapitan draws a distinction that is similar to the one I am drawing here between direct and indirect self-reference accounts of intention.

to which intentions are subject. And the cognitivist may achieve this aim by positing certain conditions for intending to ϕ, even if these conditions cannot be understood without an independent grasp of the notion of intention.

The indirect self-reference account of intentions solves several of the problems we have seen for the standard cognitivist account of intentions as consisting in directly self-referential beliefs. First, unlike directly self-referential beliefs, indirectly self-referential beliefs have a content that can be represented without the belief in question ever having existed. For this reason, the existence of indirectly self-referential beliefs is compatible with the claim that whenever one can believe a proposition, it is possible instead to suspend judgment concerning this proposition. Second, it is possible to specify the content of an indirectly self-referential belief without having independently specified the identity conditions of this belief, and for this reason, indirectly self-referential beliefs can have specifiable identity conditions. Third, indirectly self-referential beliefs have a content that can be entailed by beliefs that do not involve direct reference to these beliefs. And so indirectly self-referential beliefs can be formed via valid inferences. And fourth, as we will now see, the indirect self-reference account of intentions does a better job than the direct self-reference account at explaining the means–end coherence requirement.

2.2. Explaining the Weak Means–End Coherence Requirement

Kieran Setiya proposes a cognitivist explanation for a means–end coherence requirement in "Cognitivism about Instrumental Reason." Here he endorses, and attempts to explain, a principle that we may call the *Weak Means–End Coherence Requirement*:

WME If a fully rational agent intends to ψ, and believes that she will ψ only if she ϕs-because-one-now-intends-to-ϕ, then she intends to ϕ.

Setiya's explanation of this principle involves the following *Modus Ponens Requirement*:

MP If a fully rational agent believes that p, and believes that (if p then q), then she believes that q.

Since, on Setiya's account of intentions, intending to ψ involves believing that one will ψ, it follows from this account that if someone intends to ψ, and believes that she will ψ only if she ϕs-because-she-now-intends-to-ϕ, then she is required, by the Modus Ponens Requirement, to believe that she will ϕ-because-she-now-intends-to-ϕ. And so, in order to explain WME,

Setiya need only claim that anyone who believes she will ϕ-because-she-now-intends-to-ϕ is rationally required to intend to ϕ. And this claim follows from the following principle:

X One ought rationally never to falsely believe that one intends to ϕ.

WME follows from the conjunction of principle X and the Modus Ponens Requirement. And so if the latter two principles are genuine requirements of theoretical rationality, then Setiya will have succeeded in deriving WME purely on the basis of requirements of theoretical rationality. Note, further, that if we accept these two principles, then we can explain WME on the basis of any account of intentions whatsoever that includes the Strong Belief Thesis. For the only assumption about the nature of intentions that figures in this argument is the assumption that anyone who intends to ψ believes that she will ψ.

However, many would question whether principle X is a genuine requirement of rationality, let alone a genuine requirement of theoretical rationality.[8] Fortunately, if we move from the direct to the indirect self-reference account of intentions, we can explain WME without invoking principle X.

Suppose an agent intends to ψ, and believes that he will only ψ if he ϕs-because-he-now-intends-to-ϕ. Since he is required, by means–end coherence, to intend to ϕ, it follows that he satisfies the non-cognitive background condition of the intention to ϕ. Hence, in order to show that he is rationally required to intend to ϕ, it will suffice to show that he is rationally required to have the belief component of the intention to ϕ. And this, according to the indirect self-reference view, is the belief that he will ϕ-because-he-now-intends-to-ϕ. But since he intends to ψ, and hence, on the direct self-reference view, believes that he will ψ, and since he also believes that he will ψ only if he ϕs-because-he-now-intends-to-ϕ, it follows from the Modus Ponens requirement that he is rationally required to believe that he will ϕ-because-he-now-intends-to-ϕ. And this, according to the direct self-reference account of intentions, is precisely the cognitive component of the intention to ϕ. Hence, in intending ψ, and in believing that he will only ψ if he ϕs-because-he-now-intends-to-ϕ, he is rationally required to intend to ϕ. And so, if we assume the indirect self-reference account of intentions, we can explain WME purely on the basis of the Modus Ponens requirement, without invoking principle X.

Another advantage of the indirect self-reference account is that it enables us to understand instances of instrumental reasoning as valid inferences.

---

[8] For criticisms of this principle, see Michael Bratman's "Intention, Belief, Practical, Theoretical."

For suppose one begins with the intention to ψ and the belief that one will only ψ if one ϕs-because-one-now-intends-to-ϕ—and hence one satisfies the background conditions for intending to ϕ—and on the basis of this intention–belief pair one forms the intention to ϕ. On the indirect self-reference account of intentions, this process of reasoning is equivalent to the following inference:

(1) I will ψ because I now intend to ψ.
(2) I will only ψ if I ϕ because I now intend to ϕ.

---

(3) I will ϕ because I now intend to ϕ.

And this is a valid inference.

It seems, therefore, that the indirect self-referential belief account of intentions is highly successful. For in addition to solving the problems for the direct self-reference view we discussed earlier, it also does a better job at explaining both the means–end coherence requirement and instrumental reasoning. But we aren't out of the woods yet. For while the indirect self-reference view provides a good explanation of WME, the latter, as I shall now argue, is too weak to count as the proper formulation of the requirement of means–end coherence.

2.3. Why the Weak Means–End Coherence Requirement is Too Weak

I will now argue that since there are often circumstances in which it would be rational to intend to ϕ, but in which it would not be rational to believe that we will ϕ only if we so intend, WME cannot be the proper formulation of the means–end coherence requirement.

Consider a case in which I am the designated driver for a party that I will be attending this evening. I intend to drive home safely, and I believe that remaining sober is a necessary means to my driving home safely. Suppose I know that it is very difficult for me to resist the temptation to drink alcohol, and so if I want to ensure that I remain sober at the party, I must form the firm intention to do so before I arrive at the party. Suppose, however, that I recognize that there is a chance that I might remain sober even if I don't form this prior intention prior to going to the party: there might not be any alcohol at the party, or there may be no alcohol that appeals to me, or I may find that I am unusually resistant to its tempting influence. In this case, it seems clear that I am rationally required to intend to remain sober at the party. But this conclusion does not follow from:

WME One ought rationally to be such that (if one intends to ϕ, and believes that one will ϕ only if one ϕs-because-one-now-intends-to-ψ, then one intends to ψ).

For WME would imply that I am rationally required to intend to stay sober only if I believe that (I will drive home safely only if I remain-sober-because-I-now-intend-to-remain-sober). But in the case in question, I do not have this belief.

The case just considered involves a prior intention directed toward a future action. But similar problems arise for concurrent intentions concerning our present actions. Consider a case in which Daria intends to win a game of darts. Her opponent is doing very badly, and so all Daria needs in order to win the game is to hit one of the three central rings of the five-ring dart board. She is a very good darts player, and so she knows that if she intends to hit one of the three central rings, she will do so. Of course, if she merely had the general intention to hit the dartboard, without specifically intending to hit one of the three central rings, she might nonetheless hit one of these central rings. Let us suppose that she is agnostic on the issue of whether she would hit one of the three central rings if she had no specific intention to do so: she thinks there is a reasonable chance that she would, but that there is also a reasonable chance that she would not. In this case, it would seem that, given Daria's other beliefs and intentions, she cannot rationally fail to intend to hit one of the central three rings. But again, this requirement does not follow from WME. For Daria does not believe that she will hit one of the three central rings only if she does so because she intends to do so.

It seems, therefore, that WME is too weak to count as the proper formulation of the requirement of means–end coherence. However, as I will now argue, the Strong Means–End Coherence requirement is too strong. Fortunately there is a third formulation of this requirement, the *Moderate Means–End Coherence Requirement*, which, like Baby Bear, is just right. And this formulation, it will turn out, can be explained on the basis of the indirect self-referential account of intention.

2.4. Explaining the Moderate Means–End Coherence Requirement

Recall that according to the Strong Means–End Coherence Requirement, one cannot rationally intend an end without intending what one believes to be a necessary means to this end. This formulation appears to be overly strong. For when we intend to carry out some action in the future, there may be a large number of intermediate actions that we believe to be necessary means to this future action, but to have an intention, in the present, to carry out each one of these intermediary actions would seem to involve superfluous mental clutter. Thus, I intend to bicycle to campus tomorrow afternoon. And I believe that the following are all necessary means to my doing so: walking to my front door; turning the handle of my front door; opening my front door; walking to my bicycle; removing my keys from my pocket; inserting my bicycle key into my bicycle lock; turning the key; etc., etc. But surely I am not rationally required to already have all these intentions. It would suffice for me to form these intentions tomorrow afternoon.

And there is a further reason to deny that SME is the proper formulation of the means–end coherence requirement. Suppose I am in prison, and I intend to keep my mind occupied tomorrow by counting the cracks in the wall of my prison cell. And suppose I believe that remaining in my prison cell is a necessary means to counting these cracks. In this case, it follows from SME that I am rationally required to intend to remain in my prison cell. But this hardly seems plausible. For I know that I have no choice but to remain in my prison cell. Hence, whether to remain in my prison cell is not a possible object of rational deliberation. But it would seem that I cannot be rationally required to have an intention that I could not form by way of rational deliberation. And so it would seem that I cannot be rationally required to intend to remain in my prison cell, contrary to SME.

In the above example, the necessary means is something I believe I will never be able to choose. But other counterexamples can be given that do not involve this feature. Suppose it is now Monday. I have a crystal ball that enables me to see everything that I will do on Tuesday, but that does not reveal any events after Tuesday. Suppose, further, that tonight I will forget everything I learned from the crystal ball, and so tomorrow I will no longer have foreknowledge of all my actions. Suppose that today, as I gaze into the crystal ball, and I observe that tomorrow I will pick up my suit from the dry cleaners. After observing this, I might deliberate concerning what to do on Wednesday. Since I know my sister's wedding is on Wednesday, I may form the intention to wear my suit to her wedding. And I may believe that picking up my suit from the dry cleaners is a necessary means to wearing my suit to her wedding. But since I already know, on the basis of compelling evidence, that I will be picking up my suit from the dry cleaners, I am not in a position to deliberate concerning whether to pick up my suit from the dry cleaners. For deliberation concerning whether to ϕ must proceed from a state of uncertainty concerning whether one will ϕ, and this is ruled out in my present case. In the words of Isaac Levi, prediction crowds out deliberation. And since I am not in a position to rationally deliberate concerning whether to pick up my suit from the dry cleaners, it seems I cannot be rationally required to intend to do so.

One possible response to this problem is to say that one is never under a rational requirement to intend to ϕ if one has sufficient evidential reason to believe that one will ϕ. But the cognitivist should not welcome this proposal. For, at least very plausibly, a belief is only rational if it is theoretically or epistemically rational, and a belief is only theoretically or epistemically rational if there is sufficient evidential reason for this belief. Hence, if intending to ϕ involves believing that one will ϕ, then whenever one lacks sufficient evidential reason to believe that one will ϕ, it would be irrational to intend to ϕ. And so, if one accepts the current proposal, and holds that one can only be rationally required to intend to ϕ when one lacks sufficient evidential reason to believe one will ϕ, then one must conclude that one can only be rationally required to intend to ϕ when intending to ϕ would be irrational. And this is hardly a desirable conclusion.

There is another problem with this proposed response. For when one is about to perform an action, one is generally in a position to know that one intends to perform this action, and that one is unlikely to change one's mind or to fail in the performance of this action. Thus, when one is about to perform an action, then one generally has sufficient evidential reason to believe that one will perform this action. And so if this proposed response were correct, and one is never under a rational requirement to intend to ϕ if one has sufficient evidential reason to believe that one will ϕ, then it will very seldom be true that one is rationally required to perform any action that one is about to perform.

What we should say, therefore, is not that one is never rationally required to ϕ when one has sufficient evidential reason to believe that one will ϕ, but rather that one is never rationally required to intend to ϕ when, *apart from one's intention to ϕ*, one has sufficient evidential reason to believe one will ϕ. And, if we adopt this proposal, then we must reformulate the means–end coherence requirement. According to the *Moderate Means–End Coherence Requirement*,

MME One ought rationally to be such that (if one intends to ψ, and one believes that ϕ-ing is a necessary means to ψ-ing, and if, apart from the intention to ϕ, one would have insufficient evidence for the belief that one will ϕ, then one intends to ϕ).

Note that this principle applies in many cases in which the Weak Means–End Coherence Requirement does not apply, and in which, intuitively, a principle of means–end coherence ought to apply. Consider once more the case of Daria who intends to win the game of darts, and who believes that hitting one of the three central rings of the dartboard is a necessary means to winning the game. Since she does not have the belief that she will win the game only if she hits one of the central rings *because she now intends to do so*, WME does not imply that she is rationally required to hit one of the three central rings. However, under normal circumstances, MME will imply that she is rationally required to hit one of these rings. For Daria recognizes that unless she intends to hit one of the central three rings, there is a good chance that she will not hit one of these rings. Hence, conditional on her not having the intention to hit one of the central three rings, she has little confidence that she will hit one of these rings. And so if she does not believe that she intends to hit one of these rings, she should not believe that she will hit one of them. And if she does not have sufficient reason to believe that she intends to hit one of these rings, she will not have sufficient reason to believe that she will hit one of them. But at least under normal circumstances, unless she intends to hit one of these rings, she will not have sufficient reason to believe that she intends to do so. Consequently, apart from the intention to hit one of these rings, she would not have sufficient reason to believe that she will hit one of them. Therefore, in this case, the conditions for the applicability of MME are met.

Thus, MME appears to be a plausible candidate for being the proper formulation of the means–end coherence requirement. And luckily, it is not difficult to provide a cognitivist explanation of MME. All we need to assume is the Strong Belief Thesis. For suppose this thesis is true, and that the antecedent of MME is satisfied. In this case, one will believe that one will ψ, and one will also believe that ϕ-ing is a necessary means to ψ-ing, and so one will be rationally required to believe that one will ϕ. Further, if one satisfies the antecedent of this conditional, then apart from the intention to ϕ, one would lack sufficient evidence for the belief that one will ϕ. And, at least plausibly, if one lacks sufficient evidence for the belief that one will ϕ, then one cannot rationally believe that one will ϕ. It follows that, apart from the intention to ϕ, one cannot rationally believe that one will ϕ. Therefore, if one is rationally required to believe that one will ϕ, then one is rationally required to intend to ϕ. But we have seen that if the antecedent of the conditional is satisfied, then one is rationally required to believe that one will ϕ. Therefore, if the antecedent is satisfied, then one is rationally required to intend to ϕ. In other words, one ought rationally to be such that if one satisfies the antecedent of the conditional, one satisfies the consequent. And so the Moderate Means–End Coherence Requirement is true, and can be explained purely on the basis of requirements of theoretical rationality, assuming only the Strong Belief Thesis.

So things are looking rosy. For if we accept the Strong Belief Thesis, we can explain not only the requirement of Intention Consistency, but also the Moderate Means–End Consistency Requirement, which is arguably the proper formulation of the means–end coherence requirement. And if we accept the Self-Referential Belief Thesis, then we can also avoid the problem of mere recognition that we discussed in Section 1.4. And while the direct version of the Self-Referential Belief Thesis faced a number of difficulties, we saw how these difficulties can be avoided by moving to the indirect version. But alas, two serious problems still lie ahead. In the next section, I will argue that the standard self-referential belief accounts of intention have very implausible implications concerning the circumstances in which intentions can be rational. And in Section 2.6, I will argue that any view of intentions that involves the Self-Referential Belief Thesis will be incompatible with a coherent understanding of instrumental reasoning.

2.5. The Problem of Causal Overdetermination

We have seen that there is reason to doubt the cognitivist view that intending to ϕ involves believing that one will ϕ. But the self-referential views of intention that we are now considering have much stronger implications concerning the beliefs involved in intention. First, they imply that a necessary condition for intending to ϕ is that one believe that one intends to ϕ, or at least that one believe that one has the belief-component of this intention. Second, they imply that a necessary condition for intending to ϕ is believing that one's intention to ϕ will play a role in causing one to ϕ. Are these implications plausible?

Concerning the first implication, many authors have pointed out that young children, and even some animals (e.g. chimpanzees) appear to have intentions, and yet it seems implausible to ascribe to them second-order beliefs about their attitudes. Of course, one might argue that young children and animals really do have these beliefs but in an implicit or inarticulate manner; or one might argue that young children and animals don't really have intentions; or one might argue that while they may have intentions of a sort, these intentions are not subject to rational requirements, and so the cognitivist account of intentions need not apply to them. Each of these maneuvers, however, has a cost, and so there is reason to prefer an account of intentions that does not require us to make them.

Far more problematic is the implication that in order to ϕ one must believe that one will ϕ because one now intends to ϕ. For it seems that in many cases in which intentions are called for, the belief that one will perform the intended action because one now intends to do so would not be a rational belief.

Harman considers cases of this kind in "Practical Reasoning."[9] Suppose Judy has the option of going to a party, but decides to stay home instead. In this case, Harman argues, it might not be rational for Judy to believe that she will stay home *because she so intends*. For even if she had no intention to stay home, she might do so anyway out of habit. Harman calls intentions of this kind "negative intentions."

Not all cognitivists are persuaded by such cases. Kieran Setiya argues as follows: "[Harman's] 'negative' intentions are causes, too. It is just that the action they cause is over-determined: it would have happened without them." Hence we can accept the claim that anyone who intends to ϕ believes that she will ϕ because she so intends, "so long as we reject, or qualify, the counterfactual test for causation."[10] Thus, even if, in the absence of the intention to stay home, Judy would have stayed home out of habit, it does not follow that her intention to stay home can't cause her to stay home. For her intention to stay home might preempt her habit in causing her to stay home, and might thereby be the genuine cause of her staying home.

The problem with this response, however, is that pre-emption cuts both ways. While it is true that the one's current intention to ϕ might preempt other potential causes of one's ϕ-ing, it is likewise true that other potential causes of one's ϕ-ing might preempt one's current intention to ϕ. Thus, now, at noon, I intend to brush my teeth before going to bed at midnight, but I am aware that I may brush my teeth at midnight not because of my having this intention at noon, but rather out of habit. Similarly, right now, in the summer, I intend to wear long sleeves in the winter, but I recognize that when winter comes, I may wear long sleeves not because of any intention I formed in the summer, but because I will then want to stay warm, and I will believe that wearing long sleeves is a necessary means to staying warm. Or being the designated driver, I may intend not to drink at the party I will be attending this evening, while recognizing that there is a possibility that I will refrain from drinking at the party not because of my current intention not to drink at the party, but because when I arrive at the party I will find that the only available beverages are ones that I find revolting.

Thus, a prior intention to perform a given action may be pre-empted by an independent motivation, at the time in question, to perform the action in

---

[9] Gilbert Harman, "Practical Reasoning" *Review of Metaphysics* 29 (1976), 431–63, reprinted in his *Reasoning, Meaning, and Mind* (Oxford: Clarendon Press, 1999), 46–74. Harman's discussion of the Judy example occurs on pp. 53–4 (all page references to Harman's paper will refer to the reprint).

[10] "Cognitivism about Instrumental Reason," footnote 30.

question, such as a habit, or an emotional response, or the recognition of a decisive reason. Further, a prior intention can be pre-empted by subsequent deliberation. I may now intend to retire when I'm 65, while recognizing that what causes me to retire when I'm 65 may be not my current intention to retire when I'm 65, but rather an intention to retire when I'm 65 that I form at a later stage in life when I reopen the question as to when to retire.

Finally, one can have an intention while recognizing that one may fulfill this intention not because one has this intention, but rather because of circumstances completely outside of one's control. Suppose that Ed intends to do anything Jane asks him to do on her birthday. He might have this intention while recognizing that Jane may not ask him to do anything on her birthday. But if she doesn't ask him to do anything, then although it will trivially be true that Ed does everything Jane asks him to do on her birthday, this will not be true because of Ed's intention.

Thus, in a wide variety of cases where it appears to be rational to intend to ϕ, it would not be rational to believe that one will ϕ because one now intends to ϕ. And so if, as the standard cognitivist accounts of intentions imply, anyone who intends to ϕ believes that she will ϕ because she so intends, then it follows that these apparently rational intentions are in fact irrational. This, therefore, is a very strong reason to reject such accounts of intention.

2.6. The Problem of Practical Reasoning

We saw earlier that, on the indirect self-reference account, intentions can be formed by way of valid inferences. However, on this view of intentions, they cannot be formed by way of *sound* inferences. For on this account, the intention to ϕ involves the belief that one will ϕ because one now intends to ϕ. Hence, the intention to ϕ involves a belief that can only be true if one intends to ϕ. But any premises from which one form the intention to ϕ by way of a sound inference must be premises that entail the belief component of the intention to ϕ, and so they must entail that one intends to ϕ. Now if these premises are true, then one already intends to ϕ, and so one cannot form the intention to ϕ on the basis of these premises. And if, on the other hand, these premises are not all true, then they cannot provide the basis for a sound inference. Either way, it will be impossible to arrive at the intention to ϕ by way of a sound inference.

But this conclusion, like the conclusion that on the direct self-reference view intentions cannot be formed by way of valid inference, need not trouble the cognitivist, since, as before, she may deny that practical reasoning takes the form of a logical inference. But the indirect self-reference account of intentions has a much more troubling implication, since it implies that no one who understands what intentions are could ever form the intention to ϕ by way of a conscious process of reasoning. For if an intention involves a belief, then any reasoning in which one forms this intention must be reasoning in which one forms the belief it involves. And reasoning leading to the belief that p is reasoning in which one is guided by the question *whether p*, and in which one arrives at an affirmative answer to this question. Hence, if the intention to ϕ involves the belief that p, then any self-conscious process of reasoning wherein one forms the intention to ϕ must be a self-conscious process of reasoning wherein one arrives at an affirmative answer to the question *whether p*. Hence, if the intention to ϕ involves the belief that one will ϕ because one now intends to ϕ, then one can self-consciously form the intention to ϕ only if one can self-consciously arrive at an affirmative answer to the following question:

Q1 Will I ϕ because I now intend to ϕ?

And if one understands what intentions are, then one will regard Q1 as equivalent to:

Q2 Will I ϕ because I have an attitude that involves the belief that (I will ϕ because I now intend to ϕ)?

But if one is asking question Q2, then one cannot already have made up one's mind concerning the answer. And if one is asking question Q2 self-consciously, then one will recognize that one has not yet made up one's mind concerning the answer. Thus, one will recognize that one does not believe that one will ϕ because one now intends to ϕ. And so the answer to Q2 will be obvious: "no!" And if one understands that the view of intentions under consideration is correct, and hence one regards Q1 as equivalent to Q2, then the answer to Q1 will be equally obvious: "no!" Hence one will be unable to self-consciously arrive at an affirmative answer to Q1. And so it follows, on the account under consideration, that one will be unable form to the intention to ϕ by way of a self-conscious process of reasoning.[11]

---

[11] Perhaps the problem derives from the temporal indexical, "now." There would be no difficulty, after all, in arriving, by way of self-conscious reasoning, at the conclusion "I will ϕ because I intend at t to ϕ," so long as one does not believe that the time is now t. And so if the cognitivist held that the belief-component of the intention to ϕ is not the belief that (one will ϕ because one now intends to do so) but rather the belief that (one will ϕ because one intends at t to do so) for some t other than the present, then the cognitivist could avoid the problem just described. But she would do so at significant cost. For she would no longer have a view of intentions according to which intention formation cannot consist in mere recognition. For one can certainly arrive, on the basis

We have seen that in order to explain the means–end coherence require-ment, the cognitivist must give sufficient conditions for intending a means. These sufficient conditions must include a cognitive condition. And if it also includes a non-cognitive condition, the latter must take the form of a background condition. And this implies that, in instrumental reasoning, the formation of the instrumental intention consists in the formation of the cognitive component of this intention. And this implies, in turn, that if this cognitive component is a belief that can be formed on the basis of compelling evidential reasons, then the formation of intentions can consist in mere recognition. The cognitivist may be able to avoid the conclusion that the formation of intentions can consist in mere recognition, so long as she adopts the self-referential belief thesis. But if she adopts this thesis, she will run into all the problems we have encountered in the last three sections.

Besides the constraints just given, are there any independent reasons to accept the Self-Referential Belief Thesis? Some cognitivists argue for the Self-Referential Belief Thesis on the basis of what we may call the *Self-Referential Intention Thesis*:

> Anyone who intends ϕ intends to (ϕ because of her current intention to ϕ).

In Appendix B, I argue that none of the standard arguments for the Self-Referential Intention Thesis is sound. I also argue that there is good reason to reject this thesis. Hence, arguments for the Self-Referential Belief Thesis that are based on the Self-Referential Intention Thesis are without force.

And so the cognitivist appears to be faced with a dilemma. There are a number of serious problems with the Strong Belief Thesis, that is, and so if the cognitivist claims that in order to satisfy the cognitive conditions for intending to ϕ, one must believe that one intends to ϕ, then the cognitivist is in hot water. But if, on the other hand, she claims that in order to satisfy the cognitive condition for intending to ϕ, it is sufficient to have a belief with some specified content, a content that does not entail that one intends to ϕ, then she will be committed to the conclusion that merely recognizing the truth of a proposition on the basis of compelling evidence can constitute forming an intention.

But it may be that the cognitivist can avoid both horns of this dilemma. That is, she may be able both to reject the view that intending to ϕ involves believing that one intends to ϕ; and to reject the view that believing some

---

of compelling evidence, at the belief that one will ϕ because, at some other time, one intends to ϕ. And so if such belief were the cognitive component of the intention to ϕ, one could form the intention to ϕ merely by recognizing the truth of this belief.

particular proposition that does not entail that one intends to ϕ is sufficient for having the belief component of the intention to ϕ. The way to reject both of these claims is to deny that having the belief component of the intention to ϕ is simply a matter of having a belief with an appropriate content. An alternative is that the belief component of the intention to ϕ must be a belief that not only has the right content, but that also has the right kind of basis.

3. AN ALTERNATIVE ACCOUNT OF INTENTIONS

3.1. The Basis of Intentions

Gilbert Harman has proposed that an intention to ϕ is an idea concerning the future which

(i) represents itself as causing it to be the case, or as guaranteeing, that one shall ϕ; and
(ii) is arrived at and maintained by practical reasoning.

We have seen that the kind of self-referential view expressed in (i) faces a number of problems, and in Appendix B I discuss further problems with this kind of view. But the second part of Harman's view may be more promising. Perhaps we can distinguish between intentions and mere predictions of our future actions on the ground that the beliefs involved in these two cases are arrived at by way of different kinds of reasoning. Perhaps Harman is on the right track in saying that an intention is "an idea of the future arrived at and maintained by practical reasoning."[12]

This suggestion cannot be accepted exactly as it stands, for it seems that there could be intentions that are not arrived at and maintained by practical reasoning. Suppose I intend to go to the fridge. I arrived at this intention via practical reasoning, proceeding from the intention, or perhaps the mere desire, to drink orange juice, and the belief that going to the fridge is a necessary means to drinking orange juice. It seems possible, if extremely improbable, that a swamp man could spontaneously materialize in front of my fridge with a psychology very similar to my own, and in particular, with a similar intention to go to the fridge. In this case, his intention would not have been arrived at by practical reasoning. Furthermore, once one has formed an intention, it does not seem to be always necessary to engage in practical reasoning simply in order to maintain this intention. Thus it

---

[12] "Practical Reasoning," 63.

would seem that the swamp man's intention to go to the fridge might be neither arrived at, nor maintained, by practical reasoning.

It appears, therefore, that we cannot understand intentions as beliefs about the future formed and maintained by way of practical reasoning. Perhaps, however, we can understand them as beliefs that are directly based on practical reasons. Let us say that a given attitude, A, belonging to an agent, s, is *directly based on practical reasons* just in case s's disposition to retain attitude A is directly explained by the fact that s has a set of attitudes from which she *could* arrive at attitude A by way of practical reasoning. Given this definition, we may propose that the intention to ϕ consists in the non-cognitive background condition for intending to ϕ, whatever that may be, plus a belief that one will ϕ that is directly based on practical reasons.

Thus, although the swamp man's belief that he will go to the fridge was not arrived at by practical reasoning, this intention is at least partly based, in the relevant sense, on his intention to drink orange juice and his belief that going to the fridge is a necessary means to drinking orange juice. For this pair of attitudes partly explains his disposition to retain his belief that he will go to the fridge, since apart from this pair of attitudes he would be less reluctant to form some other plan of action, and hence to cease believing that he will go to the fridge. This must be true, since we are assuming that he is a psychological duplicate of me, and in my case the corresponding belief–intention pair play the corresponding explanatory role in my psychology. And this pair of attitudes is one on the basis of which it is possible to arrive at the belief that one will go to the fridge by way of practical reasoning. Thus, since the swamp-man has a belief that he will go to the fridge that is based on a set of attitudes of the appropriate kind, he satisfies the cognitive condition for intending to go to the fridge.

So when is it true that a given belief could be arrived at on the basis of a given set of beliefs by way of practical reasoning? Clearly, the set consisting in the intention to ψ and the belief that ϕ-ing is a necessary means to ψ-ing is a set of attitudes on the basis of which one could arrive, by way of practical reasoning, at the intention to ϕ. And so if the intention to ϕ involves the belief that one will ϕ, it is a set on the basis of which one could arrive, by way of practical reasoning, at the belief that one will ϕ. But equally clearly, it is not the only set of attitudes of this kind, since not all practical reasoning takes this simple, instrumental form. And in order for the view of intentions under consideration to be complete, it would need to specify which processes of reasoning count as practical reasoning and which do not—it could not, without vicious circularity, simply say that a process of reasoning counts as practical reasoning just in case it issues in an intention, since it defines intentions in terms of the kinds of reasoning from which they issue. Of course, even once one has specified which processes of reasoning count as practical reasoning, there will still remain some circularity, since some of these forms of reasoning will proceed from sets of attitudes that include intentions. But this kind of circularity is no more vicious than that found in standard functionalist accounts of mental attitudes, on which attitudes of a given type are defined in terms of the ways in which they causally interact with other attitudes, including attitudes of the same type.

3.2. Evaluating Our Account of Intentions

We must now determine whether the account of intentions we have proposed can explain the requirements of intention consistency and of means–end coherence, and whether it can do so while avoiding the pitfalls of the other accounts of intention we have considered.

Clearly, like any account of intentions that entails the Strong Belief Thesis, the present account can explain the Intention Consistency Requirement. Similarly, like any account of intentions that entails the Strong Belief Thesis, this account, in conjunction with principle X, can explain the Weak Means–End Coherence Requirement. And, much more importantly, like any account that entails the Strong Belief Thesis, this account can explain the Moderate Means–End Coherence Requirement.

Can it provide a cognitivist explanation of the Strong Means–End Coherence Requirement? It seems it cannot. For any such explanation would need to show that it is a requirement of theoretical rationality that:

> Anyone who intends to ψ, and believes that ϕ-ing is a necessary means to ψ-ing, must believe that she will ϕ *on the basis of a set of attitudes from which she could arrive, by practical reasoning, at the belief that she will ϕ.*

And while it is clear, on the current account, that any such agent would be rationally required to believe that she will ϕ (since this belief follows straightforwardly from her other beliefs), it is unclear why she should have to believe this on the basis of a set of attitudes of a specified kind. For she might have other sufficient reasons to have this belief, and if this is the case then it would seem perfectly theoretically rational for her to have this belief entirely on the basis of these other sufficient reasons.

Suppose, for example, that I am driving home, and I know that I will soon be approaching a stop sign. And suppose I intend always to obey the traffic regulations, and I believe that a necessary means to my doing so is that I stop at the upcoming stop sign. In this case, I will have a belief–intention pair on the basis of which I could form the belief that I will stop at the stop sign by way of practical reasoning. Suppose, however, that I have abundant evidential reason for believing that I will stop at the stop sign. Suppose, for example, that in my long driving history, I have never failed to stop at a stop sign. In this case, I have a surplus of attitudes on the basis of which I could form the belief that I will stop at the stop sign. And it would seem that I could be perfectly theoretically rational without basing my belief that I will stop at the stop sign on all these attitudes: I could, with perfect theoretical rationality, believe that I will stop at the upcoming stop sign purely on the basis of my knowledge of my own perfect track record.

In response to a similar difficulty, Harman has suggested that it is a requirement of rationality that one never form a belief by way of theoretical reasoning that one could form by way of practical reasoning. Such a principle would imply that, in the case just described, I could not rationally form the belief that I will stop at the stop sign by theoretical reasoning, on the basis of my knowledge of my track record, since I am in a position to form this belief by practical reasoning, on the basis of my intention always to obey the traffic regulations. However, even if the proposed principle were a requirement of rationality, it surely isn't a requirement of theoretical rationality: if I were to form the belief that I will stop at the stop sign on the basis of the available evidence, I would not thereby be theoretically irrational. And so the cognitivist cannot appeal to such a principle in explaining the means–end coherence requirement.

It seems, however, that there is no reason to look for supplementary principles by which we could explain the Strong Means–End Coherence Requirement. For, as we saw in Section 2.5, there is reason to believe that SME is considerably too strong. And so we should regard that fact that our theory does not entail SME as a virtue of this theory, not as a vice. Since it does explain the Moderate Means–End Coherence Requirement, and since the latter appears to be a formulation of the right level of strength, our account appears to provide an adequate cognitivist explanation of the requirement of means–end coherence.

In this respect, however, it does not differ from any other account that entails the Strong Belief Thesis. But our theory has a number of additional virtues. First, like the self-referential belief accounts of intentions, it avoids the implication that the recognition of the truth of a proposition on the basis of compelling evidence can constitute the formation of an intention. This view can avoid this conclusion, not by claiming that the belief component of the intention to ϕ is a belief with a special content, but rather by claiming that the belief in question must be based on a set of attitudes by which it could be formed by way of practical reasoning. So long as the view includes an account of practical reasoning according to which purely evidential reasons can never be an adequate basis for such reasoning, the view will entail that intentions can never be based on purely evidential reasons. And so the view under consideration shares the principal virtue of the self-referential belief account of intentions. But it avoids many of the problems of the latter account.

First, because, on this view, to intend to ϕ one needn't believe that one will ϕ because of this very intention, this view does not imply that, in cases in which we think the causal efficacy of our intention may be preempted by other factors, we cannot rationally intend to ϕ. Thus, this view does not suffer from the problem of causal overdetermination discussed in Section 2.3.

Second, this view allows for a very satisfying account of instrumental reasoning. Suppose I intend to ψ and believe that ϕ-ing is a necessary means to ϕ-ing. On the view we are considering, I will be in a position to reason my way to the intention to ψ. For on the view under consideration, in intending to ψ, I will believe that I will ψ, and from this belief, together with the belief that ϕ-ing is a necessary means to ψ-ing, I can infer that I will ψ. The belief that I thereby form will be based on a pair of attitudes of the right kind (namely an intention and an instrumental belief), and so in having this belief I will satisfy the cognitive condition for intending to ϕ. And since I am required, by means–end coherence, to intend to ϕ, I must antecedently satisfy the non-cognitive conditions for intending to ϕ, whatever they may be. And so since, in forming the belief that I will ϕ, I come to satisfy the cognitive condition for intending to ϕ, I will come to satisfy all the conditions for intending to ϕ, and will thus acquire the intention to ϕ. Hence, I will arrive at the intention to ϕ by way of a valid inference.

And third, on the present view, it is possible to form the intention to ϕ by way of an inference that is not only valid, but sound. For on the present view, the belief involved in the intention to ϕ is simply the belief that one will ϕ, not the belief that one will ϕ because one so intends. And so the relevant belief is one that can follow from a set of premises that do not entail that one has this belief. Hence it can follow deductively from a set of premises all of which are already true before this belief is formed. And since the belief component of the intention to ϕ does not imply that one has this belief, it can be formed by way of a self-conscious process of reasoning.

I conclude, therefore, that if one is to be a cognitivist about practical reason, then this is the account of intentions one should accept. And so we have sketched an answer to the question of *how* to be a cognitivist about practical reason. There remains, of course, the question of *whether* to be a cognitivist about practical reason, a question whose answer goes beyond the scope of this chapter.

APPENDIX A: INTENTIONS AND PRACTICAL ACCEPTANCE

Even if we reject the Strong Belief Thesis, we might still hold that a related thesis is true. That is, we might hold that while intending to ϕ needn't involve believing that one will ϕ, it does involve planning on the basis of the supposition that one will ϕ, or in other words, taking it for granted, in the context of practical reasoning, that one will ϕ. Let us use the term "acceptance," or "acceptance from the practical point of view," to refer to this attitude of taking a proposition for granted in the context of practical reasoning. We may then formulate this suggestion as the *Strong Acceptance Thesis*:

> A necessary condition for intending to ϕ is *accepting* that one will ϕ in all contexts of practical reasoning.

The view that intending to ϕ involves accepting that one will ϕ, and that rational requirements on intentions can be explained in terms of rational requirements on the attitude of acceptance, should not be described as a purely cognitivist view. For the attitude we are calling acceptance is not a purely cognitive attitude: it does not aim at truth, accuracy, verisimilitude, knowledge, understanding, or any other cognitive aim. More generally, practical acceptance does not have a mind-to-world direction of fit: it does not aim to represent the world as it really is. It aims rather at the effective guidance of action, and for this reason it can be rational to accept a proposition from the practical point of view even when one lacks sufficient reason to believe that it is true, and even when one has sufficient reason to believe that it is false. Thus, in some cases, we can take one theory for granted in the context of practical reasoning (say, classical mechanics) which we do not believe to be true, because the theory we believe to be true (say, quantum mechanics) is too complicated or unwieldy to employ in the context of practical reasoning, and we can serve our interests better by treating the simpler theory as true.[13] In some cases, we can rationally take things for granted in the context of practical reasoning because doing so puts us in a beneficial frame of mind. Hence, one can rationally take it for granted, in certain contexts of practical reasoning, that the client one is representing is innocent, or that one's spouse is faithful, or that one will recover from one's illness, even though one does not have sufficient reason to believe these claims. And in some cases, we can rationally take a proposition for granted in the contest of practical reasoning without believing that it is true

---

[13] Someone may object that what we take for granted is not that classical mechanics is true, but rather that classical mechanics is approximately true. But this is not right. For reasoning on the supposition that something is approximately true is very different from, and far more complicated than, reasoning on the supposition that it is true. For example, on the supposition that p and q are true, we can infer any conclusion that is entailed by the conjunction of p and q. But from the supposition that p and q are approximately true, we cannot infer that the propositions that are entailed by their conjunction are approximately true.

because we know that, if the proposition is false, it will make little difference to how we act.[14]

But while practical acceptance should not be described as a cognitive attitude, we might describe it as a quasi-cognitive attitude. For one thing, while it does not, in general, have a mind-to-world direction of fit, it doesn't in general have a world-to-mind direction of fit either: someone who accepts classical mechanics in the context of practical reasoning does not thereby have a tendency to bring it about that classical mechanics is true. Further, like belief, to accept a proposition from the practical point of view is in some sense to treat it as true. Like belief, acceptance seems to be governed by a norm of consistency, as it seems that in the context of practical reasoning, one cannot rationally accept inconsistent propositions. Similarly, like belief, it seems to be governed by a principle of closure, in the sense that there is rational pressure to accept, or take for granted, the propositions that follow from other propositions that one accepts. But if we assume that intention involves acceptance, and that acceptance is governed by analogues of all the norms on belief that figure in standard cognitivist explanations of the norms on intention, then we might expect to be able to give an explanation of these norms on intention that has all virtues of the standard cognitivist explanation, but without invoking the Strong Belief Thesis. And since acceptance appears to be a quasi-cognitive attitude, it would seem that such an explanation should count, if not as a purely cognitivist explanation of the requirements of practical rationality under consideration, at least as a quasi-cognitivist explanation—or, to borrow an expression from Olivier Roy, who proposes an explanation of this kind, a "hybrid cognitivist explanation."[15]

We saw that the intention consistency requirement can be explained in terms of the Strong Belief Thesis in conjunction with *Belief Consistency*:

> One ought rationally to be such that the set of all the propositions one believes is logically consistent.

But if we move from the Strong Belief Thesis to the Strong Acceptance Thesis, then we must move from the requirement of Belief Consistency to *Acceptance Consistency*:

> One ought rationally to be such that the set of all the propositions one accepts is jointly consistent with one's beliefs.

For if Acceptance Consistency is true, and if a necessary condition for intending to ϕ is accepting that one will ϕ, then one ought to be such that the set of propositional contents of one's intentions is jointly consistent with one's beliefs. Hence, Acceptance Consistency, in conjunction with the Strong Acceptance Thesis, entails Intention Consistency.

---

[14] I discuss this last type of case in "Rejecting Ethical Deflationism" (*Ethics* 116, July 2006) and in my dissertation, "Rational Acceptance and Practical Reason" (2006, Rutgers University).

[15] For an explanation along these lines, worked out in much more detail than I have provided here, see ch. 6 of Olivier Roy's *Thinking before Acting: Intention, Logic, Rational Choice* (Amsterdam: Institute for Logic Language and Computation, 2008).

Unfortunately, there are problems with this account. For one cannot plausibly accept the Strong Acceptance Thesis while denying the Strong Belief Thesis. For suppose the strong belief thesis is false, and hence that one can intend to ϕ without believing one will ϕ. Suppose, in particular, that Michael intends to stop at the bookstore on his way home from work, but he does not quite believe that he will do so, since he knows he might forget. And suppose he is offered a bet, called bet X, with the following payoff structure: if he accepts bet X, and he goes to the bookstore, then he will make a profit of 25 cents, but if he accepts bet X and fails to stop at the bookstore, then he will be tortured for the rest of his life. It seems clear that, in this case, Michael might well not take it for granted that he will stop at the bookstore in the context of deciding whether to take bet X. Indeed, if Michael is rational, then he will not take this for granted, since taking this for granted would license taking bet X, and taking bet X would be a rational choice only for an agent who, unlike Michael, is fully confident that he will stop at the bookstore. Hence, it would seem that, if Michael can intend to stop at the bookstore without being fully confident that he will do so, then he can also intend to stop at the bookstore without taking it for granted that he will do so whenever he is engaging in practical reasoning. More generally, if it is possible for an agent to intend to ϕ without believing that she will ϕ, then it is possible for an agent to intend to ϕ without taking it for granted that she will ϕ in every context of practical reasoning. In other words, if the Strong Belief Thesis is false, then the Strong Acceptance Thesis must also be false.

And so the latter thesis must, at the very least, be weakened. One possible weakening, endorsed by Olivier Roy, is the *Moderate Acceptance Thesis*:

A necessary condition for intending to ϕ is accepting that one will ϕ in every context of practical reasoning in which the intention to ϕ is relevant.

But the above example is as much a counterexample to the Moderate Acceptance Thesis as it is to the Strong Acceptance Thesis. For in the context of deciding whether to accept bet X, Michael's intention to stop at the bookstore is clearly relevant. And yet, if we deny the Strong Belief Thesis, then we should allow that Michael could intend to go to the bookstore, without accepting the proposition that he will do so in the context of deciding whether to take bet X.

We might try weakening the thesis still further, by the *Weak Acceptance Thesis*:

A necessary condition for intending to ϕ is accepting that one will ϕ in *some* contexts of practical reasoning.

Unfortunately, however, this weaker requirement does not suffice to explain the requirement of intention consistency. For if all that is involved in intending to ϕ is accepting that one will ϕ *in some context or other*, then an agent who has two contradictory intentions may accept that she will ϕ in one context of practical reasoning, and she may accept that she will not ϕ in a distinct context of practical reasoning. But when contradictory acceptances are compartmentalized in this manner, then they need not involve any irrationality. It would not be irrational, for example, if an agent took it for granted that space is Euclidean in the context of planning a trip to Kalamazoo, and if this same agent took it for granted that the space is non-Euclidean in the context of planning a trip to Mercury. Nor would it be irrational for a lawyer to take it for granted that her client is an upstanding citizen when she is defending him in court, and yet to take it for granted that he is a scroundrel when she encounters him in non-professional contexts.[16]

Thus, if the cognitivist aims to provide a cognitivist explanation of the Intention Consistency Requirement, she has little to gain from moving from the claim that intention involves belief to the claim that intention involves practical acceptance. For if the latter claim is given a weak formulation, and states only that intending to ϕ involves accepting that one will ϕ in some contexts of practical reasoning, then it will not suffice to explain the Intention Consistency Requirement. And if, on the other hand, this claim is given a stronger formulation, and states that intending to ϕ involves accepting that one will ϕ in every context of practical reasoning, or in every relevant context of practical reasoning, then this claim will be implausible apart from the Strong Belief Thesis.

What about the means–end coherence requirement? Can it be explained on the basis of a quasi-cognitivist view of intentions according to which intending to ϕ involves accepting that one will ϕ? Recall that when we were considering straightforward cognitivist views according to which intending to ϕ involved the *belief* that one will ϕ, the most promising attempts to explain the Means–End Coherence Requirement appealed to *Modus Ponens Requirement*:

> One ought rationally to be such that (if one believes that p and one believes that (if p then q) then one believes that q).

This principle, together with the Strong Belief Thesis, entails that if one believes that one will ψ, and believes that one will ψ only if one ϕs, then one is rationally required to believe that one will ϕ. Now if we move from the Strong Belief Thesis to the Strong Acceptance Thesis, then we will need to explain why anyone who intends to ψ, and hence accepts that she will do so, and believes that ϕ-ing is a necessary means to ψ-ing, is rationally required to accept that she will ϕ. And to explain this, we will need something like the principle *Hybrid Modus Ponens*:

> One ought rationally to be such that (if one accepts that p and one believes that (if p then q) then one accepts that q).

However, Hybrid Modus Ponens appears to be false. For suppose I am convinced that Einstein was right, and that space is non-Euclidean. Indeed, suppose I believe the following material condition: if space is Euclidean, then I am a monkey's uncle. Suppose, however, that in a context of practical reasoning in which I am planning a trip to Kalamazoo, I accept, or take it for granted, that space is Euclidean. This would not seem to involve any irrationality. But in this case, Hybrid Modus Ponens implies that in planning my trip to Kalamazoo, I am rationally required to accept

---

[16] For a discussion of such contextual variations in acceptance, see Michael Bratman's "Practical Reasoning and Acceptance in a Context."

that I am a monkey's uncle, or in other words, that the only way I can be fully rational, given the beliefs and acceptances just described, is to take it for granted, in this context, that I am a monkey's uncle. And this, of course, is not a very plausible implication.

Even if this problem could be solved, there is a remaining problem. For it is not plausible that accepting that one will ϕ, along with whatever non-cognitive background conditions there may be for intending to ϕ, is sufficient for intending to ϕ. Recall the example from Section 2.1 in which Barry the banker intends to protect the million dollars, and he believes that locking the money in the safe is a necessary means to protecting the money. Recall that he also believes that he will lock the money in the safe, but he believes this simply because he has read that he will do so in his putative biography he was given by Robbie the robber. In this case, Barry clearly satisfies the non-cognitive background conditions for intending to lock the money in the safe. We might further suppose that Barry is so convinced by the statements he reads in the biography that he accepts them all from the practical point of view. Thus, he takes it for granted, in practical reasoning, that he will lock the money in the safe. Even so, such acceptance will not amount to the intention to lock the money in the bank. And so while Barry is taking it for granted that he will lock the money in the safe, Robbie will be able to run off with the money.

It seems, therefore, that the quasi-cognitivist view of intentions, like the pure cognitivist view, fails to provide a satisfactory account either of the consistency requirement or of the means–end coherence requirement.

APPENDIX B: THE SELF-REFERENTIAL INTENTION THESIS

In "Practical Reasoning," Harman argues for the following two theses:

Strong Belief Thesis (**SBT**): Anyone who intends to ϕ believes that she will ϕ.

Self-Referential Intention Thesis (**SRI**): Anyone who intends ϕ intends to (ϕ because of her current intention to ϕ).

Together, these two theses entail the Strong Belief Thesis. For it follows from these two theses that anyone who intends to ϕ believes that she will (ϕ because of her current intention to ϕ). And so it follows from these theses that the intention to ϕ involves a belief that refers to this very intention. But if a belief is a component of an intention, then in referring to this intention, it will refer, at least indirectly, to itself. And so it follows from the above theses that intentions involve self-referential beliefs.

Since I discussed the Strong Belief Thesis in Section 1, here I will focus on the Self-Referential Intention Thesis. I will begin by criticizing the standard arguments in favor of this thesis, and I will then present an argument against it.

The first argument for SRI to consider, presented by Harman, can be stated as follows:[17]

A1. One cannot arrive at the intention to ϕ by way of practical reasoning if one believes that one's intention to ϕ would not result in one's ϕ-ing.

A2. The only natural way to explain A1 is to assume that every intention to ϕ is an intention to ϕ-because-of-that-very-intention.

A3. Hence we can conclude, by inference to the best explanation, that anyone who intends to ϕ intends to (ϕ because of her current intention to ϕ).

I believe that the first premise of this argument is true, but that the second is false. There is another natural way to explain A1, namely this: intending to ϕ is an attitude one has *in order to* ϕ. And there is a *negative* causal belief condition on the in-order-to relation: one cannot ψ in order to ϕ if one believes that ψ-ing would not result in one's ϕ-ing. For example, one cannot practice in order to win a contest if one believes that practicing would not result in one's winning the contest. However, there is no corresponding *positive* causal belief condition on the in-order-to relation: it is not the case that one can only ψ in order to ϕ if one believes that one's ψ-ing would result in one's ϕ-ing. For example, it is not the case that one can only practice in order to win the contest if one believes that one's practicing would result in one's winning the contest; one might, after all, be uncertain as to whether practicing would have this result. Thus, if the correct explanation of A1 is the fact that intending to ϕ is something one does in order to ϕ, then there will be a negative causal belief condition on intending to ϕ: it will be impossible to intend to ϕ while believing that one's intending to ϕ will not result in one's ϕ-ing. There need not, however, be any positive causal belief condition on intending to ϕ, and so it may be possible to intend to ϕ without believing that one's intention to ϕ will result in one's ϕ-ing. Thus, if we assume that intending to ϕ is something one does in order to ϕ, which is an assumption that Harman himself makes elsewhere, then we can give a very straightforward explanation of A1 that does not commit us to A2.

A second, and closely related, argument for SRI, presented by Kieran Setiya, can be stated as follows:[18]

B1. One cannot coherently intend to (ϕ, but not because of one's current intention to ϕ).

B2. The only natural way to explain B1 is to assume that every intention to ϕ is an intention to ϕ-because-of-that-very-intention.

B3. Hence we can conclude, by inference to the best explanation, that anyone who intends to ϕ intends to (ϕ because of her current intention to ϕ).

But again, the second premise is false, because there is an alternative explanation of B1. For B1 follows from a negative causal belief condition on intentions, discussed

---

[17] See Harman's "Desired Desires," in Ray Frey and Chris Morris (eds.), *Value, Welfare, and Morality* (Cambridge: Cambridge University Press, 1993), 138–57.

[18] See his "Cognitivism about Instrumental Reason" *Ethics* 117 (July 2007), 649–73.

above, in conjunction with the strong belief thesis. That is, B1 follows from these two premises:

NC. One cannot intend to ϕ while believing that one's current intention to ϕ will not result in one's ϕ-ing.

SB. Anyone who intends to ϕ believes that she will ϕ.

For by SB, if one intends to (ϕ, but not because of one's current intention to ϕ), then one must believe that one's current intention to ϕ will not result in one's ϕ-ing. And hence it follows, by NC, that one cannot intend to ϕ. But anyone who intends to (ϕ, but not because of one's current intention to ϕ) must intend to ϕ. Therefore, if NC and SB are true, then it is impossible to intend to (ϕ, but not because of one's current intention to ϕ). And so one can explain B1 without appealing to B2.

Of course, one might reject the above explanation of B1 on the grounds that one rejects the strong belief thesis, SB. But, as we have seen, this move is not available to the cognitivist about practical reason.

A third argument for RI, again from Harman, can be presented as follows:[19]

C1. Intending to ϕ is something that one does in order to ϕ, and that one recognizes that one does in order to ϕ.

C2. But if one intends to ϕ, and recognizes that one is ψ-ing in order to ϕ, then one intends to (ϕ because one now ψs).

C3. Therefore, if one intends to ϕ, and recognizes that one (intends to ϕ in order to ϕ), then one intends to (ϕ because one now intends to ϕ).

C4. Therefore, in intending to ϕ, one intends to (ϕ because one now intends to ϕ). That is, anyone who intends to ϕ intends to (ϕ because of her current intention to ϕ).

Once again, the second premise is false. Suppose I will be competing in a musical contest. Suppose I know that my competitors are incompetent, and so I will win the contest so long as I practice adequately. I don't know, however, what instrument I will be required to play: it may be the harpsichord, or it may be the kazoo. So I practice playing both. In this case I intend to win the contest, and I recognize that I am practicing playing the harpsichord in order to win the contest, but I do not intend to (win the contest because I am practicing playing the harpsichord). After all, I recognize that I may not play the harpsichord in the contest at all, and so my current practicing may not play any causal role in my winning the contest. Hence, it would seem that one could intend to ϕ, and recognize that one intends to ϕ in order to ϕ, without intending to (ϕ because one intends to ϕ).

A final standard argument for RI, presented by John Searle, can be stated thus:[20]

D1. The content of a propositional attitude is the proposition that is true just in case that mental state is satisfied.

---

[19] See his "Practical Reasoning," *Review of Metaphysics* 29 (1976), 431–63.
[20] See his *Intentionality: An Essay in the Philosophy of Mind* (Cambridge: Cambridge University Press, 1983).

D2. The intention to ϕ is a propositional attitude that is satisfied only if one ϕ-s because of that very intention.

D3. Therefore it must be part of the content of the intention to ϕ that one ϕ-s because of that very intention.

D4. Therefore, anyone who intends to ϕ intends to (ϕ because of her current intention to ϕ).

Once again, the second premise can plausibly be rejected.[21] Suppose that now, at noon, I intend to brush my teeth tonight before going to bed. And suppose I do brush my teeth tonight before going to bed. In such a case, we would normally say that my prospective intention to brush my teeth is satisfied. And if we learned that in the evening I brushed my teeth out of habit, and that the prospective intention I had formed at noon to brush my teeth in the evening played no causal role in bringing about my evening tooth-brushing activity, we would not normally say that my prospective intention was therefore unsatisfied. Thus, one can plausibly maintain that an intention to ϕ can be satisfied even if it is not the case that one ϕ-s because of this intention.

Now it may be that prospective intentions (intentions we have prior to the time of the intended action) refer to concurrent intentions (intentions we have at the same time as the intended action). That is, it may be that whenever we have a prior intention to ϕ, we intend that at some future time we ϕ *because we then have a concurrent intention to be ϕ-ing*. In this case, the prior intention to ϕ will refer to a concurrent intention ϕ, and will only be satisfied if one ϕ-s because of a concurrent intention to ϕ. But the former intention still needn't be self-referential, since it may be that the only intention that figures in the content of the prospective intention is the later, concurrent intention, and not the prospective intention itself.

Thus, the standard arguments for SRI do not appear to be successful. Moreover, there is strong reason to reject SRI. For it seems that if we have reason to intend to ϕ, then we have reason to perform actions that are necessary in order to guarantee that we ϕ. Therefore, if intending to ϕ involved intending to ϕ because of this very intention, then anyone who has reason to intend to ϕ has reason to act in ways that are necessary to guarantee not that his ϕ-ing result from his current intention to ϕ. But this does not seem to be the case. Suppose, for example, that it is noon, and I intend to brush my teeth at midnight. Suppose I believe that if I leave my toothbrush in its usual place, I may brush my teeth not because of my current intention. In this case, moving my toothbrush to an unusual location would be a necessary means to ensuring that I brush my teeth because of my prior intention, and not merely out of habit. And yet it would seem that I could have reason to intend to brush my teeth tonight without having reason to move my toothbrush to an unusual location. Hence, it seems that in intending, at noon, to brush my teeth tonight, I needn't intend to brush my teeth tonight because of my current intention to do so.

---

[21] Alfred Mele discusses this argument in "Are Intentions Self-referential?" *Philosophical Studies* 52 (1987), 309–29. His diagnosis is that we should reject the first premise and retain the second.

10

Archimedeanism and Why Metaethics Matters

Paul Bloomfield

It may seem that, in a forum such as this, it is only preaching to the choir to argue for the thesis that metaethics both exists as a discourse in its own right and is important too. It is not unfair to say that philosophers are more prone to reflection than most, so it would not be surprising to find metaethicists engaged in self-justification as a matter of course. We are familiar with moral philosophers asking why anyone should care about morality, and we expect morality to be able to justify itself to our satisfaction. Something similar would be expected for metaethics. Why should anyone care about metaethics? But this essay is not a defense of metaethics in the name of idle self-justification, nor is the forum necessarily filled with choir members. For metaethics is under a sort of attack, and one of the attack's ironies is that it is being staged by those we would ordinarily think of as philosophers who have contributed significantly to metaethical discourse. In particular, putting cards on the table, leading the charge against metaethics, we have a self-proclaimed pragmatist and rejecter of all ontological claims, Richard Rorty, the progenitor of quasi-realism, Simon Blackburn, and the "face value" realist who wants to base the law on morality, Ronald Dworkin. While certainly not the only ones, these three, despite what appears to be massive metaethical disagreement amongst them, seem to all agree that metaethics is not an independent discourse, with a recognizable subject matter all of its own.[1]

In addition to the people I have thanked in the notes, I'd like to thank Ben Bradley, Christian Coons, Robert Johnson, David Lambie, Don Loeb, Andrew Sepielli, Ian Smith, and an anonymous referee.

[1] The irony should not escape us that Rorty, Blackburn, and Dworkin have had many significant, and often quite heated, disagreements about the foundations of ethics, or lack thereof, in the face of their agreement about the debilitated status of metaethics. Ultimately, it gives rise to Rorty's righteous insouciance, Blackburn's reluctant queasiness, and

They would all agree with Rorty's idea that we cannot "step outside our skins",[2] and with Blackburn's thought that all questions *about* ethics are actually *within* ethics.[3] It is Dworkin, however, who has made the fulcrum of the current debate out of the idea that metaethics has no Archimedean leverage on ethics.[4] Blackburn and Dworkin both think that all metaethics is actually a part of standard normative ethics, and that one's so-called "metaethical" views are in fact not independent from the engaged, substantive ethical views which we take on matters such as abortion and slavery. Rorty at least acknowledges that academics are discussing something that is not wholly a part of normative ethics, but he thinks that this part in particular is a third spinning wheel that does nothing important whatsoever. The degree to which metaethics is distinct from normative ethics is the degree to which he thinks we should stop talking about metaethics; it is all a useless legacy of a misbegotten dialogue which Plato started long ago. We would be better off not doing it at all.[5] Metaethics is faced with two bad choices: either it does not exist or it does exist but does not matter.

Dworkin's frustrating quietism. For Rorty's insouciance, see Introduction to *Consequences of Pragmatism* (Minneapolis: University of Minnesota Press, 1982), p. xvi; for Blackburn's queasiness, see "Realism: Quasi or Queasy?" in J. Haldane and C. Wright (eds.), *Reality, Representation, and Projection* (Oxford: Oxford University Press, 1993), 365–83; for Dworkin as a quietist, see Nick Zangwill, Symposium commentator on R. Dworkin. *Brown Electronic Article Review Service*, ed. J. Dreier and D. Estlund, World Wide Web, http://www.brown.edu/Departments/Philosophy/bears/9612zang.html, Dec. 2, 1996.

   [2] Introduction to *Consequences of Pragmatism*, p. xix. Rorty continues: "But we must be careful not to phrase this analogy [language as a tool] so as to suggest that one can separate the tool, Language, from its users and inquire as to its 'adequacy' to achieve our purposes. The latter suggestion presupposes that there is some way of breaking out of language in order to compare it with something else." Later is his earliest use of "Archimedean" that I've found: "The modern Western 'culture critic' feels free to comment on anything at all … He is the person who tells you how all the ways of making things hang together hang together. But, since he does not tell you how all possible ways of making things hang together hang together—since he has no extra-historical Archimedean point of this sort—he is doomed to become outdated" (p. xl).
   [3] *Ruling Passions* (Oxford: Clarendon Press, 1998), 295.
   [4] "Objectivity and Truth: You'd Better Believe It" *Philosophy and Public Affairs* 25/2 (spring 1996), 87–139.
   [5] Rorty writes: "The pragmatist takes the moral of this discouraging history [the failure to find a successful metaphysical account of either Truth or Goodness] to be that 'true sentences work because they correspond to the way things are' is no more illuminating than 'it is right because it fulfills the Moral Law.' Both remarks … are empty metaphysical compliments—harmless as rhetorical pats on the back to the successful inquirer or agent, but troublesome if taken seriously and 'clarified' philosophically" (*Consequences of Pragmatism*, p. xvii). It is my sense, by the way, that from Rorty's point of view the final word of this quotation should have been capitalized to indicate his pejorative sense of "Philosophy".

Getting philosophical work out of a metaphor based on Archimedean leverage is not a new trick. It may have been Descartes who got things under way when he wrote in his Second Meditation:

Archimedes once demanded just one firm and immovable point, that he might move the whole earth. Great things are no less to be hoped for if I should find even one thing, however slight, that is certain and unshakeable.[6]

There are probably earlier philosophical applications of the metaphor of which I am not aware. The first contemporary use I have found of it is from a 1960 essay on language and knowledge by Isaiah Berlin; here, Berlin makes much the same use of the non-existence of an Archimedean point from which to evaluate our knowledge as Neurath had earlier made of the idea that knowledge, as a whole, is like a raft adrift.[7] It was Rawls, however, who first used the metaphor in a particularly moral way. Though not quite applying the idea in a metaethical context regarding the foundations of moral claims, in *A Theory of Justice*, Rawls does discuss the idea of an Archimedean point by which particular moral judgments may be found justified.[8] His "Original Position" was intended to be just such a standpoint. He writes that: "justice as fairness is not at the mercy, so to speak, of existing wants and interests. It sets us an Archimedean point for assessing the social system without invoking a priori considerations" (p. 261). It is written about in this vein by David Gauthier and Bernard Williams as well.[9]

Of course, it is Dworkin's "Objectivity and Truth: You'd Better Believe It" that has brought the metaphor into its current place in the form of a challenge to metaethics. Dworkin says that a theory is "Archimedean" if it

---

[6] *Meditations on First Philosophy*, trans. D. Cress (Indianapolis: Hackett Publishing, 1993), 17.

[7] Berlin writes: "Most of the certainties on which our lives are founded [...] the vast majority of the types of reasoning on which our beliefs rest, or by which we should seek to justify them [...] are not reducible to formal deductive or inductive schemata, or a combination of them [...] The web is too complex, the elements too many and not, to say the least, easily isolated and tested one by one [...] we accept the total texture, compounded as it is out of literally countless strands [...] without the possibility, even in principle, of any test for it in its totality. For the total texture is what we begin and end with. There is no Archimedean point outside it whence we can survey the whole and pronounce upon it [...] the sense of the general texture of experience [...] is itself not open to inductive or deductive reasoning: for both these methods rest upon it." Reprinted as "The Concept of Scientific History", in *Concepts and Categories*, ed. H. Hardy (New York: Viking Press, 1979), 114–15; ellipses added by J. Cherniss and H. Hardy in "Isaiah Berlin", *Stanford Encyclopedia of Philosophy*, 2007, World Wide Web at http://plato.stanford.edu/entries/berlin/.

[8] (Cambridge, MA: Harvard University Press, 1971).

[9] See, respectively, *Morals by Agreement* (Oxford: Clarendon Press, 1986), ch. 8, and *Ethics and the Limits of Philosophy* (Cambridge, MA: Harvard University Press, 1985), ch. 2.

purports to "stand outside a whole body of belief, and to judge it as a whole from premises or attitudes that owe nothing to it" (p. 88). As a result, all explicitly metaethical theories are Archimedean in this sense. Dworkin, in a way to be sketched below, argues that all Archimedeanism leads to one form or another of skepticism, regardless of what the theorists may think about the commitments of their theories. This includes metaethical theories like error theories or relativistic theories, which are not too hard for Dworkin to interpret as "skeptical" of ethics and morality. It also includes, however, many metaethical positions which are prima facie not skeptical about morality in the least, including all the various forms of moral realism, secondary quality theories of value, subjectivism and expressivism of all stripes. According to Dworkin, all Archimedean metaethics leads to moral skepticism since it all ultimately leads to the conclusion that there are no right answers in ethics or morality. Some forms of Archimedeanism, such as error theories or cultural relativism, directly imply that there are no correct answers in morality. The rest will have to accept that there are no *right* answers to moral questions when they realize their various attempts to explicate the metaphysics and epistemology of "rightness", in this context, all fail, for one reason or another. Dworkin argues "against the case" of each Archimedean metaethical position, purportedly showing each to fail. (To this degree Dworkin and Rorty agree on the use of an "argument by cases" to conclude that we should give up on metaphysics.) Metaethics is the start of a road that invariably leads to skepticism, regardless of the intentions of the theorists, and this, were it true, would be a good reason to stop the discussion.

Dworkin's argument against Archimedeanism is based on an idea of neutrality, which for him is a technical term.[10] We can begin with a standard way of putting the standard distinction between so-called "first-order" and "second-order" moral propositions (what Dworkin calls "I" and "E" propositions).[11] On the one hand, we have engaged, substantive

[10] Dworkin's also discusses "austerity" at length, which there is no room to discuss here as well. Neutrality is, however, a necessary ingredient in his argument against metaethics and if it fails, as I hope to show it does, then attending to austerity is superfluous.

[11] John Mackie expresses the Archimedean view in distinguishing between first and second order points of view: "Since it is with moral values that I am primarily concerned, the view I am adopting may be called moral scepticism. But this name is likely to be misunderstood: 'moral scepticism' might also be used as a name for either of two first order views, or perhaps for an incoherent mixture of the two. A moral sceptic might be the sort of person who says 'All this talk of morality is tripe,' who rejects morality and will take no notice of it. Such a person may be literally rejecting all moral judgements; he is likely to be making moral judgements of his own, expressing a positive moral condemnation of all that conventionally passes for morality; or he may be confusing

moral or ethical propositions, such as "Abortion is wrong" or "The life of pleasure is best," and on the other we have supposedly metaethical "further claims" or propositions about them, such as "What I said about abortion and pleasure was not just my venting my feelings." Archimedeans claim neutrality about the content of engaged moral claims since they claim to take "no sides" in engaged, substantive debates ("Objectivity and Truth", 93). Given this, Dworkin says that Archimedean neutrality is an "illusion" if two conditions apply (ibid. 97). The first is that for metaethical propositions, we can find "a plausible interpretation or translation of all of them that shows them to be positive moral judgments." The second condition obtains if we cannot demonstrate how metaethical claims are "philosophically distinct" from engaged propositions. It is "easy enough", Dworkin says, to see that the first condition obtains: "because the most natural reading of all [metaethically] further claims shows them to be nothing but clarifying or emphatic or metaphorical restatements or elaborations of [the engaged] proposition that abortion is wrong" (ibid.). Blackburn makes this same point, when he claims that affirming:

(1) Slavery is wrong.

(2) Slavery is objectively wrong.

(3) Slavery is truly, factually, really wrong.

all amount to the same thing. Rorty makes a similar point about propositions invoking "the Moral Law" (see n. 5 above). To use Blackburn's terminology, there is no semantic difference between affirming (1), (2), and (3), only a difference in "emotional temperature." Blackburn follows Ramsey, in thinking that like affirming "p", "it is a fact that p", and "it is true that 'p'" all mean the same, affirming (2), and (3) do not "mark an addition" to affirming (1): these affirmations all mean the same thing.[12] One may think one is distinguishing between a personal opinion and a claim about

---

these two logically incompatible views, and saying that he rejects all morality, while he is in fact rejecting only a particular morality that is current in the society in which he has grown up. But I am not at present concerned with the merits or faults of such a position. These are first order moral views, positive or negative; the person who adopts either of them is taking a certain practical, normative, stand. By contrast, what I am discussing is a second order view, a view about the status of moral values and the nature of moral valuing, about where and how they fit into the world. These first and second order views are not merely distinct but completely independent: one could be a second order moral sceptic without being a first order one, or again the other way round" (*Ethics: Inventing Right and Wrong* (Harmondsworth: Penguin, 1977), 16).

[12] *Ruling Passions*, 78. F. P. Ramesy, "Fact and Propositions", in *Foundations: Essays in Philosophy, Logic, Mathematics, and Economics*, ed. D. H. Mellor (London: Routledge, 1978), 40–57.

how the world actually is, while in effect all one is doing is making a further move in a normative debate by adding emphasis in the form of these "further claims". Blackburn, Dworkin, and Rorty agree that making further metaethical claims about one's engaged normative claims adds nothing to their content, though they may help a person gauge how strong one's moral commitments are. This is "metaethical minimalism".[13]

So, Dworkin thinks the first condition obtains that shows the illusory nature of Archimedean neutrality. Dworkin's argument that the second condition obtains is, as mentioned, an argument by cases. None of the going metaethical theories out there, according to Dworkin, succeeds in giving an adequate account of the metaphysics of ethics: he gives arguments that are supposed to show that realism fails, secondary quality theories fail, quasi-realism and expressivism fail, subjectivism fails, error theories fail, etc. Dworkin concludes that Archimedean neutrality is an illusion. Metaethical theorists are really taking part in engaged, substantive normative debate, whether they realize it or not. Moreover, they are all ultimately committed to moral skepticism, for reasons it is now time to explain.

Dworkin argues that some theories, like subjectivism, expressivism, and some forms of relativism, as well as error theories, are immediately skeptical about morality, since they are committed in one way or another to thinking there are no right answers to moral questions as there are to questions about, say, science. As a result, they are committed to claims such as:

(4) There is no right answer to the question of whether slavery is wicked.

Contrary to what these metaethicists may think, Dworkin argues that agreeing to (4) is agreeing to a substantial moral claim, a claim that "must be" evaluated as a claim "internal to the evaluative domain rather than archimedean about it" ("Objectivity and Truth", 89). He thinks uttering (4) implies adopting a position which condones slavery. The inference, which Dworkin never explicitly spells out, seems to be that from (4), we can derive:

(5) It is false to say that slavery is wicked.

And this seems to imply:

(6) Slavery is not wicked.

---

[13] See e.g. Simon Blackburn, Symposium commentator on R. Dworkin. *Brown Electronic Article Review Service*, ed. J. Dreier and D. Estlund, World Wide Web, http://www.brown.edu/Departments/Philosophy/bears, as well as *Ruling Passions*, 77–9 and 294–7.

As such, the theories of these metaethicists commit them to immoral views, whether they realize it or not.[14] According to Dworkin, any metaethical theorist who claims that there are no right answers to moral questions is committed by the tenets of his or her theory to particular engaged, substantive moral views, particularly skeptical moral views, whether they realize it or not. Moral realism, secondary quality theories of value, or any attempted positive account of the nature of morality, will lead to skepticism since the failure of their various theories to give a coherent metaphysical account of the truth-makers for moral claims will lead them to accept (4), and (4) again leads to (6). So, all forms of Archimedeanism lead to skepticism.

One may begin to question these arguments by wondering whether or not this anti-Archimedeanism can be argued for without itself taking an Archimedean stand on the subject matter of metaethics: doesn't it require Archimedean leverage on reality to conclude that gaining Archimedean leverage on reality is impossible? Arguing against the possibility of meta-physics is itself to adopt a metaphysical position; one need only think of Hume. Rorty acknowledges how hard it is for a pragmatist to engage in debates with traditional Archimedean philosophers without getting pulled back into their debates. Rorty says, "Stop the debate" and as soon as we ask why, the very activity of his giving a response starts philosophy up again. Even if Rorty, qua pragmatist, says "Stop, because it doesn't work", we should still expect an Archimedean explanation for why it does not work and this he cannot consistently give. Blackburn ("Realism") is acutely aware of the problems of embracing a global form of quasi-realism, since it seems to leave us with no ontically firm categorical basis for our evaluative dispositions; it is, rather troublingly, dispositions "all the way down". A quasi-realist is committed to acknowledging a fact/value distinction, but then must go on to claim that this distinction is itself evaluative and not factual. We are left without a value independent world. The further problem for Blackburn comes from his arguing for quasi-realism against, say, realists and subjectivists, since it certainly seems like he is telling us that realism and subjectivism are false, not just internally from the quasi-realistic point of view, but in Archimedean fact. In order to conclude that affirming the claims (1), (2), and (3) above all come to the same thing, one must have already concluded that there is no robust objectivity, factuality, or substantial (non-minimalisitic) truth about morality. One wants to reply

---

[14] Dworkin does not think these metaethicists themselves are immoral people who think that slavery is not wicked, but rather that they contradict themselves without knowing it. My thanks to Ronald Dworkin for discussion on this and other issues (see esp. n. 17 below).

to Blackburn by saying that when he says that all questions about ethics are actually within ethics (see n. 3 above), he is himself making a claim *about* ethics that fails to have any substantial, normatively loaded ethical implications for how we ought to live our lives.

The same problem can be extended to cover Dworkin's anti-Archimedeanism: in order to make his claims about the non-existence of an Archimedean standpoint that metaethics can occupy, he must either acknowledge that these are themselves metaethical claims, made from an Archimedean standpoint, or acknowledge that they are not really metaethical claims (the subject matter of which does not really exist anyway) but are really only a part of normatively engaged moral philosophy. If he adopts the former option, his claims are self-refuting. If he adopts the latter option, then he is taking part in a debate by denying the existence of the debate: his denial constitutes a performance error.[15] Dworkin cannot claim his anti-Archimedeanism is the truth about metaethical debate without denying his anti-Archimedean standpoint: in order to privilege the claim that there is no Archimedean standpoint over the claim that there is an Archimedean standpoint, one must adopt an Archimedean standpoint.

At this point, the rhetoric begins to spiral out of control and the dialectic becomes close to pointless. There are other ways, however, to defend metaethics. One is to look more closely at the sort of argument given above, beginning with (4). (4) is in fact an unusually constructed proposition and this is revealed by considering its negation. Normally, we do not think that the addition or removal of a negation can turn a normative proposition into a non-normative one, or vice versa.[16] One may negate (4) by placing the

[15] A similar point is made by Kenneth Ehrenberg, "Archimedean Metaethics Defended" *Metaphilosophy* 39/4–5 (2008), 508–29.

[16] See e.g. James Brown's, "Moral Theory and the Ought-Can Principle" *Mind* 86 (1977), 206–23; George Mavrodes', " 'Is' and 'Ought' " *Analysis* 25/2 (1964), 42–4; and D. G. Collingridge's, " 'Ought-Implies-Can' and Hume's Rule" *Philosophy* 52 (1977), 348–51. These philosophers assume the negation of a normative judgment is itself a normative judgment in their attempts to show a contradiction between Kant's dictum that "ought implies can" and Hume's dictum that "is does not imply ought". I take these issues up in more detail in my "Two Dogmas of Metaethics" *Philosophical Studies* 132 (2007), 439–66. In "Metaethics and Normative Commitment" *Philosophical Issues* 12 (2002), 241–63, James Dreier says the assumption is "safe" but points out that Humberstone's taxonomy does not support it. See I. L. Humberstone, "First Steps in a Philosophical Taxonomy" *Canadian Journal of Philosophy* 12 (1982), 467–78 and "A Study in Philosophical Taxonomy" *Philosophical Studies* 83 (1996), 121–69.

In Madison, Peter Vranas pointed out that there are some trivial logical moves involving disjunctions of moral with non-moral propositions, similar to moves made by Arthur Prior to bridge Hume's "is/ought gap", which show that the above claim about negation and normativity admits of counterexamples. While technically both Vranas and

negation in different spots, and the meaning of the resulting proposition may vary according to where and how the negation is used. One natural reading of (4) when negated involves a double negation, which when eliminated leaves it reading:

(7) There is a right answer to the question whether slavery is wicked.

("It is false that there is no right answer" = "There is a right answer".) One might think that since (7) seems to be consistent with thinking that slavery is wicked as well as with thinking that it is not, its "Archimedean neutrality" is preserved, and that should make us reconsider the status of (4). But there are contexts in which (7) seems to be engaged: suppose that a recalcitrant bigot maintains (4), that there is no determinate answer to the question whether slavery is wicked, because the moral considerations that tell in favor of classifying it as wicked are exactly evenly balanced with the moral considerations that militate against such a classification. In response, (7) might be uttered by someone who disagreed about the balance of considerations, thinking either that slavery is wicked or that it is not wicked, or (7) may also be uttered by someone who, perhaps due to the determinate nature of the utilitarian calculus, thinks there are no genuine moral dilemmas, there are always right answers, even if we cannot always figure out what "the right answer" is. There are undeniably engaged contexts in which (4) and (7) figure.[17]

Prior are right, most do not think that Prior has really bridged Hume's gap, nor do I take it that Vranas' counterexamples really tell against the distinction between normative and non-normative propositions indicated here. I am much indebted for discussion on this point to Peter Vranas, David Copp, Jon Tresan, Michael P. Lynch, Daniel Massey, and Jeffrey Wisdom.

[17] I thank Matthew H. Kramer for a very helpful and extended discussion of the entire debate. In particular, he made me see the engaged reading of (7). In personal communication, Ronald Dworkin reminded me of his original discussion of comparisons between Picasso and Braque, on the one hand, and Beethoven, on the other: one might say there is a right answer about who is a better artist between Picasso and Braque, but that there is no right answer about whether Picasso is a better artist than Beethoven. He noted that (7) may be the result of a belief that there are no genuine moral dilemmas, which is surely a substantial and engaged position. Of course, someone who asserted (4) and (7) might have something like this in mind. The point is that nothing substantial is entailed by (4) or (7) when the context of its utterance is a metaethical debate between, e.g., a realist and a relativist. See also the quote from Mackie in n. 11 above.
    Another way to read (4) and (7) as engaged was suggested by Gil Harman during discussion in Madison. Harman read (6) ("Slavery is not wicked") as a rejection of the presuppositions involved in the debate. This is to read (6) as entailing both (5) ("It is false to say that slavery is wicked") and what I'll call (5′) "It is false to say that slavery is not wicked". (6) would be true if there is no such thing as wickedness; this would be similar to saying that a particular person is not a witch because there are no such things as witches. On this interpretation, (4) entails (5), which is inconsistent with what I'll

The problem for Dworkin's account of neutrality is that there are ambiguities in these propositions, and the appearances do not lie: there are other non-engaged, metaethical, contexts in which (4) and (7) may be uttered where their Archimedean neutrality is preserved. As examples (to be discussed in the following paragraphs), they might also be uttered in the context of an argument between a moral realist and a cultural relativist; or in a different argumentative context, (4) can be read as entailing a contradiction while (7) can be seen as an empty tautology. There are a variety of meanings of these propositions which come through when considering different contexts in which they could be asserted.

On the natural reading of (7) mentioned above, it is consistent with both the idea that slavery is not wicked (which was (6)), and that it is wicked. On this reading of (7), it does not imply (6) or its negation, since these give determinate answers to the pertinent question, whereas (7) only asserts that such answers exist without saying anything about what they are. Whatever the truth is with regard to slavery's wickedness, one can take any substantive position with regard to it, say either (6) or its negation, and still accept (7). In this context, (7) might be agreed upon by all parties to an engaged debate over whether or not slavery is wicked. So, in a context such as this, it looks like (7) cannot be a substantive ethical claim; (7) is normatively neutral. On this reading, (7) is a metaethical claim that retains Archimedean neutrality. Such a claim is contested ground in a debate between, say, the realist and relativist (or a realist and an error theorist). The former asserts (7) and the latter denies it. In this context, however, uttering (7) is not to take a stand on whether or not slavery is wicked.

In still another context (7) can be read as a tautology.[18] If the inference from (4) to (6) is a good one, then the following would have to be good as well:

(4) There is no right answer to the question of whether slavery is wicked.

(5′) It is false to say that slavery is not wicked.

(6′) Slavery is wicked.

call (6′) "Slavery is wicked", and hence (4) rules out any moral view saying that slavery is wicked, but (4) still does not entail (6). (4) will also entail (5′), which is inconsistent with (6), and hence rules out the view saying that slavery is not wicked, while not entailing (6′). So (4) is consistent, despite ruling out both (6) and (6′). Since that is so, it follows from Harman's interpretation that (7), which is the negation of (4), is a substantive normative claim. I thank Mark Schroeder for his help in reconstructing Harman's thought.

[18] I again thank Mark Schroeder, this time for pointing out this reading of (7).

Recall that (6) was that "Slavery is not wicked". So, if there are good arguments from (4) to both (6) and (6′), then these latter together yield:

(6&) Slavery is wicked and slavery is not wicked.

And this is obviously a contradiction. But if (4) entails a contradiction, and (7) is a negation of (4), then (7) is a tautology, which again makes it substantially neutral. Someone might assert (7) in this way if they wanted to sum up a thought like the following:

> Look, at the normative level, either the abolitionist or the slave-trader is right or there's a draw between them (in which case 'the right answer' is that there is no right answer); so, no matter what there is a right answer at the normative level; or, at the metaethical level, either the realist is right or the relativist is, or error theorist or expressivist is right, but somebody has got to be right, and so too at that level, of course, there is always going to be a right answer. So, no matter what, there is always going to be a right answer (even if, again, 'the right answer' is that there is no right answer). (7) is an empty tautology and implies nothing substantially.

What we may conclude is that there is no reason to draw any specific conclusions about the meaning of (7) or how it is best interpreted or "translated", since its meaning and/or best interpretation will vary from one context of utterance to another. There is, as Dworkin suggests, a sense in which (4) is odious and implies (6), but if (4) were ever actually uttered, it need not be meant in this way; it could be, but, as we have seen, it certainly need not be. (4) may imply (6), but it certainly does not entail it. The Archimedean neutrality of both (4) and (7) may be preserved, given that they may be uttered as contested metaethical propositions which happen to focus, as an example, on the debate over the status of slavery.

What we learn is that the first condition of Dworkin's account of neutrality is far too weak to do its job. Recall, this first condition is that, for each purported metaethical proposition, we can find "a plausible interpretation or translation of all of them that shows them to be positive moral judgments" ("Objectivity and Truth", 97). Simply considering sentences in isolation and finding a way to interpret them as part of an engaged debate is not sufficient for showing a lack of neutrality. While there may be some utterances of (4) and (7) that make them fit to be interpreted as positive and engaged moral judgments, what we have seen is that there are other contexts in which such an interpretation is not plausible.

So there is reason to think that Dworkin is wrong to hold that the first condition obtains: not all metaethical claims can be "plausibly interpreted" as a part of engaged morality. And Dworkin's argument by cases in support of the second condition is not satisfying either. For example, one need not be sympathetic at all with naturalistic moral realism to think Dworkin's saddling them with so-called "morons" or "moral fields" will philosophically settle the matter; an argument like that may satisfy a jury of philosophical lay people, but not one of people trained in philosophy. As another example, James Dreier has done an excellent job in articulating a neutral form of secondary quality theory that turns on a sophisticated three-dimensional semantic model.[19] Nor will Dworkin's quietism about his own metaphysical commitments be satisfying on its own terms: after all his criticism of others, his own reticence sounds like a cop-out. In any case, showing how weak all the available *explanans* are does not suffice to show that there is no *explanandum* "out there" to be explained. (For another comment on Dworkin's second condition, see n. 20.)

In any case, there are reasons, contra Dworkin, to think that an account of Archimedean neutrality should not hang on what interpretations or translations of a person's language are possible, as much as it should hang on what a person's commitments actually are. (Dreier (n. 19) argues for this point as well.) What we really want to know is if being committed to one metaethical theory over another ipso facto commits one to some particular substantial moral position and/or vice versa. We can establish a more plausible understanding of the "neutrality" of a metaethical claim from the claims of a substantive normative debate by establishing two conditions (*a*) and (*b*). We may say that a metaethical claim X is neutral with respect to substantial debate over an engaged thesis Y, just if (*a*) one can consistently hold that X is true while also holding either the truth or the falsity of Y and (*b*) that one can consistently hold that X is false while holding either the truth or the falsity of Y.[20] So, consider (8) as X:

(8) The ontology of the actual world lacks mind-independent moral properties.

and (9) as Y:

(9) Abortion is immoral.

(*a*) obtains because one can consistently assert (8) by denying the existence of mind-independent moral properties while also thinking either (9) is true

---

[19] "Metaethics and Normative Commitment" *Philosophical Issues* 12 (2002), 241–63.

[20] It is worth noting that if this account of neutrality is both cogent and has application, then, by itself, it vitiates Dworkin's second condition for the illusory nature of Archimedean neutrality, even before his "argument by cases" can begin. This condition obtains if we cannot demonstrate how metaethical claims are "philosophically distinct" from engaged propositions. But if one can hold a metaethical position X, while adopting either the truth or falsity of engaged position Y, and vice versa as laid out above, then it is hard to see what more could be needed for being "philosophically distinct". I thank Jeffrey Wisdom for pointing this out to me.

and that abortion is immoral, or that it is not immoral, taking (9) to be false. Condition (*b*) obtains as well: one can consistently deny (8) and assert that (9) is either true or false. Whatever the truth is with regard to immorality of abortion, one can take any position in the metaethical debate over the existence of mind-independent moral properties. Therefore, the substantive ethical debate over the morality of abortion is neutral with respect to the debate over the existence of mind-independent moral properties.

To borrow a page from Rawls, we can imagine a "normative veil of ignorance" that blocks people from knowing all their engaged ethical positions. We could then go on to ask whether people behind the veil could pursue metaethical debate. For example, take George, Osama, and Friedrich and put them behind this sort of normative veil of ignorance. We can easily imagine George and Osama agreeing on the idea that moral truth (whatever it may be) comes from God and arguing with Friedrich who is both an atheist and a skeptic about morality; and this is consistent with these characters agreeing or disagreeing in any combination on engaged normative issues when not behind the veil. Indeed, we can imagine a different scenario where we have Richard, Simon, and Ronald all being fairly liberal and tolerant in their engaged moral and political views and yet, behind such a veil, they might find plenty to argue about, such as whether insouciance is really an apt attitude to take toward morality, whether it makes sense to see all facts as being at least partly constituted by our values, or whether or not law ought to take morality as its foundation.

Moreover, metaethicists need not see neutrality as a black and white issue. Of course, we should expect there to be some sort of logical relations that obtain between some moral and metaethical views. And there might even be some metaethical positions that rule out or rule in some engaged points of view. It might be possible for some to make direct inferences from their metaethical views to engaged views: if one were a moral nihilist, one might take the non-existence of morality as license to act in ways conventionally deemed "immoral". We could also, however, imagine a nihilist who is as committed to being morally good as a master chess player is to being a good chess player; it might just all be a game to a nihilist, but it might also be a game the nihilist cares about deeply.

It is important to note that metaethicists need not claim that metaethical theorizing is completely value neutral. No one wants to dispute the value-ladenness of all theoretical dispute: at bottom, all theories are chosen for their simplicity, elegance, and explanatory power, among other considerations, all of which are epistemic values. (The metaphysical realist argues that simplicity, elegance, and explanatory power are, in some robust way, truth conducive.) What metaethicists of all stripes want to insist upon, however, is that the nature of morality can be truly described: among the variety of extant metaethical positions (or perhaps one not yet conceived), one of these is correct or true, and the others are incorrect or false, in the same way that most physicists assume that one interpretation of quantum physics is true and the others are false, even if they are not in a position to say which is which. All metaethicists need to claim is that morality is a phenomenon in the world whose nature is best described by one metaethical theory over the others: for example, either expressivism or constructivism or moral realism or error theory or cultural relativism is the truth about morality. Perhaps again the truth is some position no one has thought of yet. None of this implies that metaethical theories lack normative import or are wholly value free. Metaethical theorizing must obey the same normative canons of logic and theoretical reasoning as any other sort of theorizing: at the very least, it must meet normal epistemic standards.

It is worth noting that there is value-laden normativity running through most philosophical pursuits and at some level, all discourses are entwined with each other, none seem wholly independent from all others. (This is certainly true of any sort of Quinean "web of beliefs".) In the end, there may be no sharp line to be drawn between engaged ethics and metaethics; all distinctions between discourses may be to some degree vague. Nevertheless, a vague distinction is still a distinction, just as day is distinct from night, though twilight be vague, and acorns are not oak trees, despite the lack of a sharp line distinguishing them.

Engaged ethics and metaethics share conceptual underpinnings, for example, both take the same concept, namely that of *ethics* (or perhaps *morality*) as their starting point, if we are arguing from first principles, and as their goal, if we are arguing toward first principles. But ethics is intended to be practical while metaethics is theoretical. And one might say that since we have shown the neutrality of metaethics and that its import is theoretical, have we not, thereby, shown metaethics to be unimportant? Is it not a third wheel, spinning along, affecting nothing? Spurious? Otiose?

Nicolas Sturgeon once wrote a paper called "What Difference Does it Make Whether Moral Realism is True?", arguing against what he called the "So What Thesis" which is itself a common response to the claims of moral realism.[21] We can globalize the question of his title, at least with respect to metaethics, and ask of any particular metaethical theory, what difference it makes if it is true. Why should anyone care which metaethical theory is true? Isn't it enough that we just go on being engaged, to the

---

[21] *Southern Journal of Philosophy* 24 suppl. (1986), 115–41.

best of our ability, in our practical, ethical lives? And, again, haven't we just seen how the answers to metaethical questions do not determine the outcome of engaged normative debates, like that of slavery, abortion, or capital punishment? Arguing for the neutrality of metaethics seems to be arguing it into irrelevance.

This appearance is, however, deceptive. There are, of course, ways in which theory does affect practice. Examples outside metaethics are rife. The debate over scientific realism is one. Consider an analogy of (8) and (9), where in place of (8), we have a statement of Bas van Fraassen's constructive empiricism.[22] We then get:

(10) Science takes empirical adequacy (not truth) as its goal and to accept a theory is to accept it as empirically adequate.

Imagine (11) as the statement of a position, taken from a journal in applied physics, in a recherché debate regarding the behavior of quarks. (10) would be as neutral to (11), as (8) is to (9). It is hard to imagine that the outcome of the debate about quarks would be settled by the debate between a scientific realist and a constructive empiricist, especially since both theories about science can adequately explain all the empirical data. Yet, no one accuses Bas van Fraassen of surreptitiously engaging in substantial scientific debates in the way that metaethicists are accused of being engaged. Nor does anyone think that there is nothing important at stake in this debate in the philosophy of science. To foreshadow the discussion below, consider the differences between how a constructive empiricist and a realist conceive of disagreement in science. On the constructivist's view, there is no problem in adopting two mutually inconsistent theories since inconsistent theories can both be empirically adequate; one may use whichever theory is most convenient. Realism, on the other hand, is not so permissive, since it is assumed by all that the truth, whatever it may be, cannot contradict itself. Permissiveness, in this regard, may affect the argumentative standards at play in a disagreement about quarks, and this is the sort of difference theory can make to practice: it can open up or close off areas of discussion, it can affect what counts as evidence or as a "relevant consideration" in the debate. Theory will not settle the debate, but it may constrain it. This can help us see how metaethics can be relevant to normative ethics while maintaining its Archimedean neutrality.

A defender of metaethics may begin a more direct articulation of how the truth about it matters by noting the ubiquity of normativity and

---

[22] *The Scientific Image* (Oxford: Clarendon Press, 1980). I thank Tom Bontly for very helpful discussion of the analogy to this debate in the philosophy of science.

why we think it matters. It is nowadays a commonplace to note that both epistemology and semantics have normative aspects to them.[23] One might think that understanding the phenomenon of normativity could, indeed, affect how we conceive of the practical endeavors of knowing and communicating. There are ways we ought to behave, ways we ought to think, and ways we ought to speak, and understanding what is meant by these various "ought"-s might teach us something useful about ourselves, what sort of creatures we are, what sort of world we live in. The already mentioned value-ladenness of theorizing in general secures the usefulness of understanding the nature of value and the proper bearing of it on our lives, however indirect this usefulness might be. We should be surprised to find the truths of epistemology determining which statistical analysis to use in garnering the truth from some set of data, just as we would be surprised to find the truth about universal grammar settling a particular dispute about the meaning of a slang expression. Perhaps some extreme or out-lying counterexamples to these ideas might be found in bizarre or exceptional circumstances, but no general truths follow from this about epistemology or philosophy of language, their autonomy or their importance. Metaethics is in the same boat.

Still, this is only to gesture at the way in which metaethicists may respond to the Global So What Thesis. What metaethics can teach us is how much of ethics is "up to us", to be decided by personal choice or social convention, and how much is not "up to us". Metaethics will tell us how much of ethics is detected and how much is invented, and this could affect our engaged practices in at least four different ways, which may not be more than little mentioned here. The four ways are that metaethics will (i) explain the authority morality actually has over us, as well as the nature and extent of that authority; (ii) determine what the proper moral epistemology is; (iii) affect how we manage the moral education of the young; and, finally, and perhaps most importantly, (iv) affect how we conceive of and handle engaged moral disagreement. Though settling these matters will not, by itself, be sufficient to determine the outcome of engaged debates over issues such as abortion or capital punishment, it would be invalid to conclude from this that metaethics is useless and this is the minimum required to rebut the Global So What Thesis.

There are many metaethical theories. Roughly grouping them, while leaving some hybrids out for the sake of simplicity, we might say that there are four groups: realist theories, expressivist theories, constructivist

---

[23] For a well-developed account of the close relations between moral and epistemic normativity, see Terence Cuneo, *The Normative Web* (Oxford: Oxford University Press, 2007).

theories, and error theories. Equally roughly, we may say that realists hold moral truth to be determined by mind-independent reality; expressivists think that the nature of morality is exhausted by the expression of (non-cognitive or quasi-cognitive) attitude; constructivists hold that moral facts are constructed by personal or social choice (and hence include cultural relativists); and error theorists who think that our pre-philosophical concept of *morality* implies the existence of entities that do not in fact exist. Given these four types of theories, not to mention the many, many distinctions available within each type, and the four ways mentioned above that metaethics can matter, there is no present room for discussing each of the sixteen resultant combinations. Even if it turned out that each group did not dictate a distinct answer for each of the four ways, the remainder would still require a lot to thoroughly discuss. We must settle for sketches.

What is the nature of moral constraint, or of the demands of morality, and the extent of these demands? What is the origin of moral authority? Why ought I (or we) be moral? First, perhaps, is the question of whether figuring out the nature of moral authority is relevant or irrelevant to actual engaged morality. It seems hard to resist answering "Relevant", since we typically think there is a difference between the authority of morality and the authority of prudence; we think the authority behind proper table manners is different from the authority of conscience. At the very least, there will be differences in motivation and psychology regarding moral decision making. To deny this would be like thinking that there is no difference between doing something of one's own free will and being coerced into doing it. To put these differences of authority in terms of value, we can all think of some cheap-quality snapshot that has great "sentimental value" to us, and it is obvious that sentimental value does not have the same authority over us as moral value. Even if one did answer by saying "The nature of moral authority is irrelevant to engaged morality", an apt response would be to point out that ruling out as irrelevant whole ranges of considerations from a deliberative process is certainly pragmatically relevant to that process. Undeniably, ruling out astrology and superstition from scientific consideration has had pragmatic effects on scientific practice. Realists, expressivists, constructivists, and error theorists will all answer these questions about the nature of moral authority differently. Who is right among them will therefore make a difference to engaged morality, though it is hard to see how the answer could count one way or another in a debate about what to do in a particular situation. Take, for example, the impermissibility of slavery. Each metaethical theory had better be consistent with the impermissibility of slavery, or it is not even in the running. In a case where we are not quite as confident as we are about slavery, when claiming, for example, that capital punishment is never permissible under any circumstances, it is nevertheless hard to see how taking a position in the metaethical debate entails one outcome or another at the engaged level. It is one thing to agree on what ought to be done, it is another to agree on how important or authoritative this prescription is.

Moving on, it is not hard to see how knowing which moral epistemology is true for us, knowing how we gain moral knowledge, can have an effect on our engaged moral practices. It is hard to see how to deny it. The differences between being an intuitionist, a rationalist, or an empiricist with regards to moral knowledge should be apparent, and agreeing on these matters will make an engaged argument go differently. What counts as evidence will certainly be affected. For example, intuitionism seems necessary for being any sort of non-naturalist about morality. If, say, one believed in God as the source of all morality, and that we have knowledge of what is moral and immoral, one probably would think we gain moral knowledge through intuition (or perhaps revelation plus testimony). And this lets in and rules out all sorts of different considerations. If one is rationalist, then one is likely to think that moral knowledge is a priori, and if it is, this can give us certainty, or perfect confidence in moral claims. One might think that even God could not deceive us into thinking that $2 + 2 = 5$, and the knowledge of the wrongness of torturing babies for fun could be equally certain. We would likely lack just that sort of confidence if we were naturalists who think that moral knowledge is a posteriori, but we can of course have almost certain confidence in our knowledge of, say, evolutionary theory, and our confidence in morality may be of the same ilk. Constructivists will say that the moral properties are importantly different than biological or chemical properties, and the way we gain knowledge of morality is correspondingly different than how we gain knowledge of biology or chemistry. Moral epistemology must be sensitive to such distinctions. Expressivists must shoulder the burden of explaining how we can have moral knowledge, despite the fact that it is not fully cognitive as knowledge of chemistry is. And if error theorists are right, and there is literally no such thing as moral knowledge, it will be their challenge (if they choose to accept it) to show how this result can or should make no practical difference, such that we can be error theorists and go on just as we had been going on without being unjustified in our behavior.

At this point, it should be obvious how the answers to metaethical questions might influence moral education, which is of undeniably pragmatic value. If, for example, a Stevensonian emotivism is correct, then teaching our children to think morally will require different pedagogical strategies and tactics than if, say, the Cornell realists are right and moral knowledge is empirical and a posteriori. If moral argumentation has as its point the suasion of attitude, then we should teach our children differently than if moral argumentation is no different than rational argumentation about a mathematical proof or a scientific theory. If we are error theorists and we still want our children to behave in ways that are conventionally called "moral," then we will have to consider how to train them, given the knowledge that down the road, they will learn that morality has much in common with Santa Claus and the Tooth Fairy.

But perhaps the "knock-down" argument for the import of metaethics comes from looking at moral disagreement. There are, of course, many different kinds of disagreement among humans. Indeed, we can probably disagree over just about anything. Typically, in disagreements, there are what might be called "ground rules" or "rules of engagement" in the disagreement that determine which sorts of considerations are relevant and which are irrelevant. Disagreements, when conducted fairly, proceed based on these ground rules, though it could hardly be maintained that, in general, determining the ground rules determines the outcomes of the disagreement. Different kinds of disagreements have different ground rules. So, from the engaged point of view, disagreements are handled differently in morality, etiquette, baseball, science, and math, while there is, of course, non disputandum for mere gustibus. In general, we think it matters to how a dispute is to be engaged whether, in the end, we think it will be decided by a determination of the truth or by an exercise of power. And even if the latter is the case, we may nevertheless think it apt to "speak truth to power". If it turns out that cultural relativists are right about morality, then this should affect how we handle some, if not all, cross-cultural moral disputes; at the very least, relativism weighs in favor of tolerance, though of course relativists have no exclusive rights to tolerance. If morality is conventional in its foundations, precedence and tradition will probably deserve more weight in deliberation than if morality is founded upon rationality. If non-naturalistic realism carries the metaethical day, then the value of empirical data or arguments that are a posteriori in character will have a different significance in moral disagreement than if naturalistic realism turns out to be true. As noted above, if Stevensonian emotivism is correct, then moral disagreements, when not based on fact, will be settled by non-cognitive forms of suasion. If an error theory turns out to be the truth, such that no moral claims can reasonably be thought of as "literally true", then this should, at some level, affect how we argue, if our argument is currently predicated on the idea that we are, indeed, arguing over what is true. When considering how we ought to handle engaged moral disagreement, determining what the true ontology is for morality, whatever it may be, may make a clear practical difference: not everything is equally worth dying or killing for.

One might think that, by responding to the Global So What Thesis, have we then fallen back toward the idea that there is no such thing as

Archimedean neutrality?[24] Any answer that might be given might seem to play right into the hands of Rorty, Blackburn, and Dworkin. This appearance, however, can be easily dispelled by noting that it is wrong to let one party to a dispute settle the rules by which the dispute is to be settled. It would be question-begging in all sorts of ways to let, for example, a deontologist or a consequentialist be the arbiter of the "ground rules" for a dispute between them. This would be like letting one team in a competition determine what the rules of the game are. Archimedean neutrality is required of metaethics, at the very least, because it is the metaethicists who are charged with determining the ground rules of engaged morality or the rules of the moral game. Anything less than neutrality at the metaethical level may very well have question-begging and unfair consequences at the engaged level. Just as we should fix the laws of the land and the procedures for how cases are to be tried prior to trying the first case, so too is there a priority for figuring out what we think about metaethics before we try to answer engaged questions about how one ought to live.

Metaethics matters because the truth about it should affect, should constrain the form of engaged ethics and morality. It may have a direct effect on the content or substance of morality, in the way that it is possible for syntax to have an effect on what counts as semantically meaningful. And just as one may nevertheless find syntax to be independent of semantics, and vice versa, one may also find metaethics to be independent of engaged ethics. This analogy may not be perfect. Neither, however, is the metaphor of metaethics as Archimedean. Metaethics does not give us enough leverage on engaged moral debate to settle its outcomes. Still, answering metaethical questions can help determine the way engaged ethical debates are pursued, and this may in turn, indirectly, help settle them, if only by setting argumentative constraints, ruling-out and/or ruling-in types of consideration, and determining what counts as evidence. Therefore, metaethics is substantially independent of engaged ethics, and yet it matters nonetheless.

---

[24] I thank both Daniel Massey and Douglas Edwards for independently bringing this worry to my attention.

11

Constitutivism and the Inescapability of Agency

Luca Ferrero

1. INTRODUCTION

1.1. The norms of rationality and morality have special authority; they are *categorically* binding. They bind agents regardless of their contingent motives, preferences, and intentions. By contrast, the norms of particular games, institutions, and practices are only *conditionally* binding. They have normative force only for agents who have a good enough reason to participate in them. A statement that one ought to move the knight along the diagonals, for instance, expresses an ought-according-to-the-norms-of-chess. But the oughts of rationality and morality are not qualified with the clause '-according-to-the-norms-of-rationality/morality'; they rather tell us, as Stephen Darwall writes, 'what we ought to do *simpliciter, sans phrase*.'[1]

How can we account for the categorical force of the norms of rationality and morality? Some philosophers have argued that the grounds of these

An earlier version of this chapter was presented at the Metaethics Workshop at the University of Wisconsin at Madison in 2007. I am grateful to the audience for their comments and criticisms, especially to David Copp, Connie Rosati, Mark Schroeder, Jacob Ross, and Peter Vranas. Many thanks to Russ Shafer-Landau for the wonderful job he did in organizing the workshop and editing this volume. My interest in constitutivism was first sparked by an invitation to comment on Peter Railton's work at a symposium in his honor at the University of Rome. I thank Tito Magri, Peter Railton, and Barry Stroud for the comments and encouragements I received on that occasion. I thank Jennifer Morton and Assaf Sharon for illuminating conversations at the early stages of this project. I am very grateful for the extensive written comments I have received from David Enoch, Elijah Millgram, and two anonymous reviewers.

[1] Darwall (1992: 156).

unconditional oughts are to be found in the nature of agency.[2] In a rough outline, their basic claim is that the norms and requirements of practical rationality and morality can be derived from the constitutive features of agency. Hence, a systematic failure to be guided by these requirements amounts to a loss of agency. But there is a sense in which we *cannot but be* agents. It follows that we are necessarily bound by the oughts of rationality and morality, we are bound by them *sans phrase*.

1.2. The success of this argumentative strategy—which goes under the name of 'constitutivism'—depends on establishing the following two claims. First, that the norms of rationality and morality can be derived from the constitutive features of agency. Second, that we cannot but be agents, that agency is non-optional.[3]

Constitutivism has been criticized on both counts. Some have argued that the constitutive features of agency offer too thin a basis for the derivation of substantive normative principles and requirements.[4] Others have objected that agency does not have any special status vis-à-vis ordinary games and practices; that our participation in agency is *optional* in the same sense as our participation in ordinary games and practices.

1.3. In this chapter, I will offer a partial defense of constitutivism. I will show that there is something special about agency that makes engagement in it significantly different from the participation in other ordinary enterprises (by which I mean games, practices, institutions, and the like). I will argue that agency is 'inescapable' in a way that could help explain its role in grounding unconditional oughts. My defense of constitutivism, however, is limited in scope since space restrictions prevent me from discussing the prospects of deriving substantive norms from the nature of agency.[5]

---

[2] Constitutivist views are defended by Korsgaard (1996; 1997; 1999; 2002), Railton (1997), Millgram (1997: ch. 8), Schapiro (1999), Velleman (2000; 2004; forthcoming), and Rosati (2003).

[3] A further problem with constitutivism concerns how it handles errors and imperfections in attempts at complying with the constitutive standards of agency. The worry is that constitutivism might implausibly imply that agents can only exist as perfect agent, which in turn would preclude the possibility of any genuine criticism for failures to abide by the standards of agency; see Cohen (1996: 177), Railton (1997: 309), Lavin (2004), Kolodny (2005), FitzPatrick (2005), and Coleman (unpublished).

[4] See Setiya (2003; 2007). Railton (1997: 299) hints at a similar worry in the attempt at deriving epistemic norms from the constitutive features of belief. A related concern (raised in conversation by Jacob Ross and Mark Schroeder) is that the constitutive features of agency might be necessary but insufficient for the derivation of specific normative principles.

[5] The aspiration of grounding unconditional oughts and deriving substantive normative principles are arguably the most ambitious aspirations of constitutivism but by no means the only ones; see Velleman (2004: 288–9).

2. THE SHMAGENCY OBJECTION

2.1. The constitutive standards of an ordinary enterprise *E* determine what the agent is to do in order to engage in it. If a subject systematically fails to abide by the standards of chess, say, she is not a chess player. The rules of chess are binding on anyone who intends to play that game. But their normative force is *optional.* An agent is not *actually* bound by them unless she has a good enough reason to play chess in the first place. Moreover, whether one has a reason to play chess is not something that can be derived from the constitutive standards of chess alone.

If agency were like an ordinary enterprise, the same would be true of its constitutive standards. First, the standards of agency and what could be derived from them would be binding only on those subjects who have a good enough reason to be agents, to engage in the 'enterprise of agency,' as I will sometimes say. Second, whether one has reason to be an agent could not be derived from the constitutive standards of agency alone.

2.2. David Enoch has recently argued that agency is indeed optional like any ordinary enterprise, and that constitutivism is therefore untenable.[6] It is impossible to ground unconditional obligations in the constitutive standards of an enterprise that is only binding if one has an independently given reason to engage in it.[7] The normative force of the reason to be an agent, assuming that there is indeed such a reason, would elude the constitutivist account of normativity.

Enoch's argument is based on what might be called the 'shmagency objection.' He asks us to imagine a subject—a 'shmagent'—who is indifferent to the prospect of being an agent. The shmagent is unmoved by the constitutive standards of agency. For instance, in response to Korsgaard's version of constitutivism—according to which agency is the capacity for self-constitution—the shmagent says:

Classify my bodily movements and indeed me as you like. Perhaps I cannot be classified as an agent without aiming at constituting myself. But why should I be an agent? Perhaps I can't act without aiming at self-constitution, but why should I act? If your reasoning works, this just shows that I don't care about agency and action. I am perfectly happy being a shmagent—a nonagent who is very similar to agents but who lacks the aim (constitutive of agency, but not shmagency) of

---

[6] Enoch (2006). See also Sharon (unpublished).
[7] Millgram (2005) is the first one to have pointed out that constitutivism might be the target of a criticism of this kind, although he does not go as far as Enoch in objecting to the ultimate viability of constitutivism.

self-constitution. I am perfectly happy performing shmactions—nonaction events that are very similar to actions but that lack the aim (constitutive of actions, but not shmactions) of self-constitution.[8]

2.3. A shmagent is unmoved by the constitutive standards of agency in the same sense in which someone who is indifferent to the game of chess, let's call him a chess-shmayer, is unmoved by the standards of chess. A chess-shmayer could successfully challenge the force of the constitutive standards of chess by saying, 'I don't care about chess. I am perfectly happy being a chess-shmayer—a nonplayer who is very similar to chess-players but who lacks the aim of chess playing (say, making legal chess moves with the ultimate goal of checkmating my opponent). I am perfectly happy performing chess-shmoves—non-chess moves that are very similar to chess-moves but that lack the aim of chess playing.'

The challenge of the chess-shmayer is *external* to the game of chess. Attempts at convincing the chess-shmayer to care about chess cannot be made *within* the game of chess since he is neither moved nor bound by its rules.[9] Likewise, a chess-player who is worried that her playing might not be justified has to get outside of the game in order to find out if it is. In the meantime, she might still continue to play chess, but figuring out whether she has reason to do so is not part of the game of chess.

Enoch's suggestion that there might be shmagents is supposed to show that the standards of agency can only be binding for those subjects who have an independently established reason to be agents, whether or not they are already participating in the agency-enterprise. This reason, if it exists, must in principle be accessible to shmagents and effective in moving them; that is, it must be both available and binding outside of the enterprise of agency.

2.4. The shmagency objection is targeted at all versions of constitutivism. Whatever standards are held to be constitutive of agency, one could always imagine a shmagent who is indifferent to those standards.[10] Hence, whether the objection succeeds or fails is something to be determined in abstraction from particular versions of constitutivism and their specific suggestions about the constitutive features of agency.[11] In this chapter, I will argue for the

---

[8] Enoch (2006: 179).

[9] This is not to say that the constitutive standards of the game are *irrelevant* to its justification. The standards matter, for instance, for the individuation of the object of the justification. The point that I am making in the text is only that the process of justifying the playing of the game is not part of the playing itself, it is not a series of moves internal to the game.

[10] Enoch (2006: 170 n. 1).

[11] Constitutivism is sometimes presented as being about the constitutive standards of action rather than agency. As far as the discussion of the grounds of categorical

viability of the constitutivist strategy on the face of the shmagency objection, but I will not try to defend any particular version of constitutivism. My argument appeals only to those general features of agency that are accepted by all constitutivist theories. The discussion requires nothing more than an agreement on a very general characterization of the concept of full-fledged intentional agency, on agency as the capacity to shape one's conduct in response to one's appreciation of reasons for action and to engage in the practice of giving and asking for these reasons (both about one's own conduct and that of others).

2.5. The shmagency objection is even more general in scope than it might appear at first. The objection can be extended to undermine all forms of constitutivism, even those that are not centered on agency. If Enoch is right that agency is optional, the same appears to hold of shmagency as well. The question whether there is reason to be an agent rather than a shmagent is thus to be adjudicated outside of both agency and shmagency. This adjudication is a move in a distinct enterprise, one that provides a standpoint external to both agency and shmagency. Let's call it 'uberagency.'

Could constitutivism be relocated at the level of uberagency, of the more comprehensive enterprise that includes both agency and shmagency as optional sub-enterprises? The problem is that an Enoch-style objection could still be moved to this kind of constitutivism. Couldn't we always imagine the existence of shm-uberagents, subjects who are indifferent to the constitutive standards of uberagency? That is, subjects who would be bound by the standards of uberagency only if they had an independently established reason to be uberagents? The same move used to show that agency is optional can thus be used to show that uberagency is optional. Moving at an even higher level would not help because the move could be repeated ad infinitum. The possibility of this regress shows that, *pace*

normativity is concerned, however, constitutivism is better formulated in terms of *agency* as the capacity to engage in intentional action. This is because the argument revolves around the comparison between the exercise of this capacity and the participation in ordinary enterprises. I think that versions of constitutivism originally cast in terms of action can be reformulated easily, for present purposes, in terms of agency. This is not to deny that the agency/action distinction might be relevant—as argued by Setiya (2003), for instance—for the derivation of substantive norms and requirements. Particular versions of constitutivism might also be differentiated on the basis of the *kinds* of features that they hold to be constitutive of agency/action (which could be aims, motives, capacities, commitments, or principles) and on whether these features operate at the personal or subpersonal level. (For instance, Velleman puts the emphasis on aims—which up to Velleman (2004) he presented as operating at the subpersonal level; Korsgaard and Railton present constitutivism in terms of personal-level compliance with principles; Rosati talks in terms of (sub-personal?) constitutive motives and capacities of agency.) None of these differences is relevant, however, for the main topic of this paper, the discussion of the viability of the general constitutivist strategy.

constitutivism, appeal to the constitutive standards of *any* enterprise (be it agency, uberagency, or what have you) could never account for any *categorical* ought.

3. THE INESCAPABILITY OF AGENCY

3.1. The initial appeal of the shmagency objection rests on the impression that there is a close analogy between agency and ordinary enterprises. If one can stand outside of chess and question whether there is any reason to play this game, why couldn't one stand outside of agency and wonder whether there is any reason to play the agency game? The problem with this suggestion is that the analogy does not hold. Agency is a very special enterprise. Agency is distinctively 'inescapable.' This is what sets agency apart from all other enterprises and explains why constitutivism is focused on it rather than on any other enterprise.

3.2. Agency is special in two respects. First, agency is the enterprise with the largest jurisdiction.[12] All ordinary enterprises fall under it. To engage in any ordinary enterprise is *ipso facto* to engage in the enterprise of agency. In addition, there are instances of behavior that fall under no other enterprise but agency. First, intentional transitions in and out of particular enterprises might not count as moves within those enterprises, but they are still instances of intentional agency, of bare intentional agency, so to say. Second, agency is the locus where we adjudicate the merits and demerits of participating in any ordinary enterprise. Reasoning whether to participate in a particular enterprise is often conducted outside of that enterprise, even while one is otherwise engaged in it. Practical reflection is a manifestation of full-fledged intentional agency but it does not necessarily belong to any other specific enterprise. Once again, it might be an instance of bare intentional agency. In the limiting case, agency is the only enterprise that would still keep a subject busy if she were to attempt a 'radical re-evaluation' of all of her engagements and at least temporarily suspend her participation in all ordinary enterprises.[13]

3.3. The second feature that makes agency stand apart from ordinary enterprises is agency's *closure*. Agency is closed under the operation of reflective rational assessment. As the case of radical re-evaluations shows, ordinary enterprises are never fully closed under reflection. There is always the possibility of reflecting on their justification while standing outside of

---

[12] For the idea of the jurisdiction of an enterprise, see Shafer-Landau (2003: 201).
[13] On radical re-evaluation, see Taylor (1985: 40 ff.).

them. Not so for rational agency. The constitutive features of agency (no matter whether they are conceived as aims, motives, capacities, commitments, etc.) continue to operate even when the agent is assessing whether she is justified in her engagement in agency. One cannot put agency on hold while trying to determine whether agency is justified because this kind of practical reasoning is the exclusive job of intentional agency. This does not mean that agency falls outside the reach of reflection. But even reflection about agency is a manifestation of agency.[14]

Agency is not necessarily self-reflective but all instances of reflective assessment, including those directed at agency itself, fall under its jurisdiction; they are conducted in deference to the constitutive standards of agency. This kind of closure is unique to agency. What is at work in reflection is the distinctive operation of intentional agency in its discursive mode. What is at work is not simply the subject's capacity to shape her conduct in response to reasons for action but also her capacity both to ask for these reasons and to give them. Hence, agency's closure under reflective rational assessment is closure under agency's own distinctive operation: Agency is closed under itself.[15]

3.4. To sum up, agency is special because of two distinctive features. First, agency is not the only game in town, but it is the biggest possible one. In addition to instances of bare intentional agency, any engagement in an ordinary enterprise is *ipso facto* an engagement in the enterprise of agency. Second, agency is closed under rational reflection. It is closed under the self-directed application of its distinctive discursive operation, the asking for and the giving of reasons for action. The combination of these features is what makes agency *inescapable*. This is the kind of nonoptionality that supports the viability of constitutivism.

3.5. The inescapability of agency does not mean that there can be no entities that are utterly indifferent to it. It goes without saying that agency is *ontologically* optional. It is so even for us *as* biological organisms. Human animals are not necessarily rational agents. But this is not the kind of optionality that is at stake in the debate on the grounds of normativity.

---

[14] The clearest statements of what I call the 'closure' of agency under reflective rational assessment are found in Velleman (2000: 30–1; 142) and Velleman (2004: 290 ff.); see also Railton (1997: 317) and Rosati (2003: 522). For a similar closure in the theoretical domain, see Rysiew's (2002: 451) discussion of Thomas Reid's suggestion that the first principles of cognition are constitutive principles that operate as the fixed point of cognition.

[15] Notice that closure under reflection is not to be confused with *stability* under reflection. The closure is not even a guarantee of this stability. As I discuss in Section 7 below, there might be no guarantee that agency is able to validate itself.

In addition, the inescapability of agency does not imply the impossibility of dropping out of agency. First, there are brute and involuntary ways of both exiting from and entering into agency: one might nondeliberately fall asleep and wake up, lose and regain consciousness, die and (possibly) resurrect. Second, it is in principle always possible to opt out of agency in a deliberate and intentional manner; to act so as to bring about one's temporary or permanent exit from agency. An agent may commit suicide or, less dramatically, take the steps necessary to fall asleep, lose consciousness, or induce her temporary irrationality. But the subject who raises the question whether to commit suicide or interrupt her agency is not a shmagent. While she ponders whether to commit suicide, she is still living up to the standards of rational agency. For she is trying to figure out whether there is a good enough reason to leave agency. And if she decides to do so, she is still committed—as a rational agent—to sustaining her participation in agency as long as required to implement her intention to drop out of it (such as taking the necessary means to secure her successful suicide).[16] The deliberate loss of rational agency—whether temporary or permanent—is supposed to be achieved as the culmination of an exercise of rational agency.[17] The agent who contemplates the possibility of opting out of agency is not challenging the binding force of agency's standards. She is rather wondering whether there is *reason to continue* sustaining her participation in that enterprise in light of her particular circumstances. She is not professing an utter indifference to agency as such. She defers to and abides by the standards of agency in determining the fate of her future participation in it.[18] In sum, agency can be inescapable in the sense required by constitutivism even if individual agents might deliberately opt out of it if they are offered a compelling reason to do so.

3.6. The inescapability of agency shows that the analogy between ordinary enterprises and agency on which the shmagency objection rests cannot be sustained. The idea of a 'shmagent' is introduced by Enoch to show

[16] See Velleman (2004: 291). Notice that a permanent exit from intentional agency might not coincide with biological death. The subject might go into a permanent coma, revert to a lesser kind of agent (a 'wanton,' say), or turn into a 'weather-watcher' (see Strawson 1994). These entities are shmagents in the sense that they are indifferent to the constitutive standards of agency but, as I argue in the paper, they are not sources of troubles for constitutivism on account of their utter indifference to the standards of agency (which is not to say that some agents might find existence in the non-agential mode attractive and deliberately try to bring about their metamorphosis into a wanton or a weather-watcher).

[17] See Velleman (2004) and Railton (1997/2003: 313–17).

[18] This is not to be confused with the sort of unacceptable conditional commitment to one's agential unity that characterizes some *defective* forms of agency, as discussed by Korsgaard (1999: 22–3).

that there might be subjects who are indifferent to agency and would therefore need a reason available *outside* of agency to be convinced to take part in it. The inescapability of agency, however, shows that there is no standpoint external to agency that the shmagent could occupy and from which he could launch his challenge. If the shmagent is supposed to be an actual interlocutor in a rational argumentation, his professions of utter indifference to the standards of agency are self-undermining. Professing one's indifference, challenging the force of the constitutive standards of agency, and engaging in a rational argumentation are all instances of intentional agency. The subject who genuinely participates in this sort of philosophical exchange is not truly indifferent to the standards of the practice of giving and asking for reasons. However, if he is already inside that enterprise, he cannot be pictured as asking to be offered a reason to opt into it. He might ask about reasons to continue staying inside but this would make the shmagent indistinguishable from a genuine agent, although one that might be contemplating the possibility of committing suicide.

Finally, the ontological optionality of agency allows for the existence of genuine shmagents in the sense of beings who are truly and completely indifferent to the standards of agency. But these are not the kinds of beings that can raise philosophical challenges to constitutivism. We might even imagine running into a genuinely indifferent shmagent that makes sounds indistinguishable from the alleged professions of indifference like the one previously quoted ('Classify my bodily movements and indeed me as you like,' see Section 2.2). But this encounter would be only a bizarre coincidence of no philosophical significance. It would pose no more of a threat to constitutivism than a parrot that has been taught to recite a 'shmagency mantra.'

3.7. It is only under extraordinary circumstances that entities that are truly indifferent to the constitutive standards of agency might appear to be engaged in anything that resembles genuine intentional agency for sufficiently long stretches of time. Hence, there is something puzzling about one feature of Enoch's description of the shmagent. He presents the shmagent as 'being perfectly happy performing shmactions—nonaction events that are *very similar to actions* but that lack the aim (constitutive of actions, but not of shmactions) of self-constitution.'[19] Why does it matter that shmactions are supposed to be *very similar* to actions? Given the shmagent's utter indifference to agency, there is no basis to expect a systematic non-accidental similarity between the conduct of agents and that of shmagents. There is no reason to believe that the lives of shmagents

---

[19] Enoch (2006: 179, my emphasis).

could be very much like those of agents *but for* the shmagents' indifference
to the constitutive standards of agency.[20] Insisting on the similarity might
make it easier to persuade us to think that the jurisdiction of agency
is not as encompassing as it might initially appear, and that we should
regard the shmagent as able to raise actual philosophical challenges. But the
expectation of this similarity is unwarranted.[21]

4. ALIENATED PARTICIPATION

4.1. Can the shmagency objection be reformulated so as to circumvent
the inescapability of agency? Enoch suggests that, if agency is indeed
inescapable, the shmagent should be conceived not as standing outside of
agency but as an *alienated participant*. This alienated shmagent is introduced
as someone who claims: 'I cannot opt out of the game of agency, but I can
certainly play it half-heartedly, indeed under protest, without accepting the
aims purportedly constitutive of it as mine.'[22]

What kind of objection to constitutivism is raised by alienated participation? Presumably, an alienated participant still needs to be given a
good enough reason to be an agent, although not in order to participate
(given that she is already in) but rather to overcome her alienation, to
wholeheartedly embrace agency and internalize its constitutive standards.
And this reason cannot be produced simply as a result of her inescapable
although alienated participation.

4.2. The initial appeal of this response to the inescapability of agency
comes, once again, from drawing an analogy between agency and ordinary
enterprises. Alienated participation seems to be unproblematic in the case
of ordinary enterprises. For instance, one might play chess half-heartedly,
without internalizing its aim. This alienated chess-player would simply go

---

[20] The suggestion that the lives of shmagents might be just like those of agents but
for the shmagents' indifference to the standards of agency is similar to the explanation
of the working of a radio offered in the following philosophical joke (which I first heard
in Warren Goldfarb's lectures on Wittgenstein at Harvard University): 'X asks Y: How
does a telegraph work? Y: Think of it this way. There's a large, long dog with his head
in Boston and his tail in Springfield. When you pat him on the head in Boston, he wags
his tail in Springfield; and when you tweak his tail in Springfield, he barks in Boston. X:
OK. But tell me: How does a radio work? Y: Just the same, but without the dog.'

[21] The similarity would matter if the shmagency objection were interpreted as making
a much weaker point against constitutivism; if it were interpreted as raising issues with
the specific conception of agency adopted by particular constitutivist theories rather than
with the constitutivist strategy in general, as I discuss more extensively in Section 6
below.

[22] Enoch (2006: 188).

through the motions of chess; she would just *pretend* to be playing chess. She moves the chess pieces in ways that externally match the legal moves of chess. Perhaps, she even moves them in ways that externally match the strategically deft moves of someone who genuinely intends to win the game. Because of her alienation, however, she is not truly playing chess. She is not making an earnest attempt either at winning or even at making legal chess moves. If she is presented with the opportunity to terminate her alienated participation or to make an illegal move, she is ready to take immediate advantage of this opportunity if it helps her to advance whatever ulterior goal motivates her pretense. This is because the constitutive aim of her alienated playing is not the same as the constitutive aim of chess; it is only parasitic on it.

Under special circumstances, a simulation or a pretense might be 'inescapable' in the sense that the agent might be forced to sustain it until the game is over (say, she might be forced to 'play' it at gunpoint). When such circumstances obtain, all the moves that the agent makes as part of her sham playing might *look* exactly like those of a genuine chess player, given that she might find that it is better for her to continue her sham playing through the end of the game. The apparent completion of the game, however, does not make her into a genuine player, since she continues to be moved by a different constitutive aim.

4.3. Alienated participation in ordinary enterprises is a genuine possibility but not one that can be used to show that there is a problem with constitutivism. Alienated participation in ordinary enterprises is not a good model for the alleged alienated participation in agency. In the absence of a plausible analogy with ordinary alienated participation, however, I do not know what to make of the suggestion that there could be an alienated participation in inescapable agency. To begin with, as we have just seen, pretending to participate in an enterprise is not a genuine instance of participation in that enterprise, not even when one is forced to sustain the pretense until the simulated enterprise is over. This means that no ordinary enterprise is strictly speaking inescapable. One is *not* playing chess when one is just pretending to.

In addition, the ways in which an ordinary enterprise might be said to be inescapable have nothing to do with the inescapability of agency. Agency is not inescapable in the sense of being coerced or forced to participate in it, which are the ways in which ordinary enterprises can be said to be inescapable. Agency is inescapable in the sense that it has the biggest jurisdiction and it is closed under its distinctive operation.

4.4. Ordinary examples of alienated participation, such as pretending, playacting, and simulating, are still instances of intentional agency, no less than the genuine participation in the simulated enterprise. This is another manifestation of the inescapability of agency. This means that any kind of alienated participation in agency, if modeled on this kind of pretending, would have to count as an instance of genuine participation in agency. 'Pretending to be an agent' or 'going through the motions of agency,' if they are to be understood on the only plausible model of alienated participation that we have, are ultimately instances of non-alienated intentional agency. One can playact or simulate any particular action and activity, including particular instances of playacting and of simulation, but playacting and simulating are still instances of genuine intentional acting. What about pretending to be an agent *tout court*? If this is something that is done *outside* of agency, it offers no example of alienated *participation*, which is what Enoch is after. Instead, if the pretense is carried out within agency, it cannot be an instance of genuine alienated participation.[23] One cannot pretend to be an agent as such without genuinely being an agent at least as far as one's intentional pretense is concerned.[24]

4.5. Are there other possible interpretations of alienated participation? I could think of two, but neither helps Enoch's case against constitutivism. First, one might think of inescapability in terms of some kind of psychological compulsion. This suggestion does not work, however, because the very possibility of being dissociated from the springs of one's conduct, which is the kind of alienation that accompanies this kind of compulsive behavior, is incompatible with the identification required by the very notion of full-blooded intentional agency.[25]

---

[23] In a footnote, Enoch (2006: 190 n. 47) appears to concede this point but he mentions it almost in passing, which suggests that he does not think of it as especially damaging to this overall position.

[24] It is only in the context of the *development* of agency that a being that is not yet a full-fledged agent might genuinely pretend being such an agent. This is what might happen, for instance, in certain forms of child play (see Schapiro 1999). This possibility, however, does not offer any support for the shmagency objection. There is nothing in Enoch's presentation of shmagents that suggests that they are like children, that they perform less than full-fledged intentional actions as part of a process of maturation into adult rational agents. (This is not to deny that constitutivism faces some intriguing philosophical questions about the nature of developmental transitions into full-fledged agency, given that we come to adulthood not via abrupt and brute transitions but as a result of an extended and gradual process that includes browbeating, manipulative inducement, and simpler forms of rational argumentation.)

[25] This is the point missed by Marmor (2001: 38–9) in his presentation of the idea of estranged and alienated participation, which is one of the sources of Enoch's discussion of the alienated shmagent. The fact that one might think of oneself as alienated from the springs of action does not prove that one can be estranged from one's intentional agency. The argument rather runs in the opposite direction. Those aspects of one's psychology from which one could be alienated or dissociated are, because of the very possibility

Second, couldn't we think of alienated participation as a sort of reluctance to abide by the constitutive standards of agency? There is no denying that being an agent can be hard work. It is not unusual to balk at the prospect that we are expected to satisfy all the demands of rational agency. There might be times when we wish that the job of agency were easier, and we might therefore meet its demands with some 'reluctance.' Those agents who are especially sensitive to temptation, more prone to akrasia, or lacking in resolve might exhibit considerable recalcitrance in meeting the standards of agency and not be as wholehearted at it as an Aristotelian *phronemos*. But these familiar psychological phenomena do not raise any objection to constitutivism. The existence of imperfect and defective agents, and the half-heartedness that might be experienced by enkratic ones are not evidence that participation in agency is normatively optional. They are only evidence that this participation might be psychologically arduous.

5. SHMAGENCY AND SKEPTICISM

5.1. In the previous sections, I have argued that the shmagency objection fails because it rests on untenable analogies between agency and ordinary enterprises. Both the original version of the objection and its restatement in terms of alienated participation fail to acknowledge properly the distinctive inescapability of agency. The failure of the shmagency objection, however, offers only indirect support for constitutivism. It does not eliminate the possibility of other challenges and objections.

5.2. One worry is that the strategy used to reject the shmagency objection exposes a troubling inherent weakness of constitutivism. Constitutivism responds to the shmagency objection by denying the possibility of shmagents as rational interlocutors who could launch a genuine philosophical challenge. Entities that are utterly indifferent to agency do exist but they pose no threat to constitutivism since they raise no rational challenges or objections. This means that constitutivism succeeds at *defusing* the shmagency objection by showing that there can be no shmagents. As a result, however, constitutivism is unable to *defeat* the shmagent by refutation.

According to Enoch, this shows a serious limitation of constitutivism. The problem arises because of the anti-skeptical aspirations expressed by some constitutivists. If constitutivism is expected to offer a refutation of skepticism about normativity, the appeal to the inescapability of agency

of alienation, inadequate to account for intentional agency (see Velleman 2000: chs. 1 and 6).

might backfire. Constitutivism could only show that the skeptic is impossible but could not prove that he is wrong.[26]

5.3. This problem does not arise if we are dealing with the shmagent rather than with the skeptic. The shmagent is not necessarily skeptical about the categorical force of the norms of practical rationality and morality. The shmagent only rejects the suggestion that the ultimate grounds of normativity lie in the constitutive standards of agency. The shmagent does not necessarily deny that those grounds could be found elsewhere. He might even accept the suggestion that the constitutive standards of agency play a crucial role in the derivation of the norms of practical rationality and morality. Even so, he would claim that their categorical force ultimately depends on the existence of a conclusive reason for us to be agents; a reason which cannot be provided, however, by the constitutive standards of agency.

Although the shmagent does not have to be a skeptic about normativity, a skeptic might try to argue for his position by taking the shmagency route. This skeptic-as-shmagent would grant the relevance of the standards of agency for the derivation of substantive norms but argue that the possibility of shmagents shows that there is no categorical reason to be agents.

5.4. Against this kind of skepticism, constitutivism could effectively use the strategy already deployed against the shmagent. If there can be no space for the shmagent as a rational interlocutor, *a fortiori* there can be no space for the skeptic-as-shmagent. This kind of skepticism is defused by being disarmed rather than defeated by being refuted.

This conclusion is troublesome for those who insist that constitutivism provide a refutation of all versions of skepticism. But it is hardly evidence of some serious difficulty with constitutivism as a general argumentative strategy. The issue is only whether constitutivism should be embraced by those philosophers whose primary aspiration is the refutation of the skeptic in all of his possible guises, including the skeptic-as-shmagent one.

5.5. In any event, if one is willing to settle for a less ambitious anti-skeptical strategy, constitutivism still offers a variety of anti-skeptical tools. In addition to the defusing of the skeptic-as-shmagent, constitutivism is not barred from attempting actual refutations of those skeptics who do not take the shmagency route but launch their challenges while standing *inside* agency. Likewise, constitutivism is not barred from engaging in rational conversations with (and, if necessary, refutations of) *defective* agents—including massively defective ones, at least as long as they have not yet stepped outside of agency.

---

[26] See Enoch (2006: 190 n. 44).

In sum, although constitutivism might be unable to refute every kind of skeptic, it still offers a combination of anti-skeptical weapons—including the possibility of actual refutations—that many should find reasonably satisfactory. Whatever limitations constitutivism might exhibit on this front, they hardly count as a devastating objection to it.

5.6. The indispensability of agency does not rule out the possibility of genuine skeptical challenges launched inside of agency. This is why constitutivism might be able to engage in actual rational argumentations with these 'internal' skeptics and attempt to refute them. At the same time, this shows that constitutivism might still be vulnerable to a *reductio ad absurdum*. This is what any skeptic who does not take the ill-fated shmagency route is going to attempt against constitutivism.[27] Nonetheless, the inability of constitutivism to rule out a priori the *bare* possibility of a *reductio* can hardly count as a criticism of it. In the absence of any specific suggestion of how the *reductio* is supposed to work, all that one might ask of constitutivism is a generic profession of intellectual humility, that is, the acknowledgment that it is not in principle immune from a *reductio*. But the burden of proof still lies with the skeptic; he is the one who has to show that constitutivism fails on the face of inconsistent commitments. In addition, this skeptic cannot find any support in the discussion of shmagency. None of the characterizations of shmagency that we have encountered thus far suggests that constitutivism might suffer from any internal inconsistency. There is one last concern with the anti-skeptical implications of constitutivism. In adopting a kind of transcendental argument against the possibility of the shmagent (and the skeptic-as-shmagent), constitutivism might exhibit the same limitations the transcendental arguments used against epistemic skepticism.[28] In 1968 Barry Stroud famously argued that transcendental arguments fail at deducing substantive truths about the world from nothing more than the necessary conditions for the possibility of our thoughts and experiences. The transcendental arguments are unable to establish non-psychological conclusions—truths about how things are—from mere psychological premises.[29] This failure leaves room for more modest arguments, which remain confined within the psychological realm but establish connections between different

---

[27] Here I am in agreement with Enoch's suggestion that skeptical challenges are best interpreted as 'highlighting tensions within our own commitments, as paradoxes arguing for an unacceptable conclusion from premises we endorse, employing rules of inference to which we are committed' and that the philosophical task thus is 'not to defeat a real person who advocates the skeptical view or occupies the skeptical position (what view or position?) but, rather to solve the paradox, to show how we can avoid the unacceptable conclusion at an acceptable price,' Enoch (2006: 183–4).

[28] See Wallace (2004: 458), cf. Gibbard (1999: 154).

[29] See Stroud (reprint in 2000).

ways of thinking that are indispensable for us.[30] The weaker arguments
show that some of our beliefs are invulnerable in the sense that 'no one
could consistently reach the conclusion that although we all believe that
things are as that belief says that they are, the belief is false.'[31] The limitation
of these more modest arguments is that they cannot prove that the skeptical
possibility is false. They offer *no refutation* of skepticism. For beings with
radically different cognitive faculties or conceptual schemes, the skeptical
possibility might be a live one. But the skeptical possibility is inaccessible
to us as rational subjects because it is *inconsistent* with the correct operation
of our own judgment-sensitive attitudes.[32]

5.7. What are the implications for constitutivism of the modesty of the
transcendental arguments? The problem seems to be that constitutivism
leaves the logical possibility of normative skepticism open. However, I think
we should be cautious about accepting this conclusion. This conclusion is
based on an analogy with the transcendental arguments adopted against
epistemic skepticism. Couldn't it be that the kind of confinement or
inaccessibility of the skeptical possibility might be specific to the epistemic
domain and not extend to the practical and normative one? There might
be enough differences between the nature of these domains and the
skepticisms that they invite to warrant a closer look at the specific structure
of the transcendental arguments applied against normative skepticism before
declaring them modest.

In any event, how troubled should we really be about the modest import
of transcendental arguments? As modest as they are, they tell us that in
the *correct* exercise of our *full rationality*, and while relying on our own
most basic conceptual schemes, we cannot be persuaded by skepticism
given that it is *inconsistent* with the operation of our rational faculties
and our conceptual commitments.[33] For a modest claim, this seems to
be quite strong to me.[34] But this might just be a matter of philosophical

---

[30] See Stroud (1999: 165).

[31] Stroud (1999: 166). See also Hookway (1999: 177) and Taylor (1995: 26, 33).

[32] See Hookway (1999: 177–8).

[33] See Hookway (1999: 178). The inaccessibility of the skeptical possibility is not
a matter of some psychological *impediment*, as if we were unable to get rid of some
obsessive thought or hang-up. It is rather a matter of the fully rational operation of our
judgment-sensitive attitudes.

[34] If what the transcendental arguments prove is that the skeptical possibility is
inaccessible to us because of the nature of rationality and the structure of our conceptual
schemes, this limitation is not a fault of the transcendental *argument*, but a liability
of *our nature* as rational beings. It seems to follow that even other anti-skeptical
arguments, as long as they are launched inside of our conceptual schemes and while
relying on our rational faculties, will be unable to refute skepticism. Likewise, if
the transcendental arguments against normative skepticism prove to be similarly modest,

temperament. However, isn't talk of clashing temperaments the place where many discussions of skepticism eventually lead?

Finally, let's remember that the transcendental argument of constitutivism is successful against the shmagency objection, at least in its non-skeptical version. The issue raised by the shmagency objection is about the optionality of the engagement in agency, not about our dealings with all possible kinds of normative skepticism. With respect to the former issue, I maintain that the transcendental claims of constitutivism suffer from no troubling limitations. And this is all that we need to establish the viability of constitutivism.

6. CONSTITUTIVISM WITHOUT AGENCY

6.1. Despite the failure of the shmagency objection, the idea of shmagency might still be relevant to investigating the plausibility of constitutivism. In particular, concerns might be raised about the special role played by agency in constitutivism. Could we have constitutivism without agency? One might accept the central claim of constitutivism—that categorical oughts are grounded on the constitutive standards of a special kind of enterprise—but reject the suggestion that agency qualifies as the special enterprise.

This proposal might take two forms. First, one might argue that the truly inescapable enterprise is some sort of uberagency, that is, an enterprise that includes both agency and shmagency as optional subordinate enterprises.[35] Alternatively, one might argue that there is more than one inescapable enterprise. Shmagency might be as inescapable as agency.[36]

6.2. These suggestions pose no serious threats to constitutivism if the notions of shmagency and uberagency are ultimately intended not to replace the *concept* of agency but to articulate a different *conception* of it. By

then one cannot blame constitutivism for the weakness of its anti-skeptical import. Other meta-ethical views are supposed to suffer from exactly the same limitations, since they are *our own* limitations, not constitutivism's.

[35] The regress argument against uberagency presented in Section 2.5 above does not apply here, since the proposal under consideration accepts the constitutivist claim that the regress is stopped once we reach the level of the genuinely inescapable enterprise.

[36] Velleman (forthcoming) appears to read Enoch's shmagency objection as suggesting something somewhat along these lines. I do not think that this is the best interpretation of Enoch's argument, although this reading might be suggested by some remarks that Enoch makes in the original presentation of the shmagent, especially in his discussion of the similarity between shmactions and actions (see Section 3.7 above). In any event, many aspects of Velleman's response to Enoch can be persuasively applied to both readings of the shmagency objection (see Sections 6.6 and 7.5 below).

a 'conception of agency' I mean a substantive articulation and specification of an otherwise uncontested concept of agency.[37] For instance, a discussion about whether agency is better understood in terms of self-understanding (as Velleman suggests) or self-constitution (as Korsgaard does) is a dispute among competing conceptions of agency. The undisputed concept of agency, instead, is meant to outline the basic structure of agency at a more general level. The concept is individuated by its role in relation to other equally general concepts such as—to mention a few—those of choice, intention, open alternatives, and autonomy. To illustrate, conflicting conceptions of agency would not disagree over statements like 'agency is the capacity exerted when a subject acts intentionally as a result of her autonomous choice over alternatives she believes to be open to her.' Statements of this sort are part of the articulation of the shared concept of agency.

Notice that, in spite of its generality, the concept of agency is sufficiently substantial to be the object of sustained philosophical scrutiny. The inescapability of agency, for instance, is a feature of agency that can be derived from the general features of the concept of agency. The defense of constitutivism presented in this paper is conducted at this level of generality. Nothing that I say here takes any stance about particular conceptions of agency.

6.3. The appeal to the possibility of shmagency or uberagency raises no concern about constitutivism if this appeal is interpreted as suggesting an alternative conception of agency, even if only in the guise of the more radical replacement of the concept of agency. Under this interpretation, the shmagent who says, 'Classify my bodily movements and indeed me as you like,' and 'I am perfectly happy being a shmagent—a nonagent who is very similar to agents but who lacks the aim (constitutive of agency, but not shmagency) of self-constitution,'[38] is only targeting a *specific* account of the substantive constitutive standards of agency—the one formulated in terms of self-constitution. He is not really objecting to constitutivism. What he really means to say is something along these lines, 'It is fine by me if you want to reserve the term "agency" and its cognates to describe the enterprise aimed at self-constitution; the problem is that this enterprise is optional as evinced by my indifference to it and my ability to engage in a conduct that is very similar to agency in spite of my indifference to self-constitution. Therefore, agency *in the sense of the enterprise of self-constitution* cannot be the ground of the normativity.' According to this interpretation, the shmagent is only making a linguistic concession to his opponent; he is promoting a different conception of agency under the label of shmagency. He is not

---

[37] For the distinction between 'concept' and 'conception,' see Rawls (1971: 5–6, 9).
[38] See Enoch (2006: 179) and Section 2.2 above.

really trying to replace the concept of agency as the genuine inescapable enterprise that plays the uncontested conceptual role articulated in terms of such notions as choice, intention, autonomy, etc. This kind of shmagent, therefore, is not really raising any problem for constitutivism about agency.

6.4. A true criticism of the focus of constitutivism on agency requires that the notions of uberagency and shmagency be meant as genuine replacements of the *concept* of agency. This is, however, no easy task. One cannot single out 'agency' as the only concept to be replaced. Doing without it requires finding a suitable replacement for the entire set of *agential* concepts, that is, the set of all those notions—such as action, choice, autonomy, reactive attitude, etc.—that are at least in part individuated in relation to the very idea of agency. The problem is that this constellation of agential concepts is one of the fundamental features of our conceptual scheme. It is only in terms of these agential notions that we can articulate some of the most fundamental distinctions that we make in our attempts at making sense of the world and of our relations to its denizens. The concept of 'agency' is essential to delineating the shape of a basic domain of reality—the domain of the 'practical.'

6.5. For shmagency or uberagency to qualify as genuine conceptual alternatives to agency, they must be able to play a role in the shaping of conceptual schemes that is comparable to the one played by agency. This requires more than an abstract structural isomorphism with the distinctive features of agency. In principle, we might be able to make sense of phenomena that, at a suitably abstract level, might be said to be inescapable. That is, of phenomena that are closed under their distinctive operations—whatever those might be—and that have the largest possible 'jurisdiction' in their relevant domains—whatever those might be. But these structural similarities are not sufficient to show that we have a replacement for the concept of agency. The inescapability of agency is more than a formal property. The inescapability of agency is part of its distinctive *substantive* role, the role that makes the concept of 'agency' the linchpin of our understanding of the practical domain. Even the notions of 'enterprise' or 'jurisdiction,' which are used to characterize the structure of inescapability, seem ultimately to be concepts of a practical/agential kind.

6.6. The notions of uberagency and shmagency could aspire to be adequate conceptual replacements of the concept of agency only if they could support a more *substantive* ontological and conceptual role comparable to the one of agency. They would have to do so, however, in their own *non-agential* terms. For instance, shmagency should bear comparable relations to the 'shm-' counterparts of such notions as action, autonomy, reactive attitude, and the like; that is, to *shmaction, shmautonomy,* and *shmreactive* attitude. In other words, as agency stands to the practical domain, shmagency should stand to a comparable domain, although one conceived in shmagency's own terms—the *shmractical*, maybe?

What are we to make of a conceptual substitution of this kind? We could certainly make sense of the 'shmractical' notions as a mere notational restatement of the agential concepts but, of course, this would not be a genuine alternative to them. On the other hand, if the proposal purports to be more than a notational restatement, we need to get some grip on what this 'shmractical' domain is supposed to be like. But I think that if we are pushed to this point, we have no conceptual resources in our repertoire that can help gain any insight into what this proposed replacement of the concept of agency is supposed to amount to. We have outstripped the limits of our conceptual imagination.[39] We cannot really do without the concept of agency. There is no problem with disputing about alternative conceptions of agency, but a replacement of the concept of agency in its role as a fundamental element of our conceptual scheme seems out of the question. This shows that there is a further sense in which agency is inescapable: agency is inescapable as an enterprise and indispensable as a concept.[40]

7. THE SELF-VALIDATION OF AGENCY

7.1. In the previous sections, I have argued that the shmagency objection is unconvincing. Because of the special status of agency—the inescapability

---

[39] See Velleman (forthcoming: ch. 4) for a similar conclusion.

[40] Velleman (forthcoming: ch. 6) supports what he calls a 'mild version' of shmagency. He argues that, according to his conception of agency in terms of self-understanding, the principles of self-intelligibility might take a variety of forms. Some might consider a behavior intelligible in terms of a narrative understanding, others in terms of a causal-psychological explanation, others in terms of any combination of these two forms of explanation. The constitutive standards of agency remain silent on which principle of self-intelligibility should be adopted. Velleman points out that this pluralism is not necessarily a problem for constitutivism about agency. The choice of principles might be arbitrary, but constitutivism about agency does not purport to claim that there can be no space for arbitrary choices. I think that Velleman is correct on this point. There might actually be other dimensions along which the concept of agency is underdetermined (for instance, the temporal extension and structure of the unit of agency, on which see Ferrero (forthcoming)). I take issue, however, with his suggestion that this is a concession to the shmagency objection. The underdetermination in the concept of agency suggests that there might be pluralism in the ways in which agents might fully specify the structure and boundaries of what they take to be the inescapable enterprise. This pluralism is nonetheless internal to a shared understanding of the basic structure of agency, including its role as the inescapable enterprise. The fact that certain features of particular specifications of the structure of agency might be arbitrary does not make agency optional in the sense required by the shmagency objection.

of the enterprise of agency and the indispensability of the concept of agency—the question whether there is reason to be an agent cannot be raised and answered outside of agency. That is, it cannot be raised outside of the actual engagement in the agency enterprise and outside of a conceptual scheme in which the notion of agency plays an essential role. This does not mean, however, that constitutivism is exempt from the need to address the question, nor that it lacks the resources to do so. Nevertheless, the question whether we have reason to be agents has to be taken up *within* agency. It has to be taken up by subjects who are not indifferent to the standards of agency and thus try to answer it in deference to these standards.

7.2. As previously remarked, the distinctive operation of agency in its discursive mode is the practice of giving and asking for reasons for action. Because of the inescapability of agency, when an agent wonders whether she has reason to engage in agency, she can do so only by applying the distinctive operation of agency over her own agency. How does this self-directed operation affect the justification of one's engagement in agency? Does it guarantee that there is always reason to be an agent? That is, is agency necessarily self-validating? Or is this self-directed operation unacceptably circular?

7.3. Let's consider circularity first. One concern is that, as an agent begins investigating whether she is justified in being an agent, she must already be taking this justification for granted. After all, because of the inescapability of agency, she has to conduct her investigation in deference to the standards of agency. True, but the agent need only assume that her participation in agency is *provisionally* justified. As an agent, she cares about her participation in agency. As she embarks in the investigation, however, she is not yet assured that her care is eventually going to be proven justified (although she might hope that it is going to). Because of the inescapability of agency, however, there is no other place from which she could launch this investigation. Given that the acceptance of the standards of agency is only provisional, the agent is not really begging the question when she begins pondering whether she should be an agent.

7.4. The provisional character of one's deference to the standards of agency, however, does not dispel all worries about circularity. There is also a concern about the validity of the criteria used in determining what counts as a correct answer to the practical question about agency, to the question whether one should be an agent. When one asks whether one should engage in an ordinary enterprise, one adopts the criteria of correctness set by the nature of intentional agency. This is because one is to answer the question whether one is to engage in that enterprise *as* an intentional agent; that is, one is to show her engagement to be supported by reasons for action.

When one asks the practical question about agency itself, one is to defer to the same criteria of correctness since this is what asking a practical question consists in. But here lies the problem. If the validity of the criteria set by agency depends on our being justified in engaging in that enterprise in the first place, there seems to be an unacceptable circularity in justification: The criteria used in determining whether one is justified in being an agent are the same criteria whose validity depends on one's being justified in being an agent.

7.5. I will argue that, in spite of the appearances, there is really no unacceptable circularity here. To show this I need to make some preliminary remarks about the kind of circularity that might affect ordinary enterprises. (In the following discussion, I take my cues from an argument recently made by Velleman in support of a similar conclusion.[41])

When trying to validate a *move* made within a given enterprise, one has to appeal to the criteria of correctness set up by the constitutive standards of that enterprise. A move in the game of chess, for instance, is correct if and only if it abides by the rules of chess. These rules are given prior to and independently of that move. Questions about the validity of the game's criteria of correctness, rather than of its moves, cannot arise within that game. This is because the criteria determine what it is for a particular conduct to count as a correct move in that enterprise. It would be a misunderstanding of their role as correctness-setting if we were to ask whether these criteria are valid in their own terms. The rules of chess are not chess-valid, so to say, since they determine what chess-validity amounts to. To ask for the self-validation of these criteria would be meaningless rather than circular.

7.6. For some more complex enterprises, such as theoretical or practical reasoning, there is the possibility of a genuinely vicious circularity. One might reason theoretically about one's theoretical reasoning, or reason practically about one's practical reasoning. For instance, one might want to establish whether a rule of inference like *modus ponens* is theoretically valid. In doing so, one cannot rely on that very rule. This would be unacceptably circular. For there is an independently established criterion of theoretical correctness—conduciveness to the truth—that must be used to validate the rule of inference. To validate the rule of inference, one is to show, *without relying on that very rule*, that the rule meets the criterion of theoretical validity; that the rule is conducive to the truth. No similar question arises, however, for the criterion of theoretical validity, as opposed to a rule of inference. The criterion of theoretical validity cannot be *theoretically*

---

[41] See Velleman (forthcoming: ch. 4).

validated since its role is to determine what counts as being correct in theoretical reasoning.

7.7. Although it makes no sense to ask for the self-validation of the correctness-setting criteria of any enterprise, these same criteria might be said to be 'justified,' 'valid,' or 'correct' if they meet the standards set by some other enterprise. For example, one might be concerned with the playability of a game (Is it too easy? Too tedious? Are the rules inconsistent?) and thus speak of the validation of the game's rules in terms of playability. Alternatively, one might speak of the validation of the criteria in terms of the practical question, 'Should I be playing this game?,' 'Should I be engaged in this enterprise?' In this case, one might say that the criteria are valid if playing that game is justified, that is, if one is justified in *adopting* the game's criteria. But this practical validation, as it might be called, does not make the game's criteria valid *qua* correctness-setting criteria for that game. The rules of chess determine what counts as a legal chess move whether or not there is ever any reason to play chess. Finally, one might ask whether the criteria of a particular enterprise are constitutive of that enterprise. As part of the investigation in the metaphysics of chess, for instance, one might ask whether 'castling' is a valid rule of chess, by which one means to ask whether 'castling' *is* one of the rules of chess.[42]

7.8. Similar considerations can be made about the criteria of agency. First, whether a particular move in the game of agency is a valid move in that game depends on the criteria of correctness set up by the constitutive standards of agency. Second, any attempt at giving a practical justification for the use of a rule of practical inference that relies on that same rule is viciously circular. A rule of inference is to be practically validated in terms of the independently given criteria of correctness in practical reasoning (whatever they are supposed to be). Third, it is a misunderstanding of the role of the criteria of correctness of practical reasoning to try to validate them in their own terms, to show that they are *practically* valid. Fourth,

---

[42] A further issue with the criteria of both theoretical and practical reasoning is whether one is justified in adopting them as *explicit* guides in shaping one's conduct. For instance, there might be cases in which the goal of reaching the truth is better achieved if one does not explicitly conceive of one's conduct as aimed at that goal. Likewise for practical reasoning. For such cases, one might be justified in adopting some criteria as determining the *objective* correctness of her conduct but not as the standards that she is to follow as *subjective guides* in determining her conduct (see Railton 1997). There is no circularity, therefore, in wondering whether there is reason to use an objective criterion of correctness of an enterprise as one's subjective guide in that enterprise. Nor is it a failure of practical justification of an enterprise, if the use of its objective criteria as subjective guides cannot be practically justified. This is true even about the objective criteria of agency.

one might validate these criteria in terms of the standards set by a distinct enterprise. In particular, one might embark on an investigation into the metaphysics of agency in order to discover the nature of the constitutive standards of agency and of the criteria of practical correctness.

In other words, the following questions are to be kept separate: The metaphysical question about agency: What are the true criteria of practical reasoning? The question of correctness in practical reasoning: How do I go about telling whether the answer to a practical question is correct? The practical question about agency: Do I have reason to be an agent?

7.9. We are now in a position to see why the self-application of the criteria of correctness of agency is not viciously circular. When one asks the practical question about agency—'Is there reason to be an agent?'—one relies on the criteria set by the nature of agency to answer this question given that this is a *practical* question. What one is asking is whether one should *adopt* these criteria in shaping one's conduct. One is not asking whether the criteria are valid in their status as setting what counts as correct in practical reasoning. This status is rather presupposed in raising the practical question. The status remains unaffected by the answer that one is going to give to the practical question. Like in the chess example above, the standards of agency continue to set what counts as practically correct *whether or not* one has any reason to adopt those standards. The worry of circularity arises only because of the mistaken impression that the practical question is supposed to establish that the criteria are valid as the criteria that sets what counts as practically correct.

7.10. It is worth remarking that, in addressing the practical question, there is no provisional assumption of the criteria that determine the nature of practical correctness. We accept them as independently established. What is provisional is rather our *adoption* of them in shaping our conduct. The adoption is provisional since we are still trying to figure out whether we are eventually justified in adopting them (see Section 7.3 above). Once again, there is no objectionable circularity in the provisional adoption of them. It is nonetheless true that because of the inescapability of agency the practical question can only be addressed within agency. This implies that the criteria of practical correctness determine the ultimate fate of their own adoption. *If* the engagement in agency turns out to be justified, the criteria turn out to be *self-ratifying*: they justify in their own terms our actual use of them in the shaping of our conduct.[43] This is not a matter of circularity, but of closure.

---

[43] Millgram (2005) suggests that there are two strategies that constitutivism might adopt to show that agency is non-optional. First, there is the metaphysical strategy directed at showing that we *cannot but be* agents. Second, there is the practical strategy

7.11. Notice the conditional nature of the conclusion reached above. The fact that, when raising the practical question about agency, constitutivism is not threatened by vicious circularity offers no guarantee that we necessarily have reason to be agents. The constitutivist strategy offers no guarantee about the self-justification of agency and the self-ratification of its criteria. That agency operates over itself wherever we raise the practical question about agency, leaves open what the answer is going to be (at least to a point, see Section 8.2 below).[44] The only thing that appears to follow immediately from the inescapability of agency is that the investigation about the justification of agency cannot be conducted by someone who is indifferent to agency. But nothing immediately follows about the outcome of this investigation.

7.12. Whether we are justified in being agents is a substantive question whose answer depends on the particular criteria of correctness suggested by individual versions of constitutivism as spelled out in their specific *conceptions* of agency. I see no reason to deny that some of the criteria that might be advanced by specific versions of constitutivism might fail to prove that agency is self-justifying. However, to establish whether particular versions succeed at this task is a question that falls outside the scope of this chapter.[45] For present purposes, all that matters is the proof that constitutivism does not produce a self-justification of agency that is either trivial or viciously circular.

8. A PARADOX OF SELF-VALIDATION?

8.1. I have just argued that the inescapability of agency allows, although it does not guarantee, that there might be an unproblematic self-validation

directed at showing that we *cannot refuse the offer* to be agents. It is interesting to notice that, if the self-justification of agency proceeds according to the structure illustrated in this chapter, the validation of agency is the result of both strategies. To begin with, the self-justification depends on the inescapability of agency, which is a matter of the metaphysics of agency. The self-application of the operation of agency is mandated by the fact that we cannot but be, in the relevant sense, agents. At the same time, the self-validation is a matter of practical necessity: a fully rational agent cannot refuse the offer to participate in the enterprise of agency: participating in the enterprise is what her reflective practical reasoning tells her *to do*.

[44] Rosati (2003: 522) might thus be too hasty in suggesting that the operation of the motives and capacities constitutive of agency is self-vindicating just in virtue of their self-application.

[45] Velleman (forthcoming) explicitly argues that his own constitutivist view in terms of self-understanding is self-ratifying.

of the engagement in agency. In this final section, I will argue that the inescapability of agency seems also to imply that, at least in one particular respect, agency might be *beyond* validation. This is what might follow from the pragmatic paradox that would be faced by any agent if one were to discover that agency does not self-validate and that one has no reason to be an agent.

8.2. What happens if the criteria of practical correctness fail to ratify their own adoption? What is a rational agent to do if she were to discover that she has reason *not* to be an agent? If, while playing chess, a rational agent discovers she has a conclusive reason never to play chess, she is to immediately stop playing. The same should also be true of agency. Giving up one's participation is what reason demands in response to the discovery of unjustified engagements. Hence, if a rational agent discovers she has reason not to be an agent, she is supposed to give up immediately her participation in agency, that is, to stop being responsive to her acknowledgement of reasons for action. However, part of what she is no longer supposed to respond to includes the very reason that she has just discovered to hold of her, namely, the reason not to be an agent. The conclusion of her practical reasoning requires her to give up *hic and nunc* her rational agency *tout court*.

But this is not something that she can intentionally do as a *rational* agent. Any step that she would take in order to intentionally exit from agency would be *in compliance* with the demands of rationality, since in doing so she would be appropriately responding to the conclusion of her reasoning. At the same time, any step she would take to exit agency would also be *in violation* of the same demands of rationality. For, in taking that step, she would still be behaving, even if for the last time, *as* a rational agent, which is exactly what she has discovered she *is not to do*. Hence, the pragmatic paradox induced by the discovery that one's own agency fails to self-validate, that it fails to justify practically our own engagement in it.

8.3. The situation faced by the agent who discovers she has reason not to be an agent is different from the *non*-paradoxical cases of 'rational irrationality'; cases where one has reason to suspend temporarily one's rational responsiveness in order to increase long-term success as a rational agent (for instance, when one might induce one's temporary irrationality in order to avoid being the successful target of a coercive threat).[46] Rational irrationality is not problematic. It has the same structure as rational suicide, which—as previously discussed in Section 3.5—is not paradoxical. In both situations, when the agent is implementing her decision, she does exactly what she is

---

[46] See Parfit (1984: 13).

supposed to do in response to the dictates of practical reason. Throughout this implementation she continues to see herself as justifiably bound by the constitutive standards of agency, since even if she is eventually going to opt out of agency forever, she is not giving up on agency *tout court*.

By contrast, if there is no reason whatsoever to be an agent, one cannot be required to *intentionally* opt out of agency. Rather, the demand should be that the agent immediately *disappear*, but not as a result of any exercise of her intentional agency, of her responsiveness to reasons. What practical reason seems to demand in this case is not that the agent *do* something, but that something *happen* to her. However, happenings are exactly the kind of things whose occurrence cannot be directly *demanded*.[47] The paradox is that the rational agent is required to respond to reasons by immediately and permanently ceasing to be responsive to them. But at that point any intentional action would be one intentional action too many.[48]

8.4. How does this paradox bear on constitutivism? What generates this paradoxical possibility is the inescapability of agency. This does not mean that constitutivism is weakened by it. The paradox does not show that constitutivism would *fail* at the self-validation of agency. The paradox does not show that the conceptions of agency championed by individual versions of constitutivism are unable to provide a self-justification of agency. Rather, the paradox raises some doubts about the *legitimacy* or the *intelligibility* of asking that agents validate the exercise of their own agency. This is because there is something peculiar to raising a practical question whose negative answer would throw the agent into the pragmatic paradox illustrated above.

But even if we do not go as far as claiming that the question 'Should I be an agent?' could not be legitimately raised, the pragmatic paradox that would be generated by a negative answer to this question reinforces one of the basic claims of constitutivism about agency: the special status of agency vis-à-vis the issue of its practical justification. Agency is an enterprise of a very different kind and nature from ordinary enterprises. Drawing analogies

---

[47] There can only be an *indirect* rational demand for happenings in that an agent might be required to create the conditions for something to happen at a later time. But this indirect demand is not what reason requires in the case discussed in the main text.

[48] The problem is not one of the timing of the response. The problem is not that the action would be one action too late, as it might happen if one discovers that one *has no reason* to do something that one *has just done*. If agency fails to self-validate, it fails to self-validate atemporally. If an agent discovers that there is no reason to be an agent, she would thereby find out that she was never justified in her past actions. With respect to those actions, there is nothing that she can do, now or ever. But this is not paradoxical. It is simply the consequence of the impossibility of changing the past. The paradox arises, however, about the present exercise of agency in its necessary projection into the immediate future, which is the time where one is supposed to begin discharging the rational demand (Don't be an agent!) that one has just discovered to apply to oneself.

between agency and other enterprises is a very risky strategy, since the purported analogies might be more misleading than illuminating, as the arguments in this chapter have shown. It is even questionable whether it is really appropriate to speak of agency as a 'game' or as an 'enterprise,' as is often done in the literature on constitutivism, this work included.

8.5. In closing, let me briefly mention some ways in which the special structure of agency as the inescapable 'enterprise' affects questions about its practical justification.

For any ordinary enterprise, the basic form of the question whether to engage in that enterprise looks the same whether or not the agent is already engaged in that enterprise.[49] Not so for agency. To begin with, it is unclear whether there could really be a reason to participate in agency for any subject who is not yet an agent. It might not make sense to ask for reasons to opt into agency, given that there is no intentional action of *opting into* agency. *Transitions into* agency cannot be imputed to the agent: the agent is the end product, not the initiator, of these transitions.[50] In a similar fashion, the pragmatic paradox discussed above might suggest that it makes no sense to ask about the practical justification for the agent's *current* exercise of her agency. At the same time, questions about the justification for intentionally opting out of agency in the future are perfectly in order, as already shown in the discussion of suicide and rational irrationality.[51]

8.6. Another important issue concerns the 'guise' of agency under which the question of the justification of agency is raised. In this chapter, the discussion has been conducted not at the level of specific conceptions of agency, but at the level of the undisputed but general *concept* of agency (see Section 6.2). At the latter level two significant negative results have been achieved: the rejection of the threat of circularity and the discovery of a paradox in the self-validation of agency. But the concept of agency might

---

[49] This is a claim about the 'basic form' of the question. I am not denying the obvious fact that answers to specific practical questions are often path-dependent: in particular cases, whether one is already engaged in a given enterprise often makes a difference to the practical question whether she is to engage in that enterprise.

[50] Cf. the 'paradox of self-constitution' in Korsgaard (2002: sections 1.3.2–1.3.3).

[51] David Wiggins raises the possibility of a similar asymmetry in the case of the related issue of the existence of reasons to support the temporal continuity of individual lives: "[O]ne may muster the courage to ask the question what is so good, either absolutely or for me, about my own mental life's flowing on from now into the future. Surely this depends on what kind of person I am or think I am, and what sort of mental life it is. Well, not quite. There is something instinctive here and as irreducible as the rational commitment to make prudent provision for the future. These are things that we need reasons to *opt out of* rather than things that we have to look for reasons to *opt into*," Wiggins (1979: 307, my emphasis).

turn out to be too generic for a constructive argument in support of the actual self-validation of agency. It seems that a positive self-validation can only be found by looking at the more concrete characterizations of agency spelled out in the *conceptions* of agency championed by specific versions of constitutivism.

8.7. The difference between concept and conception is also relevant to the derivation of substantive normative claims from the constitutive standards of agency. The concept of agency might offer too thin a ground for this job. The richer characterization of agency offered by specific conceptions appears to be a more plausible starting point for the derivation of substantive norms and requirements. Whether this is sufficient to assuage the worries about the normative fertility of constitutivism, however, is not a question that can be addressed in this chapter. My goal has only been to prove the general viability of constitutivism against the shmagency objection and the worries about circular self-validation. Putting these concerns to rest only completes half of the job in defense of constitutivism. We still need to consider whether constitutivism can be true to its other ambitious aspiration, the derivation of *substantive* norms and principles from the constitutive standards of agency. But this is a question for another occasion.

REFERENCES

Cohen, G. A. (1996) 'Reason, Humanity, and the Moral Law,' in C. Korsgaard, *Sources of Normativity* (Cambridge: Cambridge University Press).

Coleman, Mary C. (unpublished) 'Toward Modest Constructivism.'

Darwall, Stephen (1992) 'Internalism and Agency,' in J. E. Tomberlin (ed.), *Philosophical Perspectives* (Atascadero, CA: Ridgeview), 155–74.

Enoch, David (2006) 'Agency, Shmagency: Why Normativity Won't Come from What Is Constitutive of Action' *Philosophical Review* 115: 169–98.

Ferrero, Luca (forthcoming) 'What Good is a Diachronic Will' *Philosophical Studies*.

FitzPatrick, William J. (2005) 'The Practical Turn in Ethical Theory: Korsgaard's Constructivism, Realism, and the Nature of Normativity' *Ethics* 115: 651–91.

Gibbard, Allan (1999) 'Morality and Consistency in Living: Korsgaard's Kantian Lectures' *Ethics* 110: 140–64.

Hookway, Christopher (1999) 'Modest Transcendental Arguments and Sceptical Doubts: A Reply to Stroud,' in R. Stern (ed.), *Transcendental Arguments: Problems and Prospects* (Oxford: Oxford University Press), 173–87.

Kolodny, Niko (2005) 'Why Be Rational?' *Mind* 114: 509–63.

Korsgaard, Christine (1996) *The Sources of Normativity* (Cambridge: Cambridge University Press).

—— (1997) 'The Normativity of Instrumental Reason,' in G. Cullity and B. Gaut (eds.), *Ethics and Practical Reason* (Oxford: Clarendon Press), 215–54.

Korsgaard, Christine (1999) 'Self-Constitution in the Ethics of Plato and Kant' *Journal of Ethics* 3: 1–29.

—— (2002) 'Self-Constitution: Action, Identity and Integrity. *The John Locke Lectures.*'

Lavin, Douglas (2004) 'Practical Reason and the Possibility of Error' *Ethics* 114: 424–57.

Marmor, Andrei (2001) *Positive Law and Objective Values* (Oxford: Oxford University Press).

Millgram, Elijah (1997) *Practical Induction* (Cambridge, MA: Harvard University Press).

—— (2005) 'Practical Reason and the Structure of Actions,' in E. N. Zalta (ed.), *The Stanford Encyclopedia of Philosophy.*

Parfit, Derek (1984) *Reasons and Persons* (Oxford: Oxford University Press).

Railton, Peter (1997) 'On the Hypothetical and Non-Hypothetical in Reasoning about Belief and Action,' in G. Cullity and B. Gaut (eds.), *Ethics and Practical Reason* (Oxford: Clarendon Press), 53–79; reprinted in Peter Railton, *Facts, Values and Norms: Essays toward a Morality of Consequence* (Cambridge: Cambridge University Press, 2003), 293–321.

Rawls, J. (1971) *A Theory of Justice* (Cambridge, MA: Harvard University Press).

Rosati, Connie (2003) 'Agency and the Open Question Argument' *Ethics* 113: 490–527.

Rysiew, Peter (2002) 'Reid and Epistemic Naturalism' *Philosophical Quarterly* 52: 437–56.

Schapiro, Tamar (1999) 'What is a Child?' *Ethics* 109: 715–38.

Setiya, Kieran (2003) 'Explaining Action' *Philosophical Review* 112: 339–93.

—— (2007) *Reasons without Rationalism* (Princeton: Princeton University Press).

Shafer-Landau, Russ (2003) *Moral Realism: A Defence* (Oxford: Oxford University Press).

Sharon, Assaf (unpublished) 'Unreflected Glory: A Challenge to Metanormative Constructivism.'

Strawson, Galen (1994) *Mental Reality* (Cambridge, MA: MIT Press).

Stroud, Barry (1999) 'The Goal of Transcendental Arguments,' in R. Stern (ed.), *Transcendental Arguments: Problems and Perspectives* (Oxford: Oxford University Press), 155–72.

—— (2000) 'Transcendental Arguments,' in B. Stroud, *Understanding Human Knowledge* (Oxford: Oxford University Press), 9–25.

Taylor, Charles (1985) 'What is Human Agency?' in C. Taylor, *Human Agency and Language: Philosophical Papers* (Cambridge: Cambridge University Press), 15–44.

—— (1995) 'The Validity of Transcendental Arguments,' in C. Taylor, *Philosophical Arguments* (Cambridge, MA: Harvard University Press), 20–33.

Velleman, J. D. (2000) *The Possibility of Practical Reason* (Oxford: Oxford University Press).

___ (2004) 'Replies to Discussion on *The Possibility of Practical Reason*' *Philosophical Studies*, 277–98.

___ (forthcoming) *How We Get Along* (Cambridge: Cambridge University Press).

Wallace, R. J. (2004) 'Constructing Normativity' *Philosophical Topics* 32: 451.

Wiggins, David (1979) 'The Concern to Survive,' repr. in D. Wiggins, *Needs, Values, Truth* (New York: Blackwell, 1998).

Index

Lightning Source UK Ltd.
Milton Keynes UK
UKHW010613130223
416869UK00001B/38